GOD
& MRS
THATCHER

GOD
& MRS
THATCHER

THE BATTLE FOR BRITAIN'S SOUL

ELIZA FILBY

Biteback Publishing

First published in Great Britain in 2015 by
Biteback Publishing Ltd
Westminster Tower
3 Albert Embankment
London SE1 7SP
Copyright © Eliza Filby 2015

ISBN 978-1-84954-785-7

10 9 8 7 6 5 4 3 2 1

A CIP catalogue record for this book is available from the British Library.

Set in Goudy Old Style

Printed and bound in Great Britain by
CPI Group (UK) Ltd, Croydon CR0 4YY

CONTENTS

'Economics is the method; the object is to change the soul.'
— MARGARET THATCHER, *THE TIMES*, 1981

Not odd, said God, I'd have you know,
It may seem easy down below
To keep the Bishops all in tow
Just propping up the Thatcher show
Up here, you see, there's hell to pay
She wants to tell ME what to say!
— MICHAEL FOOT MP, *THE TIMES*, 1984

PROLOGUE

GOD AND
MRS THATCHER

'All the great political questions of our day are primarily theological.'
– ARCHBISHOP WILLIAM TEMPLE, 1942[1]

THE OBITUARIES HAD long been composed; the commemorative pull outs were ready to be printed. Much ink would be spilled over Lady Thatcher's passing as commentators and journalists filed in earnest to have their say on the first draft of history. Tweets rather than pin-badges were now the chief form of popular protest but it was a more fleeting and disposable kind. Summations of her reign in 140 characters clogged up the Twitter feed, both the sweet chirps of birds and the raspy hiss of vultures. Reporters were dispatched across the kingdom – to Tyneside, Toxteth, Basildon, the Clyde and, of course, to her childhood home of Grantham – all in a desperate bid to gauge that ill-definable thing: the national mood. 'Thatcher gave me my first home', 'Thatcher took away my livelihood', came the cries, but anyone born after she had left office in 1990 looked on in bemusement. 'Wasn't she an old lady who had lost her memory?' was the response from one seventeen-year-old.

For a brief moment, Britain appeared to have rewound itself back to the 1980s. In Trafalgar Square, anti-Thatcher protestors geared up for a re-run of the poll-tax riots, although on this occasion the officers on horseback were not necessary. The left tried in vain to resuscitate the lost passion and solidarity of yesteryear, all together now for one last chorus of 'Maggie, Maggie, Maggie, out, out, out'. It was as if they were at a reunion gig of a group they had loved in their youth; they could remember the lyrics but somehow the anthem was not as resonant or powerful as it had once been. Meanwhile former ministers rehearsed well-worn anecdotes of Thatcher hand-bagging foreign dignitaries or of her rustling up shepherd's pie in the No. 10 kitchen; all revelling in that kinky mix of the regal and domestic that so defined the Iron Lady. Her admirers immediately began the process of canonisation heralding the miracle worker St Margaret, while her detractors were determined to cast her as the Antichrist, the Iron Lady who had had the nation in the jaws of a vice and mercilessly tightened until it could stand no more. How could the media sustain this for nine days until her funeral? How did it ever sustain it for the eleven years she was in power? It was, however, a purely domestic preoccupation. American broadcasters soon lost interest, while one Spanish television channel simply re-hashed material it had used for *The Iron Lady* film starring Meryl Streep.

Lady Thatcher's funeral in the City was an extraordinary day. The crowd was a mixture of tourists out to see the London they had been promised in the guidebooks, day-trippers from Middle England there to 'pay their respects' and City folk hanging out of their office windows avoiding work. All waited until the ceremony was over, not in mourning as such, rather as respectful observers. The British spectator stood patiently and seemingly in harmony with British pomp and ceremony, occupying the narrow City streets not designed for such spectacles.

I spent the day in the media tent opposite St Paul's Cathedral telling any broadcaster that would give me airtime that Lady Thatcher was a devout Christian, that she had been a preacher before she had entered politics and that the funeral service reflected her Methodist roots. 'So for our listeners at home, who may not know, could you tell us what exactly a Methodist is?' enquired one interviewer, who I noticed was sporting a pair of 'Gotcha!' engraved cufflinks.[*] I had an inkling that Margaret Thatcher would have been appalled, both by his question and by his choice of accessory.

Even from the grave, it seems, Margaret Thatcher was determined to tell the Church of England what true Christianity was: a heavy dose of 'hell and damnation' from the King James Bible and a rousing rendition of 'I Vow to Thee, My Country'. The Bishop of London's sermon certainly went down better than his words had done thirty years previously. Back in 1982 he had scripted the Archbishop of Canterbury's notorious 'pacifist' sermon delivered at the Falklands War thanksgiving service in St Paul's. On that occasion, Thatcher was reportedly 'livid', but on this day, one would imagine, she would have had no such quibbles.

It was not a send-off like Winston Churchill's: there were no steel cranes bowing in unison along the Thames. Perhaps the equivalent would have been if that towering shrine to Thatcherism, Canary Wharf, had ceremoniously switched its lights on and off. But Thatcher wanted no such show, no lying-in-state either. In the end, she had judged it about right, seemingly rekindling her populist antennae in death, which some would say she had lost at the end of her political life. Nonetheless, few could ignore the incongruity of a woman lauded as Britain's greatest peacetime Prime Minister being given a funeral with full military honours. This was not the burying of an international stateswoman

---

* 'Gotcha!' was the headline used by *The Sun* newspaper during the Falklands War when British forces had successfully sunk the Argentinian ship, the *Belgrano*. The headline was withdrawn by 8 p.m. that evening, but not before 1.5 million copies had been printed and dispatched.

(as evident by the congregation turnout at St Paul's), rather it was a fitting send-off for the lower-middle-class girl from Grantham who had spent her life rattling the British establishment, but who in death had the Queen, the Church, the BBC, the military, even former enemies in her party, finally celebrating her as one of them.

If George Orwell described England as 'a family with the wrong members in control', then Margaret Thatcher was the cruel but indomitable aunt whose favoured nieces sang her praises while those black sheep whom she had disregarded waded in with tales of woe. In death as in life, Thatcher's presence cast a piercing spotlight on Britain, but instead of revealing it to be either in discord or harmony, her passing simply demonstrated how much it had changed. As a sombre and respectful silence greeted the gun carriage and the pallbearers carried the coffin up the steps into St Paul's, that woman's shadow, which had loomed so large for so long, gently faded as the sun burst out over Paternoster Square. The mood was not morbid nor was it celebratory, but rather one of relief. Thatcherism had finally been laid to rest. As the renowned historian Peter Hennessy reflected: 'The 1980s is no longer politics, but history.'

•   •   •

I DOUBT MANY people have uttered the words 'God' and 'Mrs Thatcher' in the same sentence. To some it may border on blasphemy, even heresy; to the less religiously or politically sensitive, the idea that religion played any significant part in the 1980s is not immediately obvious in a decade dominated by union conflict, deindustrialisation, market liberalisation and the Cold War. Scour any books on the decade and you will find little reference to religion, the Church of England, and next to nothing on Margaret Thatcher's personal faith. To a large degree this absence is indicative of a broader problem: the secular mindset of most historians of contemporary Britain, which has meant that religion is largely omitted from writings on the twentieth century (although, for obvious reasons, historians and commentators have been forced to confront the issue in the twenty-first). Crudely speaking, those analysing Britain's experience hang their work on two central narratives. Firstly, Britain's withdrawal from empire and its decline as a global economic superpower and, secondly, its transition to a mass democracy and the development of its welfare state. Yet few ponder on that other major change, which was no less dramatic and would have as great an impact on Britain's political culture, namely the collapse of Christianity. Historians of the nineteenth century, of course, find it impossible to ignore religion. Victorian politics, to a degree, was dominated by the tussle between Nonconformists, Catholics and the Church of England, as Britain's religious minorities and non-believers, no longer silenced by persecution, fought the long, hard battle for equal recognition before the law. Christians of varying shades spearheaded the great causes of the century from the anti-slavery movement and temperance to social and electoral reform. Parties and votes were sliced along denominational lines, with the Conservative Party firmly positioned as the protector of the Church of England and the Liberal Party forwarding the interests of the Nonconformists. These bonds were not so fixed as to prevent a High Anglican (William Gladstone) from becoming leader of the Liberals, nor an Anglican of Jewish origin (Benjamin Disraeli) to take charge of the Conservatives, but the lengths to which both went to reassure their separate Christian constituencies reflected the enduring strength of these allegiances.

It is commonly assumed that Christianity ceased to have a pivotal role in British politics from the Edwardian period onwards. Disillusionment replaced faith as Britons dropped the cross somewhere amidst the muddy mass slaughter of the Somme, and so it followed that with declining observance came the de-Christianisation and the eventual secularisation of British politics. Nonconformist grievances became faint cries, the pulpit was no longer the training ground for would-be

MPs and the ties between parties and denominations, which had defined the previous century, withered away as class replaced religion as the central dividing line in the mass democratic age.

And yet Christianity in twentieth-century Britain was remarkable not for its sudden death but for its lingering influence on both the left and the right. The formation of the Labour Party owed much to its Christian impetus. It was this spiritual inspiration, which distinguished British socialism from its more secular and radical manifestations on the European continent, that was one of the many reasons why the party was able to quickly evolve into a centrist force. A survey of the first intake of Labour MPs, that was conducted in 1906, revealed that only two out of the forty-five had actually read Karl Marx, with many more citing the Bible as their chief influence.[2] The sacraments could still arouse as much passion as protectionism in Parliament, as the Church of England's failure to secure the revision of the Prayer Book in 1927–8 demonstrated. Led by Conservative evangelical laymen, Home Secretary Sir William Joynson-Hicks and the Attorney General, Sir Thomas Inskip, MPs twice rejected the proposed new version out of fears that the Church had gone too far in accommodating Romanist practices. The cause of Protestant England had been defended and protected by parliamentarians although the debacle was to have important consequences for Church–state relations. A red-faced Church was determined that no such intervention would ever happen again and thus set itself on the path towards greater autonomy from Parliament.

All three parties – Liberal, Conservative and Labour – could claim a Christian ethos and continued to feed off their spiritual heritage. The post-war settlement, which massively expanded the responsibilities of the state in the areas of education, health, welfare and housing, was not simply a political consensus but more profoundly a moral consensus forged out of the shared hardships of the Depression and the War and the common ground between Tory Anglicans and Christian socialists. In many senses, the post-war settlement, which was to be baptised the 'New Jerusalem', was the pinnacle moment in Britain's Christian politics and one in which the churches, especially the Church of England, played a pivotal role. Things were, however, beginning to change. When, in 1964, Harold Wilson proclaimed that the Labour Party 'owed more to Methodism than to Marxism', it was a sentiment with which most party activists could agree, but not for much longer. Soon a more radical form of secular socialism took hold: one that embraced identity politics (that of sexuality, race and gender) but, oddly, seemed to ignore religion as a form of identification. At the same time, One-nation Conservatism began to detach itself from the Church of England and in membership and tone was no longer exclusively Protestant or even Christian.

Nonetheless, most of Britain's post-war prime ministers were men of faith even if they became wary of preaching the Gospel to an increasingly secular electorate. Harold Macmillan would always reach for his Bible in times of trouble, Harold Wilson could claim a solid Nonconformist underbelly, while Edward Heath was one-time correspondent for the Church Times and cited Archbishop William Temple as one of his chief influences. Labour's Jim Callaghan was born into a devout Baptist household and had been a Sunday school teacher in his youth and, even though he later became a semi-detached member, he always acknowledged the debt he owed to Christianity.[3] The exception was Winston Churchill who, when asked whether he was a 'pillar of the church' replied, 'Madam, I'd rather describe myself as a flying buttress – I support the church from the outside.'[4]

Despite declining religious observance, priests did not hide behind their altars and retreat from public life; indeed political engagement was believed to be one way that the Church could connect with the ungodly masses. The Anglican bishops, still with their treasured twenty-six seats in the House of Lords, persisted in offering well-intentioned (but not always well-informed) interjections on the pressing issues of the day. On the key matters that dominated post-war politics – the evolution of the welfare state, decolonisation of empire, legislation on sexual morality, immigration and industrial conflict – the Church of England did not simply let its views be known, but, in many instances, was crucial in shaping the outcome.

To a certain extent, all this activity has been obscured by the blanket theory of secularisation. But this sociological concept – that is, an understanding that modernisation precipitates the gradual erosion of religion in the public and private sphere – is a relatively unhelpful explanation in the case of Britain, which even today maintains a somewhat complex relationship with Christianity. Crudely speaking, whereas America has a secular state but a largely devout public, Britain has a Christianised state and a predominantly secular electorate. Statistics on churchgoing, which clergymen have morbidly obsessed over since the first religious census in 1851, have traditionally been the litmus test for the strength of belief in Britain. Yet the notion that the spiritual health of the nation should be judged on the number of those who spend a few hours in a church on one day of the week is a rather restricted method of calculation to say the least. Throughout the ages, people went to church for a myriad of reasons, including poor relief, education, compulsion and social expectation as well as out of genuine faith. Christianity has always filtered into and shaped various aspects of British life, be it philosophy, culture, politics or class.

It is, however, an undeniable fact that from the late 1960s, Britain, like most other Western countries (with the exception of the United States) experienced a dramatic decline in Christian worship and affiliation. Yet, on the eve of the Thatcher years, Britain could hardly be called 'secular', for in education, broadcasting, law and, of course, in ceremonial character, Britain remained identifiably Christian. Enoch Powell was surely right when he wrote in 1981: 'The nation was once not as religious as some like to believe, nor is it now as secular as people

now like to assume.'⁵ The blend between the secular and sacred may
have been less obvious by the late-twentieth century and no longer a
decisive factor at election time but it remained a notable undercurrent
running through political thought and action. In short, Christianity
still mattered, and it would matter significantly during the fractious
years of the 1980s.

The broad aim of this book is to examine the interrelationship
between religion and politics in post-war Britain. It is thus a two-
pronged story concerning the politicisation of Christianity on the one
hand and the Christianisation of politics on the other. It therefore
seeks to demonstrate how the political class sought inspiration (and
legitimisation) from the Gospel for their political ideas and policies
and how the Established Church, to the same degree, viewed engagement in politics as part of its spiritual mission. The 1980s represent a
key juncture in this narrative for two reasons. Firstly, in 1979, unbeknownst to most of the public at the time, Britain had elected its most
religious prime minister since William Gladstone, one who from the
very first moment of her premiership referenced her spiritual motivation by reciting a prayer on the steps of No. 10. Margaret Thatcher,
though, did not simply draw on Christianity for rhetorical ornamen-
tation for, as the daughter of a Methodist lay-preacher, she had a clear
understanding of the religious basis of her political values. In fact, it
was no accident that Britain elected a Nonconformist woman precisely
at the time that its 'Nonconformist conscience' died; the conviction
politics of the Iron Lady satisfied a thirst for certainty in an age of
profound doubt. Just as the emergence of Thatcherism needs to be
set within the context of Britain's economic and industrial decline,
so too does it need to be analysed within the context of the country's
religious decline.

Secondly, one of the most politically damaging and forceful challenges that Margaret Thatcher faced throughout her premiership was
from the Church of England. While the Labour Party endured a period

of self-inflicted paralysis, it was the Established Church which, rather surprisingly and often willingly, stepped up as the 'unofficial opposition' to defend what they considered to be Britain's Christian social democratic values. In the pulpit, at the picket line, on the Lords' benches and in the inner cities, the Anglican clergy routinely condemned neoliberal theory and practice as being fundamentally at odds with the Christian principles of fellowship, interdependence and peace. How and why the Established Church sought and gained such prominence at a time of declining faith is one of the central themes of this book.

The Conservative Party and the once-dubbed 'Tory Party at Prayer' became locked in a conflict that would have political, spiritual and, in some cases, personal consequences. For many, though, this was not a minor political spat; it reflected a serious theological gulf. Was the biblical message principally about individual faith and liberty as Margaret Thatcher enthusiastically proclaimed, or collective obligation and interdependence as the bishops preached? Of all the biblical references that littered the sermons and speeches of politicians and clergy in the 1980s, it was the parable of the Good Samaritan that was most frequently evoked. For Margaret Thatcher, the story of a Samaritan helping an unknown, battered man, who was lying helpless in the road, demonstrated the supremacy of individual charitable virtue over enforced state taxation. In her uncompromising words: 'No one would remember the Good Samaritan if he'd only had good intentions; he had money as well.'[6] For the Anglican leadership, on the other hand, the parable meant something quite different, namely the universality of human fellowship and the scriptural justification for the indiscriminate redistribution of wealth. As the Bishop of Stepney made clear: 'The point of the story is not that he had some money but that the others passed by on the other side.'[7] Behind these differing interpretations of one parable lay contrasting conceptions of Christianity, of political values and, indeed, of the nation itself.

It is, of course, possible to examine the 1980s not in terms of competing theologies but in terms of ideologies, namely the polarisation between left and right. If the contribution of the Labour Party is downplayed slightly it is because the left had abandoned the post-war consensus (to an even greater degree than the right) and was entangled in a civil war, which had much to do with the decline of its traditional working-class support base and very little to do with Christianity. This is a book chiefly about the conflict between the Established Church and the Conservative Party, not about the various fortunes of Christian denominations in post-war Britain. But, of course, it is impossible to tell this story without reference to them and, in particular, to the rise of the ecumenical movement. Nor does this narrative deal sufficiently with that province where the convergence between religion and politics was most apparent and most damaging: Northern Ireland. This is in part because the Troubles were a sectarian conflict rather than a theological war of words on the rights and wrongs of capitalism. If anything, the toxic mix of the religious and the political in Northern Ireland revealed the tameness of the debate in Britain.

Of course Christians can be found on both sides of the political spectrum and Christianity itself has been both a progressive and a conservative force throughout history. If there is one scriptural certainty, it is that biblical interpretation is elastic and can be moulded to justify whatever one wishes to endorse, be it the 'invisible hand' of the market or the socialist utopia. In this specific case, the Church of England shifted further leftwards while the Conservative Party took a sharp turn to the right, causing an irrevocable breach between two institutions that had been close allies for over 200 years or more. Cracks in this relationship could be dated back to the early 1900s but the final break would only come in the 1980s under Margaret Thatcher.

It might be said that both the Church of England and the Conservative Party have transformed more than any other British institutions in the twentieth century. Paradoxically, for two organisations supposedly concerned with tradition and preservation, both have shown a remarkable ability to adapt in order to survive. That the Church of England was not only able to maintain, but, in many ways, strengthen its role as the Established Church in a secular pluralised society may have been by default rather than explicit design. Arguably, it has proved remarkably successful. The Conservative Party has gone through a similar process of reinvention. In the age of mass enfranchisement, the party of land and privilege gradually morphed into promoters of the free market and the upwardly mobile class, while maintaining its paternalistic tone and old establishment associations. It was not an easy transition and, like the Church, it consistently faced complaints from within its membership. But, by doing so, the Conservatives were able to become the most successful political party of the twentieth century. Collectively, what it does suggest is that all the heated debate over what is 'true' Conservatism or 'true' Anglicanism – a favourite navel-gazing pastime of both Anglicans and Conservatives – ultimately reflects a wilful misreading of their complex histories.

Margaret Thatcher, however, stands apart from this narrative. This is due to the fact that both the left and the right (for different reasons) have chosen to grant her an almost mythical-like status. Your opinion of Margaret Thatcher is immediately given away by how you refer to her; some literally spit out her surname with an emphasis on the first syllable, others prefer the overly familiar 'Maggie'. Even after her death, the political class and the public still struggle to speak of the former Prime Minister as a part of history, consumed as they are in a seemingly exhaustive debate over whether her time in power offers the cause or the remedy for today's problems. This hints at one of the main motivations of this book: a wish to consign Margaret Thatcher to the past and locate her place within it rather than see her as an ahistorical phenomenon of either saintly or devilish proportions.

By and large, the British prefer their prime ministers to be pedestrian rather than charismatic characters. One need only compare the palatial grandeur of the White House to the poky flat above No. 10

to illustrate this point. The post of prime minister, curtailed as it is by a parliamentary chamber and constitutional monarch, facilitates the British dislike and distrust of strong leadership. Yet Margaret Thatcher is one of the few occupiers of No. 10 to have subverted this tradition.

The legend of the Iron Lady is well known and remains remarkably intact. Margaret Thatcher, it appears, was gifted with superhuman capabilities. She was a woman from humble origins whose great mental and physical resilience made her the 'best man for the job'. She emerged unscathed without a hair out of place from the ashes of the bombed-out Grand Hotel in Brighton and successfully crushed the enemies within as well as threats beyond our shores. She was Boudicca, beating the bureaucrats in Brussels; she was Elizabeth I, always flirtatious but firm with her ministers; and in the end she was sacrificial St Joan, burnt at the stake having been betrayed by her own party. Margaret Thatcher has now been accorded a place at the dinner table with these high priestesses of history. She bulldozed her way through the New Jerusalem, unleashed Britons from the chains of socialism and set the people free.

Recent biographers and historians have quite rightly put a dent in this mythology as Richard Vinen, John Campbell and others have reminded us that Thatcher was in fact an incredibly pragmatic and canny politician and that the 'ism' she spawned was not as coherent an ideology as she herself liked to proclaim nor as the left liked to presume. Charles Moore's highly illuminating and balanced official biography offers a detailed portrait of her character and time in Downing Street that is never likely to be surpassed. God and Mrs Thatcher is not strictly a biography, rather Margaret Thatcher's life and times are used as narrative hinges to explain the fundamental shifts that took place in Britain's political and religious values in the second half of the twentieth century, and the ensuing debate in the 1980s (chiefly between the Established Church and the Tory Party) about those values. In short, the aim is not only to show how Margaret Thatcher recreated Britain, but also to address a much more intriguing question: how did Britain create Margaret Thatcher?

Margaret Thatcher was very much a product of provincial inter-war England. But, crucially, she escaped and then benefited from the opportunities that were opening up to women. In one sense, her story is a classic tale of mid-twentieth-century social embourgeouisement: a grammar school girl 'done good', although marrying a millionaire certainly eased the journey. She was not a throwback to Britain's Victorian past, but most definitely a twentieth-century woman: one who witnessed Britain's imperial decline and accepted the new American empire, indeed more readily than some of her contemporaries.

The two defining moments that shaped the politicians of her generation – the Depression of the 1930s and the Second World War – she experienced from a distance. What Margaret Thatcher did experience (albeit via her father) was the collapse of Nonconformity and the decline of the Liberal Party as its central mouthpiece. She was a product of Britain's changing religio-political landscape and it is this, possibly more than any other factor, which explains why a lower-middle-class girl of Nonconformist origins was able to become the leader of the male-dominated party of the establishment.

Margaret Thatcher would often indulge in the fact that she was an outsider in her party, and it is true she was. Although she respected and often displayed an embarrassing reverence for the old establishment, it was always an admiration she felt from a distance. She married into it, she worked for it, adopted its habits, tastes and values more than she cared to admit, but throughout her life she always understood that she was never truly a member of the club. Much like Methodist founder John Wesley's semi-attachment to the Church of England, Margaret Thatcher always had one foot in and one foot out of the British establishment. On the surface, it was her gender that marked her out, but in fact it was her Nonconformist class-consciousness, formed at a time when such distinctions still held sway, which was the source of her anti-establishmentarianism.

The religious faith of leaders is not to be underestimated. It can drive some to war, others to peace; some left, others right. One's faith and religious heritage is not something that is confined to the head or the heart, it manifests in different ways: in personality, outlook, style and language. When speaking of Margaret Thatcher's Nonconformity, one cannot simply consider personal faith, but also her class and principles. If Thatcher was a conviction politician, then at the root of her politics were her religio-political values. These were assumed and accepted precepts about God and man applied to the political sphere. This is not a book about policies, but ideas. It is less about what Margaret Thatcher and her contemporaries did, more about what they believed.

CHAPTER ONE

'GOD BLESS GRANTHAM'

'My "Bloomsbury" was Grantham – Methodism, the grocer's shop, Rotary and all the serious, sober virtues cultivated and esteemed in that environment.'
— MARGARET THATCHER, 1995[1]

'In Grantham it was like swimming in a very small pool: you keep bumping into the sides.'
— MARGARET THATCHER, 2010[2]

IT IS NECESSARY for all modern political leaders to construct a personal narrative. Their journeys must be enlightening tales demonstrating their sound character, verifying their populist credentials and making them flesh in the public mind. The result is often a series of self-conscious, politically motivated, dewy-eyed reminiscences, which often do little more than provide material for satirists.

Margaret Thatcher's tales of growing up in Grantham were different. She paraded the family's humble origins and upbringing more than any other modern politician. The parable of the young Margaret schooled in the principles of the market in the family grocery shop in Grantham became central to Iron Lady mythology. 'I had precious little privilege in my early years,' she would declare, in a calculated swipe at the gentlemen squires that dominated her party and the champagne socialists that filled the Labour benches.[3] Her predecessor, Edward Heath, was actually from lower stock – the son of a carpenter and a maid from Broadstairs in Kent – but few voters knew it. Heath never hid his heritage, but he never traded on it either. Few could say that about Margaret Thatcher.[4]

In fact, Thatcher rarely referred to her Grantham beginnings until her bid for the Conservative leadership in 1975 when, in a radio interview just before the first ballot, she marked out her provincial roots and class credentials as key to understanding her political values:

> All my ideas about life, about individual responsibility, about looking after your neighbour, about patriotism, about self-discipline, about law and order, were all formed right in a small town in the Midlands, and I've always been very thankful that I was brought up in a smaller community so that you really felt what a community could be.[5]

What began as a simple rebranding exercise to alter the public perception of Margaret Thatcher as a privileged millionaire's wife would later come to serve as the moral foundations for the reformulation of the Conservative Party under her leadership. Out went the Disraelian ethos of 'one nation' and in came the shopkeeper's ethic of 'getting on'.

Thatcher's purposeful reminiscences supposedly harked back to a time when the community governed rather than the state, when free enterprise and personal responsibility reigned and when the church (in her case the Methodist chapel) was the focal point of town life and the fountain of moral guidance. She weaved the historical with the personal in what amounted to a seemingly naive but damning critique of Britain's record since 1945. Her recollections were a conscious exercise in historical revisionism, a narrative that challenged the deeply entrenched view that the pre-welfare age was a blot on the nation's conscience; far from it, according to Thatcher, it was a time when hard work, pride and patriotism prevailed. In the 1960s, at the height of modernist optimism and Prime Minister Harold Wilson's 'White Heat' technological revolution, Thatcher's quaint provincial tales would have been laughed out of the conference hall. But in the hazy and chaotic years of the mid-1970s, they touched a nerve. Hers was, of course, a highly edited narrative for obvious reasons: the grocer's daughter rather than the millionaire's wife suited the austere times of 1970s Britain. From the moment Thatcher became leader of the Conservative Party, Grantham was routinely referenced as a worthy guide for a nation in crisis.

Thatcher's evocation of her early years was so deliberately political that it is easy to dismiss it all as pure spin. And yet, as the local archives reveal, Margaret Thatcher's account of Grantham was not too distant from the reality; although it was not always as benign or as simple as she liked to claim. Understanding Grantham, however, is key to understanding Thatcher; not only the religious and political values to which she subscribed but also crucial to explaining some of the naivety and short-sightedness in her political thinking.

As a former minister and one of Thatcher's loyal lieutenants, Lord Parkinson, made clear: 'It all goes back to Grantham. Grantham was the essence of Thatcherism.'[6]

I. Open all hours

GRANTHAM, A SMALL town in the heart of the East Midlands, has always been a stop-off point en route to somewhere more exciting.

Today, its buildings are uncomfortably meshed together and act as layered sediments of centuries of social and economic change.[7]

There is medieval Grantham with its quaint alms-houses and timber-
framed thatched-roof pubs that are dwarfed by St Wulfram's Church,
whose steeple still dominates the skyline. There is also Georgian Grantham; no sweeping circular crescents like that of Bath or Bristol, just a
few rows of houses in perfect symmetry, which still house the town's professionals. The dominant architectural style is Victorian, reflective of the
fact that in the nineteenth century Grantham developed into an important engineering centre and railway depot. But there are no vast factories
or affiliated culture of working men's clubs as in the industrial north, only
endless rows of small terraced houses designed for Grantham's workers.
All roads lead to the main square with its faux-grand town hall honouring
the moment in 1835 when Grantham assumed charge of its own governance. There are signs too of Margaret Thatcher's inter-war childhood: the
bustling high street and those 'palaces of escapism', the (now redundant)
cinemas. Finally, there is post-war Grantham with its brutalist maze-like
shopping centre and municipal post-office, which is awkwardly plonked
on the edge of the square. Today, with Woolworths and Marks & Spencer
gone, it is pound shops and charity shops that dominate, with the largest
employer the local hospital and the mammoth supermarket warehouses
situated on the fringes of town.

With a population of approximately 20,000, Grantham between the
wars was a medium-sized place run by the local borough council, then
in the hands of the small businessmen: the brewers, tradespeople, man-
ufacturers and shopkeepers such as Margaret Thatcher's father, Alfred
Roberts. On the periphery were the working class, a mixture of agricul-
tural, railway and industrial workers. The nobility's influence, although
fading, still lingered with Lord Brownlow, the local grandee of the nearby
Belton estate. Brownlow served once as mayor and served as Lord Lieutenant of Lincolnshire between 1936 and 1950, but was clearly content
to leave the day-to-day governing to Grantham's petite bourgeoisie.

Grantham did not escape the Depression although in her memoirs Margaret Thatcher offered a somewhat sanitised description of the queues outside Grantham's labour exchange, remarking 'how neatly turned out the children of those unemployed families were', which in her view was evidence of the 'spirit of self-reliance and independence … in even the poorest people of the East Midlands towns.'[8] Importantly though, Grantham was no Stockton-on-Tees, where widespread unemployment and poverty in that deprived part of the north-east would compel the local MP, Harold Macmillan, to pen *The Middle Way* in 1938: the founding tract of twentieth-century One-nation Conservatism. The 1930s Hunger Marchers only travelled through Grantham, they did not originate from there. The Depression was a defining moment for the ruling class, which swung the political barometer firmly in favour of statist solutions, but as Thatcher later remarked in her memoirs: 'Things look different from the perspective of Grantham than from that of Stockton.[9] It was true, they did.

Alfred Roberts, a working-class man whose family had been in the shoe-making trade, had arrived in Grantham via Northamptonshire in 1913. Over the course of three decades, he would go from grocer's apprentice to owner of two shops and mayor of the town. Roberts immersed himself in Grantham's social, religious and political life in his multiple roles as lay-preacher at Finkin Street Methodist Church, trustee of Grantham Savings Bank, governor at the local school, president of the Chamber of Trade and the Rotary Club, as well as alderman on Grantham's borough council. In Margaret Thatcher's eyes, he was the embodiment of individual aspiration and social responsibility, but he was no exception. In these days of genuine local autonomy, men like Alfred Roberts not only felt a social and religious expectation but also enjoyed genuine power and prestige. Her mother, Beatrice, in contrast, is a lightly sketched figure in the Grantham parable. Thatcher once remarked that 'at fifteen we had nothing more to say to each other'. Speaking in 1985, Margaret Thatcher likened her mother to

Martha in St Luke's Gospel. In the story, Mary dutifully sits and listens intently at the feet of Jesus while Martha is preoccupied with household chores. The biblical comparison is an unfavourable one and suggests that Margaret considered her mother, like Martha, a woman with the wrong set of priorities.

Margaret was born above the shop on the 13 October 1925, four years after the Robertses' first child, Muriel. Thatcher once compared living in the No. 10 flat to living above the shop, for 'you are always on duty'. In one sense she was right; being a grocer did mean unsociable hours. The shop was open until 7 p.m. on weekdays and 9 p.m. on a Saturday, although it was closed on the Sabbath. More importantly, as one of Thatcher's biographers has noted, the grocer was the centre point of trade at its most basic level, the intermediary between the market and the home.[10]

The small grocer was king in the inter-war period. Supermarket chains had not yet achieved their dominance, while the expansion of the high street and a rise in disposable incomes precipitated an increase in independent shopkeepers from 275,000 in 1911 to 362,000 by 1931. The establishment of the National Federation of Grocers' Associations in this period reflected the independent grocers' strength but also a desire to protect their interests against the emerging threat of the Co-op and chains such as J. Sainsbury, which even in the 1930s took 30 per cent of all sales. The grocery business was more than just a profitable trade, for during the 'hungry thirties' food inevitably became a politically potent issue, especially as women – traditional regulators of the household budget – now had the vote. As the political class clashed over whether protectionism and imperial preference was the solution to Britain's economic woes, so consumer behaviour assumed ever-greater importance. The Empire Marketing Board, established in 1926, urged consumers to buy only imperial goods: an initiative that was adopted sporadically in Grantham. Under such circumstances, Alfred Roberts must have felt the threat of competition and political pressures on his business, but it was equally possible that, in his role behind the counter, he felt that he was dutifully serving the nation and the empire too.

Whereas Grantham's working class would have shopped at the nearby Co-op, Alfred Roberts's store catered for a distinctly middle-class clientele. The fact that Roberts's shop also had a sub-post office, however, meant that the working-class residents would stop by to collect their pension, unemployment benefit or deposit money into their savings accounts. This did not make Roberts's shop an off-shoot of the state, but did mean that the heterogeneous mix of Grantham society would come through its door, all assured of their place and defined by which part they used. As one Grantham resident, Vic Hutchinson, has recalled:

> I remember how proud I was when made school prefect and Captain of Newton House, tassel and all! My pride, however, was deflated somewhat, but only temporarily, by of all people the aforementioned Alfred Roberts who when serving me in the post-office, commented, 'what on earth is the school coming to?' The veneer of humour failed to hide his lack of confidence in this jumped-up Co-op shopper.[11]

During the Depression, though, it is highly likely that the Co-op store posed a threat to Roberts's business. Situated not far from his shop on St Catherine's Road, it offered cheaper priced goods and the additional incentive of the 'divi'. Queuing for the dividend was an annual event for Grantham's working-class residents as it was for the other four million Co-op members of Britain. Redistribution through consumption had been its founding principle; however, in practice, this meant taking business away from private small shop-owners. It is little wonder that Alfred Roberts and other tradesmen in Grantham viewed the Co-op's arrival with even greater suspicion than the local Labour Party.

Margaret Thatcher later claimed that she had 'little privilege' in her childhood, but this was down to her parents' thrifty values, rather than a lack of money. Funds were made available for things deemed

worthwhile, such as Latin or piano lessons, while birthday gifts and
pocket money were invested in saving stamps. The Robertses purchased their first radio set in 1935 (relatively late for an inter-war
household) and their first car (second hand) just after Margaret left
for university in 1942. If thrift was considered a virtue, then debt was
the ultimate vice. In a presidential speech to Grantham's Rotary Club
in 1936, Roberts spoke of the 'manacles of debt' as the 'curse of mankind' and, as bank trustee, publicly pledged to 'get Grantham saving'.[12]
From the archives, it is striking how often debt is a recurring theme in
Alfred Roberts's dealings, whether it be balancing the council budget
or maintaining the church finances.

As a grocer, Roberts was especially sensitive (but not necessarily
sympathetic) to the dangers of credit. His business was vulnerable if
account holders did not settle up and thus eyeing up people's ability
to pay was crucial. But, above all, it was his Methodist gut that told
him that debt was wrong. Methodists tended to view credit as being
just as corrupting and damaging as drink or gambling. 'Before I ever
read a page of Milton Friedman or Alan Walters,' Thatcher claimed
in her memoirs, 'I just knew … thrift was a virtue and profligacy a
vice.'[13] It is therefore not without irony that her government oversaw an unprecedented expansion in personal credit. In the inter-war
years, as Margaret Thatcher admitted, to say that an individual 'lived
up to the hilt' was the worst possible insult.[14] This was in part down
to the rise in hire-purchase consumerism, which increased twenty-
fold between 1918 and 1938 with 80 per cent of cars, 90 per cent of
sewing machines and 95 per cent of pianos all bought on credit. An
existence financed on the 'never-never', rather than through hard
work, which could literally be taken away as quickly as it was delivered, contravened what it meant it be part of the stable middle class.
The key indication of middle-class status – home ownership – which
even in 1939 included nearly 60 per cent of the middle classes, was of
course the biggest gamble on the 'never-never' of them all.

II. Methodism maketh the man

ALFRED ROBERTS MAY have spent the majority of his time behind the counter but he defined himself in terms of his religion rather than his trade. Methodism was not a compartmentalised aspect of his life but a seven-day-a-week preoccupation, which underlined every thought, word and deed. The chapel was where he met his first (and indeed his second) wife, it was where he both received and bestowed spiritual instruction, and it would also act as the springboard for his entry into public life. For the Roberts family, their class, religion and politics were an indistinguishable set of allegiances headed by a man who was a leader in each sphere, as a shop owner, lay-preacher and town councillor.

'Our lives revolved around Methodism,' so said Margaret Thatcher.[15] Even by inter-war standards, her religious upbringing would have been considered austere; viewed through the lens of today's post-Christian Britain it seems positively archaic. The family would say grace before and after every meal and her parents were strict teetotallers – only keeping an old bottle of sherry in the house for guests. 'For us, it was rather a sin to enjoy yourself by entertainment ... Life was not to enjoy ourselves. Life was to work and do things,' Margaret Thatcher later pondered, evoking a childhood frustration for what must have been a stifling upbringing.[16]

To the contemporary reader, the classifications of Baptist, Presbyterian, Congregationalist and Methodist may seem a little blurred or inconsequential, but in inter-war Britain, distinct denominational identities still mattered. Since its advent in the eighteenth century, Methodism had made the impressive leap from breakaway sect to a prominent place in the mainstream of British life. Founder John Wesley was Lincolnshire-born – in Epworth about fifty miles from Grantham – but it was while at Oxford that he had established his Holy Club. Wesley's group soon became known as 'Methodists', a derogatory name given because of their orderly and pious approach to life. But like most labels that begin as an insult, it stuck. Wesley's aim was to create a Bible-based 'new model army of saints' as an antidote to what he considered to be the self-serving and unholy preoccupations of the Established Church. Wesley, however, never saw himself as a Nonconformist but always considered himself a member of the Church of England.

Methodism had started life as an evangelical revival society, but officially broke away from Anglicanism following the Plan of Pacification in 1795 and soon emerged as a substantive force in its own right. Missionaries were sent out to spread the Word, first to colonial America (where Wesley himself preached), then to other parts of the British Empire, and Methodism soon became one of the leading forms of Christianity in the colonies. Like all Reformist sects, it was defined by its missionary zeal and prioritisation of Scripture over tradition and reason. 'Methodism was born in a revival' and the 'evangelistic spirit is the breath by which it lives' affirmed the Wesleyan Conference in 1912. It differed, however, from Calvinism and Presbyterianism, in its rejection of predestination (the idea of a division between elect and non-elect) and upheld the concept of free will bestowed by God's universal grace. It thus centred on man's individual relationship with the Almighty, which was made explicit through Covenant services in which worshippers would publicly reaffirm their faith. Other identifiable features were its communal expression through congregational singing (most notably through the hymns of John's brother, Charles Wesley) and the precedence of the sermon over the sacraments. Even so, Methodism was always closely aligned with the Church of England, modelling its worship on the Book of Common Prayer. For this reason, its distance from Anglicanism was always more cultural than theological.[17]

Like other Nonconformist sects, Methodism was devoid of land and patronage, thus its growth was largely dependent on its laity and communities. As the ecclesiastical historian Adrian Hastings has made clear, initiative and liberty were woven into its culture: '[Nonconformity] stood for a freedom seen theologically and evangelically, but they expressed it at every turn as a sociological and political freedom too.'[18] Methodism may have had a nominally centralised structure with its yearly gathering of ministers, but it was not hierarchical (in that there were no bishops) and therefore its growth relied on the local chapels and circuits led by ministers and aided by lay-preachers. A lack of hierarchy meant that the laity played their part, but it also made orthodoxy hard to enforce.

From its earliest beginnings, Methodism had always been an uncomfortable agglomeration of disparate groups, but by the 1850s it had split into two identifiable strands (in addition to other splinter groups). Primitive Methodism was strong in Cornwall, Wales, the Potteries, Yorkshire and the coalfields of Durham and Northumberland, while Wesleyan Methodism was the dominant strand amongst the lower-middle-class communities of Lincolnshire, Bristol and the central halls of the northern towns of Manchester, Sheffield and Leeds. Whereas Primitive Methodists were 'low church', Wesleyan Methodists tended to be 'higher' in both their practices and composition. Socially conservative and the most conformist of all Nonconformists, Wesleyan Methodists tended to take a somewhat disparaging and snobbish view of their more radical Primitive counterparts. Needless to say, it is significant that the Robertses were Methodists and not Anglicans or Quakers, but it is equally important that they were from the Wesleyan rather than the Primitive branch of Methodism.

The changing of labels, from 'Dissenters' to 'Nonconformists', and, at the turn of the century, 'Free Churches', was an indication of growing acceptance and legitimacy. The building of Westminster Central Hall in 1912, directly facing both Westminster Abbey and Parliament, was a symbol of Methodism's specific achievement and the fact that it was no longer seen as the rebellious cousin of the Established Church. Paradoxically, just at the point of acceptance, Methodism began to decline, although in the 1930s there were still approximately 860,000

Methodists, of which just over half, 500,000, were Wesleyans. This evangelical flame would eventually be snuffed out in the 1960s; the inter-war years would prove to be its last flicker.

Scripture and individual salvation may have been at the heart of Methodism, but there was no denying its communitarian impulse. 'Christianity is a social religion,' so said John Wesley, 'to turn it into a solitary religion is to destroy it.' But the definition of what was meant by 'a social religion' differed within the strands of Methodism and changed over time. Wesley himself had been a champion of the anti-slavery movement and prison reform. As these battles dissolved, so the next generation of Methodists channelled their energies into education, temperance, sabbatarianism and disestablishmentarianism, reflecting the distinct priorities of Methodism as well as the unifying Nonconformist battle against the privileges of the Established Church. By the 1920s, these issues had more or less dissipated (or become irrelevant) and Methodists, like all Christian denominations, embraced the new causes of the age, principally social reform and pacifism. The development of what became known as the 'social gospel' within the Christian churches closely paralleled and contributed to the social democratic shift then taking place within British politics.

In 1932 the various branches came together under the Methodist Union. That this merger came at a time of declining membership was no accident; the hope was that it would revive the fortunes of Methodism. But the cause of religious unity, much like that of a political coalition, is often an indication of weakness rather than strength. The amalgamation of Primitive and Wesleyan chapels, with their differing practices, communities and associational cultures, was an awkward process for all involved. In Grantham, however, unification would not take place for another twelve years, in 1944, after Margaret Roberts had left for university. In this period, Grantham boasted three Methodist chapels as well as Baptist and Congregational congregations, a Roman Catholic church (directly opposite Roberts's shop) as well as the Anglican parish of St Wulfram's. Rivalry between the churches was still evident, but at a time when the cinemas were beginning to attract a greater number of devotees than the church, ecumenicalism slowly became the order of the day. Civic and political culture was no longer arranged so tightly around denominational lines, especially as new clubs such as Rotary established themselves as non-denominational and open to all.

During the inter-war period, what was deemed respectable secular culture such as classical music concerts, sporting events and dances began to infiltrate chapel life. Handel, Haydn, Mendelssohn and Elgar had never been so popular and bridged the gap between sacred worship and secular entertainment in the same way that Christian rock would attempt to do thirty years later. Musical concerts at Finkin Street Church were the highlight of the Robertses social calendar and were probably the only occasions when the chapel would be filled to capacity. These events proved a hit with a young Margaret Roberts who later confessed that 'it was the musical side of Methodism which I liked best'.[19] Such developments, however, represented piecemeal changes. Much like a suited man loosening his tie, inter-war Methodism may have been more relaxed but it was still restricted.

The temperance movement had been the great battle of the nineteenth century but by the inter-war years many had abandoned the cause. Teetotalism was no longer a condition of Methodist membership although it was still widely encouraged, especially at Finkin Street Church, which had its own temperance secretary well into the 1950s. Despite tight legal restrictions, betting achieved greater respectability in this period largely down to the popularity of American-imported greyhound racing, which the British embraced as something of their own. For Methodists, however, a flutter on the dogs, horses or football pools was tantamount to a false belief in luck over the will of God. In 1925 the Wesleyan Methodist conference banned the use of raffles or lotteries, judging that they debased the spirit of charity and appealed to man's selfish motive. Tellingly, speculation in the realm of finance was also considered a morally reprehensible activity that capitalised on other people's loss without rendering commensurate Christian service: a judgement that seemed vindicated following the Wall Street Crash of 1929. By Margaret Thatcher's own admission, her father too viewed the financial dealings of the City of London as institutionalised gambling.[20]

That the Robertses piety was out of step with changing times is best illustrated in Alfred Roberts's uncompromising stance on the preservation of the Sabbath, which as councillor he fought hard to maintain in Grantham. Dubbed by the local paper as the 'most controversial and revolutionary subject' ever to be debated, in 1938 he passionately argued against a Labour proposal for the playing of games and amusements in the local parks on Sundays.[21] In a debate that hinted at both the religious and class tensions in Grantham, Councillor Goodliff pointed out that as golf clubs were permitted to open on a Sunday and the public parks were not, the restrictions whiffed of one rule for the middle class and another for the working man. In a spiritual plea, Roberts responded that although 'there was no such thing as compulsory Christianity' (pointed words from a Nonconformist), 'there was such a thing as drifting into a life which was absolutely and totally devoid of any spiritual inspiration'. The proposal was rejected, it was said, largely due to Roberts's performance. The idea was raised once again by Labour councillors, in altogether different circumstances, during wartime in 1942 for the benefit of the munitions workers. Showing little sympathy for leisurely pursuits, Roberts remarked somewhat bitterly that he worked harder than any munitions worker and had enjoyed fewer days off since 1939. On this occasion, he reluctantly accepted defeat, although he coupled it with a warning that Sabbatarianism (and by implication Christianity) was losing its hold: 'We are eating into our English Sunday as fast as we can.' He was later to be proved right.[22]

Roberts may have struggled to enforce the Sabbath in Grantham but he had more success within his own household. 'Bach not bowls' should define the day according to the guidelines of the Methodist *Christian Observance of Sundays*, published in 1939, which in the Robertses home meant that board games, sewing and even newspapers were forbidden.[23] The family would attend chapel both morning and evening services, while the daughters would also twice attend Sunday school. Margaret had the additional role as pianist for the younger children until she was relieved of her duties when she went to university. For the Robertses, the chapel was a social centre as much as it was a place of worship. On Fridays the two sisters would attend the Methodist Youth Guild, Tuesdays evenings were set aside for the ladies' sewing club, while Alfred and Beatrice also had their separate weekly prayer meetings. Speaking in 1993, Margaret Thatcher admitted that she frequently tried to get out of going to chapel: 'I think it was a little bit too much. I was the only person at school who went to church quite as often. It would have been a little bit better to have a little bit less.'[24]

A copy of Margaret Thatcher's childhood catechism kept in her personal archives at Churchill College, Cambridge reveals the type of religious instruction she received. The catechism (a Greek word literally meaning 'indoctrination') was conceived as a spiritual 'Q&A' covering redemption, sin and judgement as well as the Ten Commandments, Beatitudes, Lord's Prayer and the Apostles' Creed. Margaret Roberts's copy is heavily annotated but there are no signs of boredom: no doodles or boys' names encased within a heart and arrow, only the markings of an attentive and serious scholar. The young Margaret seems to have been extremely taken with the notion of sin and service, which she underlined at several points: 'What is sin?' 'Sin is disobedience to the will of our heavenly father in thought, word or deed.' This was a Methodist instruction, which principally stressed the individual relationship with God, the Christian notion of service and the all-encompassing nature of sin.[25]

The Sunday service at Finkin Street Church would follow the standard form of six hymns alternated with prayers and lessons before climaxing with the preacher's sermon. Most of the children of the congregation were spared the sermon, sneaking out before its commencement, but the Roberts sisters were made to dutifully listen. Margaret Thatcher later recounted how she and Muriel used to impatiently time the preacher and would get agitated if the sermon went over fifteen minutes. After-wards, it was common for the speaker to be invited to supper by one of the congregation, with Alfred Roberts, lay-preacher and local grandee, often willing to step in as host.

Alfred Roberts was given his first taste of leadership at Finkin Street Church, serving on both the Leaders' and Trustee boards. It was here, sitting round a table discussing age-old problems such as the appall-ing state of the lavatories, that Alfred Roberts learnt the tedious art of governance by committee. The minutes reveal a preoccupation with declining membership particularly in the weekly Bible-study classes which, in 1928, had an average of thirty-two but by 1946 had decreased to just seven: a downwards slide that was never halted. It was customary for all churches to administer a poor fund for destitute mem-bers of the congregation and records reveal that a Mrs Wright, whose husband was seriously ill and could not work, was deemed deserving and was regularly sent one pound throughout the 1920s. Chapel finances remained the chief worry, and, as chairman of the Circuit Finance Committee, something with which Alfred Roberts was inti-mately involved. Account books for Finkin Street reveal that it was seriously in debt, sinking under the weight of two-pound per week inter-est payments to Midland Bank; a situation that was only resolved when the Wesleyan Conference agreed to step in. Thrift was not always prac-tised as much as it was preached, it seems. One contemporary accused Finkin Street of offering 'cheery chats for weary wives' while the min-isters shamelessly profited from their flock.[26] There is no evidence of any wrongdoing in the archives; the truth was that the building was nearly a century old and substantial funds were required to maintain it.

Finkin Street Church is an imposing stone building, situated down an intimate side street of Georgian houses. Until 2013 it had been

registered for sale but the only potential buyer – a chain of Italian piz-
zerias – had been forced to pull out once it was realised that the interiors
were protected under its Grade II-listed status. It is still used by a small
congregation of Grantham's (now amalgamated) Free Churches but
in a building with a capacity of 600 that takes ten hours to heat in the
winter, it is ill-suited to the contemporary demands of this small, dedicated congregation. The church may have escaped the common fate
of commercialisation that has befallen many former places of worship
in Britain, but preservation has not helped its cause. Unlike other
recycled sites of Britain's industrial landscape – the factories converted
into gentrified apartments, the quarries buried under new shopping
complexes, the redundant chapels transformed into mosques – Finkin
Street Church remains a shell to Britain's lost Nonconformist age.

Finkin Street, c. 1920. 'Wesleyan Chapel' is carved in stone on its exterior

Built in the Tuscan style of the 1840s, Finkin Street's denominational
tradition is proudly carved in stone on its exterior. Inside, the layout
looks much like a civic chamber with its semi-circular two-tiered

auditorium. Closer inspection reveals it to be a spatial representation of the 'priesthood of believers', with no altar dividing the shepherd and his sheep. All eyes are directed towards the organ for the hymnody and the elevated pulpit, which is situated in the middle rather than to the side. Most churches tended to have two separate (often encased) pulpits, one for the ordained, another for the laity. Finkin Street is testimony to the spirit of egalitarianism in Methodism, with its singular stand.

Inside Finkin Street. All eyes are focused on the pulpit and the organ for the source of Methodist worship: the sermon and the hymnody

At Finkin Street, sermon duty would alternate between the chapel minister, local circuit preachers and, as its records reveal, even visiting speakers from distant parts of the empire, including Australia, West Africa and Hong Kong. In 1918, the same year that women were granted the vote, Wesleyan Methodists lifted the ban on female preachers. Several women officiated at Finkin Street, particularly in wartime, although there is no evidence that Margaret Thatcher's mother, the ever-practical, ever-in-the-background Beatrice, ever took the plunge. Watching would have been the young Margaret Roberts, probably fidgeting on the hard uncomfortable wooden pews with her legs impatiently swinging to and fro as the sermon reached beyond the reasonable quarter of an hour. In her memoirs, Thatcher recounts how those Sunday sermons left a lasting impression, particularly one on Christian charity and illegitimacy, and a wartime sermon linking the fighter pilots of the Battle of Britain with the Apostles and another on God's providence. By far the most inspiring figure in the pulpit, however, must have been her father. Standing at over 6 ft tall with his shock of white albino hair and in Thatcher's own description, affected 'sermon voice', one would imagine that Alfred Roberts assumed the air and authority of an Old Testament prophet. Margaret Thatcher later remarked that he was a 'powerful preacher' whose sermons were full of 'intellectual substance'.[27] It was certainly true that Roberts was a famed local preacher who would tour the local chapels it is said, often with his youngest daughter in tow. A circuit calendar from 1944 shows that Roberts preached at least four times a month in different locations, at both afternoon and evening services.

Lay-preachers were not simply foot soldiers, but esteemed officers, particularly those gifted with a rhetorical flair and an ability to rouse the troops. They were required to undergo some training and would be responsible not just for the sermon, but the entire service. For a man like Alfred Roberts, who had left school at an early age, it is quite possible that this tutelage, and the respect he gained from preaching in various pulpits across Lincolnshire, stirred a sense of self-belief that fuelled his political ambitions. Methodists sought to stir the individual's imagination through the sermon in the hope of leading the flock to a deeper, more conscious faith. As far as we know, Alfred Roberts did not partake in open-air preaching; religion, like politics, had gone 'inside' by the inter-war years. His sermons therefore would have been delivered within the confines of a chapel and preached to the faithful. Yet this was no easy mission. Roberts had the unenviable task of keeping the laity 'converted' at a time when many were drifting away.

But if we have the image of Alfred Roberts in the pulpit, what of his words? A collection of his sermon notes, kept by Margaret Thatcher and now housed in her personal archive, serve as a fertile source into the mind and manner of a man to whom so much has been attributed, but so little is known. Mostly dating between 1941 and 1945, these handwritten notes were jotted down at the back of his daughter's chemistry book, possibly due to the paper shortage during the war. They reveal an impassioned man at work, with some parts illegible with frequent crosses out, underlining, capital letters for emphasis as well as bullet points to be hammered home to the flock.

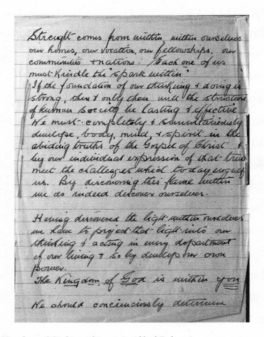

'The Kingdom of God is within you': Alfred Roberts's sermon notes c. 1940

Like a musical score, the underlying aspect here is the rhythm of the preacher's delivery: all staccato sentences, repetition of phrases, a built crescendo followed by exaltation. But there is little appreciation of language for its own sake: no flowery semantics, just simple words of faith.[28]

As would be expected, the notes contain the essential ingredients of the dissenting tradition: individual salvation ('The Kingdom of God is within you!') and the Protestant work ethic ('It is the responsibility of man ordained by the creator that he shall labour for the means of existence. It is a supreme act of faith.'). 'You possess all you need,' Alfred Roberts insisted. 'There is nothing to acquire. Learn to recognise what is already yours.' All that was necessary was hard work, for 'a lazy man' was one who had 'lost his soul already'.

Roberts would remind his audience why they were not Roman Catholics, evoking Martin Luther's edict 'individual salvation by faith alone' and also why they were not Anglicans, judging that a church 'under the tutelage of Kings and Princes' was merely a temporal vehicle hosed in holy water. Alfred Roberts, however, appreciated the nature of Christian unity: the 'diversity of administration but the same Spirit and Lord.' Above all, Christianity in Roberts' view concerned free will, a spiritual inwardness and an individual Covenant with God. Roberts was not rigid and prescriptive but intellectually curious when it came to his faith. As historian Antonio Weiss has highlighted, references to Alexander Pope and William Wordsworth in the sermon notes reveal a man who was 'un-Piestistic' who liked to be challenged by secular thought.[29]

Contained here are also instructions to prospective preachers, with Roberts setting out the requirements necessary to lead and inspire a following. First, it demanded absolute conviction: '…[in order to] kindle the flame in the heart of your hearer, you will have to keep the flame burning on your own altar.' Secondly, he was cautious that it would be a slog: 'Your task demands and deserves sheer hard work. Sweat of brains and discipline of soul … [if] you desire your sermon to make a difference to human lives and lead them more thoroughly to surrender to the sovereignty of Christ.' Finally, he recognised the importance of being at one with the flock: 'Never allow yourself to become aloof and out of touch with the realities of other men's lives.' Thatcher never made any direct reference to these guidelines even though she often quoted other pieces of advice given to her by her father. And yet these qualities can be readily associated with her leadership. There is little doubt too that Margaret Thatcher self-consciously embraced the style and tone of a preacher. As she told interviewer Brian Walden in 1983: 'There would have been no great prophets, no great philosophers in life, no great things to follow, if those who propounded the views had gone out and said "Brothers, follow me, I believe in consensus." No, Brian, no.'

Politics, according to Margaret Thatcher, was about conviction: an understanding which she had been taught 'in a small town by a father who had a conviction approach'.[30] Examining her father's sermon notes, there is little reason to doubt her on this point.

Historically, Methodism always applied itself more readily to politics than Anglicanism. The Established Church was tied too closely to the state to question it. Unsurprisingly, there is clear evidence of a fusion between the temporal and spiritual in Roberts's sermons. In a coded reference to the leading debate of inter-war politics – protectionism versus free trade – Roberts let slip where he stood on the matter: 'God refuses to put grace on a tariff' with the implication being that the universal freedom of market mirrored the universal availability of grace. This was a doctrinal legitimation of the 'invisible hand', which echoed that of nineteenth-century free trade Liberals and one that his daughter would annunciate with equal passion forty years later.

As would be expected of a dissenter, Alfred Roberts also extolled the virtues of religious liberty and condemned its opposite: religious uniformity. But this too was laced in political terms, with religious conformism likened to 'a denominational closed shop', thereby betraying a belief that compulsory trade union membership and mandatory affiliation to a particular faith were both infringements on personal freedom. In another extract, Alfred Roberts aligned spiritual conformity to totalitarianism: 'Uniformity can be a soul destroying agent, as evil as totalitarianism, and totalitarianism, can end in the systematic dehumanisation of man.' Addressing the party-faithful at the annual conference in 1989, Thatcher served up a similar homily on individual liberty in reference to her ideological battle against communism: 'Remove man's freedom and you dwarf the individual, you devalue his conscience and you demoralise him.'[31]

There is an indication though that her father, in line with other men of his generation, acknowledged the social evils of the age. In a clear reference to the Beveridge Report, published in 1942, Roberts preached that 'ignorance, squalor, hunger and want, injustice and oppression' was a 'betrayal of our Lord and Master'.[32] Yet, in another sermon from 1950, five years into Attlee's Labour government, he offered a coded warning to those who invested too much faith in temporal power: 'Men, nations, races or any particular generation cannot be saved by ordinances, power, legislation. We worry about all this, and our faith becomes weak and faltering.' Roberts also revealed himself to be sceptical when it came to the Church's involvement in social affairs. Going against the then consensus within Methodism, Roberts thought 'social issues' a diversion, which turned the church into 'a glorified discussion group'. Margaret Thatcher would make a similar point in a speech to the General Assembly of the Church of Scotland in 1988: 'Christianity is about spiritual redemption, not social reform.'[33] In her father's view, the real danger in the modern world was not poverty but affluence. 'No man's soul can be satisfied with a materialistic philosophy' only 'the stern discipline and satisfaction of a spiritual life'. The struggle of how to morally square the free market with the materialist culture it inspired was something his daughter would struggle with throughout her premiership.

In Finkin Street Church, to the right of the pulpit, there stands a lectern with a small plaque honouring Alfred Roberts's service to both the church and community placed there following his death in 1970. It is apt that the only mark of remembrance to Alfred Roberts in Grantham is here in Finkin Street Church and in the form of a lectern.

Margaret Thatcher obviously thought so too, making a rare trip to Grantham for the commemoration.

A brief return to Grantham: Margaret Thatcher posing with her step-mother, Cissie Roberts (left) and sister, Muriel (middle), for her father's commemorative lectern at Finkin Street Church

III. Translating the Gospel into everyday life

ALFRED ROBERTS MAY have been a prominent lay-preacher but he clearly felt his calling was in civic rather than religious life. He was not unique in this respect. Methodist lay-preachers tended to have the public-speaking skills and the networks necessary for politics; the Salem chapel in Halifax, for example, was known locally as the 'Mayor's nest' because it was the source of so many mayors in the town.

In her memoirs, Margaret Thatcher described her father as an 'old-fashioned Liberal'.[34] Alfred Roberts had certainly supported the party in his youth, had endorsed the National Government in the 1930s (with which many Liberals were aligned) but later came out as a Conservative. He publicly declared his conversion in 1949 at his daughter's adoption meeting for her parliamentary candidature for the Dartford constituency. On this occasion, according to press reports, Roberts claimed that the Conservative Party 'stood for very much the same things as the Liberal Party did in his young days.'[35] In Alfred Roberts's political journey we find one of the important shifts in twentieth-century British politics: the movement of lower-middle-class Nonconformists from the Liberals to the Conservatives.

Historically, the Nonconformist vote had overwhelmingly but not exclusively gone to the Liberal Party, yet this affiliation, while strong amongst Primitive Methodists, Baptists, Congregationalists and Unitarians, was decidedly less so amongst the Wesleyans, who in fact had been Tories until the mid-nineteenth century and remained distrustful of the Liberal Party's irreligious and radical tendencies.[†] Wesleyans continued to be ambivalent about their religious association with other Nonconformists and the political connection with the Liberals. Liberal Nonconformity, as a political force, suffered its first major blow in 1886, when Gladstone's dogged fight for Home Rule in Ireland prompted seventy-eight Liberal MPs led by Nonconformist Joseph Chamberlain to enter into an alliance with the Conservatives as Liberal Unionists. Liberal Nonconformity did, however, enjoy a brief revival in the Edwardian period – chiefly during a fight over denominational education and at the 1906 election – but the drift of the dissenters into separate Conservative and Labour camps had already begun and by the eve of the Second World War this realignment would be practically complete.

The influence of Nonconformity was, of course, evident in the formation of the trade union movement and later the political party with Labour's first leader, Keir Hardie, promoting 'Labour and Liquor don't mix' as one of his key electoral slogans. The decline of the Liberal Party in the 1920s prompted a second wave of converts to the socialist cause. One such MP was Anthony Wedgwood Benn's father, William, who defected in 1927. Indeed many future Labour stars, such as Anthony Wedgwood Benn and Michael Foot were of Liberal Nonconformist ancestry. Michael Foot's father, Isaac, for example, had been a Methodist and Liberal MP in the West Country between 1922 and 1935 where he led campaigns against drinking and betting.

Thatcher, too, had a Liberal-voting father but he represented a different phenomenon. Alfred Roberts, born in 1892, would have cast his first vote in the 'coupon election' of 1918, held after the First World War and

---

[†] John Wesley himself had been a Tory.

the passing of the Representation of the People Act, which had removed all property restrictions on voters. One would have imagined that Roberts would have put an 'X' for Lloyd George's coalition, the eventual victors, but possibly for the last time. The Liberal Party was already in decline and soon internal factionalism and competing forces would see it collapse as a ruling electoral force. The Nonconformist vote, already fragmented, split irrevocably as the Labour Party shored up the working-class constituencies while the Conservative Party made successful appeals to wavering Liberal voters, chiefly Wesleyans. Paradoxically, just as the various factions within Methodism unified in 1932, so the political divisions within it were more exposed than ever before.

Over time the electoral map of Britain transformed as urban and industrial areas turned from Liberal to Labour, and the new suburbs, small towns and rural areas turned Tory blue. But this was far from systematic. In areas such as Cornwall and parts of Wales, the Liberal allegiance held firm even after Nonconformity itself collapsed. It was, above all, a gradual and patchy development, shaped as much by local tensions (Grantham for example shifted between Conservative, Liberal and Independent in these years) as it was by a chaotic national scene which saw two coalitions, a National Government, the entry of women into the political sphere and the largest extension of the franchise in British parliamentary history. For these reasons, it was not until after the Second World War that the dust settled on these new partisan allegiances, but the aftereffects of the Liberal Party's decline would be felt right up to the 1980s.

Some within the Conservative and Unionist Party understandably greeted the extension of the franchise in 1918 with paranoia, but party managers soon realised that capturing floating Liberal voters would be crucial in order to counter Labour's natural advantage. This they proved remarkably effective in doing: its proportion of the vote never fell below 38 per cent while it managed to hold office (either in coalition or as a single party) twenty-five out of the twenty-nine years between 1916 and 1945. That the Conservative and Unionist Party was able to seize the initiative was largely due to the unassuming but canny leader Stanley Baldwin, in charge from 1923–37. Baldwin saw his mission as refashioning Conservatism for the mass democratic age, which involved targeting potential voters like Alderman Roberts. Even though Baldwin was a practising Anglican, he was of Wesleyan heritage; a fact he never ceased to remind Nonconformist audiences. Baldwin addressed more Free Church gatherings than any Tory before him where he would promote his party 'as the natural haven of rest' for the 'independent and sturdy individualism' of Nonconformists.[36] During the 1929 election, Baldwin's schmoozing of Nonconformists even prompted the Anglican *Church Times* to remark somewhat bitterly that the Conservatives 'show themselves far more eager to gain sympathy from Nonconformists than from Church-people'.[37] At the 1931 election, most of the Free Church press came out in support of the National Government. The result was a landslide for the Conservative and Unionist Party and, while some Liberals served in the Cabinet as part of the National Government, factionalism within the party would in the long run ensure that it would no longer be the dominant party at Westminster. Baldwin excelled in converting a crucial band of Nonconformists in much the same way that Margaret Thatcher would later successfully appeal to 'upwardly mobile' floating voters in the 1980s. This shift was to be a lasting change. Recent converts felt reassured by Baldwin's successor, Birmingham Unitarian and Liberal Unionist Neville Chamberlain, and later Winston Churchill, who, although in character was the complete antithesis to the Nonconformist conscience, he nonetheless had been a Liberal before crossing the floor in 1924.

It was for these reasons, then, that Alfred Roberts switched his allegiance to the Conservatives and why in 1935 he, along with his youngest daughter, campaigned for the National Government Conservative candidate, the Eton-educated, ex-military officer Sir Victor Warrender for the constituency of Grantham and Rutland. On polling day, the ten-year-old Margaret acted as the runner, relaying information to the committee room in Lord Brownlow's Belton House; it was to be her first taste of politics. Margaret Thatcher was every inch a true-blue, but her political heritage was Nonconformist Liberalism. Even in the 1950s, the heterogeneous mix of Liberals and Conservatives within the Conservative and Unionist Party was still clearly evident, although it had now firmly established itself not in terms of religion but in ethos. There was deep division between libertarians and paternalists. The paternalists would have their run of it during the 1950s and 1960s; Margaret Thatcher's ascent in 1975 would symbolise the eventual victory of the libertarian strand within the party.

Stanley Baldwin's other great ability was to stir up bourgeois and non-unionised working-class fears about socialism, which was particularly virulent amongst men like Alfred Roberts, whose paranoia stemmed more from domestic and parochial concerns than events in Moscow. The English petite bourgeoisie now defined themselves not against the landed Tory squires, but the unionised working class. Nothing, therefore, did more to alienate them from the Liberal Party than when Lord Asquith, with the agreement of Lloyd George, allowed the Labour Party to govern for the first time in 1924. And nothing did more to further endear them to the Conservatives than when, two years later, the Baldwin government crushed the General Strikers in 1926.

In 1919 the *Daily Mail* had somewhat loosely defined the middle class as 'those folk who become below the peerage, but who do not have [national] insurance cards'.[38] Over the next twenty years, aided by the consumer and property boom, the middle class expanded exponentially even though this was to be a geographical divide as much as it was a class one, with the south prospering while the industrial north felt the full effects of the Depression. Importantly, though, the Roberts family did not live in the new towns – the Dagenhams or the Brents – those areas defined by light industries, the new professional and skilled working-class inhabitants, a weak religious presence and the dominance of American consumer culture. Although Thatcher would later electorally triumph in southern suburbia, she was not a product of it. Grantham, on the other hand, was still shaped by its rural and aristocratic connections, its old industries, services and traditional vocations. Alfred Roberts may have made it into the middle class, but as a self-employed grocer, he was not of professional rank. Instead, the Robertses were members of the most fluid and frustrated section of British society: the lower middle class, who tend to take a disparaging view of both the established middle class (who do not need to strive) and the lower class (who do not bother). Unlike some members of her party, Margaret Thatcher's attitude towards the working man was never paternalistic: she was too close to the working class to be either sympathetic to it or frightened by it.

Given his strong political leanings, why then did Alfred Roberts stand as an independent on the council? The truth is that this label is misleading. Borough councils, unlike metropolitan ones, tended not to adopt party political labels during these years, although this began to change from the late 1930s onwards. Moreover, Alfred Roberts was not an independent at all but the appointee of the local branch of the Chamber of Trade. Founded in 1897, the chamber was a members-only organisation designed to protect and promote local businesses against unfair competition and to keep a watchful eye on legislation, tax and insurance. The chamber operated its own debt-collecting service and was particularly effective in curbing black-market activities during wartime. Its membership included businessmen, shopkeepers and (in this pre-NHS era) even doctors, although it refused entry to representatives of the Licensed Victuallers Association of Trade (pub landlords) and when the major industries were nationalised in the 1950s, it also barred members of those sectors from joining. Alfred Roberts's association with the chamber dated back to 1927 and he would later serve twice as its president. One particular success noted in its minute books was over the purchasing of uniforms for Margaret Roberts's school. The chamber fought against a monopoly, appealing to the school governors (of which Alfred Roberts was one) to ensure 'that parents could buy clothing where they liked'.[39] The chamber also hosted regular lectures on topics including business-finance, banking and the rise of the Co-op, which one would imagine only reinforced their hostility to organised labour and possibly international capitalism, for this was an organisation born out of the interests of provincial capitalism designed to protect the interests of provincial businessmen.

Even though the chamber asserted its non-partisan credentials, this was a dubious claim. Politically speaking, the chamber may not have been exclusively Conservative or Liberal but it was certainly anti-Labour. In the 1931 general election, for example, the chamber took out an advertisement in the *Grantham Journal* urging businessmen to support the local National Government (Conservative) candidate. The chamber worked alongside the Ratepayers Association (a lobby group for homeowners) in vetting and sponsoring new candidates for council elections. This was local democracy in action, and was, in no uncertain terms, a stitch-up. Records suggest that the chamber's majority on the council and even its seats on the county council was largely down to fixed agreement between candidates. In 1928, a resolution was sent to the Labour Party concerning the forthcoming county council elections stating that if they did not agree to the terms set down, the chamber would fight all seventeen seats. A deal was struck where candidates would run uncontested. The independents' run of the town council was also reinforced by their control over the aldermanic elections, voted for by councillors rather than the electorate, and awarded to ex-councillors who were judged to have given great service; one of whom would later be Alfred Roberts.

Long before Grantham became synonymous with Margaret Thatcher, it gained national notoriety as a place of corruption. In 1937, local journalist and author Oliver Anderson (pseudonym) published *Rotten Borough*, a parody of the dodgy dealings and self-serving pontifications of the petite bourgeoisie that ran the town.

> Upon every side I see graft, complacency, hypocrisy and petty provincialism. I see the poor left to wallow in their poverty. I see the bourgeoisie blossoming in vulgarity. I see professional classes stewing in snobbery and the aristocracy static in stupidity.[40]

Anderson, though, reserved his greatest criticism for those who ran the Chamber of Trade and the town council, whom he considered 'the very root of all evil:'[41]

> the small-town bourgeois is not a man, he is not a human, he is a pub-
> lic nuisance, and as such, should be suppressed. Let a man make money
> … but not, as he does, money for money's sake. To make money for any
> other reason than for what money can buy is low, brutish and immoral.[42]

Far from the quaint picture of Grantham life portrayed by Margaret Thatcher as one of civic duty and service, *Rotten Borough* is a tale of self-interest and material gain. One character, greengrocer Councillor Nurture, who bears an uncanny resemblance to Alfred Roberts, is accused of fixing the street lighting with gas rather than electricity in order to profit from his shares in the local gas company (he also has a reputation for being overly familiar with his female staff). Unsurprisingly, the book was withdrawn after just three weeks, when an avalanche of libel claims reached the publishers. The claims of corruption aside, what Anderson had got right were the distinct class and power networks in the town. There was undoubtedly a Grantham clique – men such as Stanley Foster, George Mills, Frederick Cheshire, George Green, Arthur Eatch, as well as Alfred Roberts – whose names can be found dominating the records of the town council, Rotary, Chamber of Trade and carved on the roll call of mayors in the town hall.

Rotten Borough: The men (and two women) running Grantham.
Alfred Roberts can be seen on the second row, second from the right

When the council was established in 1835, its chief purpose had been to administer public health and highways, but by the time Alfred Roberts was elected in 1927, its responsibilities, funds and sphere of influence had expanded exponentially to include sanitation, maternity and child welfare, roads and slum clearance, as well as the monitoring and licensing of public spaces. In 1929, Parliament extended these responsibilities even further by transferring the administration of the poor relief to local councils with the idea of loosening the social stigmatisation of destitution under the new bureaucratic guise of social welfare. Then borough councils were not considered as a mechanism of the state or a sphere for party politics, they were an organ for the community and a realm of local influence. This was beginning to change however. In the 1920s, as council responsibilities expanded, so did the flow of funds from central government. Grantham was not alone in seeking a central grant from the Public Works Loan Board at the Ministry of Health to invest in local housing, but what is perhaps more interesting is how it operated. Council discussions clearly demonstrate a preference for buyers rather than renters in a belief that the occupier would demonstrate more care and responsibility 'if the property were his own'.[43] The fiscal and social benefits of encouraging homeownership were discovered long before Margaret Thatcher's great 'Sale of the Century', it seems. If the operations of Grantham council reveal anything, though, it is that welfare provision rarely fits into such neat patterns of public versus private, charity versus state. Grantham's mixed economy of welfare and governance is perhaps one lesson that Margaret Thatcher did not take with her from Grantham.

It was in his role as head of the finance and rating group that Alfred Roberts became known as Grantham's 'Chancellor of the Exchequer'. Clearly a keen advocate for low rates and fiscal prudence, in 1936 Roberts pushed through the contracting out of the maintenance of public housing, arguing in the name of cost, efficiency and what was the best deal for ratepayers. What Alfred Roberts's council would do for ninety council houses in Grantham, his daughter would later enforce as a principle across the land. Year after year, Roberts successfully managed to balance the books, but in 1937 he controversially set the rates at fourteen shillings in the pound, which was then above the Ministry of Labour's Standard of Living Index and an unreasonable level for a town of Grantham's size. In one of the lengthiest and most fractious debates in his years as councillor – which eerily foreshadow that of the Poll Tax – Roberts defended his policy by explaining that the hike was necessary because of unexpected debts relating to the local mental hospital. Only when probed did he reluctantly admit that it was also to pay for the alterations and furnishings of the town clerk's new offices and an increase in council salaries.

Correctly sensing that the rate was unjustifiable, Roberts put the blame on those who did not pay, who were, in his words 'sponging on the people who do'. Bad collection rates was a moot point, but when it was suggested that harsh proceedings be taken against defaulters, Roberts feared a backlash: 'If I did that I don't know whether I would dare walk about the streets of Grantham … I am sorry to have to be the man to move it and more sorry than ever to be one of the men who will have to pay it' he remarked bitterly.[44] Even in this period, local rates were known as the 'unfair tax', for, as responsibilities of local councils increased (especially in relation to social welfare), homeowners complained, somewhat legitimately, that they were paying for services for which they themselves did not benefit. It remained a contentious issue and one which Margaret Thatcher would attempt to solve, disastrously, when Prime Minister.

Local borough councils reached their peak of authority and influence in the 1930s, but soon Westminster started to usurp these powers and so began the process of centralised control. It developed an unstoppable momentum during wartime and continued apace in the late 1940s and early 1950s under successive Labour and Conservative administrations in what might be interpreted as the evolution of centralism rather than a fundamental ideological switch. Grantham's councillors may have regretted the loss of their powers but they also recognised that their small borough council was ill-equipped to deal with growing expectations and responsibilities.

In 1945, Alfred Roberts would reach the pinnacle of his career by becoming Mayor of Grantham. At the election, one of his arch-rivals, Councillor Foster, generously heaped praise on a man whose 'forthrightness' and 'unchallengeable integrity' made him worthy of the role. The outgoing mayor, Councillor Dale, then placed the robe and chain on Alfred Roberts's shoulders and handed him the seal. According to the *Grantham Journal*, Roberts was overwhelmed by the occasion, his stern face softening momentarily.[45] The role itself was chiefly ceremonial and one often bestowed on long-serving members of the council, but Alfred Roberts (like his daughter) clearly revelled in the ceremonial side of politics; no more so than in 1945 when he led the victory parade to celebrate the end of the war. How the people of Grantham greeted his time in office is impossible to judge, although the *Grantham Guardian*, a paper that took a very dim view of proceedings at the town hall, often portrayed him somewhat unfavourably as Napoleon Bonaparte.

Post-war reconstruction brought great changes in Grantham, as it did elsewhere in Britain. The borough council promised an ambitious programme of house building, state education and full employment. It appeared, though, that the old guard would have no place in the new regime as the newly elected council declared its intention to work for the working class of the town and not be beholden to private or sectional interests. It would take seven years before the Labour Party would finally achieve a majority on the council in 1952 and, naturally, it was only fair that the number of aldermen reflected this majority. On the day of the election, it came down to a division between two candidates, with Roberts losing by a not insubstantial five votes. The *Grantham Journal* recorded the scene that followed:

He stood, took off his robe, looked longingly at it as he laid it on the aldermanic bench and then said with tremendous emotion and so quietly it was almost inaudible: 'No medals, no honours, but an inward satisfaction. May God bless Grantham forever.'[46]

Alfred Roberts throws down his robes as he is voted off the council in favour of Labour councillor Audus

After more than twenty years of service, Roberts had been unceremoniously booted off his beloved council. Margaret Thatcher famously wept when she recounted this story in a TV interview in 1985, calling it a 'tragedy'.[47] Years later, after her own traumatic demise, she returned to those events in 1952: 'I thought my father's example was so wonderful. So hurtful, but so wonderful, and so dignified ... I didn't forget it.'[48]

IV. There *was* such a thing as society

WHEN, IN 1987, Margaret Thatcher clumsily uttered the immortal words, 'There is no such thing as society', she handed a gift to her critics. 'There is no such thing as society because Margaret Thatcher has destroyed it' came the reply. But her explanation that followed is perhaps more revealing:

There is living tapestry of men and women and people and the beauty
of that tapestry and the quality of our lives will depend upon how much
each of us is prepared to take responsibility for ourselves and each of
us prepared to turn round and help by our own efforts those who are
unfortunate.[49]

Here Thatcher was evoking a concept of civil society (those mediating
institutions between the individual and the state), which had legitimate intellectual roots on both the left and right. Admittedly though,
Thatcher had a very narrow understanding of what constituted civil
society. It was characteristically middle class, socially conservative and
religiously inspired, with no room for co-operatives, unions or solidarity of any kind. Nonetheless, on this subject, Thatcher spoke not from
an ideological perspective but personal experience for it was exactly
what she had witnessed first-hand as a child.

Grantham had a vibrant and extensive network of charities, philanthropists and associations. The logo of local engineering firm, Ruston
& Hornsby, adorned the fire engines, the library was built courtesy of
the Carnegie Trust, while Grantham's Rotary, the Chamber of Trade
and local philanthropists provided the 'bread and circus' events. Associational culture certainly thrived in inter-war Grantham, but while it
may not have been party-political or denominational, it was certainly
class-based. The power and initiative lay very much in the hands of the
bourgeoisie, with some paternalistic injection from the local landown-
ers, while Grantham's poor remained silent and compliant beneficiaries.
Grantham's civic life, much like its politics, was chiefly the means by
which local dignitaries such as Alderman Roberts were able to exercise
their public service, forward their interests and satisfy their religious
conscience. One such occasion was the week-long Civic Centenary
Celebrations in June 1935 to commemorate 100 years of Grantham
council. Organised by the Chamber of Trade, it seems to have had less
to do with celebrating the town and more to do with keeping the tills

ringing with events such as a 'shopping week', a window-dressing competition and a 'buy British goods' day. The ten-year-old Margaret, then
a pupil at Huntington Primary School, took part in a parade of children
singing a hymn composed by local parson, Rev. E. Stancliffe, entitled
'Grantham's Jerusalem':

> *The present yours, the future ours; we promise that, When reaping*
> *What now you sow, you yet will know*
> *A Grantham in safe keeping…*
> *We swear to serve with heart and nerve*
> *Our God, our town, our nation*

Margaret Thatcher remembers being 'immensely proud of our town;
we knew its history and traditions; we were glad to be part of its life.'[50]
But, as the daughter of Alderman Roberts, she had a unique view of
its importance and her family's place within it. She witnessed Remembrance Day, for example, from the windows of the Guildhall ballroom
as she watched her father take part in the procession with his fellow
councillors. Her attitude may have been different had he fought and
been parading in his uniform.‡

In 1937, the town centre was once again adorned in flags, festoons
and bunting for the Coronation of George VI, which Alfred Roberts had
orchestrated as head of the council's celebration committee. Grantham
residents were treated to a week-long series of events which included
brass bands, a classical music concert, religious services (naturally both
Anglican and Methodist), a coronation carnival with acrobats and jugglers and a firework display culminating in a live outdoor radio broadcast
of the coronation. It is worth remembering that during that summer
of 1937, as the twelve-year-old Margaret was watching jugglers in
Grantham Dysart Park, Michael Foot, then a journalist at the *Tribune*,

---

‡ Despite trying to enlist several times, Alfred Roberts was unable to fight in the First World War
owing to poor eyesight.

was busy keeping the various strands of the left together under the 'Unity Campaign', while the young Edward Heath was observing the rise of National Socialism in Germany, attending the Nuremberg Rally and coming face-to-face with Goering, Goebbels and Himmler. If Foot was always the left-wing intellectual holding the movement together, Heath, forever the internationalist, then Margaret Thatcher was always the provincial girl. It is through such formative experiences that one's political values are formed and future battles are forged.

Margaret Thatcher may have later rhapsodised about Grantham's civic life, but, as a child, the cinema clearly held more allure and attraction. By the 1930s, Grantham could boast four cinemas, the grandest of which, the State Cinema, was said to have a staircase like that out of a Busby Berkeley musical. Finkin Street Church tried in vain to compete by establishing its own film club, although the content was strictly regulated and attendees had to endure a sermon and hymns as part of the show. Margaret Roberts was in no doubt where she would rather be. She later recorded how, as a child, she was 'entranced with the glamorous world of Hollywood', the historical epics of Alexander Korda and the dramatic heroines played by Barbara Stanwyck, Greta Garbo and Ingrid Bergman, as well as the musicals of Fred Astaire and Ginger Rogers: 'I roamed to the most fabulous realms of the imagination. It gave me the determination to roam in reality one day,' she wrote in her memoirs.[51] This was her first taste of Americana and she revelled in it.

British actors do not appear in her list of favourites nor does she reference the visit to Grantham of arguably the biggest British film star of the 1930s, Lancashire lass Gracie Fields. Thousands of Granthamsonians reportedly turned out to hear Field's Rochdale roar from her hotel window but not the Robertses. Admittedly, it is hard to imagine Alderman Roberts and his daughters parading through the streets of Grantham leading a chorus of 'Sing As We Go!' Anti-Americanism may have stirred in Conservatives such as Enoch Powell and writers such as J. B. Priestley, but not Margaret Thatcher. She may have always been a 'little Englander', but Thatcher was someone who from an early age eagerly embraced all the romantic possibilities of the new American empire.

One American import, in which her father was heavily involved, was Rotary International. Started by a small group of businessmen in Chicago in 1905, Rotary migrated to Britain in 1911 and by 1939 had 400 clubs with 20,000 members and Prince George as its patron. Rotary explicitly forbade partisan and sectarian affiliations and encouraged social and commercial responsibility as well as an active engagement in local, national and international affairs. Alfred Roberts had helped establish the Grantham branch in 1931, later becoming its president in 1935. Of her father's attachment, Thatcher wrote in her memoirs: 'The Rotary motto, "Service Above Self", was engraved on my father's heart.'[52] Its ethic certainly complemented Roberts's faith with its emphasis on service and individual effort for the greater good. At its annual dinner in 1934, the *Grantham Journal* recorded the toast delivered by Rotarian C. Bispham:

> Rotary International realised that man was a gregarious and social ani-
> mal, and has to live in communities where it was essential for his very
> existence that he should have the cooperation and help of all the rest
> of the members of his community. In fact, the individual was, as it were
> a cog in a vast machine, and for that machine to run smoothly, it was
> essential that every cog should give its maximum service.[53]

C. Bispham had articulated in 1934 what Margaret Thatcher had tried to do in 1987 with her 'no such thing as society' comment. This was the 'living tapestry', or at least how Margaret Thatcher understood it.

Given the international nature of Rotary's organisation and spirit, it is perhaps unsurprising that events on the European continent soon dominated the weekly luncheon discussion. Not long after Hitler came to power, Rotary hosted a presentation from a Professor H. Brose of Nottingham University who had just returned from Germany. Brose was clearly impressed, remarking that 'everybody was clothed and fed' and there was no sign of the 'unemployed about the streets', as in places such as Nottingham. Welcoming the rise of fascism as an antidote to communism, Brose reassuringly concluded that Britain had nothing to fear from Germany's 'defensive rearmament' and that having read *Mein Kampf*, he considered Hitler 'extremely straightforward and sincere'.[54] Four months later, local cinema owner J. A. Campbell visited Germany as part of the British Rotary delegation. Like Brose, Campbell believed fascism preferable to communism and was pleased to report that Hitler, whom he had heard speak at a rally, looked favourably on Rotary even though Campbell remarked that it was below its normal strength because of the 'boycott of the Jew'.[55] It is not until 1939, seven months before war broke out, that we hear what Alfred Roberts thought of all this. By this time, Rotary had been banned in Germany and international events were conspiring towards war, even though the people still clung to Chamberlain's promise. Roberts praised the man who had gone to Munich 'armed only with a neatly-rolled umbrella with his mind made up and his will intent on peace'. Roberts, though, coupled this with a stark warning that although fascism may suit Germany there were fundamental principles that all should adhere to: 'Justice, truth and liberty'. For Roberts, the primacy of the latter was paramount: 'Liberty in its proper realm and sphere [is] vital … principles [are] greater than personality, and more important than any form of government.'[56]

Roberts's take on international affairs undoubtedly hardened during the war. In one of his first speeches as mayor in 1945, entitled 'From Bombing to Building', Roberts judged that in a nuclear age it was imperative that those who adhered to the Christian Gospel 'blast their way through the barricades and the obstacles of evil which opposed the peace of the world'. Offering a reassessment of Chamberlain, he concluded: 'We were becoming a race of sentimentalists ... in trying to appease an aggressive people.' Now was no time for pacifism or compromise, he affirmed, but upholding moral truth against the Soviets: 'They have got to be made to understand quite firmly and definitely that what they ask for is wrong.' In light of Margaret Thatcher's Manichaean approach to international affairs it may be that her father's dismissive take on what he termed the 'stupid sentimental type of diplomacy' had some influence.[57]

In the run up to the war, the troubles in Europe impacted in a very direct way on the Robertses' household. Following Hitler's absorption of Austria in 1938, the family agreed to give sanctuary to Muriel's Jewish pen pal, seventeen-year-old Edith Muhlbauer. Edith clearly considered Grantham rather dull, while the locals reportedly found her cosmopolitan and quixotic. She smoked tobacco, wore beautiful clothes and make-up and was said that Alfred Roberts feared that she might turn into 'one of those girls in Amsterdam'. It appears not to have been a happy encounter on both sides; Edith only spent a few weeks at the Robertses before going to live with Mr Wallace, the dentist, and eventually travelling to South America to live with her aunt.[58] Margaret Thatcher later claimed that Edith's tales of persecution in Austria were the origins of her life-long sympathy for the Jewish community. This may have been true, but much more likely was that her encounter with Edith was yet another reminder that there was a bigger world outside Grantham.

The war inevitably impinged on Grantham life like it did on most British towns. With the introduction of rationing, Roberts may have found his role in the community enhanced, but he also must have felt the creeping tentacles of the state intruding on his business more than ever before. Margaret Roberts lived out her teenage years during wartime, but while those on the battlefields quickly realised that Germans were also human beings, to her they were the anonymous enemy buzzing in the sky or the 'strutting brownshirts' demonised in newsreels.[59] The scene of Thatcher's wartime experience that is often depicted is of her doing her homework sheltered under a rickety kitchen table during air raids as her father fulfilled his duties as chief welfare officer directing Grantham's civil defence. The town was indeed a target for the Luftwaffe, with seventy people killed and approximately 200 people injured as a result of raids. Grantham was certainly of strategic importance, with its railway depot, RAF base and armaments factory, BMARC, yet it appears to have been hit more than most provincial towns.

'Grantham has provided us with more inquiries and problems than any other town in the Region', ran a secret memo from Major Haylor soon after the bombing of the BMARC factory in June 1941.[60] It advised that all Grantham telephone calls and post should be put under special surveillance. Why? It was not the factory that was of concern, but its owner –industrialist, playboy and suspected fascist sympathiser, William Kendall. A notorious figure in Grantham, Kendall was councillor and later MP when he successfully stood as an Independent MP against the Conservative War Coalition candidate. Kendall was a huge hit with Grantham workers, whom he won over with decent pay, parties and a morale-boosting visit by Clark Gable. He was also a close acquaintance of the Robertses. On the most dramatic day of Alfred Roberts's political career, when he was voted off the council in 1952, Kendall was the only man to speak in his defence. Kendall would also be the one to accompany Margaret Roberts on the train when she left Grantham for Oxford University in 1942.

William Kendall, who, it was said, 'talks like Beaverbook and looks like [James] Cagney', had had a spell in the Royal Navy, been in Russia for the 1917 Revolution ('on the side of the pretty girls' according to Kendall) and had worked at a car-manufacturing plant in Philadelphia before arriving in Grantham in 1938 as managing director of BMARC.[61] MI5 had monitored him from the start of the war and had recently released files revealing his links with the fascist British

National Party and suspicions that he was supplying photographs of his factory to the Germans (the bomber which hit BMARC was found to have detailed photographs of the grounds). MI5 were also wary of Kendall's Jewish servants, Leo and Milada Borger and especially local doctor Dr Jaugh, a known Nazi-sympathiser and Rotary member, who Margaret Thatcher remembers as a 'cold man' who used to give her father pro-Hitler literature in the mid-1930s.[62]

Also implicated was Lady Ursula Manners, then women's officer at the factory and a one-time girlfriend of both Lord Brownlow and Lord Beaverbrook, who was suspected of trading secrets to Kendall. Grantham was awash with rumours about spies at BMARC. The town hall was aware of the investigations, but given that Kendall reportedly used to entertain councillors with trips to Paris, they may have felt a little uneasy themselves. It was in 1942, when Alfred Roberts visited BMARC to preach a sermon to the munitions workers that Kendall suggested that he accompany his daughter, Margaret, to London to ensure that she reached the Oxford train safely.

In 1980, William Kendall wrote to Margaret Thatcher from America, where he was now living, to congratulate her on her election victory. Thatcher replied in warm tones, remarking that she indeed remembered him as an MP and 'as a very successful industrialist'.[63] Things were not always what they seemed in Grantham, nor were they always as Thatcher remembered.

In many ways, Thatcher's Grantham can be seen as a microcosm of inter-war British society with the dominant influence of the petite bourgeoisie, the diminishing input of the landed gentry and the provincial working class beginning to flex their muscles through the Co-op and the Labour Party. Grantham also reflected the changing religious make-up of Britain. The chapel was in decline but still the source of civic energy, while closer relations between all denominations symbolised the end of sectarianism but ultimately reflected the weakening hold of Christianity over the populace. Grantham's class structure was prejudicial and undoubtedly full of tension, yet ultimately harmonious. This was a situation which would ensure that, on the national scene, Britain did not fall to fascism or communism and in a small town like Grantham, why men such as Alfred Roberts and Lord Brownlow could get along. Yet it was in a state of flux. The arrival of party politics in the town chamber, the influence of American consumer culture and post-war pledges of reconstruction challenged the dominance of the petite bourgeoisie and gave hope for a more egalitarian age. As Prime Minister, Thatcher would frequently speak of the harmony between capitalism and civil society, but in Grantham she had experienced a distinctly provincial form of capitalism and a complementary civic culture that served a clique and was built on a set of values and class structure that was under increasing threat.

Thatcher may have eulogised Grantham later in life but as a teenager she probably had a better understanding of what it really was: a dull, stifling environment one wanted to escape from. In her memoirs, she remembers looking rather enviously out of her bedroom window at the Roman Catholic Church opposite with the girls celebrating their first communion 'dressed in white party dresses with bright ribbons, and carrying baskets of flowers'. She admitted that the Methodist look was 'much plainer ... If you wore a ribboned dress an older chapel-goer would shake his head and warn against the "first step to Rome"'.[64] Clothes for the future Margaret Thatcher would be an outward expression of her delight in decadence.

There was, however, one crucial reason she escaped Grantham and hardly went back. Unlike Churchill, who had a bullying father whom he was constantly trying to please, Thatcher had a doting father whom she soon outgrew. She had lived her early years in black and white; Margaret Roberts yearned for life in Technicolor.

CHAPTER TWO

THE PATH OF
CONFORMITY

*'As a Methodist in Grantham, I learnt the laws of God. When I read
Chemistry at Oxford, I learnt the laws of science, which derive from the
laws of God, and when I studied for the Bar, I learnt the laws of man.'*
— MARGARET THATCHER, 1999[1]

WARTIME OXFORD WAS a far cry from the romanticism of
Evelyn Waugh's *Brideshead Revisited*. The City of Dreaming
Spires had succumbed to the tedious practicalities of war
as air-raid instructions dominated the noticeboards, the infamous com-
memoration balls were abandoned and courses shortened to two years.
The student population was different too. Disproportionately women,
there was also a mix of younger students and men whose medical con-
dition had kept them out of the war. Margaret's base was Somerville
College, situated at the end of Woodstock Road, which unlike the
Anglican college, Lady Margaret Hall, was non-denominational and

catered for grammar-school sparks just like Margaret Roberts. The girl from Grantham, however, did not initially feel at home. 'I felt shy and ill at ease in this quite new environment' Thatcher later admitted.[2] To use a well-worn phrase, Margaret Roberts had gone from being a big fish in a small pond (winning a place at Oxford had caused a stir in Grantham) to a small fish in a very big pond.

Intimidated by the worldliness of Oxford, Wesley's Memorial Chapel in the centre of town initially proved a safe haven. 'Methodism provided me with an anchor of stability and, of course, contacts and friends who looked at the world as I did.'[3] Thatcher became a committed member of the University's Wesleyan Society, attending its study groups and socials as well as preaching in nearby chapels. She was in the home of Methodism, literally following in John Wesley's footsteps as she toured the local circuit evangelising to congregations. Nigel Gilson, who after university became a Methodist minister and would later preach at Finkin Street, describes Margaret Roberts's faith as 'effervescent'; she was both spiritual and inquisitive and took prayer meetings and discussion groups seriously. Another contemporary, Jean Southerst recalled one of Margaret's sermons – 'Seek ye first the Kingdom of God; and all these things shall be added onto you' – as 'outstanding'.[4] It is worth reiterating a point made by her biographer John Campbell, that 'Mrs Thatcher was a preacher before she was a politician'.[5]

Where more flighty souls may have floundered, Margaret Roberts's faith remained unchallenged by the social and intellectual temptations of Oxford: 'I never felt in any danger of that,' she later said.[6] Nonetheless, Margaret did experiment with the city's various spiritual offerings, attending the college chapel and the centre of intellectual Anglicanism, the University Church of St Mary, which she noted had 'a certain official formality which [made] it a somewhat cold place of worship'.[7] She also invested time in her other passion, music, joining the joint Balliol and Somerville choir, and the Bach choir.

Margaret returned to Oxford for her third year in October 1945 to find it a completely different place. The constraints of war had been loosened, the blackouts were no more, and, with demobbed soldiers now overrunning the lecture halls and the labs, the place had an altogether freer groove. She relished her newfound freedom and indulged even more in those things that had been denied her for most of her adolescence. She had joined the Oxford University Conservative Association (OUCA) on her arrival in Oxford, but it was not until her third year that she made her mark, firstly on the policy sub-committee, then serving as its secretary, treasurer and, finally, its president in the Michaelmas term of her fourth year. As she became more involved in OUCA, so she attended the Wesleyan Methodist chapel less and less. The boundless energy she had channelled into preaching the Word was now redirected into rallying the Tory troops.

Margaret Roberts gained a reputation within OUCA not for her right-wing convictions but for her persistence and dedication. She was admired for her willingness to canvass in those places where upper-class Tories would not have dared, such as the Morris Cowley Motor Works just outside Oxford.[8] While she undoubtedly gained respect from her OUCA colleagues, it was not the case within her own college. 'Somerville had always been a radical establishment and there weren't many Conservatives about then,' remembered wartime college principal Janet Vaughan. 'We used to argue about politics; she was so set in steel as a Conservative. She just had this one line.'[9]

Her first political tract 'The Basis of Conservatism', which she co-wrote for OUCA soon after the Labour election landslide, included a nod to individual enterprise but also to the redistribution of wealth. The overriding tone, however, was one of urgency: a desire for the Conservative Party to firmly and quickly frame its response to the 1945 result. This was certainly being done by those in the higher echelons of the party, principally R. A. Butler, who, under the guise of the Advisory Committee on Policy and Political Education, had been tasked with the difficult job of formulating economic planning and social welfare in a Conservative guise.

Margaret Roberts revelled in the social as well as the political life of OUCA, attending the dinners and balls and enjoying the company of the raffish Tory boys who were very much in charge. She was in awe of their wealth, connections and lifestyle and would be susceptible to such charms throughout her life. Her Oxford contemporaries also included future *Times* journalist William Rees-Mogg, Labour minister Anthony Crosland and writer and campaigner Ludovic Kennedy, but she appears not to have made a great impression, nor they on her.[10]

One future sparring partner whom Margaret Roberts did encounter was Labour stalwart Anthony Wedgwood Benn. She attended his election party as President of the Oxford Union, a strictly non-alcoholic affair. Thatcher later said that although she and Benn 'rarely agreed on anything', they shared a 'sympathy' based on their 'religious roots'.[11] When interviewed, Benn rejected such affinity and dismissed any notion that Thatcher's politics had a Christian basis, although he did concede that Thatcher's Methodist heritage was probably the source of her conviction style.[12] According to Benn, Thatcher, like himself, was a 'sign-post' politician, as opposed to a 'weather-cock' (those politicians who fluttered in the wind such as Tony Blair). In this respect at least, Benn always preferred to identify himself as the left-wing equivalent of Thatcher rather than the socialist antidote to Blair. Benn and Thatcher stemmed from the same robust Reformist tradition, even if their politics sprouted in opposite directions. Seen together, they personify the divergent paths of Nonconformist Liberalism in the second half of the twentieth century.

It was as President of OUCA that Margaret Roberts first encountered Robert Runcie, her future Archbishop of Canterbury. With foppish auburn hair, good looks and Merseyside charm, Runcie had a social confidence and ease that enabled him to mingle freely with the upper classes. A war-hero for the boys and a hit with the girls, Runcie had returned to Oxford from the Normandy beaches having been awarderd a Military Cross and soon became notorious for chatting up ladies in the Bodleian Library and for his ability 'to sink a pint of beer straight off'.[13] Keeping his political options open, Runcie had initially joined both the Labour and Conservative clubs but had stumbled onto the OUCA committee as representative of the newly established university wing of the Carlton Club (he had been one of its founding members). Despite being from similar stock, Runcie remembered: '[Thatcher] obviously associated me with those lordly characters who were giving Conservatism as a serious philosophy a bad name ... I always regarded her as rather tubby, with rosy cheeks. Not my sort of girl!' Clearly nor was he her sort of boy, for Margaret Roberts reportedly sacked him from the OUCA committee because of his 'rather frivolous attachment to politics'. 'She was trying to turn the Conservative Association into a serious political force ... and I was nobody to have on board,' Runcie later said with a hint of glee.[14]

In many ways, Robert Runcie was the complete antithesis to Margaret Thatcher in both personality and politics. He once remarked that he was 'the meringue to [Thatcher's] roast beef'.[15] He was always suspicious of dogmatism and distrusted those with no sense of humour. As his son, James Runcie, later said of his father: 'He had a sort of detached liberalism, which made him conscious of the ridiculousness of people and situations, yet this was combined with an enduring respect for the conservatism of institutions.'[16] This was to be an outlook and demeanour that would both help and hinder him as leader of the Church of England and in his relations with the Prime Minister.

These two different personalities, the humorous and carefree Runcie and the overly serious Margaret Roberts, had originated from two very different Englands. Runcie's Crosby, near Liverpool, was a world away from Thatcher's Grantham, and his father, an electrical engineer for Tate & Lyle, was certainly no Alfred Roberts. Life in the Runcie household was about leisure and pleasure: the world of Saturday football and the greyhound, the music hall and the working men's club. Runcie's Scottish father was not a religious man and was distrustful of those who paraded their piety; he liked to recite chunks of Robert Burns on the hypocrisy of Calvinist ministers. One of Runcie's abiding images of his father was of him belting out the songs of music-hall star Harry Lauder while shaving with a cut-throat razor. Runcie's mother was a glamorous hairdresser who would often escape the drab confines of Crosby to serve on Cunard cruises, returning months later with tales from exotic locations such as Cairo or San Francisco. By Runcie's own account, he did not enjoy his Methodist Sunday school (the non-Catholic option in the area) and only enrolled in confirmation classes because he had a crush on a girl. His devout sister had encouraged him to attend the local Anglo-Catholic church but he was unmoved by it and used to sit at the back with his friends chewing toffee and impersonating the vicar: 'We tended to leave in giggles.'[17] Runcie later admitted that his early flirtation with the church was rather like joining a gang.

Like most men of his generation, his war experience defined him. Runcie had managed to talk his way into a gentleman's regiment, the Scot's Guards, which was a remarkable achievement for a man of his class and income. His time as a lieutenant in the Guards would lead to lasting friendships and act as a fast track into the establishment, where he would first encounter future Conservative minister, Willie Whitelaw, the Lord Chamberlain, Charles Maclean, and Tory donor and businessman, Hector Laing (who would later help in the refurbishment of Lambeth Palace). More importantly, the war proved a pivotal moment in the development of Runcie's faith. During the Normandy invasion, he was awarded a Military Cross for taking out an enemy gun and for rescuing his fellow soldiers from a burning vehicle. His regiment was also one of the first to liberate Belsen concentration camp, an experience Runcie later described as 'having touched evil'.[18] Runcie is the only modern archbishop who knew what it was like to kill a fellow human being and to bury his comrades. Years later,

Runcie pondered in a rather modest way on how the war had ignited his sense of vocation:

> I have interviews with anti-blood sports campaigners, and when they say: 'Have you ever killed an animal?' I say, 'No, I've only killed people' … When I'd been very successful in knocking out a German tank, I went up to it and saw four young men dead. I felt a bit sick. Well, I was sick, actually. The other time was when a German tank was shelling our position, and a very eager little man in specs came up to me and he said: 'Shall I go and discover where that tank is?' … I said: 'Yes, why don't you go?' And I saw him shamble off … Half an hour later, he was dead. I won't say that incident led directly to my becoming a priest, but it had a lot to do with it. I thought, 'I'll make up for that someday'.[19]

Based on childhood experience alone, Margaret Roberts appeared the more likely of the two to take up religious vows, but Runcie was part of a generation of educated gentlemen who still saw ministry as a desirable profession in which one's lofty liberal aspirations could be fulfilled. This was a reflection of the strength of Anglicanism in the 1940s, in particular liberal Anglican social thought.

By the early twentieth century, the 'social gospel' had evolved from being a preoccupation amongst a group of committed Anglo-Catholic reformers to the orthodoxy amongst the Church leadership. Five Anglican bishops, including the Conservative Cosmo Gordon Lang, then Archbishop of York, had backed Lloyd George's 'People's Budget' of 1909, which was Britain's first step towards redistributive taxation and a social welfare system. Three years later, the votes of the episcopal bench were crucial in pushing through the Parliament Act of 1911, which transformed the balance of power from the Lords to the Commons.

The evangelical conscience, which had guided the Church through the Victorian era, was gradually replaced with a deeper focus on the corporate morality of society, economics and the state. Nineteenth-century laissez-faire capitalism and its complementary individualistic theology was increasingly denounced as 'unchristian', while Anglo-Catholics forwarded statist solutions and an incarnational theology in its place. The Bishop of Exeter, William Cecil, noticed the change at the Pan-Anglican Congress as early as 1908, complaining that he felt 'almost out of place in speaking as a person with no belief in socialism'.[20] Cecil was right to note the difference in tone even if he had perhaps exaggerated the left-wing influence.

The wave of strikes that dominated the Edwardian years forced the specific issue of industrial relations onto the Anglican agenda. In 1917, William Temple, then the Bishop of Manchester, published a compendium of essays calling for a 'New Reformation' to subvert the 'evils of capitalism'.[21] His prayers would be answered a year later in the Church's *Christianity and Industrial Problems* Report. Co-authored by his close friend, Christian Socialist and historian R. H. Tawney, it outlined in unequivocal terms the culture of selfishness, greed and mutual distrust that pervaded the capitalist system. In the 1920s, the label of the 'Tory Party at Prayer' was still bandied about, but in tone and political outlook the Church was no longer so. This old spiritual-political marriage was quietly being dissolved, yet it was the Church rather than the Conservative Party that had taken the adulterous step and renounced the vows that united them. Importantly, though, the Church did not fly into the arms of the Labour Party (whose rise it welcomed) but increasingly came to view itself outside partisan boundaries, as independent actors in the political sphere, free from such murky affiliations and constraints. William Temple had initially joined the Labour Party but later cancelled his membership when he became a bishop, convinced that high ecclesiastical office and partisan groupings did not mix. 'I want no Christian party,' Temple explained in 1924, 'I want Christians to leaven and control all parties' – a sentiment which by the 1920s had become the common hope rather than the reality within the Church.[22] But while many clergy considered this growing independence as a proactive and positive step, it was in fact an indication of the weakening of religio-political allegiances in Britain, which was then being mirrored at the opposite end of the political spectrum with the separation of the Nonconformists from the Liberal Party.

'Not individual charity, but the administration of social righteousness is the test by which the Lord of Glory will condemn or will commend the nations of earth', so preached Rev. F. Lewis Donaldson of the Christian Socialist League in 1917.[23] With the Depression exposing the limitations of Britain's piecemeal welfare system, Donaldson's perspective on the inadequacy of charity quickly became the consensus amongst Anglican social reformers, from those slum priests involved in housing projects to the theologians in their ivory towers drafting a Christian sociology.[24] As one of the main providers of education, housing, welfare and health, ecclesiastical opinions naturally received a hearing, although the reception was not always favourable and clergy were often accused of being too idealistic in their thinking and amateurs when it came to specifics. In all this, it was not evangelicals (whose social conscience would only be awakened in the 1960s) but Anglo-Catholics who were by far the most vocal in calling for change. Some lent heavily on an incarnational theology, others on a pre-Reformation notion of an obligation to the poor, while others called for a universalised welfare system to mirror the universality of God's grace.

In 1924, Anglicans came together for the 'Conference on Christian Politics, Economics and Citizenship' (COPEC) in Birmingham, a gathering that was endorsed by all the political parties and received a supportive message from the King. Led by William Temple, the conference was ecumenical and included the Free Churches (although not Roman Catholics); this was no tokenistic inclusivity but reflected the level of convergence across the Protestant denominations on social issues. COPEC may have demonstrated a unity of purpose but it was not without tensions, particularly from radical Christian socialists who pressed the churches to go further. There was, however, a consensus on the unchristian nature of economic individualism, the exploitative nature of capitalism and the immorality of inherited privilege: 'We have realised with a fresh intensity the scandal to our civilisation and religion involved in the fact that thousands of our fellow-countrymen are without decent homes, are without work, are without education that would develop their faculties to the full.'[25]

Two years later the ecclesiastical leadership, in alliance with the Free Churches, would attempt to intervene in the biggest industrial dispute Britain had ever faced: the General Strike. But it turned out to be a clumsy affair, with the Archbishop of Canterbury, Randall Davidson's reasoned call for an end to the dispute deemed too controversial by the Director-General of the BBC, Lord Reith, who refused to broadcast the Primate's statement on the BBC. Prime Minister Stanley Baldwin reprimanded the Church for intruding on terrain over which they were ignorant while it was left to the Cardinal Bourne, the Roman Catholic Archbishop of Westminster, who denounced the strike as 'a sin against the obedience which we owe to God', to preach the message Conservatives wanted to hear.[26] The Church of England was ready to act as independent mediator in defence of the commonweal, but the Conservatives were clearly not prepared to tolerate it.

In this period, Christian social thought mirrored and incorporated progressive secular political thinking to the extent that some Anglicans complained that it was now impossible to distinguish between the two. The man who can be credited for doing the most to bridge this gap was R. H. Tawney, who would later be heralded as the godfather of twentieth-century British socialism, but may also be lauded as the mastermind behind twentieth-century Christian social thought. In his *Acquisitive Society* (1920) Tawney set out why a materialist and mechanistic philosophy was the source of contemporary social and economic malaise. He offered an historical dimension to his thesis in his *Religion and the Rise of Capitalism*

(1926), which both complemented and challenged sociologist Max
Weber's account on the association between Calvinism and capitalist values, *The Protestant Ethic and the Spirit of Capitalism* (1905).
Tawney evoked pre-Reformation Catholic teachings in his denigration of a Christian-endorsed capitalism, which he maintained was
a corruption of the original medieval teachings on usury, the common good and the biblical obligation to the poor. He followed this
with *Equality* (1931) in which he explained why inequality was an
obstruction to harmony, commonality, cooperation and even economic efficiency. Tawney's vision, although rooted in the Gospel,
was always articulated in ethical rather than explicitly biblical terms.
This was deliberate, for Tawney realised that it was much easier to
convert Christians to socialism than socialists to Christianity. It was
for this reason he was to have equal influence on both the left and
in Christian circles.[27]

Anglicans may have been forwarding the same arguments as secular socialists, but there was a notable difference in language and tone.
Anglicans, particularly the ecclesiastical hierarchy, tended to talk
not in terms of class hostility or the potential of the proletariat but
of fellowship, fair competition and cooperation in industrial practice
and profit. What may be called 'establishment radicalism' was to a
large degree conditioned by the upper-middle-class background and
culture of those Anglican clergy advocating it.[28] Centrism, inclusivity and paternalism, rather than revolution and class conflict, always
characterised the Anglican approach to social and economic issues
right up to the 1980s.

Importantly, liberal Anglicanism did not go unchallenged. 'The
Church affects the world not directly, but indirectly,' preached Rev.
Hensley Henson in 1891, 'not by prescribing a scheme of society, but
by providing true principles of action.'[29] By 1920, Henson was Bishop
of Durham and had firmly established himself as one of the leading
critics of social thought within the Church of England. Henson was

unconvinced by the clergy's apparent 'solidarity' with the working class, which he suspected was not out of compassion, knowledge or brotherhood but crude expediency: 'The clerical toadies of the age do not flatter princes but mobs ... They worship the new possessors of power,' he wrote in his journal in 1919 in response to the then Bishop of Peterborough's support for railway strikers.[30] Henson's was not a partisan critique of Christian socialism; he was no Conservative and in fact always considered himself a Liberal. Rather, his main objection to Temple and others was the way in which they tended to pronounce political progressive aims as 'divine will'. William Inge, Dean of St Paul's, was one who shared Henson's scepticism. Inge's views on the incompatibility of socialism with Christianity was summarised in his rather cynical phrase: 'Socialism always assumes that the sty makes the pig, while Christianity declares that the pig makes the sty.'[31] Christian Conservatives would rehearse similar arguments against the turbulent priests of the 1980s.

The work produced by the COPEC conference in the 1920s was followed up by two major church reports on the great concerns of the 1930s – housing and unemployment – but the aim was to provoke moral outrage rather than provide a detailed plan. By far the most important and widely read document on Christian social prophecy was William Temple's *Christianity and the Social Order*. Published in 1942, the same year as Beveridge's blueprint for the welfare state, Temple set out a Christian communitarian vision for Britain's post-war society incorporating now well-worn orthodoxies on housing, employment, education and health provision. But it was not Temple's objective to endorse particular proposals, rather his aim was to set out the Christian ethos or 'middle axioms', which should guide such decisions. His chief fear in the 1940s was not that these plans would be shelved, but that they would be set within a secular rather than a Christian framework. In the end, Temple's wish would be granted. Prime Minister Attlee's post-war settlement was christened the 'New Jerusalem' and given a suitable Christian gloss by those in Westminster: although Temple would not live to see the final result, dying in office in 1944. Of the Beveridge Report, Temple considered that it was 'the first time anyone had set out to embody the whole spirit of the Christian ethic in an Act of Parliament'.[32] Temple's *Social Order*, however, was equally influential and deserves to stand alongside both Beveridge's Report and Keynes's *General Theory of Employment* as one of the founding tracts of Britain's social democracy.

The historian Frank Prochaska has argued that the welfare state had in effect put the churches out of a job, referring to how the state assumed full responsibility in areas where the Church had previously enjoyed influence.[33] But perhaps a more accurate statement would be that the Church of England, increasingly aware of its own limitations, had taken voluntary redundancy. Nowhere was this more apparent than in the sphere of education. For his 1944 Education Act, R. A. Butler managed to convince the Church, many of whose numbers were reluctant, of the need for Anglican schools to become fully integrated into the state system; the Catholic Church however opted to for 'voluntary aided' status and thus were required to provide 50 per cent of the funds, but retained greater control over their schools. In a further move designed to satisfy the Anglican bishops, the Act stipulated that all children would be taught 'Religious Instruction' (a watered-down Protestantism) and partake in a communal daily act of worship. The settlement did not satisfy some Anglicans who feared a loss of autonomy and a dilution of denominational education, but it was a more than favourable deal for the Church of England in economic terms and, more importantly, established religious schools as a major player within the state system.

The term 'post-war consensus' is a loaded and simplistic one. The policies arising from this vision were fiercely contested, not least within the Conservative Party, and with a reluctant Churchill at the helm it would take time for the party to become fully 'converted'. It was a Christian consensus concerning the moral responsibilities of the state and its presumed Christian citizenry. It was a noble but flawed vision, layered as it was over existing measures and provisions, constrained by competing interest groups and priorities, and framed around an idealised vision of the family unit and economic behaviour that would eventually unravel over subsequent years as expectations increased, lives got more complicated and the economy faltered.

I. Conservative conformity

MARGARET ROBERTS LEFT Oxford in 1946 just as the Attlee government was beginning to put these measures into place. Her immediate concern, however, was not politics, but settling into her graduate role working for BX Plastics in Manningtree, Essex. Marooned from familiar surroundings, Methodism once again became her anchor. She attended the Culver Street Methodist Church in Colchester and offered her preaching skills to the local circuit. In a letter to Muriel, however, she complained that the local Methodists were not very welcoming, unlike the local Conservative Association and the Young Colchester Conservatives, with whom she spent most of her spare time.[34] Her father was worried about his youngest daughter and wrote to Muriel relaying his suspicions that Margaret may have fallen under the spell of a Catholic friend, Mary. In his letter, her father delivered a wonderful diatribe on the dangers of Roman Catholicism, which he explained was an intolerant religion that oppressed individual freedom and likened it to totalitarianism.

Muriel immediately wrote back to allay her father's fears, informing him that in fact the reverse was true: it was Mary who was under Margaret's spell.[35] But her father had been right to sense a change in his daughter. Margaret had not been seduced by Rome but she was becoming more and more distanced from her father, Grantham and her Methodist roots.

Her goal of pursuing a political career remained unabated. A whiff of an opportunity came in 1948 in a chance meeting with an old Oxford friend at the Conservative Party conference in Llandudno, who set up a luncheon with the Dartford Conservative Constituency Association in Kent, which was then scouting for a candidate. Margaret Roberts's Dartford campaigns in the general elections of 1950 and 1951 would not only prove to be excellent training for a political career but would turn out to be a turning point in her life. What kind of Toryism did Margaret Roberts offer the constituents of Dartford? A clue is given in a short piece she composed for the *Young Kent Forum* in 1949. Entitled: 'Two Contemporaries – Marx and Disraeli', the article was scrappy history, but offers an intriguing insight into her political beliefs. According to Roberts, Marx and Disraeli were men who had both experienced the Industrial Revolution but had come to quite different conclusions. Marx was dismissed as a 'German' intellectual who had devised his thesis in the 'musty air of the British Museum'. Disraeli, on the other hand, appalled by 'poverty and misery', had come to the sensible conclusion that only a combination of social reform, collective bargaining with the workers and opportunity for all would bridge the gulf between the 'rich and poor'.

While Margaret Roberts cast Marxism as a foreign and abstract materialist creed, her claim was that One-nation Conservatism aspired to something higher: the moral law of Christianity.[36] In this, Margaret Roberts was mirroring arguments that Quintin Hogg, her future Lord Chancellor Lord Hailsham and then MP for Oxford, had recently set out in his *The Case For Conservatism*. Intriguingly, though, Margaret Roberts articulated a more libertarian vision of Conservatism when canvassing at an event in Erith, Kent, in 1950. Drawing on the words of her father and echoing sentiments of Hayek's *Road to Serfdom*, which she had read while at Oxford, she criticised socialism not from a One-nation perspective as a threat to a harmonious social order but as a threat to individual liberty. According to the *Erith Observer*: 'Recalling what her father had said about the bird in the cage, Miss Roberts concluded: "It has social security. It has food and it has warmth, and so on. But what is the good of all that if it has not the freedom to fly out and live its own life?"'[37]

Here we have both Margaret Roberts 'the paternalist' and Margaret Roberts 'the libertarian'. In this, the young candidate was in fact reflecting the ideological tensions within her party at the time.

Above all, the general elections of 1950 and 1951 revealed Margaret Roberts's natural ability to run a campaign. 'She was like someone who had made a vow to take up a religious life, she was so dedicated,' remembered one Young Conservative from her Dartford days.[38] If Margaret Thatcher had one natural gift as a politician, it was not in aspects of philosophy or policy, but in the congregational side of politics. The importance of this cannot be overstated and would be an area where she would later outshine her contemporaries. Much like a religious leader, she was at her best when mingling with the party faithful and converting people to the cause.

Dartford was a solid Labour seat with strong trade union support, yet Margaret Roberts proved herself adept at targeting potential voters, such as the non-unionised working class, women and, particularly, Nonconformists. During the election in 1951 she addressed the local Free Church Council, delivering a speech that tied together themes of patriotism, Christian decency and the religious calling to public service; qualities that she, reportedly a politician of 'sound Christian convictions', sought to personify.[39] She offered some rousing words to the Dartford Congregational Church, pledging: 'If we [do] not revive Christianity in this country it [is] not only ourselves, but the whole world that [will] suffer.'[40] In the 1950s, chapels were still the main access point to the community and its votes; a fact that Margaret Roberts, more than anyone would have been conscious of. She may have also have recognised the potential rewards of canvassing to Nonconformists, given that they were likely to be aspirational lower-middle-class voters and possibly wavering Liberals. In both elections, Margaret Roberts was unsuccessful in defeating the incumbent Labour MP, Norman Dodds, but she managed to cut his majority by a third and, more importantly, had impressed Conservative Central Office with the energy she had brought to an unwinnable seat.

'She stood for Dartford twice and lost twice and the second time she cried on my shoulder I married her', so said Denis Thatcher, who had first encountered his future wife at her adoption meeting for the Kent constituency. Born into an upper-middle-class family, Denis Thatcher was a son of the empire, whose father had emigrated to New Zealand in the 1870s and founded a paint and chemicals business, Atlas Preservatives. Denis had joined the family firm in 1933, serving until war broke out. He had married in 1942 but, like many wartime unions, it had ended in divorce soon after he returned home in 1948. He was a default Anglican, but, by all accounts, was not an active believer, with the war only enhancing his scepticism. He always insisted on calling clergymen by the deferential term 'padre', yet would deliver it with a touch of irony that hinted at underlying contempt.

In many ways, Denis Thatcher was the perfect match for Margaret Roberts, even though she herself did not immediately recognise it. They had met at the right time in their lives. At thirty-three, Denis was then considering that he should find a wife, while she was increasingly aware of the disadvantages of being a single woman of little means in politics. Yet this union was not mere expediency. Politically, of course, they shared a great deal in common, but they were from quite different spheres: he was worldly, she was provincial; he was establishment, she was Nonconformist; he was rich, she was not. Margaret Roberts's marriage to Denis represented the final severing from her roots. This process had begun in Oxford, continued in Essex, but was only made permanent once she was married.

The gap between Margaret's old life and new was made blatantly apparent when it was time for her prospective husband to meet her parents. Soon after the engagement, Denis whisked his new fiancée up to Grantham in his sports car. On the way, Margaret felt compelled to tell him the bad news: 'I think you ought to know, my parents don't drink.' The renowned tipple-loving Denis may have felt a compulsion to slam down on the brakes, but he drove on in silence. Passing Grantham town hall, Denis quipped, 'I bet they're awfully proud of that!' Misinterpreting Denis's irony for sincerity, Margaret gushed with pride, 'Daddy thinks it's wonderful.' Denis silently cautioned himself: Watch it, Thatcher.

After introductions, Margaret told her father that her fiancée would like a drink: 'I swear her father had to blow the dust off the South African sherry bottle,' Denis later recalled. They didn't stay for long, and afterwards Denis insisted that they stop off somewhere for a stiff gin.[41] Pitted against her father's strait-laced Nonconformity, Denis undoubtedly offered the prospect of a more exciting life. Yet this tension between the two central male figures in her life is crucial to understanding the mix of Roundhead and Cavalier in Margaret Thatcher's personality – a tension that would become even more pronounced when she was Prime Minister.

The wedding took place in December 1952 at the spiritual home of Methodism, Wesley's Chapel in the City of London. The discreet splendour of Wesley's over Finkin Street was no contest, but the location was also further evidence of Margaret Roberts's determination to escape her small-town roots; her sister, in contrast, had been married in Grantham. The fact that Denis was divorced may have been a factor too. Methodist guidelines published in 1948 permitted that the innocent party could be remarried in chapel but only on the personal discretion of the abiding minister. Historically, Methodists had always dealt with divorce with a lighter touch than Anglicans (and certainly Catholics), while maintaining a firmer line on what was considered to be the true ungodly diversions: gambling and drink. It is quite possible then that the Robertses found Denis's taste for gin more problematic than his first marriage.

The service was conducted by the minister of Wesley's Chapel, Rev. R. V. Spivey and assisted by an old family friend of the Roberts', Primitive Methodist and socialist, Rev. Skinner. The ceremony had been full of Margaret's favourite music, including Handel's 'Water Music' and the hymn 'Lead us, Heavenly Father, lead us'. Alfred Roberts, according to Denis Thatcher, thought the ceremony 'halfway to Rome'.[42] The reception was held at Carlton Gardens, in the home of Thatcher's friend, Conservative MP Alfred Bossom, who had made his fortune building skyscrapers in New York and was renowned as one of the great party-givers of his generation, particularly for his free-flowing champagne. Bossom took charge of the toast. Standing in the wings were Alfred and Beatrice Roberts, presumably raising a cup rather than a glass and possibly feeling a tad uncomfortable in the plush metropolitan surroundings and lifestyle that their daughter had so willingly embraced. This provincial girl had definitely 'married up' and Margaret Roberts severed, albeit temporarily, her links with her town, class and religion and adopted the life of a southern millionaire's wife. As John Campbell has neatly surmised: 'Grantham remained in her blood; but for the next twenty-five years she steadily suppressed it.'[43]

Margaret Thatcher wrote of these years: 'To be a young married woman in those circumstances in the 1950s was heaven.'[44] Indeed, Margaret Thatcher had never had it so good. It was a time for holidays on the Continent, dinners at the Ivy and a four-bedroom country house in Kent, which they had seen advertised in *Country Life*. She once said: 'I remember having a dream that the one thing I really wanted was to live in a nice house, you know, a house with more things than we had.'[45] Margaret Thatcher had grown up yearning for frivolity and with Denis she got it. The Thatchers watched the coronation of Queen Elizabeth II in 1953 under the seated covered stand in Parliament Square opposite Westminster Abbey. This was a long way from Grantham's Dysart Park where Margaret Thatcher had last celebrated the crowning of a monarch sixteen years previously.

It is often remarked that the coronation of Queen Elizabeth symbolised the Conservative mood of the 1950s and to a degree this is true. Discontent undoubtedly bubbled under the surface but this was far away from Westminster and its impact would not truly be felt until the 1960s. Meanwhile, a sort of genial Conservatism, almost neo-traditionalism prevailed: the calm before the storm. The coronation, which was brought to the masses through the new medium of television, was a majestic and monumental display of faith in Britain's institutional life, especially the Established Church. Archbishop Fisher (1945–61), known as the 'headmaster archbishop', successfully resisted pressure from modernisers, including the Duke of Edinburgh, to ensure that no fundamental changes were made to the Rite last used for George VI in 1937. The one innovation was the relaying of the event on television, but even on this Fisher imposed restrictions. The anointing – the moment when the archbishop marked a cross on the Queen's forehead with holy oil – was concealed from the cameras with a blackout interrupting the live event. Such things were still deemed sacrosanct in 1950s Britain.

Church and state enjoyed congenial relations in this period. The Conservative administration, which was overwhelmingly Anglican in character, would hold regular consultative meetings with the bishops and, although it was sometimes an uneasy relationship, this was only because there were still expectations and responsibilities. Gambling reform was halted in its tracks in 1951 on the insistence of Archbishop Fisher and the Cabinet again ruled it out in 1959, despite pressure from progressive Tories. Fisher also thought Harold Macmillan's infamous 'never had it so good' remark a 'dreadful current phrase' that encouraged materialism: 'Whenever I hear it I say to myself in the words of Our Lord, "How hardly shall they that have riches enter into the Kingdom of Heaven?"'[46] R. A. Butler wondered whether the archbishop would have preferred 'you've never had it so bad'.[47]

In this period, however, the Church of England had more pressing concerns than politics, chiefly the rebuilding churches and congregations after the damage and upheavals of war. Anglican worshipping figures quickly recovered from its wartime dip, although the recovery was not sustained enough to be called a revival. Even in these years of so-called 'strength', nearly half of all Britons were not regular churchgoers. The main growth area was in suburbia, following the mass migration away from the cities; but this had the effect of exacerbating the enduring problem of the middle-class bias of Anglican congregations. Despite the dedicated efforts of some urban and industrial priests, the Church's weak presence amongst the working class was insurmountable and remained unresolved.

Anglicanism, however, did seem to be in communion with the national mood. The resurrection of Coventry Cathedral, which was eventually consecrated in 1962 with Benjamin Britten's *War Requiem* composed especially for the occasion, was a wondrous tying of Christianity and culture and a lasting symbol of reconciliation and reconstruction in the aftermath of war. When England cricket captain David Sheppard became an ordained priest in 1955, it seemed fitting that the nation should have a man of the cross at the crease. With his Dirk Bogarde looks and muscular Christianity, Sheppard became the housewives' pin-up and, in these days before agony aunts and horoscopes, was given his own pastoral column in *Women's Own*.

In 1954, American evangelist Billy Graham arrived for the first of his evangelical crusades to Britain. Graham received a big welcome in the UK, as he did in any state in the US, and over the course of three months preached to 1.3 million (predominantly young) Christians, in stadiums across the country, and to many more through live relays in cinemas, concert halls and churches. The bishops' initial cynicism was put to one side when they saw the mass crowds, with even a reluctant Archbishop Fisher consenting to give the benediction at Graham's last crusade at Wembley Stadium. Prime Minister Churchill, who had turned down an invitation to attend the Wembley event, was so impressed that he requested Graham's presence at Downing Street the next morning. An uncharacteristically nervous Churchill pressed his aides as Graham was due to arrive: 'What do you talk to an American evangelist about?'[48]

If the 1950s was a period of stability and consolidation for the Church of England, it was not so for the Nonconformists. Chapel life had been in decline since the Edwardian period and continued on this downward trend after the Second World War. It was especially acute amongst working-class communities and specifically the young, with Sunday school attendance halving between 1939 and 1959. Methodist chapels merged while lay-preachers were taken from an ever-decreasing pool and soon the idea of full communion with the Established Church – once deemed a total anathema – began to be seriously contemplated. Like once-rival companies in a dying industry, it made sense to merge. The majority of Methodists voted in favour (despite some serious misgivings), but it was the Anglican 'shareholders' who rejected the deal, largely due to the vociferous opposition from Anglo-Catholics.

In the inter-war years, tentative steps had been made in the ecumenical movement but it was embraced with renewed vigour amidst the spirit of reconciliation after the war. Relations between Protestant denominations were solidified through the establishment of the British Council of Churches (BCC), while the cause also found an international vehicle through the World Council of Churches (WCC), which owed much to Anglican input and was conceived as a kind of Christian UN. Roman Catholicism was not represented on either of these bodies. The Catholic Church was busy forging its own course in this period, establishing schools and churches to accommodate the post-war wave of Irish immigration; it would be a further twenty years before the Catholic Church would gain full recognition on the national and ecumenical stage. The movement towards Christian unity as well as the break-up of traditional partisan-church allegiances strengthened rather than weakened the position of the Church of England, allowing it to enjoy, in the words of one ecclesiastical historian, 'a spiritual superiority over all other churches, and a confident sense of its growing political, social and even intellectual claim to a place in the mainstream of national life'.[49]

It was precisely at this time that Margaret Thatcher moved away from Methodism and became an Anglican, albeit of a 'low church' variety. It is hardly unknown for those who have risen socially to also rise spiritually. Margaret Thatcher, however, justified it differently, stating in an interview with the *Catholic Herald* in 1978 that she had longed for a 'little bit more formality' in religion and given that John Wesley had always regarded himself as a member of the Church of England, she did not feel that a great theological divide had been crossed.[50] Technically, this is true, although one wonders whether her parents agreed. Much more likely was that the strict and sober Nonconformity into which she had been raised did not complement the new world Thatcher was now operating in. Political expediency may have played a part in her decision too: in the 1950s, Conservatives were still expected to be Anglicans. Margaret Thatcher also took the conscious decision not to enforce any form of worship on her children. 'I did not insist that they went to church. I think that was probably because I'd had so much insistence myself,' she later admitted.[51] Her decision provoked consternation from her mother, who reprimanded her daughter for not raising the twins in the Methodist faith. If ever there was a sign that Thatcher had escaped her childhood by this point, it was in her attitude towards her own children's religious education.

It would take Margaret Thatcher just under a decade to get into

Parliament but finally, in 1959, she entered through the doors of
Westminster as the MP for Finchley. At a dinner for the new intake,
Harold Macmillan recommended Disraeli's 1845 novel *Sybil, Or the
two Nations*, on the plight of the working class, as preparatory reading for his cohort of MPs. Thatcher later admitted that she did not
take his advice. When Prime Minister, Thatcher tended to caricature
the Macmillan era as one of complacency and misdirection. If this is
what she felt at the time, she never voiced it. All evidence points to
the fact that she fully subscribed to Macmillan's paternalistic vision
of Toryism. During the election of 1963, in a speech entitled 'What it
means to be a Christian Member of Parliament', for example, Thatcher
offered a classic Tory-Anglican defence of the Established Church and,
in a sentiment worthy of William Temple, affirmed that freedom and
democracy could not be sustained on 'an empty stomach' and that
Britain as a 'Christian nation' provided this political nourishment
through its welfare state.[52] Macmillan certainly considered her in his
camp; appointing her as a junior minister of Pensions and National
Insurance in 1960; a post she held until the fall of the Conservative
government in 1963.

One-nation Tories may have been leading the government during the long period of Conservative power between 1951 and 1964,
but those of a classical liberal persuasion proved a constant source of
agitation. Tensions came to a head in 1958 when the entire Treasury
team – Enoch Powell, Nigel Birch and Chancellor of the Exchequer,
Peter Thorneycroft – resigned in protest to Macmillan's refusal to rein
in public spending. The Prime Minister may have shrugged it off as 'a
little local difficulty' but the fact was that most of the Tory grassroots
were in sympathy. Under Macmillan, Conservative Party conferences
were often frustrating encounters, not helped by the fact that party
activists were treated with a large degree of contempt by the leadership. Macmillan's Treasury team had resigned over technicalities
of economic policy, however the concerns of the libertarians at the

grassroots encompassed broader ideological concerns about the demise of civil society and state encroachment on the individual. Macmillan's 'little local difficulty' in 1958 was a sign of much bigger things to come.

II. Fragile altars

THE 1950S WERE not as harmonious as some people like to claim nor were the 1960s as radical as some people like to remember. The term 'the sixties' has become convenient shorthand to describe the arrival of affluence, the end of deference, the relaxation of social mores and the intensification of sexual and identity politics that occurred in Britain between 1963 and 1973. But, if Britain was swinging, it was not to a particularly vigorous rhythm, it seems. There were more bingo players than Buddhists; *The Sound of Music* outperformed *Last Tango in Paris* at the box office; subscribers to *Reader's Digest* outnumbered those of underground satirical magazine *Oz*; and far more people visited National Trust properties than marched on anti-nuclear demonstrations with CND.[53] Britain did experience a culture war of sorts but it was not as divisive or as deep-rooted as that in the US. Three institutions, however, did undergo profound transformation: the BBC, the universities and the Church of England. Once the fabric of the conservative establishment, they morphed into paragons of the new liberal values and would later become key targets for the New Right.

If the post-war settlement of the 1940s had reformulated the relationship between the state and the public citizen, then the liberalising legislation of the 1960s undoubtedly signalled a new consensus between the private individual and the law. Stitch by stitch, Britain undid the restrictive legal corset that had been in existence for 100 years or more and ushered in a flurry of reforming legislation, which some heralded as civilising measures while others denounced it as encouraging permissiveness. The Macmillan government set the bandwagon in motion, allowing for the less contentious issues of obscenity, gambling and drinking to proceed through the House, while it would be Labour's Home Secretary Roy Jenkins who would later steer through the trickier issues of decriminalising homosexuality and abortion, the ending of capital punishment and the easing of restrictions on divorce. Most of the existing laws had been ripe for reform for a long time, but it was caution and compromise rather than radicalism that characterised their eventual passing. Nor could these laws be solely attributed to the spirit of the age: most had their origins in the inter-war period and much of the thinking had been done in the early 1950s. Puritans and progressives could be found on both sides of the House while the Labour leadership remained conscious of how these developments (particularly the decriminalisation of homosexuality) would go down with their working-class supporters. These Acts only applied to England and Wales; Scotland and Northern Ireland, largely due to religious pressures, would pursue a much more restrictive path and at a much slower pace.

Far from being instigated by a band of secular liberals, it was the Church of England, whom Parliament still entrusted to act as its conscience, which played an instrumental role in orchestrating and legitimising reform. Some Anglicans took a pragmatic view, considering that Victorian notions of 'sin', to which many citizens did not subscribe, should no longer be enshrined in law. Others took a more positive view, forwarding the Christian case for the New Morality.[54] The conservative Archbishop Fisher was clearly reluctant to lead the Church down this path, but his successor, the pious yet practical Anglo-Catholic Michael Ramsey, who arrived at Canterbury in 1961, was prepared to concede that reform was inevitable and that the Church should not close its eyes. That these changes were even being considered was itself evidence of a new tone within the Church, from a culture of condemnation to one of understanding: 'Better to deal with how people are than how we would like them to be' was the guiding principle.

The existing obscenity law dated back to 1857 and was revised just over a century later in 1959 while theatrical censorship was also taken out of the regulatory hands of the Lord Chancellor. The *Lady Chatterley's Lover* case in 1960 became an infamous show-trial for the recently passed Obscene Publications Act as daily reports from the courtroom titillated the chattering classes, particularly the contribution of John Robinson, the Bishop of Woolwich, who threw his priestly weight behind D. H. Lawrence's book. Robinson was a man who delighted in rumbling the ecclesiastical establishment and on this occasion he did not disappoint. He declared that sex was sacred and seemed to imply that Lady Chatterley's affair with the gamekeeper Mellors was a symbolic act of Holy Communion. An incandescent Archbishop Fisher immediately ushered out a public rebuke: adultery was, and remained, a sin.

The Betting and Gaming Act of 1960 had a much more profound impact on ordinary people's lives. Illegal betting was a thing of the past as gambling establishments soon popped up on the high street; 10,000 within the first six months of the Act. Gambling acquired a respectability hitherto unseen and signalled another nail in the coffin for Britain's Nonconformist past. One issue which had been preying on the minds of parliamentarians since the mid-nineteenth century was the death penalty. Even though opinion polls consistently pointed to the public's overwhelming support for its retention, parliamentarians decided that they knew best and voted for a temporary abolition in 1965, which was made permanent in 1969. Church leaders were resolutely in favour, with Archbishop Ramsey making an impassioned speech in the Lords supporting the bill. There were some law 'n' order populists, including Margaret Thatcher, who cried 'an eye for eye', but most were of the view that the removal of the death penalty was a positive Christian step.

The decision to finally decriminalise homosexuality in 1967 was the surest sign that Parliament was prepared to disconnect British law from Christian notions of sin. The initiative had in fact come from the Church, which had published a report in 1954 advocating decriminalisation. This was the prompt that the Macmillan government needed to appoint its own commission, led by committed Anglican Lord Wolfenden, whose proposals were announced in 1957 and broadly echoed the Church's position. Archbishop Ramsey backed the new law and faced the inevitable backlash from the Church and especially in the Lords, where he was accused of debasing the nation's morals and promoting homosexuality. The Methodist Conference and the Roman Catholic Church's Advisory Committee endorsed the change but the Church of Scotland refused. It would later prove to be the main obstacle to the decriminalisation of homosexuality north of the border, which would only get the green light in 1980. Some prominent Anglicans, including the Bishop of Woolwich, John Robinson, were involved in the Homosexual Law Reform Society, which fought the decade-long campaign to get Wolfenden translated into law. Few Christians, however, were prepared to go as far as the Quakers, who maintained that homosexuals should be treated equally (they compared it to being left-handed) and advocated full recognition. The Sexual Offences Act was an inherently conservative measure, which meant that the sexual act itself was no longer a crime. The 1967 Act ensured that the battle for private rights had been won; it would not be until the late 1980s that the homosexual lobby would effectively mobilise and seek full equality before the law.

Two years later, in 1969, the Divorce Reform Act was passed, but it had had a fraught history. When the first relaxation of the divorce laws had come in 1937, Archbishop Lang had abstained. Despite being privately opposed, Lang was of the view that as Britain was no longer a Christian country, it was wrong to enforce Christian standards in the law. His successors, however, did not share his view and quashed successive attempts at reform in 1951 and 1963 (of the latter, Ramsey's intervention in the Lords had been crucial in defeating the bill).

Conscious that change was inevitable, Ramsey commissioned a Church report to ensure some influence over Parliament. It proved problematic: how could the Church realistically admit that breakdown could occur without undermining marriage as a principle? *Putting Asunder*, published in 1966, however, concluded that an offence did not need to be committed for divorce to take place; in effect, it was a concession that marriage could divert from the Christian ideal. The Law Commission took much the same line and together they thrashed out a set of proposals, which accepted 'irretrievable breakdown' as a justification for separation. Ramsey, though, was displeased with the result and, when the vote finally came, he abstained. The Matrimonial Property Act, passed a year later, was equally significant, for it enabled women for the first time to claim on their former husband's earnings, thus making divorce a more viable proposition for the female spouse.

No issue more clearly demonstrates the tameness of moral reform in this decade than the debate over abortion. In the US, the 1973 Supreme Court ruling on *Roe vs Wade* became a defining moment that would subsequently divide states, parties and voters. Britain's Abortion Act in 1967, in contrast, generated much discussion, yet passed with far less controversy. Some promoted a women's right to choose (an argument reinforced by the recent introduction of the contraceptive pill), but most were of the opinion that in a country with a national health service, it was an immoral anomaly that women were forced into seeking illegitimate and archaic procedures which often led to scarring, permanent damage and even death. Introduced by the son of a Church of Scotland minister, Liberal MP David Steel, the bill did not directly sanction abortions, but provided a legal justification for carrying them out under stringent restrictions. The Church had prompted the debate in 1964 when it published a report under the chairmanship of the Bishop of Durham, Ian Ramsey, which marked a distinction between abortion and infanticide and concluded that the risk of the life of the mother was the only grounds for abortion. The

Church's intervention, while influential, was in the end limited; the Abortion Act would go much further than the bishops hoped. When it came to the vote the Lords Spiritual were divided with Archbishop Michael Ramsey refusing to endorse it. The Roman Catholics opposed it outright but its bishops were too poorly organised and too late to the negotiating table to effectively offer a voice. Catholics would later provide much of the weight behind pro-life pressure groups LIFE and the Society for the Unborn Child, which would spearhead the calls for tighter controls in the 1980s.

The Church of England's main prerogative had been to ensure that they had some input and that legislation was discussed within a Christian framework; in some cases they were successful, but ultimately there was only so far the bishops were prepared to go. What these debates revealed was not the collapse of Christian morality (as some right-wingers would later claim), but the division within the denominations themselves. The relative openness of the Church of England and Free Churches contrasted sharply with the rigidity and lack of engagement of the Roman Catholics. Contraception was a case in point. Anglicans did not oppose the permitting of free contraception on the NHS to unmarried couples. The Church had in fact been advocating sex education and birth-control clinics in the name of responsible family planning since the 1920s. The Roman Catholics' hard line on this matter was unequivocally set out in the papal encyclical *Humanae Vitae* in 1968, which forbade all forms of artificial contraception. Another striking feature was the near-complete silence from the Nonconformist left. It would be the New Right who would later take up the fight against the 'permissive age'.

Margaret Thatcher, as other MPs, voted according to her conscience, which in fact meant she sided with the reformists rather than conservatives on most issues. Margaret Thatcher, like most of her generation, took an old-fashioned view on matters of sex, but her Christian faith was not, nor had it ever been, moralistic. Thatcher supported the decriminalisation of homosexuality and abortion; on the latter, she took a surprisingly liberal position, claiming in a radio broadcast soon afterwards that 'one of the worst things anyone can do in this world is to bring an unwanted child into it'.[55] She opposed the Divorce Reform Act on the grounds that she believed it made it easier for the man to desert his wife and was prepared to speak against the liberalisation of obscene material. She had read *Lady Chatterley's Lover* for an appearance on the BBC's political panel show *Any Questions* and apparently was 'not anxious to linger on it at all'.[56] In her New Year message to her Finchley constituents in 1970, Thatcher pressed for 'a reversal of the permissive society' that, in her view, had made man a 'slave to his own appetites'.[57] But there were no signs that she was prepared to lead the charge in Parliament and, in fact, rarely spoke about such matters until her election to the leadership in 1975, when it became politically advantageous for her to do so.

Meanwhile, the Church had much bigger concerns. By the late 1960s, few could ignore the rapid pace at which the British people seemed to be abandoning the pews. Anglican baptisms dropped by 10 per cent and confirmations by 30 per cent in just six years.[58] Fewer and fewer were taking up holy orders, with the number of new ordinands shrinking by nearly a quarter between 1967 and 1972. The Free Churches fared even worse, with Methodist congregations suffering a drop of 10 per cent between 1960 and 1970 and a further 22 per cent in the next decade.[59] The downward trend, which would eventually impact on all Christian denominations, even the Roman Catholic Church, signalled the greatest crisis in British Christianity for decades, potentially more damaging than either the Industrial Revolution or the First World War. It soon became clear that this was a lasting development, which the churches had little hope of reversing.

All manner of things were blamed, from the impact of television to

the imposing style of church buildings, but of course, the biggest threat
to churchgoing was the family or, more accurately, the privatisation of
family life that came with rising home ownership and greater affluence
and leisure in the 1960s. The churches were not the only form of associational culture to suffer; clubs, organisations and political parties all
experienced a similar fate. Christian worship, though, was not simply
in decline, but was being undermined by an equally powerful force:
secularism. Churchmen and politicians, however, seemed to speak as
if this was a peculiarly British phenomenon although a quick glance at
Australia, Canada, New Zealand and Northern Europe made it clear
that this was an international trend.

Britain was unique in one respect. Immigration from the Commonwealth in the 1950s and 1960s had provided the Protestant churches
with ready-made congregations in its secular cities. But the alienation
and often racism that immigrants experienced forced many to set up
their own independent churches and they were lost to the established
denominations forever. It must go down as one of the great tragedies of
English Christianity that these new communities were not wholeheart-
edly welcomed into the fold. This was despite Archbishop Ramsey's
own leadership on the immigration issue as chairman of the National
Committee for Commonwealth Immigrants. Appointed by Harold
Wilson, Ramsey stood firm against the government's Commonwealth
Immigration Act in 1968 and later supported the citizenship rights of
Kenyan Asians. Leadership on this matter, however, appears not to
have trickled down to the parishes.

The 1960s proved to be the defining moment when faith 'became
optional'.[60] Church attendance ceased to be a social convention or a
measure of respectability. Britain's youth, with more money in their
pockets and the prospect of more exciting alternatives, were easily lured
away from Sunday school. The most significant decline was evident
amongst women (always the majority in the pews) who, with greater
opportunities in education and in the workplace, inevitably found

salvation in things other than Christianity. The decline in female piety, however, meant that the intergenerational transference of faith was severed forever. If the young were not receiving religious instruction in home, school or church, where would they encounter faith? Margaret Thatcher recognised this dilemma early on and, in a speech in 1969 to Christians in Finchley, lamented that 'it was like separating a flower from its roots'.[61]

In what would result in some worthy, and some disastrous, initiatives, Anglicanism underwent an image overhaul in the 1960s and 1970s in a desperate bid to make it relevant and credible in the modern age. The King James Bible now had to compete alongside an updated and more accessible translation, The New English Bible. The Sermon on the Mount ('Blessed are') took precedence over the more prescriptive Ten Commandments ('Thou shall not'). The Devil, damnation, and in particular the doctrine of original sin, seemed out of sync with the age, and their subtle side-lining reflected the general shift towards a more social and less condemnatory approach to faith. In all this, progressive Christians did not consider that they were pandering to the age but acting in a sincere belief that modernisation would ensure Christianity's lasting appeal. The Catholic Church would have its reforming moment – *aggiornamento* – with the second Vatican Council convened in 1962, of which its most profound and lasting reform was the switch from Latin to the vernacular mass.

Rather than shielding Christianity from popular culture, theologians sought to actively engage with it, although comments such as that from Ian Ramsey, then Professor of Divinity at Oxford, who declared that 'Beatle language was virtually theological language' hardly added credibility to the Church's cause.[62] By far the most notorious example of such 'dialogue' was Bishop John Robinson's *Honest to God*, published in 1963. Written in a rush while he was cooped up in hospital, Robinson's book was serialised in *The Observer*, sold one million copies in three years and sent shock waves rippling through the parishes. Robinson seemed to imply that the only way of being 'honest to God' was to be 'honest to yourself', which was an open-ended doctrine that appeared to put a question mark over every biblical concept. Robinson was dubbed 'the Anglican bishop who does not believe in God' by Telegraph journalist T. E. Utley in his blackening review of the book.[63] Robinson's views were hardly representative of mainstream Anglicanism, rather a reflection of a radical group of clergy known as the 'South Bank' theologians whose engagement with the New Morality certainly generated more attention and consternation than praise.

Of more pressing concern was how to revive the local parish in an era of decline. The Rector of Woolwich, Rev. Nicolas Stacey, was one such priest who opened up his church hall to counselling groups and transformed his crypt into a coffee bar during the day and a discotheque at night. Within four years, the parish was welcoming 1,500 people a week through its door, although Stacey persistently faced accusations that he was de-sacralising his place of worship: 'If [he] thinks he can build the Kingdom of God by frying eggs on the altar and percolating coffee in the organ pipe he should think again,' complained one local clergyman.[64] Frustrated by the opposition he encountered and convinced that he would not be promoted, Stacey eventually resigned the priesthood and later became director of social services for Kent County Council. Even the clergy were now questioning whether the Church was the best arena for living out their faith.

Where Anglicans did prove their worth was in pioneering charities and causes both at home and abroad. Leading international organisations such as the Anti-Apartheid Movement, Oxfam, Christian Aid and Amnesty International, and domestic charities such as Shelter and the Samaritans all owe their existence to a renewed sense of Christian social engagement in the post-war years. London vicar Chad Varah had set up the Samaritans in his crypt in 1953 after officiating at the funeral of a teenager who had committed suicide. He placed an advert in a newspaper asking for volunteers and within ten years the Samaritans had over forty branches across the UK. Britons may have been turning their backs on formal religion, but their sense of compassion and volunteering impulse clearly had not died.

In the pew, 'Make Me a Channel of Your Peace' (1967) was more likely to be on the hymn sheet than 'Onward Christian Soldiers' (1871). Christian pacifism had understandably quietened during the war but in the nuclear age, it returned to its earlier intensity as men in dog collars led the Campaign for Nuclear Disarmament (CND)'s 'pilgrimages' to Britain's base in Aldermaston and opposed the Vietnam War. Events across the globe, too, proved a source of inspiration as Anglicans intellectually engaged with black liberation theology in the US, ideas about social justice emerging in the decolonised developing world, and Catholic liberation theology (an explicit tying of Christian-Marxist ideas) in South America. Exposure to these political theologies, which many clergy experienced first-hand through the World Council of Churches and in missionary posts throughout the dying empire, had the effect of gradually reshaping the Anglican mindset towards a more radical and global perspective.

A crucial facet of 1960s post-materialist culture was its moral assault on Western capitalism, of which the ecological and fair-trade movements were its obvious and most fruitful manifestations. Many at the grassroots and those working abroad began to highlight some of the failures and restrictions of inter-war liberal Anglicanism. The Christian critique of capitalism in this era was more combative and less centred on British experience or even the 'poor'; it now became about confronting a global system in which all were implicated. José Miguez Bonino, an evangelical Argentinian theologian who had been involved in the World Council of Churches and was a pioneer in both liberation theology and the ecumenical movement, delivered a lecture in London in 1974 which seemed to encapsulate where the Christian perspective on economics was heading: 'The basic ethos of capitalism is definitely anti-Christian; it is the maximising of economic gain, the raising of man's grasping impulse, the idolising of the strong.'[65]

•   •   •

THE CHRISTIAN DENIGRATION of capitalism was not something that concerned Margaret Thatcher; it was only when she became leader of the Conservative Party that she would offer a rebuke. However, her own religious heritage – the world of the chapel, Rotary and the grocery shop – was clearly on the wane. Alfred Roberts had sold his business in 1958 just at the right time. The age of the small grocer was no more as the removal of pricing restrictions ensured that the big supermarket chains with cheaper goods assumed a monopoly. By the 1960s, Finkin Street Church had amalgamated with its old Primitive rival and now rented its space out for dance classes and other activities once deemed ungodly. Grantham town hall would eventually be dissolved in 1974, under the 1972 Local Government Act, which also abolished the post of alderman.

In late 1969, Alfred Roberts developed emphysema and lived his last days confined to his bed with an oxygen mask. The preacher was silenced. Alfred Roberts died on the 12 February 1970, soon after hearing his daughter on a radio panel show. Thatcher later pondered in her memoirs: 'He never knew that I would become a Cabinet minister, and I am sure that he neither imagined I would eventually become Prime Minister. He would have wanted these things for me because politics was so much a part of his life and because I was so much his daughter.'[66] Alfred Roberts's passing is significant for one more reason, for it came just ten days after the Conservative shadow Cabinet (of which Thatcher was now a member) held a conference at Selsdon

Park. It was here that the Conservative Party first began to explore free-market solutions to the nation's growing economic woes. The death of Nonconformist England would eventually trigger a reinvention of Conservative Britain.

CHAPTER THREE

THE GREAT REAWAKENING

'The other side have got an ideology they can test their policies against. We must have one as well.'
— MARGARET THATCHER, 1975[1]

'Her greatest intellectual gift was for simplification ... she saw life in primary colours.'
— ALFRED SHERMAN, 1995[2]

CONSERVATISM IN BRITAIN has always been a disparate group of ideas and influences and in this regard the New Right that emerged in the 1970s was no exception. As historian Maurice Cowling on the right and Marxist sociologist Stuart Hall on the left recognised, Conservatism underwent a profound and uncompromising transformation in the 1970s, reordering itself intellectually, culturally, religiously, and finally, politically with the elevation of Margaret

Thatcher as leader in 1975. Signs of a 'right turn' in British public life were discernible long before it took hold in Westminster; in the senior common room of Peterhouse, Cambridge, the seminar halls at the Institute of Economic Affairs (IEA), at the annual meeting of Mary Whitehouse's National Viewers' and Listeners' Association (NVLA) and in the debating chamber of the Church's General Synod. Collectively, these represented variations on the same theme: a conservative reaction against liberal progressivism and the post-war world. Margaret Thatcher was the political benefactor of a right-wing mood that she did not initiate, but crucially she would come to symbolise it, give her name to it and put flesh on its ideological bones.

I. 1968 'n' all that

THE YEAR OF 1968 is generally regarded as a triumphant moment for the left when pacifists, feminists, socialists and civil rights activists engaged in a simultaneous and seemingly spontaneous orgy of protest across the globe. But in many ways it was an equally significant moment for the right, representing as it did the beginnings of radical reactionary conservatism, which pitted itself not only against socialism but also what many considered to be an equally damaging and complacent force: establishment conservatism. Those on the right would eventually come to steal the language of 'liberty' and 'individualism' from the left but would attach to it very different meanings. True freedom, they judged, was not sexual liberation, but owning one's house.

It was in 1968 when the post-war consensus came off the rails. Political centrism was in crisis mode from that point onwards as radicals on the right as well as the left grabbed the headlines and began to set the terms of the debate. In April 1968, Enoch Powell delivered his infamous 'Rivers of Blood' speech, which sought to re-mould Tory nationalism in an anti-immigration guise. That same year, monetarist economic theory and the ideas of Milton Friedman made it into the pages of *The Times*. The following year saw the publication of the first of the notorious 'Black Papers' attacking progressive education and Labour's abolition of grammar schools. Spearheaded by literary critic and founder of the Homosexual Law Reform Society, A. E. Dyson, the Papers were lauded by those on the right for denting the social-ist myth of equality in education, which they always suspected would result in a flat-lining of opportunity.

In 1968, Margaret Thatcher, then Conservative shadow minister for fuel and power, was invited to give an address to the Conservative Political Centre's meeting to commemorate forty years since women had achieved full emancipation. Rejecting such a tokenistic notion, she instead delivered an ambitiously titled piece 'What's Wrong with Politics'. Thatcher's speech, which contained very little by way of eco-nomics or policies, offered a broad critique on post-war state expansion and its corrosive effects on individual liberty. Margaret Thatcher's contention, which many considered quite innocent and sensible at the time, was that the individual must be emancipated from such bur-dens so that the values of responsibility and duty to others could be restored. In preparation, Thatcher had studied works of Conservative philosophy, but in the end, it was to her Bible that she turned to for legitimation: 'Even the Good Samaritan had to have the money to help, otherwise he too would have had to pass on the other side.'[3] It was a foretaste of what was to come.

In 1968 though, it was Enoch Powell who was the leading light on the right. Prime Minister Harold Wilson said as much at the Labour Party conference that year, and in a calculated swipe at Edward Heath, singled Powell out as his main rival. Wilson was, of course, conscious of the support that Powell had amongst the working-class Labour vot-ers, as the pro-Powellite march by the East End Dockers had recently demonstrated. The Conservatives would later take advantage of anti-immigration feeling, but Heath condemned Powell's views in no uncertain terms as 'an example of man's inhumanity to man which is absolutely intolerable in a Christian, civilised society'.[4] Both Labour and Conservatives remained aware that in evoking the popular anguish about immigration at a time of a weakening economy, Powell had stirred up a hornet's nest that would not easily go away.

Enoch Powell always lacked the personal skills and charm required to become leader and tended to inspire admiration rather than loyalty from his colleagues. He was principled yet populist, poetic yet rational but had a kamikaze-like approach to his career, which even his closest friends could not fathom. 'I go a long way along the line with Enoch,' remarked Conservative Chancellor Iain Macleod, 'but I get off before the train crashes into the buffers.'[5] Nor was Powell easy to bracket. He had given up his schoolboy dream of becoming Viceroy of India when he realised Britain's imperial game was up and in the post-decolonised new world order, became an ardent nationalist voicing anti-Americanism and anti-Europeanism with equal aggression. Long before Powell became synonymous with immigration restrictions, it was on the free market where he had shown the lead. Powell was an advocate of privatisation twenty years before the policy was enacted and even Milton Friedman wrote to *The Times* defending his economic views. But in 1974, just when it looked like the Conservative Party might come round to his way of thinking, Powell left to join the Ulster Unionists, convinced that the Conservatives, led by his great adversary Ted Heath, was no longer the party he had joined in his youth.

Powell was the first politician to combine the two strands which would later become the central tenets of the New Right – Tory nationalism with a free-market approach to economics – although the reason he is cast as the 'Godfather of Thatcherism' is as much to do with his class as his politics. A grammar-school boy from Wolverhampton, Powell dismissed the aristocratic pretensions of Toryism and promoted a form of populism, which pitted the ruling elite against the so-called 'will of the British people', be it on immigration, economics or even

the Church of England. Even though Powell had a historical consciousness that sometimes led him astray, he did not have an anachronistic
view of the world and in important ways prompted and pre-empted
many of the debates that would later dominate the Thatcher years.

One aspect of Powell that is rarely remarked upon is his religious
belief. A devout Anglican, Powell's faith was formed not in the home
but from a conversion experience in his youth when he had been
invited into the church by the local vicar. An evangelical, Powell
later became a biblical scholar and spent his dying days working on a
revised translation of St John's Gospel. His faith, though, was always
rooted in a historic (and what many clerics considered to be inac-
curate) belief in the supremacy of Parliament as the protector of the
Church and its people. Speaking to a gathering at the East Grinstead
Young Conservatives in 1980, Powell put forward the historic case:

> In England the supremacy of the Crown in Parliament is the guarantee
> to millions that their inheritance in the Church can never be taken away
> from them by arbitrary decision or clerical fashion and that the Church
> of England will never be narrowed into one sect among other sects nor
> dissolved and lost in an international and amorphous Christianity.[6]

The constitutional basis of the Church of England was something
that Powell had been arguing since the 1950s, but it later became his
main line of defence in halting the liberal direction of the Church of
England. On the main aspects of modern Anglicanism, Powell stood
in defiant opposition. He was an instrumental figure in the parliamentary campaign against the Church's updating of the 1662 Book of
Common Prayer, considered female ordination a 'blasphemous pan-
tomime' and was deeply hostile to any ecumenical alliances against
Protestant England's old enemy, Rome. He even changed his place
of worship from St Peter's, Eaton Square, to St Margaret's, Westminster, because of the incumbent priest's 'imitation of Roman fashions'.[7]

Powell's anti-Romanism may also have been the origins of his opposition to the EEC; his paranoia seems to have led him to view it as
some kind of conspiratorial Catholic plot. Powell's views on immigration inevitably put him at odds with Archbishop Ramsey. If Powell
was a reluctant hero for the National Front, then Ramsey became one
of its targets as head of the National Committee for Commonwealth
Immigrants. Enoch Powell challenged the bishops on their support
for multiculturalism, which to him stemmed from a left-wing political bias rather than sound theology. In 1969, Powell appeared in a TV
debate with anti-apartheid campaigner and Bishop of Stepney, Trevor
Huddleston. When Huddleston denounced Powell's views on race as
incompatible with biblical teaching, Powell's response was emphatic:
'When you are gratified with the conclusions that you arrive at, you
dignify them as a consequence of Christian belief.'[8] In Powell's mind,
the clergy did not have anything original or substantive to say on
political affairs. 'They are amateurs in economics, amateurs in politics, their expertise lies in a different sphere,' was his response to the
Church's Declaration on World Poverty in 1973.[9]

Powell proved to be a thorn in the Church's side throughout the
1970s and 1980s, working with traditionalists in the Synod to thwart
Church Measures when they reached Parliament. Powell was clearly
a reassuring figure for conservative Anglicans. One parishioner wrote
a series of letters to Powell with a list of complaints about her local
vicar who had apparently allowed the use of the church for an Islamic
funeral, consented to female laity conducting Holy Communion and
whose Easter service had featured a West Indian Calypso. 'Just what
religion is this Church practising?' she complained to Powell, assured
that her frustrations would gain a favourable hearing.[10]

Powell liked to claim that his faith and his politics were separate
('My Kingdom is not of this World' was one of his stock phrases), but
no one could deny the political resonance of his statement: 'Man is born
as an individual, he dies as an individual ... It is to man the individual

that the Gospel speaks.'[11] Margaret Thatcher would later reiterate this point using almost identical language. Powell's belief in the doctrine of original sin lay behind his scepticism towards any utopian visions of state. According to Powell, the Bible did not contain a blueprint for human advancement, as he explained, in rather bleak terms, to the parishioners of St Michael and Mary in Southwark in 1973:

> Christianity does not, repeat, not, look forward to a gradual betterment of human behaviour and society or to the progressive spread of peace and justice upon earth. Still less does Christianity purport to offer a scheme or general outline for bringing that about. Quite the reverse, it uniformly teaches ... that things will get worse rather than get better before we are through.[12]

Enoch Powell was an unsettling figure for the ruling elite. He pierced holes in the ideological foundations of the post-war liberal order: its politics, its religion and the make-up of British society. Powellism foreshadowed Thatcherism in serving up a new vision of post-imperial nationalism combined with economic liberalism and, like Thatcher, Powell drew on the notion of the sanctity of the individual and God-given liberty to justify it.

Powell had merely rocked the boat in the late 1960s. It would take a further seven years and two election defeats to bring about change in the Conservative Party. But, importantly, something happened to Britain in the interim: a crisis in national self-confidence. Economic and industrial disruption following from the oil shock of 1973 exacerbated an already prevailing sense of uncertainty about Britain's place in the world in the wake of decolonisation (something, which Britain's entry into European Economic Community in 1973 did not halt). Rising immigration and Celtic nationalism, too, seemed to be corroding a traditional and cohesive notion of Britishness. The fallout in Ulster was a knock to national pride not to mention a cause of international embarrassment. In the 1970s, Britain seemed like a racehorse that had lost its rider but was still in the race, jumping limply over each hurdle and meandering all over the place. Henry Kissinger summed it up succinctly in a note to President Ford in 1975: 'Britain is a tragedy.'[13]

In 1970, Ted Heath appeared to have the answers, setting out a programme for change devised at the Selsdon Park Hotel. Selsdon was always more important for its tone rather than specifics. An enthused Keith Joseph, then shadow Minister for Technology and Trade proclaimed that it aimed for 'civilised capitalism based on competitive free enterprise in a context of human laws and institutions'.[14] This all sounded inherently sensible, but in the end Heath would not have the luck or the metal to enact the necessary changes. He would be defeated by the two great crises of the age – industrial strife and inflation – as he opted for appeasement rather than confrontation with the unions. Margaret Thatcher would learn pertinent lessons from the Heath government of 1970–74.

II. A turn to the right

NEO-LIBERALISM, AS IT became known, was not that new by the time that the Conservative Party came to fully embrace it. It could be dated back to 1947 with the formation of the Mont Pelerin Society, named after the resort in Switzerland where a collection of like-minded scholars, including Friedrich Hayek, Karl Popper and Milton Friedman, established a group committed to reasserting classical economic liberalism against the Keynesian orthodoxy. Britain soon had its own neo-liberal vehicle in the form of the Institute of Economic Affairs (IEA), set up in 1955 and led by a son of a tramways inspector and failed Conservative parliamentary candidate, Ralph Harris, and former Liberal Party activist and son of a Jewish émigré, Arthur Seldon. That the economic tide in Britain was turning away from post-war Keynesianism was clearly evident by 1976 when Labour Chancellor Denis Healey implemented cuts as a condition of Britain's embarrassing bail-out by the International Monetary Fund (IMF). Jim Callaghan declared at the Labour Party conference that year that it was now 'impossible to spend your way out of a recession'. But in this, the Labour government was merely accepting pragmatic monetary constraints; it did not represent an ideological switch. What was discernible about the economic liberals who gained prominence in the 1970s was not only their discrediting of the Keynesian model, but their fanatical belief in the alternative.

British economic liberals tended to hark back to the glory days of nineteenth-century laissez-faire capitalism as the historical precedent to be repeated, while the Keynesian post-war 'experiment' was dismissed as a tale of false idols, wrong policies and bad results, particularly in respect to the welfare state. As early as 1971, just when welfare spending was beginning to contract, Ralph Harris pleaded for a more radical overhaul. The welfare state, he wrote, 'is anything but a gift horse. Rather it is a lame nag harnessed to an outdated bandwagon ... the sovereign people should pull hard on the reins, ask for their money back and get off the overcrowded monstrosity.'[15] Harris, who had been born a Nonconformist and later became an Anglican was not averse to casually drawing on the doctrine of original sin to debunk the myth of the exalted state. According to Harris, the state was not one of utopian dreams, as socialists professed, but a heretical fantasy, which incorrectly assumed the inherent goodness of humanity and largely benefited the bureaucratic class in charge. Nigel Lawson would make an almost identical point in 1980, when as Financial Secretary to the Treasury he gave a speech entitled 'the New Conservatism'. Drawing on philosopher Anthony Quinton's notion that Conservatism rested on the imperfection of mankind (devoid of its religious associations), Lawson claimed that whereas socialism forwarded a 'creed of utopianism and the perfectibility of man', Conservatism on the other hand concerned 'the creed of original sin and the politics of imperfection'. Few Conservatives would have challenged him on the notion that Conservative philosophy was rooted in 'imperfection'; what was contentious was Lawson's application to the welfare state: 'We are all imperfect – even the most high-minded civil servant ... the civil servants and middle-class welfare professionals are far from the selfless Platonic guardians of paternalist mythology: they are a major interest group in their own right.'[16]

In both cases, Harris and Lawson were not offering a Christian vision of Conservatism or even the market (this job would later fall to Margaret Thatcher), rather they were conveniently using the doctrine of the Fall to discredit the man-made state; and in Lawson's case, to define the characteristics of what he called 'the New Conservatism'.

Friedrich Hayek never considered himself a Conservative and indeed wrote an essay refuting the claim; rather he aligned himself with 'old-fashioned Liberals', that is, the classical liberalism of the nineteenth-century Manchester school.[§] Neo-liberalism was always an intellectual movement outside the Conservative Party upon which only a handful of Conservatives would directly draw. The influence of Hayek, Michael Oakeshott and others was subtle but important in establishing the philosophical and economic critique of socialism's suppression of liberty and also the exalting of individual liberty over the concept of social equality; two doctrines which would later underscore Thatcherism. What particularly excited the political class, however, was the fanaticism and above all certainty, with which economic liberals – chiefly those at the Chicago school – spoke of the market as the antidote to collectivism. Economic theory was elevated to doctrinal heights, economists lauded as the new apostles, as monetarists claimed to have discovered the miraculous formula for controlling the money supply. The chief ingredients that made up economic liberalism from the late 1960s differed from the

---

§   Thus making the distinction between the economic liberalism of the nineteenth century and the progressive liberalism of the twentieth

Conservative libertarians of the 1940s and 1950s, who had tended to root their arguments not in the sovereignty of the market but in the moral supremacy of civil society over the state.

Few economic liberals were Christians, a number were notable atheists and a large number were of Jewish origin. Hayek did believe that the modern trend towards socialism was a denial of the key characteristics of Western civilisation that had its roots in Christianity, but both he and Friedman espoused to what may be called an atheist libertarian position. Economic liberals may not have drawn on the Bible as Thatcher would later do, but they did assert the *moral* superiority of the market over socialism. Adam Smith was heralded not an economist but a moral philosopher (which he was of course was) as neo-liberals endorsed Smith's contention that the market enabled citizens to exercise their self-interest, which ultimately was for the benefit of the greater good. In Smith's classic phrase: 'It is not from the benevolence of the butcher, the brewer or the baker that we expect our dinner, but from their regard to their own interest.' Smith's notion of a 'system of natural order' also distinctly appealed to economic liberals seeking to cast socialism as an artificial construct and thus contrary to the natural laws of man.

It took a while for economic liberalism to gain a foothold within the party; meanwhile a more traditional thread of Conservative thinking, which still went by the historic label of 'High Toryism', also enjoyed renewed prominence in the 1970s. If Balliol College, Oxford, had been the intellectual pulse of post-war progressivism (the alma mater of Heath, Temple, Tawney, Roy Jenkins amongst others), then Peterhouse, Cambridge, operated in much the same function for the New Right in the 1970s, housing the likes of historians Maurice Cowling and Edward Norman and the Cambridge base for future Thatcherites Michael Howard and Michael Portillo. It, too, had notable links in the right-wing press with Colin Welch, deputy editor of the *Daily Telegraph* and Peregrine Worsthorne, associate editor of the *Sunday Telegraph* and Patrick Cosgrave, one-time political editor of *The Spectator* and later adviser to Margaret Thatcher, all linked to Peterhouse. Also rising through the ranks, but not Peterhouse men, were the likes of Charles Moore and A. N. Wilson, who would later be dubbed the 'Young Fogeys', so called because of their old-fashioned dress and high cultural tastes. These High Tories may have acted like the 1960s had never happened but they were in fact entirely a product of it. They revelled in a traditionalist and hierarchical view of society and positioned themselves in opposition to the New Liberalism and all its manifestations: its politics, culture, education, architecture and religion. High Toryism would eventually establish its own mouthpiece, the *Salisbury Review* journal, founded in 1980 and edited by philosopher Roger Scruton.

It is in fact extremely difficult to pinpoint precisely what united these disparate figures. Indeed, it was a desire for coherence that motivated Maurice Cowling to pen his exhaustive three-volume work, *Religion and Public Doctrine in Modern England* (1980–2001), which charted contribution of Conservative thought in the twentieth century as the intellectual antidote to liberal progressivism.) Above all, it was a distinctly English intellectual movement rooted in a Whiggish understanding of the organic and harmonious evolution of the English constitution and a suspicion of anything done in the name of 'progress'. Their faith in Britain's institutions was coupled with serious misgivings about who was now running them – be it the universities, the Church or the Tory Party. This was combined with a tangible sense of England (rather than Britain), which naturally underscored their evolving attitudes towards European federalism, immigration and the nationalist causes of the Celtic fringe.

In Maurice Cowling's view, the real enemy was neither socialism nor communism, but a much more pernicious force: 'secular liberalism', which, in his view, was not liberal at all but a decidedly stringent, intolerant doctrine that had pervaded Britain's culture like an alternative religion. This was the ideological label given to establishment thinking and the inspiration behind what High Tories considered the three main disasters of post-war politics: the social-democratic consensus, the 'permissive' legislation and progressive education. Cowling's particular gripe was that secular liberalism had found intellectual credibility in the discipline of sociology; he was to fight a long but futile campaign against it becoming a degree subject at Cambridge.

Most High Tories came from the Anglo-Catholic wing of the Church of England and upheld the sovereign notion of establishment, although they considered the liberal drift within Anglicanism to be a sign that secular humanism had gained a worrying foothold in the Church. This was a high charge, but, as Maurice Cowling admitted, their own underlying prejudices could not be denied either: 'It could well be that it was a polemical conviction against liberalism rather than a real conviction of the truth of Christianity,' he later said.[17] Cowling's religious commitment was ambiguous to say the least; he had considered joining the priesthood in his youth but had ceased to be an active churchgoer in his later years.

The man to imprint a historical understanding on this critique of Anglicanism was the Dean of Peterhouse, the Very Rev. Edward Norman. In his history of the Church since 1770, Norman argued that the story of the modern Anglicanism was one of gradual capitulation to the predominant secular left-wing ideas of the age, with Hensley Henson emerging as a particular hero. Norman's aim was to undermine the theological credibility of the social gospel, although he was less inclined to see similar failings within conservative Christianity, which was equally guilty of drawing on a secular bourgeois individualism to legitimise its own version of the Gospel. Liberal Anglican priest Paul Oestreicher would later dismiss Norman's position as 'populist theology', noting 'there are as many Alf Garnetts in Oxbridge as in Stepney'.[18] Oestreicher was right to label Norman's position as 'populist', for like Enoch Powell on immigration, Norman, too, pitted the elite upper-middle-class clergy against the churchgoing mass. Norman's thesis was to prove a compelling argument and one that would be rehearsed time and time again by traditionalist Anglicans in the 1980s. High Tories would take Thatcher's side in her battle with the Church but many were uncomfortable with Thatcherism as a political doctrine, especially its libertarian emphasis. This was particularly true in the sphere of economics, where the prioritising of the market, they rightly predicted, would bring about irrevocable changes to the nation's landscape, culture and psyche.

It is impossible to overstate the sense of paranoia and frustration that engulfed the Conservative-voting middle classes in the 1970s, with fears about rising prices and union militancy mirroring an earlier wave of anti-socialist hysteria that had gripped Britain in the 1920s. The middle classes had been hit hard by the economic slump and inflation; retail prices increased by 25 per cent between 1965 and 1970 and by 16 per cent in 1976 alone. Inflation was a potent issue precisely because it was seen to break the middle-class association between 'effort and reward'.[19] Meanwhile, fears about rising 'permissiveness' compounded a sense that middle-class values – respectability, discipline and deferred gratification – were wilfully being discarded for a culture of dependency, decadence and debt. The apocalyptic fears about 'national decline' or the 'British disease' masked the actual concern; the erosion of middle-class values. Signs for this frustration could be traced as far back as the 1940s with the establishment of the welfare state, although post-war affluence had done a great deal to silence these cries. In more testing times they became impossible to muzzle. By the mid-1970s, the middle class began to wail like a persecuted and vilified interest group. 'In this time of crisis … [we] are subject to unprecedented pressures, and, at the same time, to unprecedented denigration,' wrote Patrick Hutber in his defensive tract *The Decline and Fall of the Middle Class*.[20]

The problem was that the middle classes' chief political mouthpiece appeared not to be listening. Reports from the Tory Associations gathered by Conservative Central Office in the early '70s spoke very little about fiscal management but included a long list of other complaints, including trade union power, immigration, inflation, immorality and much on the diminishing virtues of personal responsibility and individual liberty. Heath had attempted to reach out to the Conservative core with his Selsdon manifesto in 1970, but disillusionment soon reappeared as he yielded to union demands. They were to punish him in the election of October 1974, with the Conservatives suffering their worst result since 1918. Some fled to the Liberals, who amassed an increasing share of the vote in the 1970s, while others decided to take matters into their own hands and establish extra-parliamentary groups. The logic was that if trade unions were able to use bullying tactics to bargain for higher wages, why should the middle classes not deploy similar methods to defend their interests?

Nineteen seventy-four was the year when the middle class bolted with the establishment of the Middle Class Association (MCA) soon after the first election that February. The MCA was later joined by the National Association of Ratepayers' Action Group, which fought a successful campaign against the recent hike in local rates. The Labour government, then wary of another election, immediately extended grants to local councils to cover the increase. The Conservative Party, too, altered its rates policy under the instruction of the new shadow housing spokesperson, Margaret Thatcher. The National Federation of Self-Employed was later established, providing an important voice for this rapidly growing element of Britain's workforce who were suffering from the contraction in the economy and who feared big business as much as union militancy. It soon claimed 30,000 members and was later joined by the Association of Self-Employed People led by future Conservative MP Teresa Gorman. All this was a worrying development for the Conservatives. Edward

Heath had been conscious of the need to appease middle-class dis-affection but not until Margaret Thatcher became leader would the party adequately address their concerns.

The most prominent, but not necessarily the most important, of these organisations was the right-wing libertarian group, the National Association For Freedom (NAFF). Established by the founders of the Guinness Book of Records, the McWhirter brothers and former Governor-General of Australia, Viscount De L'Isle, in 1975, NAFF was an direct reaction to Heath's failure to get tough with the unions, although its involvement in a 'Self Help' press and a 'Stop the Scroung-ers' campaign hinted at a broader agenda. In 1976, NAFF was to stage its greatest coup in helping to defeat the strike at Grunwick Film Pro-cessing Laboratories: a local dispute, which escalated into a symbolic confrontation between the unions and small businesses in Britain. Norris McWhirter was an old acquaintance of Margaret Thatcher. She had backed his parliamentary candidature for the seat of Orpington in the 1960s. He in turn supported her leadership campaign in 1975 and dismissed her opponents as the 'Old Gang of the Tory Party ... a bunch of political failures, has-beens who never were'. In Margaret Thatcher, McWhirter recognised a kindred spirit.[21]

Organisations such as NAFF were important not for their individual success but for collectively triggering a wake-up call within the Con-servative Party. What these groups shared in common was not only their middle-class support base but also their geographical concentra-tion in the south of England (they were particularly weak in Scotland and Wales). When Margaret Thatcher became leader, she attended to their fears, much like a mother comforting a screaming child. In one of her first tasks as leader, she established the 'Small Business Bureau' within Conservative Central Office and, not for good reason, began to draw on her own heritage as the daughter of an independent gro-cer. By the general election of 1979, these organisations had either dissolved or ceased to pose a threat to the Conservative Party.

In his 1971 book, *The Permissive Society*, Tory parliamentary candidate John Gummer put the Conservative case succinctly when he wrote: 'The twentieth century had restricted and corseted us economically while leaving us more and more free to do as we like in bed.'[22] At the time that Gummer was writing, popular anguish over moral permissiveness had found its most prominent means of expression in the National Viewers' and Listeners' Association (NVLA) formed by Mary Whitehouse in 1964. Dubbed 'God's Rottweiler' by the press, Whitehouse emerged as the self-appointed guardian of the nation's morals, leading the fighting against what she called the BBC's 'propaganda of disbelief, doubt and dirt'.[23] Whitehouse cast herself as a sobering antidote to what she called the 'candy-floss society' and spoke in a language of sin and certainty, which even Church leaders found slightly archaic.

The moral lobby in Britain fashioned itself as populist, anti-intellectual and anti-establishment, with Whitehouse presenting her crusade as a David and Goliath tale: that of an unassuming lower-middle-class teacher from the Midlands taking on the tax-funded liberal elites at the BBC. Whitehouse, though, demonstrated an impressive capacity for self-promotion and publicity. She exploited the potentialities of the new media age as much as she condemned them and as a result attracted a level of attention that far outweighed the NVLA's support base. Whitehouse's claim that she represented the 'silent majority' was questionable; even at its height, the organisation had a membership of just 30,000 and was always more of a one-woman show than a mass movement. Nonetheless, Whitehouse's attacks on the liberal establishment, much like Enoch Powell on immigration, were both forms of a right-wing populist rhetoric, which Margaret Thatcher, in her anti-establishment flourishes, would later excel in communicating to the electorate.

Of the Christian motivation behind the NVLA, there can be no doubt. Whitehouse was an evangelical Anglican, while the NVLA's original manifesto had begun with the declaration: 'We women of Britain believe in a Christian way of life.' NVLA members were much like Whitehouse herself – predominantly middle-aged, evangelical women – although the NVLA also counted many Nonconformists, High Anglicans and Roman Catholics within their ranks. The NVLA's respectable and discreet form of middle-class female activism proved a sharp contrast to the brash ostentatiousness and radicalism of the women's movement then beginning to flower. This was Britain's culture war and it was distinctly female in its composition. At the same time that feminists were hijacking the Miss World competition and heckling host Bob Hope, Mary Whitehouse was staging silent prayer demonstrations and petitioning the Home Office to remove death metal man of darkness Alice Cooper from Britain. It hardly needs saying that the majority of Britons did not consider either Bob Hope or Alice Cooper much of a threat.

The moral right was given additional impetus in the early 1970s with the formation of the National Festival of Light, founded by evangelical Peter Hall, who, on returning to the UK from missionary work in India, was shocked to find Britain in what he described as a 'moral landslide'.[24] Hall convinced other prominent lay-Christians to join his cause, including the evangelical industrialist Sir Fred Catherwood, Catholic anti-obscenity campaigner Lord Longford (later dubbed 'Lord Porn') and Malcolm Muggeridge, a former atheist and satirist who seemed to lose his sense of humour when he found Christ. Taking its cue from American-style evangelicalism, the Festival of Light held mass rallies in Trafalgar Square in 1971 and again in 1972, attracting crowds of well over 20,000. Activists soon realised, however, that if there was to be a moral revival it would come through legislative change rather than the saving of souls.

Whitehouse's own tactic was to move the fight from the streets to the law courts where she believed, correctly as it turned out, that such causes were likely to find favour amongst the predominantly conservative judiciary. The 1970s saw a series of successes against obscenity, such as the banning of *The Little Red Book*, penned by

two Danish schoolteachers, which had asked the youths to question and challenge societal moral norms. In 1971, the publishers of
underground satirical magazine *Oz* were charged with 'conspiracy
to corrupt public morals' and although they were eventually let off,
their trial put 'obscenity' in the spotlight in the same way that *Lady
Chatterley's Lover* had done ten years previously. In 1978, Danish
filmmaker Jens Jørgen Thorsen, who was due to shoot the *Sex Life
of Christ*, was arrested at Heathrow. By far the most important case
came in 1977 when Whitehouse pursued a successful private prosecution of blasphemy against the editor of *Gay News* for publishing
a poem concerning the sexual fantasies of a Roman soldier towards
Jesus' crucified body. This was the first prosecution for blasphemy
since 1922.

Whitehouse once complained that 'the "liberators" of the '60s have
become the tyrants of the '70s'.[25] She had a point. When it came to
Mary Whitehouse and her cohort of moralists, the liberal intelligentsia did not appear to be all that liberal. Whitehouse was appalled by
the vilification she received from all quarters and by the lack of support from the one institution upon which she had assumed she could
rely: 'I was completely overwhelmed by the extent of the opposition,
and the silence of the Church' she later wrote on her blasphemy campaign.[26] Christian leaders had taken a conscious decision to distance
themselves from the *Gay News* trial with both the Archbishop of Canterbury and the Catholic Archbishop of Westminster refusing an offer
to testify. Paul Oestreicher, went so far as to question the 'Christian'
worth of the moral lobby:

> The puritan middle-class fears of Mrs Whitehouse and her friends do
> nothing to enhance Christian values. Much of the real life drama they
> want to keep off the screen and out of print shows human beings wres-
> tling seriously with themselves and the world. Sex, beautiful and not so
> beautiful, is too important to be turned into sweet romance.[27]

One of the striking features of the moral conservative revival in the 1970s was the fact that its figurehead was a female layperson rather than a man of the cloth. Whitehouse and her supporters also tended to receive a much more favourable reception in Parliament than in the Synod. Whitehouse considered this ecclesiastical reticence as evidence that the Church had embraced the New Morality. The fact that the Church had been unforthcoming in its support for the Festival of Light (the Archbishop of Canterbury had not been present) but had willingly hosted a communion service in St Paul's Cathedral for the three-year anniversary of the counter-cultural musical *Hair* seemed a shameful example of a Church gone awry.

In the 1960s, moral pressure groups had rightly pointed the finger at consumerism and materialism as well as collectivism for the decline in traditional morality in Britain. This broad analysis too reflected their support base in Parliament, which came as much from the traditional Nonconformist left as it did from the right. Yet, by the end of the 1970s, the moral lobby had more or less aligned its cause with the Conservative Party while it began to cast the left as the main perpetrators of permissiveness. How and why did moralism become the preserve of the right? It was of course easy to point the finger at the Labour Party – its government had brought in most of the offensive legislation. But, more profoundly, it was the Conservatives that initiated this move. In the mid-1970s, conscious of the disaffection at the grassroots, Conservatives started making favourable noises to Whitehouse and her followers. In his notorious Edgbaston speech in 1974, which is now best remembered for some unwise statements on eugenics, Conservative shadow minister Keith Joseph singled out Mary Whitehouse as an embodiment of individual virtue against the bureaucratic elite; that of an 'unknown middle-aged woman, a schoolteacher in the Midlands' who had set out 'to protect adolescents against the permissiveness of our time'.[28] Whitehouse was clearly flattered by the attention and duly returned the compliment: 'The people of Britain have been like sheep without a shepherd. But now they have found one,' she declared after Joseph's speech.[29] The association between the moral right and the Conservative Party would become cemented during Margaret Thatcher's years as Leader of the Opposition. Willie Whitelaw, then shadow Home Secretary, was sent off to attend the NVLA annual conference, while Thatcher purposefully began to speak of a moral revival as necessary for economic revival.

Perhaps sensing that this was where the argument was heading, Whitehouse also tied the economic argument with the moral one. 'The will to beat inflation,' Whitehouse wrote in a private plea to all party leaders before the election in 1979, was 'dependent upon the character of the people', which was 'moulded in the home'.[30] For years, issues of morality had been determined by MPs' individual conscience rather than party affiliation, yet as the left came to gradually embrace the New Morality, so the right promoted itself more prominently as the party of the family and conservative morality. Whitehouse, therefore, pinned great hopes on the new female Conservative leader who in character and demeanour seemed remarkably similar to herself: a middle-class suburban mother also armed with a handbag, a moralistic fervour and a determination to kick the ruling elite into shape.

By the mid-1970s, it was clear to most Anglicans that there was a sharp divide emerging within the Church between liberals who advocated 'accommodation' with the modern world and traditionalists who advocated 'resistance'. What is more, this fragmentation seemed to cut across the old factions of evangelicals, liberals and High Anglicans. Anglo-Catholic traditionalists, who feared what liberal reformism was doing to traditional practices, found they had much in common with evangelical conservatives concerned about the weakening of scriptural authority. This schism was not confined to the Church of England but clearly evident in the Roman Catholic Church, where conservatives were determined to halt the progress of Vatican II. Paradoxically then, just at the moment when ecumenism could have been said to have eased tensions between the churches, this was superseded by an equally damaging phenomenon: fragmentation within the Christian churches themselves.

The establishment of the General Synod in 1970 had given the Church greater control over its affairs, but it had also created a forum in which ecclesiastical factionalism and infighting could ferment. If ever there was an institution to take the sanctity out of Christianity, it was the dry, charmless debating chamber of Synod. In most instances, it showed the Church in the worst possible light with its bureaucratic class, obstructive procedure and endless series of forgettable debates. 'I regard it as a disaster, a playground for bureaucrats or bores,' wrote the Bishop of Southwark, Mervyn Stockwood, in his diocesan letter in 1972, two years into its infancy.[31]

Anglican tensions too were exacerbated by the continual decline in religious worship and sacraments, which the liberalising trends clearly had not halted. Baptisms, for example, dropped by 15 per cent in the ten years between 1970 and 1980, in line with congregation figures as a whole.[32] Under such circumstances, the ecclesiastical leadership were forced to enact a systematic overhaul of its parishes. Between 1969 and 1984 some 1,086 churches were categorised as redundant and in 1976 alone it was estimated that one parish church was destroyed every nine days.[33]

The decline of those entering the priesthood also prompted the closure of eleven of its twenty-six theological colleges between 1961 and 1977.[34] The priesthood was no longer the natural path for young Oxbridge graduates: by 1971 only 16 per cent of clergy came via this route compared with 38 per cent between 1920 and 1960; over half of new priests had no degree at all. Not that this was necessarily a bad thing; many believed that it would rid the Church of its endemic elitism, but there was little doubt that it altered the culture of Anglicanism in the process. Methodism fared even worse. Manchester, once a key stronghold, saw its congregations drop by 44 per cent between 1964 and 1984; a feat that even the most optimistic Moderators judged as irreversible.[35] Roman Catholic congregations, which had reached a peak in the late 1960s, also fell by 17 per cent in just ten years.[36] In 1978, Liverpool Cathedral, the fifth largest of its kind in the world and only the third Anglican cathedral to have been built in Britain since the Reformation, was finally opened with a thanksgiving service attended by the Queen. At the point of its inception, Victoria had been on the throne, Liverpool was a thriving port and the Church of England had just established the diocese of Liverpool to cater for the city's rapidly expanding population. By the time it was finally completed a century later, it seemed a clumsy and oversized monument to a muscular Christianity long gone. The fact that the central tower had a lift for tourists – the first of its kind for a cathedral – revealed much about the perceived intentions of its visitors.

The key growth area in the 1970s was amongst the conservative evangelicals, which accounted for nearly half of all new ordinands. These new recruits, who soon established their influence within middle-class suburban areas, tended to be individualistic in their faith and more willing than ever to challenge the liberal Anglicanism orthodoxy; they also tended to be Conservative voters. A political schism was emerging between reformers aligned with the progressive left and reactionaries associated with the right. This was a religio-political divide that would become all too clear in the 1980s.

Conservative evangelicals could feel some reassurance by the new man at the helm: the quiet, unassuming low-churchman Donald Coggan, who became Archbishop of Canterbury in 1974. Barely a year into office, Coggan launched a bold initiative, which he named his 'Call to the Nation'. With union disruption, a stumbling economy and two elections in less than a year, the archbishop entreated Britons to write to him about their concerns and hopes for the future: 'Part of our trouble is that we think the individual is powerless. That is a lie. He is not powerless. Your vote counts. Your voice counts. You count. Each man and woman is needed if the drift towards chaos is to stop. Your country needs YOU.'[37]

If there was any doubt of the sense of national disillusionment and uncertainty that prevailed in Britain in the 1970s, then the 20,000 or so letters that filled the archbishop's postbag certainly revealed it. Some predictably referred to the 'pagan, permissive ruin' and a desire for a biblical revival, but most referenced more temporal concerns, such the breakdown of communities (including the demise of the local shop), the self-interested culture of materialism and the values of thrift: 'Gone are the days, it seems, when you saved up the money to buy what you needed,' wrote one woman from Norfolk.[38] Others commented on the stifling culture of officialdom and the loss of community in the era of big business, unions and government. As one civil servant explained: 'We may all be fanned by the same breeze, but the right to put on or take off sail is ours.'[39] There were brief references to the threat of collectivism and communism, but much more on the need for the revival of the Protestant work ethic. As one man from Thames Valley offered: 'The majority who work hard and do their best are penalised, heavily taxed and vilified in order to support large numbers of idlers and scroungers. Now we all feel a kind of despair and tend to join the "take all, give the minimum" brigade.'[40] Another wondered whether salvation would come: 'Perhaps the need of the hour will bring forward someone of vision and leadership to shock us from our lethargy.'[41] Margaret Thatcher studied the published letters from the archbishop's call and in a speech in 1977 entitled 'Dimensions of Conservatism' made extensive reference to them before presenting her political philosophy of hard work, thrift, personal responsibility and moral integrity as the answer to their prayers.[42]

III. The great reawakening in the Tory Party

AS IS WIDELY recognised, it was Keith Joseph who first broke from the Heathite ranks and set the party on course for a radical change of direction. Joseph had been a proponent of the free market throughout the 1960s, although, when in power, he had overseen two of the highest spending departments in Whitehall – Housing and Social Services. The man who 'put a burr under Joseph's saddle' was his then on/off speechwriter Alfred Sherman who, in early 1974, wrote a series of articles in the *Telegraph*, which amounted to a thinly veiled personal attack on Joseph's record in office.[43] It worked. Joseph and Sherman, with consent from Edward Heath, quickly established the Centre for Policy Studies and roped in Joseph's closest Cabinet ally, Margaret Thatcher, as its deputy. CPS was not a run-of-the-mill research think-tank, rather its founders conceived it in missionary terms with a view to converting the party to neo-liberalism and translating theory into common sense to ensure mass appeal. Tone not policies was the priority.

Under Sherman's guidance, Keith Joseph delivered a series of mea culpa speeches, offering a summation of post-war Conservatism that actually had much in common with Edward Norman's assessment of post-war Anglicanism: a tale of capitulation. According to Joseph, the Conservative Party had blindly followed the post-war order and drifted away from its fundamental principles. 'It was only in April 1974 that I was converted to Conservatism (I had thought I was a Conservative but I now see that I was not really one at all),' Joseph declared in 1975 in a phrase that economic liberals greeted with relief, paternalists with despair and the general public with understandable confusion.[44] By that time, however, Joseph's momentum had already come to an abrupt halt. In a speech in Edgbaston the previous October, Joseph had attempted to broaden his analysis on the moral dimensions of economics, but had clumsily highlighted single mothers as the main social problem and eugenics as the solution. The media fury that followed convinced Joseph that he did not have the mental resilience for leadership and, when the contest was announced, he decided not to stand.

Up until the mid-1970s, nothing had distinguished Margaret Thatcher from the One-nation consensus within the party; in 1969 the *Financial Times* had her down as 'an uncommitted member of the shadow Cabinet'.[45] Her career was solid but unremarkable with the 'Milk Snatcher' episode earning her national notoriety for all the wrong reasons. Heath faced chants from Labour MPs in the Commons to 'ditch the bitch', but Thatcher had managed to weather the storm.[46] If the Edgbaston furore had forced Keith Joseph to concede that he had not the necessary mettle for leadership, then the Milk Snatcher controversy certainly convinced Margaret Thatcher that she could handle it.

In an interview with Granada TV, aired the night before the Conservative leadership ballot, Margaret Thatcher made an explicit appeal to wavering MPs. Heathite Conservatism may have alienated the middle classes, but Margaret Thatcher was determined to present herself as the candidate in harmony with the disaffected grassroots. This she did by returning to Grantham:

> My father left school at thirteen and had to make his own way in the world. I was brought up in a small town in the Midlands, for which I'm always profoundly thankful, because it's nice to be brought up in a community atmosphere in community spirit where everyone helps everyone else.[47]

Her TV performance was believed to have convinced many floundering MPs, mindful of pressures at constituency level, to vote for her. Margaret Thatcher's media persona up until that point had tended to focus on her balancing act as a working mother. From the moment that she bid for the leadership Margaret Thatcher self-consciously evoked her Nonconformist childhood – a tale of self-reliance, hard work and moral restraint – as the antidote for a nation suffering under the pressures of excessive bureaucracy, union militancy and permissiveness.

Whereas Keith Joseph's conversion had been intellectual, Margaret Thatcher's was instinctive. She had spent 1974 devouring the works of Milton Friedman, Adam Smith and John Maynard Keynes, but as

Alfred Sherman neatly put it: 'She was a woman of beliefs, and not ideas.'[48] Margaret Thatcher found that the new evangelical fervour and principles and prejudices of the New Right conveniently chimed with her Nonconformist roots. The economic arguments against excessive state spending suited her inclination towards thrift; theoretical notions of state interference went hand in hand with her understanding on the foundations of individual liberty, while the desire for moral and economic restraint fed into her innate Puritanism. This was self-conscious but it was not entirely self-constructed. Her upbringing had instilled a class and religious identity that was to be reawakened in the mid-1970s. As Alfred Sherman later said: 'The first eighteen years of her life in Puritan England shaped her forever. For her, God was a real presence ... In part I might have helped her to recognise the significance of Grantham, but much of Grantham was embodied in her, waiting to emerge.'[49]

Sherman perhaps overestimates, as he was prone to do, his own part in this. We need not delve too deeply into the psychology of Margaret Thatcher to appreciate that her father's death may have also played a part. It is not uncommon for the death of one's parents to trigger something in their offspring. Perhaps it is a desire to recreate their world or simply a romantic vision of one's childhood that takes hold; either way it is telling and perhaps understandable that Margaret Thatcher began to evoke Grantham at a time when her ties with the place had been completely severed. Although few commentators recognised it at the time, the provincial girl with Nonconformist ancestry was in many ways the right woman for the time.

IV. Conviction in an age of doubt

'TO BE A Thatcherite is, in Margaret Thatcher's own terms, to experience an epiphany, to undergo a religious transfiguration,' wrote literary critic Jonathan Raban in the late 1980s.[50] Indeed, one of the striking features of the New Right in the '70s was the number of converts that it attracted, many of whom came from the extreme left and brought with them the same energy, zealousness and a yearning for ideas. Some reached this destination on their own initiative, while others attrib-uted their conversion more personally to Margaret Thatcher. Alfred Sherman, for example, had been a former communist who had fought against Franco during the Spanish Civil War; Alan Walters, Thatcher's future economics adviser, was another who had made the leap from communist to economic liberal. Within Parliament, converts included former Labour Cabinet minister Reg Prentice (who would later serve in Thatcher's first Cabinet as Minister for Social Security) and peers Lord Robens and Lord Chalfont. Another was Labour MP Woodrow Wyatt. Elected in the Labour landslide of 1945, Wyatt had been a jun-ior minister under Attlee but would later become one of Thatcher's closest confidantes.

It is not uncommon for new leaders to adopt an evangelical tone and moral fervour in their first years, especially those considered to have a weak hold over their party, which Thatcher undoubtedly did until 1979. And yet Margaret Thatcher adopted this style more fer-vently and blatantly than most, perhaps rediscovering the flair and skills of her younger days as a Methodist lay-preacher. In one of her first speeches as leader to the Conservative Central Council in March 1975, she issued the following rallying cry to her supporters:

> It is our duty, our purpose, to raise those banners high, so that all can
> see them, to sound the trumpets clearly and boldly so that all can hear
> them. Then we shall not have to convert people to our principles. They
> will simply rally to those which truly are their own.[51]

Thatcher's evangelical style certainly stood out against the dry man-agerial tones of Edward Heath and the soft consensual words of Jim

Callaghan. Here was Thatcher presenting herself as a prophet prom-ising national renewal and a conviction approach:

> You've got to take everyone along with you ... you can only get other
> people in tune with you by being a little evangelical about it ... I'm not
> a consensus politician or a pragmatic politician; and I believe in the
> politics of persuasion: it's my job to put forward what I believe and try
> to get people to agree with me.[52]

According to these words, Thatcher saw politics as one of values not policies and the aim of leadership, like that of a preacher, as convert-ing people to the cause. This was unique to Thatcher. One can hardly imagine her leadership rivals such as William Whitelaw or Edward Heath or even those on the Labour benches such as Michael Foot or Tony Benn putting it in quite these terms. Yet Margaret Thatcher did not simply market her politics as a religious cause, but more point-edly offered a Christian legitimation for her political philosophy.

Margaret Thatcher's first foray into preaching came two years into her leadership in 1977, on the occasion of the inaugural memorial lec-ture for the Conservative Chancellor Iain Macleod. Thatcher began on a point of historical fact. Before the Conservative Party had been the party of capital or property, it 'began as a church party' she affirmed. This was indeed true but it was not an outdated mode of Erastianism that Thatcher was there to champion, but a notion of divine liberty, one that had very little to do with traditional Conservatism and was more in tune with nineteenth-century liberalism. Margaret Thatch-er's explicit tying of Christianity, individualism and Conservatism is worth quoting at length:

> Our religion teaches us that every human being is unique and must play
> his part in working out his own salvation. So whereas socialists begin
> with society, and how people can be fitted in, we [Conservatives] start

with Man, whose social and economic relationship are just part of his wider existence. Because we see man as a spiritual being, we utterly reject the Marxist view, which gives pride of place to economics.[53]

The following morning *The Times* praised Thatcher as 'a better Lutheran than Luther' with the speech representative of the best 'English Protestant Christian tradition' evoking the spirit of Wycliffe, Cranmer, Adam Smith, Wesley and Gladstone. Admittedly, this was not a very 'Conservative' list, but then as *The Times* recognised, the contents of the speech was not very Tory at all and more in line with the dissenting religious tradition: 'Is the view that a man has a religious duty to decide his own life rather than having others decide it for him, a view that now belongs to the right?' it legitimately questioned. Given Thatcher's spirited defence of the individual, *The Times* wondered whether the new leader was seeking to transform the party of the Cavaliers into the party of the Roundheads: 'King Charles I would have been surprised to be told that the men who asserted their individualism against his divine right to rule were really reactionaries, and that he was the progressive.' Margaret Thatcher, not yet leader for two years, was already playing mind games with the English historical consciousness.[54]

Edward Norman wrote a letter in support of Thatcher's speech, wryly adding that the Church of England hierarchy should read it. Not everyone was convinced though. The Vicar of Harwell and Chilton in Oxfordshire challenged Thatcher on her 'individualism based on merit' and 'a religion of "works"', which he posited was the 'very opposite of Lutheran teaching'.[55] Never one to shy away from an argument, Thatcher wrote a lengthy reply to *The Times*, in which she advised the vicar to read the works of Adam Smith:

Smith argued ... by harnessing men's natural impulse to improve their own condition and that of their families as well as to deserve the approbation of their fellow-men, the market economy visibly brought great benefits to the greater number. Smith never suggested that self-interest alone was sufficient to bring the Good Life, or that man can live by bread alone. By contrast, Marx's dialectical materialism gave pride of place to economics … perhaps the Vicar will again read Marx for himself after he has laid down Smith. He appears to believe that Marx stood for equality, as well as for benevolence and other Christian virtues. Surely then, he must have asked himself how, if this be so, can it be that wherever Marxist rule is imposed, as it is on a third of suffering mankind, it leads visibly to cruelty, misery, callousness, selfishness, new crying inequalities.[56]

Margaret Thatcher took to the pulpit a little over a year later in 1978 in a speech in the parish of St Lawrence Jewry in the City of London. Alfred Sherman was on hand to help with the drafting and suggested she speak on the revitalisation of Christianity and the Protestant work ethic. *Daily Telegraph* journalist T. E. Utley was also brought on board for expertise, yet he questioned whether it was wise for Thatcher to speak on Church matters, which risked upsetting Anglican voters just before an election:

> Public interest would be captured by using some of this autobiographical material … it is not a good idea to have the Tory Party leader leaping in to theological controversy between the liberal and conservative wings of the Church unless she makes it perfectly clear that she is doing so in a private capacity.[57]

Speechwriter Simon Webley, who also helped in the drafting, did not share Utley's desire for caution. With a sense of urgency Webley pressed Thatcher to address the decline of Christianity and the debilitating influence of 'humanistic socialism' within society. 'What has happened to the Christianity of our forefathers?' Webley asked before offering up the answer: 'It has been subsumed by an arid materialism concerned with the Gross National Product rather than the will of Almighty God.' Webley entreated Thatcher to preach a message of individual responsibility and the doctrine of original sin. In Webley's view, the public needed to be told that 'the evils of society are not due to the accident of class, education, income or region but to the inherent frailty of the individual himself'. Conscious that this would not find favour amongst the ecclesiastical and political class, Webley nonetheless drew upon the words of Montesquieu: 'When religion is strong the law can be weak, when religion is weak the law must be strong.' He too rather boldly suggested that she end with a quote from Proverbs: 'Righteousness Exalteth a nation.'[58]

Margaret Thatcher delivered a speech appropriately entitled 'I believe' incorporating Utley's suggestion that she reference her personal faith and Webley's ideas about the political application of the Fall:

> We were taught always to make up our own minds and never to take the easy way of following the crowd. I suppose what this taught me above everything else was to see the temporal affairs of this world in perspective. What mattered fundamentally was Man's relationship to God, and in the last resort this depended on the response of the individual soul to God's Grace … though good institutions and laws cannot make men good, bad ones can encourage them to be a lot worse … Christianity offers us no easy solutions to political and economic issues. It teaches us that there is some evil in everyone and that it cannot be banished by sound policies and institutional reforms; that we cannot eliminate crime simply by making people rich, or achieve a compassionate society simply by passing new laws and appointing more staff to administer them.[59]

Thatcher's speech received little by way of reaction, partly because the *Daily Telegraph* journalist present had failed to file a report and

The Times was then on strike. This may have been for the best, given that her Cabinet colleagues reportedly did not share Thatcher's enthusiasm for such sermonising. According to Sherman, the years in opposition were about saying 'as little as possible about anything'.[60]

Margaret Thatcher's message and image took time to get right with the general public, yet her affinity with the Tory Party was almost immediate. Her first party conference in 1975 had the feel of a leader reconnecting with their flock with the *Daily Mail* full of praise for the Conservative leader who had reportedly 'electrified her supporters at Blackpool ... like no party leader has done in the 1970s'.[61] It was true that Thatcher was in sympathy with rank-and-file Tories in a way that none of her rivals ever were. On seeing her perform at party conference, Harold Macmillan remarked on the contrast with his own experiences: 'We [his Cabinet] used to sit there listening to these extraordinary speeches urging us to birch or hang them all or other such strange things. We used to sit quietly nodding our heads ... But watching her ... I think she agrees with them.'[62]

Conservative strategists, though, were fearful that Margaret Thatcher appeared *too* Conservative, *too* English, and a bit *too* middle class. This was certainly how those at the US embassy in London perceived her. In a report for the US State Department on the new Leader of the Opposition, Thatcher was described as the 'genuine voice of a beleaguered bourgeoisie ... [a] quintessential suburban matron, and frightfully English to boot'.[63] This was a perception that Thatcher herself was particularly keen to refute. In a piece for the *Daily Telegraph*, Thatcher refuted the accusation that her politics were class-based:

> If 'middle-class values' include the encouragement of variety and
> individual choice, the provision of faith incentives and rewards for

skill and hard work, the maintenance of effective barriers against the excessive power of the state and a belief in the wide distribution of individual private property, then they are certainly what I am trying to defend.[64]

Margaret Thatcher, like most leaders who hope to be prime ministers, wisely avoided class labels. Meanwhile, Tory strategists aimed not only to win back traditional Conservative voters but that their policies would have a broader appeal. In short, the hope was that the affluent workers of the 1960s would become the upwardly mobile of the 1980s – they did.

The specific challenge of transforming Margaret Thatcher's image fell to smooth-talking, cigar-smoking TV executive Gordon Reece. The match was less Professor Higgins to Eliza, more Hollywood movie mogul to a young starlet. If Shirley Williams could be seen as having the boyish charm and sophistication of Katharine Hepburn and Barbara Castle, and the bolshiness of Bette Davis, then Margaret Thatcher was to be marketed as the fearless and determined Joan Crawford 'on the up'. Gone was the suburban shrill as Thatcher lowered her voice an octave, slowed it down and sharpened the intonation. She binned the hats and pearls as Reece told her to be normal and had her performing set pieces in supermarkets or doing the washing up. By the time the election came round, Thatcher's confidence in her own ability had grown. In 1978, her speechwriter Ronald Millar took her to see the new musical *Evita* by Andrew Lloyd Webber and Tim Rice. She wrote to Millar in thanks:

> It was a strangely wondrous evening yesterday leaving so much to think about. I still find myself rather disturbed by it. But if they [the Peronists] can do that without any ideals, then if we apply the same perfection and creativeness to our message, we should provide quite good historic material for an opera called Margaret in thirty years' time![65]

The genius of the Conservative campaign in the election of 1979 was its translation of complex economics into a populist message, which was projected through its leader. The image of Margaret Thatcher holding up two shopping bags of groceries – one blue, full to the brim, and the other red, half empty – crystallised in one shot how economic theory related to people's everyday lives and the Conservatives' commitment to beat inflation.

Conservatives were, of course, fortunate with the 'Winter of Discontent', which turned an already exhausted British public firmly against the unions and, more importantly, made them sceptical of the Labour Party's ability to deal with them. When, in February 1979, Archbishop Coggan initiated talks between the three party leaders, Thatcher agreed, but only on the condition of Callaghan's presence. Callaghan, however, rejected the call: a stance that showed Thatcher to be acting in the national interest without actually having to concede a word.[66] From that moment, she went on the attack. Incidentally, so did the archbishop, who in a sermon soon afterwards labelled the protest as 'pitiless' and 'irresponsible'.[67] The Winter of Discontent was important for another reason: in reinforcing fears about national decline. The understanding that Britain, the nation that had once kept Europe free, but was now going to the dogs, proved to be a potent narrative and one that the Conservatives willingly exploited: national renewal was made a key election pledge. In the end, Britons went with a woman about whom they knew relatively little but on whom they were willing to take a chance as Thatcher achieved her largest share of the popular vote in all of her three election victories.

It is customary for newly appointed prime ministers to express some vague words of thanks in their first address outside Downing Street. In 1970, Edward Heath had uttered some forgettable sentiments about recreating 'one nation'. Before the 1979 result had been confirmed, Thatcher had asked her chief speechwriter and dramatist Ronald Millar to prepare something for her to say outside No. 10. When Millar informed her of his idea for the prayer, Margaret wept. When the

moment finally came she slowly delivered the words, her eyes looking directly into the camera and only once peering down to look at
the reminder card carefully positioned in her palm:

Where there is discord, may we bring harmony.
Where there is error, may we bring truth.
Where there is doubt, may we bring faith.
And where there is despair, may we bring hope.

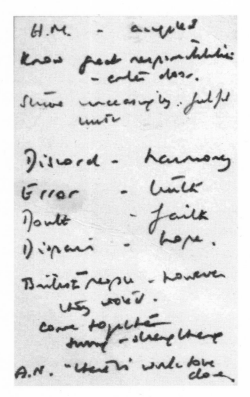

Margaret Thatcher's handwritten reminder for her first
words as Prime Minister outside Downing Street

It became an iconic moment as soon as she said it. Prompted by journalists to reflect on her historic win, Margaret Thatcher chose not to

ponder on the fact that she was the first female to occupy No. 10, but rather on the man whose influence had got her there:

> I just owe almost everything to my father, I really do. He brought me up to believe all the things that I do believe and they're just the values on which I've fought the election. And it's passionately interesting for me that the things I learnt in a small town, in a very modest home, are just the things that I believe have won the election.[68]

As she uttered these words and entered through the black door, so the era of conviction politics was born.

CHAPTER FOUR

THE GOSPEL ACCORDING TO MARGARET THATCHER

'The basis of democracy ... is morality, not majority voting. It is the belief that the majority of people are good and decent and that there are moral standards which come not from the State but from elsewhere.'
— MARGARET THATCHER, 1978[1]

'Economics is the method; the object is to change the soul.'
— MARGARET THATCHER, 1981[2]

'Although I have always resisted the argument that a Christian has to be a Conservative, I have never lost my conviction that there is a deep and providential harmony between the kind of political economy I favour and the insights of Christianity.'
— MARGARET THATCHER, 1995[3]

I N THE SPRING of 1981, Margaret Thatcher was invited to reopen the newly restored John Wesley's House, situated next door to Wesley's Chapel in the City of London. It was no great surprise she had been asked; she had been married in the chapel and at that point was the most prominent person of Methodist heritage in Britain. The house, where John Wesley had lived until his death, was to be reopened to coincide with Wesley Day, with the BBC broadcasting a special celebration service to mark the occasion.

Margaret Thatcher always made sure that she was suitably well briefed, but her level of preparation on this occasion suggests that she did not simply want to turn up and declare Wesley's house open. She read up on his early life, as well as his sermons, preaching tours and letters. Her jottings reveal a side of Thatcher rarely seen: in private study without the aid of speechwriters, unconcerned with public opinion, policy or even politics. 'The inward willingness my son, that is the proof, the strongest proof of Christianity' she had copied down from a letter from Rev. Samuel Wesley to his son John. She also made a record of the Wesley brothers' tireless work and their achievements; of the 40,000 sermons, the 400 books and the miles they had covered in their years of preaching. Speaking in the courtyard of Wesley's Chapel, Margaret Thatcher declared:

> Mr Speaker, these two men were taught the truth. They lived the truth, and they proclaimed the truth ... The zenith of their powers ... came only when they had discovered the truth within themselves. They not only taught it, not only lived by it, not only proclaimed it that they had this divine inspiration which made them discover it within themselves on this very day, so many years ago, in Aldersgate ... and so we honour them today, the very same virtues remain all the time. We had need of them then. We have need of their successors now.[4]

On the service sheet Margaret Thatcher had jotted: 'world full of global dilemmas; personal dilemmas'. At the time, she herself was no doubt feeling such burdens. The controversial 1981 Budget delivered that March had turned the entire academic economic community against the government; riots in Brixton had broken out that April while the Irish hunger striker Bobby Sands had died in early May. 'You are carrying heavy burdens, Margaret,' wrote Speaker of the Commons and Methodist George Thomas in sycophantic tones soon after her visit: 'I am convinced that the country realises that your strength of character is rooted in deep Christian convictions.'5 They did not. In fact, her unwillingness to yield to the hunger strikers' demands – as well as a personal plea from Pope John Paul II – gave rise to the public perception of Thatcher as harsh and uncaring. The *Methodist Recorder*, which had covered the visit, also hinted at other priorities. Alongside a picture of Margaret Thatcher opening Wesley's House was a call for a march against unemployment, a proposed disarmament vigil outside Parliament and a campaign by War on Want to fight global poverty.

I. The commandments of early Thatcherism

MORE THAN ANY other politician of her generation, Thatcher used her speeches as a means of asserting her personal authority and values. As is well documented, Margaret Thatcher devoted a considerable amount of time and effort into getting her public statements right. As she explained to her speechwriter on foreign affairs, George Urban: 'It's most important that the words on your lips are *your* words, that they express *your* feelings from the pit of your guts, that they mirror the stuff of which you are made.'6 There is little doubt that Margaret Thatcher, as the daughter of a preacher, believed in the power of the spoken word. She was heavily reliant on an army of speechwriters, but as her chief wordsmith Ronald Millar later confirmed: 'Her views, her opinions, her kind of language and her guidance were behind every syllable.'[7] Alfred Sherman described the process in blunter terms: 'We proposed, she disposed', hinting at the fact that it was often an agonising process for all involved.[8] The original text would be heavily marked with Thatcher's blue pen and she would often demand changes even after the final copy had been typed up. Edward Heath, in contrast, delegated the responsibility of his big speeches entirely to his staff, as did Tony Blair, who reportedly used to spend more time on fine-tuning the delivery rather than on the words themselves. For the most part, what Margaret Thatcher said, she believed, and in a language she felt comfortable with. Thatcher's rhetoric was characterised by its straightforwardness and bluntness, which in the words of Jonathan Raban, hit like the 'raw freshness of Hemingway ... after an overdose of George Eliot'.[9]

In early 1981, Margaret Thatcher was once again invited to give a sermon at St Lawrence Jewry from the same pulpit she had delivered her 'I believe' speech three years earlier. Her aides were unsure, given pressures on her time, but T. E. Utley advised in favour, judging that such an occasion 'does the PM good'.[10] Utley, though, had misgivings about the vicar at St Lawrence's, Rev. Basil Watson, whom he felt enjoyed the limelight a bit too much and whose blatantly Tory leanings Utley thought might render the association publicly disadvantageous. Rev. Watson, however, wrote to No. 10 pressuring the Prime Minister to consent: 'There are still too many in my firm who think that socialists have the undoubted monopoly of the Christian religion!'[11]

The drafting process, however, was not an easy one. Margaret Thatcher was not happy with Utley's and Webley's initial efforts. The speech was full of wishy-washy platitudes nor did it sound very Thatcherite: the Prime Minister had marked a resounding 'NO', for example, on their contention that nations were mere accidents of history. The Prime Minister clearly wanted a speech much more in tune with Edward Norman's views, whose lecture on 'Religion, Ethics and Politics in the 1980s' she had recently heard him give at a meeting of the Conservative

Philosophy Group and whose text she had marked with approving annotations. If there is any doubt that Margaret Thatcher was ever at the mercy of her speechwriters one need only contrast Webley's and Utley's first draft with the final speech she actually delivered.

Margaret Thatcher spoke on 'The Spirit of the Nation' to a packed-out congregation, although Denis was not present. He had been asked whether he would like to hear his wife give a 'major philosophical speech' but his reply was somewhat telling of what he thought of such occasions and of Downing Street life altogether: 'There are moments when all I want is to "go home" and I have blanked out 4–8 March to do just that' he informed the Prime Minister's diary secretary.[12]

Thatcher's address at St Lawrence's hinged on the central contention that 'the virtue of the nation is only as great as the virtue of the individuals who compose it'. She went on to elaborate:

> It is to individuals that the Ten Commandments are addressed. In the statements, 'honour thy father and thy mother', 'thou shalt not steal', 'thou shalt not bear false witness' and so on, the 'thou' to whom these resounding imperatives are addressed is you and me. In the same way, the New Testament is preoccupied with the individual, with his need for forgiveness and for the Divine strength, which comes to those who sincerely accept it. Of course, we can deduce from the teachings of the Bible principles of public as well as private morality; but, in the last resort, all these principles refer back to the individual in his relationship to others. We must always be aware of supposing that somehow we can get rid of our own moral duties by handing them over to the community; that somehow we can get rid of our own guilt by talking about 'national' or 'social' guilt. We are called on to repent our own sins, not each other's sins.[13]

This was in essence Margaret Thatcher's theology: the individual positioned at the centre of the spiritual and the temporal world. Her

central claim was that as the Christian faith was a call to individuals, so it should follow that the relationship between the citizen and
the state should operate along the same lines. Just as there seemed
to be little room for intermediaries (such as the priest) in Margaret Thatcher's theology, nor was there any room for intermediary
institutions (e.g. trade unions, local government) in her politics.
As Jonathan Raban put it: 'Man shall stand as nakedly before his
Government as he does before his Maker.'[14] Even more contentious
was Thatcher's assumption that because Conservative philosophy
was rooted in individualism (in contrast to socialists that prioritised
society), Conservatism was therefore closer to the Christian faith.
One-nation Conservatives would no doubt have challenged her on
this point, particularly her lack of reference to the social order, but
her prioritisation of the individual was precisely where Thatcherism
diverged from One-nation Toryism. Thatcher's main target, though,
was what she labelled the socialist 'heresy': the idea that societal salvation could come through the state.

The individual may have been at the centre of Thatcher's theological and political values, but for it to mean anything, it needed
to have one word attached to it: freedom. To reinforce this point,
Thatcher always stressed that free will was after all at the heart of
the Christian revelation: 'We are all responsible moral beings with
a choice between good and evil, beings who are infinitely precious
in the eyes of their Creator,' she had said in her first address at St
Lawrence Jewry in 1978.

A decade later, in an interview with David Frost, Thatcher referenced the notion of free will as the essence of biblical teaching: 'If
he [man] did not have the fundamental choice, well he would not
be Man made in the image of God.'[15] Frost was also the offspring of a
Methodist minister but he chose not to challenge her on this point.
That same year, in her infamous address to the General Assembly,
Thatcher even seemed to interpret the Crucifixion story as a tale of

choice rather than sacrifice: 'When faced with His terrible choice and lonely vigil [He] *chose* to lay down His life that our sins may be forgiven. I remember very well a sermon on an Armistice Sunday when our Preacher said, "No one took away the life of Jesus, He chose to lay it down".'[16]

The changing of the Conservative Party's logo from the Unionist symbol of the thistle, daffodil, clover leaf and rose to the torch of liberty in 1983 signified the new ideological focus under Thatcher. The doctrine of liberty, though, was always exalted beyond party politics and elevated to the saintly realm; it was 'not state-given' according to Thatcher, but 'God-given'. This was, of course, a distinctly Thatcherite notion of political and economic freedom. Thatcher never entertained the idea that the state could be an instrument of liberty, rather it was always characterised (either in Britain or the Communist Eastern bloc) as an instrument of oppression. Above all, liberty was only achieved through individual choice and certainly not through collective struggle. In her contention on the biblical foundations of liberty, Thatcher was prepared to confront history. When in Paris during the 200th anniversary celebrations of the French Revolution in 1989, Thatcher made the rather undiplomatic point that all hope of *liberté*, *egalité*, *fraternité* had only resulted in 'a lot of headless bodies and a tyrant'. Thatcher's history was often as subtle as her theology.

'Individual liberty' and 'choice' became the buzzwords of Thatcherism, the linguistic legitimation for government initiatives be it the extension of home ownership, the deregulation of the market or the lowering of direct taxation. Citizens would be 'free' to buy their own council houses, send their children to private schools or switch to private healthcare. Synod member and Cabinet minister John Gummer echoed his leader when, in an explicit appeal to Christian voters in 1987, he wrote: 'Choice lies at the heart of the Christian revelation … there is something wrong in believing a man is fit to choose his eternal destiny but not to decide on the education of his children.'[17] Drawing on the revelation as a justification for private education was one that few ecclesiastical leaders could stomach and yet it did find some sympathy amongst the laity. 'Haven't we all been given free will?' wrote one parishioner responding to the Bishop of Manchester's public hostility to private healthcare. 'Our way to God is free for us, we choose what prayers suit us best, we also choose the Churches that we wish to worship in […] we then have the choice as to whom we can go to for care.'[18] The notion of free will, which had historically been used against an overbearing Church was being appropriated by Thatcher to challenge an overbearing state. Indeed, what was once the scriptural justification for Nonconformity was now being articulated as the political justification for neo-liberalism.

Margaret Thatcher always maintained that unchecked and unguided liberty brought with it its own dilemmas. As she warned the congregation of St Lawrence Jewry in 1978: 'There are many difficult things about freedom: it does not give you safety; it creates moral dilemmas for you; it requires self-discipline; it imposes great responsibilities; but such is the destiny of Man and in such consists his glory and salvation.' The curtailment of liberty therefore rested not with society or the state but with the individual: freedom *with* responsibility was Margaret Thatcher's key phrase. She was, however, decidedly vague in setting out how the Church should curtail individual freedom.

According to Conservative writer G. K. Chesterton, the doctrine of original sin was the Christian creed for which there was the 'most evidence'. In the political sphere, however, the concept of sinful man (a label that tended to be heaped on the poor rather than the rich) had largely gone out of fashion in the twentieth century, for much the same reason that it had gone out of fashion in the churches. In the mass democratic age, politics on both the right and the left became about change, aspiration and hope for a better world. The pessimistic claim that man was born sinful and remained so, whatever the government did, was therefore unlikely to make it into the party manifestos or even feature in the minds of politicians whose primary concern was garnering votes. But, as we have seen, a notion of human fallibility attained new currency in the 1970s as neo-liberals deployed it as a way of undermining left-wing notions of human progress and, more obviously, as a way of reinforcing their attack on the welfare state. Margaret Thatcher fully subscribed to this view and in her address at St Lawrence Jewry in 1978 offered an explanation that was both politicised and uncompromising: 'There is some evil in everyone ... In my own lifetime, we have expended vast efforts and huge sums of money on policies designed to make people better and happier. Have we really brought about a fundamental improvement in Man's moral condition? The Devil is still with us.'[19] Socialism was characterised as morally unsound precisely because it denied human frailty, stifled freedom and thus constrained individual moral responsibility. 'You will in effect dry up in them the milk of human kindness,' Thatcher said.

Not content to speak in abstract terms, Thatcher readily applied her theological understanding to specific political problems. Spiralling prices and inflation were categorised in no uncertain terms as an 'evil' and a 'morally debilitating influence' in the way that it reduced savings, encouraged debt and created hostility between employers and employees over pay. 'It is, in my view, a moral issue, not just an economic one,' she told the congregation at St Lawrence Jewry in 1981, significantly at a time when her government was yet to control inflation. Unemployment (then running at 2.5 million), however, was merely deemed a 'concern' and was ultimately a matter of 'personal responsibility'. Here Thatcher was invoked the Protestant work ethic as the justification for her government's relinquishing of the post-war commitment to full employment. The work ethic was purportedly an inherently British characteristic that simply needed to be reawakened: 'We have always had a sense that work is not only a necessity, it is a duty, and indeed a virtue ... Work is not merely a way of receiving a pay packet but a means whereby everyone in the community benefits and society is enriched.'[20]

In an article for the *Daily Telegraph* in 1978, Margaret Thatcher had singled out R. H. Tawney and William Temple as typical of the compassionate but essentially misguided approach of Christian socialists, whom she simply dismissed as 'misunderstanding of how the modern capitalist order works'.[21] Slating the founders of Christian social thought as outdated and ignorant was bold, but tellingly Thatcher chose not to elaborate on precisely what she meant by 'modern capitalism'. As shadow leader it was perhaps not necessary to do so, but by the late 1980s, when the deregulation of the market and the excesses of the City put the spotlight on the moral credibility of the free economy, Prime Minister Thatcher would be forced to elaborate.

Remaining true to her Conservative credentials, Margaret Thatcher always maintained the rule of law as essential for the maintenance of social order and for regulating 'man's imperfection'. Law and order was of course spoken of in benign rather than authoritarian terms – although those at the sharp end of police enforcement in the 1980s may have perhaps taken a different view. The state was accorded a legitimate but limited place in Thatcher's thinking: to provide a welfare safety net and a legal framework. In her words, the purpose of the state was 'to encourage virtue, not to usurp it'. In denying that the state could either generate wealth, employment or altruism, Thatcher was deliberately targeting (and clumsily caricaturing) the main contentions of post-war political and economic philosophy.

But how did Margaret Thatcher explain the biblical obligation to one's fellow neighbour? For many Christians, this maxim was reflected in Britain's welfare state. Thatcher, however, offered a wildly different explanation of its meaning. Extending the quotation in full, 'Love thy neighbour as thyself', Thatcher offered that the 'thyself' part of the sentiment was equally as important as its prefix. In Thatcher's Gospel, it did not mean to 'elevate love of others above it' but rather that 'concern for self' was expected while the Gospel simply demanded 'that this be extended to others'. 'Self-regard' according to Thatcher was at the 'root of regard for one's fellows'.[22] We need be in no doubt of her political motives on this point; the aim was to disentangle 'love thy neighbour' from its Christian socialist associations and pin it to a Thatcherite concept of personal responsibility. 'The Good Samaritan could only have helped because he had money,' Thatcher had proclaimed in 1968, which became a neat summation of her belief that Christian fellowship could not be administered collectively through taxation nor 'manufactured by politicians', but could only be initiated by the individual.

Appearing to speak on behalf of all Christians, Thatcher explained in her article to the *Daily Telegraph*:

> For the Christian there can be no social or political panaceas, no easy escapes from personal responsibility achieved by collectivising guilt or virtue. The true ends of temporal life lie beyond it, and, though the tyrannical State may diminish virtue, the benevolent State cannot procure it.[23]

Thatcher's promise was that greater individual freedom would naturally generate a greater sense of responsibility to others. It revealed a naive hope that greater wealth would not encourage selfishness but neighbourliness, but turn us all into Good Samaritans. We would not walk by on the other side, nor would we need state-imposed traffic lights to guide us there. Thatcher set out the moral basis of a laissez-faire economy:

In a market economy, people are free to give their money and their time
for good causes. They exercise their altruism on their own initiative and
at their own expense, whether they give directly and personally through
institutions, charities, universities, churches, hospitals. When the state
steps in, generosity is increasingly restricted from all sides.[24]

Thatcher's theo-political vision was both political in its aim and
theologically reductive in its articulation. Many Christians, including Methodists, would spend a large part of the 1980s repudiating
the Gospel of Thatcherism and unmasking the social realities
of the Prime Minister's so-called 'values'. And yet, as unpalatable as
these ideas were to modern churchmen, they had legitimate roots
in Wesleyanism, nineteenth-century evangelical thought and, even
much further back, in the work of John Calvin, particularly on the
notion of the godly inspiration behind work, finance and wealth.
Margaret Thatcher was applying this theological tradition to the
contemporary age, but importantly her statements were also largely
in tune with what she had learnt as a child. In essence, she had not
strayed too far from those Sundays spent at Finkin Street. On the
few occasions that Margaret Thatcher did speak in the pulpit, it was
both necessary and appropriate for an explicit theological exposi-
tion, but whatever the forum, occasion or policy, her theo-political
values of hard work, individual freedom and personal responsibility
underscored her every word and deed.

There was, of course, little electoral advantage in preaching such
sermons, unlike in America, where Ronald Reagan would successfully
marshal the support of the Moral Majority and, along with it, many
votes. Christians in Britain, although an important constituency, did
not have the power to swing elections and could be found on either
side of the political spectrum. If Margaret Thatcher's biblical values
were to have any meaning with a predominantly non-Christian electorate, they needed to be rooted in concrete policies.

II. Thatcherism as a values project

THE 1979 CONSERVATIVE manifesto had reassuringly and rather ambitiously pledged 'to restore self-reliance and self-confidence which are the basis of personal responsibility and national success.'[25] In her first two years of government, the overriding preoccupation was getting a grip on the economy, but Margaret Thatcher always viewed economics as one aspect of a broader long-term project: 'Economics is the method, the object is to change the soul' she had told *The Times* in 1981. The following year, Thatcher set to the task of establishing the Family Policy Group (FPG) within Downing Street, which was to be led by journalist and then head of the policy unit, Ferdinand Mount, and would involve all the major ministers of state. The FPG's brief, according to John Sparrow of the Cabinet Office was to generate initiatives to reverse the 'collectivist beliefs and attitudes ... ingrained in large numbers of the population' and restore 'the spirit of individual responsibility, confidence and self-reliance' within the nation.[26] Value projects such as these were hardly new territory for politicians. One might say that Attlee's post-war reforms had also involved a deliberate re-engineering of British mindset and behaviour to fall in line with the new Keynesian economic order. So it was for the Family Policy Group in 1982, which Mount made clear was about formulating a 'general approach to social policy, which is analogous to our general approach to economic policy'.[27] Some of the ideas generated by this policy group never made it beyond briefing-paper stage, but many did and would later reappear as fully digested policies in both the 1983 manifesto (co-drafted by Mount himself) or reappear as part of the legislative programme for Thatcher's third term.

Mount begun by setting out the problems and possible solutions in a paper entitled 'renewing the values of society'. In his detailed diagnosis, Mount considered that it was an overbearing and debilitating bureaucratic culture (rather than socialism or union influence) that was the reason behind the 'loss of self-respect, disenchantment and sloth' amongst Britain's public sector workers.[28] In particular, Mount also laid the blame on the 'man in Whitehall knows best' mentality and the rise of the public sector professional class – the architects, the medics, the teachers, the councillors and social workers – who, he considered, had taken responsibility out of the hands of the citizens (now pointedly referred to as 'customers')whom they were meant to serve. Home ownership was obviously considered one of the most effective ways of generating personal responsibility and Mount was keen to extend the recent sale of council houses even further through rent-based mortgages – a proposal that Michael Heseltine actually blocked. Mount was also an early champion of greater autonomy from central and local government and the contracting out of state services; all of which the Conservative administration would later push through. University students were deemed another problem area not only because of their left-wing leanings but also as a drain on the public purse. Mount proposed that the most effective way of instilling a sense of 'personal responsibility' amongst these tax-funded rebels was to put them in debt by replacing the university grants scheme with loans; a proposal that was later made law in the Education (Student Loans) Act in 1990.

Mount was aware that changing the endemic collectivist culture within universities and the public sector would be a challenge but he was much more optimistic about the potential of instilling these values in the next generation. In a scheme that would not have looked out of place in an authoritarian regime, Mount put forward his idea for 'grammar of society' lessons in schools, which was designed as an 'antidote to the half-baked Marxism which dupes so many nineteen-year-olds'[29] and which would feature lessons on the history of common law, customs, and culture of Britain. As it turned out, the Conservative government would go even further than Mount's proposal, opting for a complete overhaul of the classroom by establishing a centralised

National Curriculum under the Education Act of 1988, which would be distinctly 'Thatcherite' in flavour. Mount also mooted the possibility of a state-sponsored children's Broadcasting Corporation that would broadcast themes of 'right and wrong' as opposed to the 'lifeless, moral-less, mindless and theme less' programmes that in his view dominated the existing children's schedule.[30] It was hoped that children might be encouraged to attend Butlin's-style summer schools, start savings accounts and get involved in voluntary initiatives such as a 'adopt a granny' scheme; on the latter Mount presumably thought that it would have the dual benefit of encouraging a communitarian ethic amongst the young and lowering the cost of care for the elderly.

Many of these child-based initiatives did not make it into the final policy package, perhaps because children were not voters or perhaps because ministers realised how unfeasible they were. Margaret Thatcher was keen though. 'I am very pleased with these ideas' she had scrawled across Mount's initial brief.[31] Cabinet Secretary Robert Armstrong, however, anticipated that Mount's paper would be met with 'cold water and faint praise' by the Cabinet and it was true, the response was mixed, although more on the specifics than the overall aims.[32] The ministers' reaction, which came in the form of individual papers submitted to the group, reveals much about the personalities, preoccupations and prejudices of those within Thatcher's Cabinet.

The Secretary of State for Transport, David Howell, who had recently authored a book, *Freedom and Capital*, but who is rarely noted as a prominent Thatcherite, was one of the most enthusiastic supporters of Mount's schemes. The Falklands War, according to Howell, had shown the government to be a 'determined and confident force' and it was only right that 'the rest of the country ... face its responsibilities in the same way'.[33] The urban riots of 1981, however, had exposed the 'defeatist' tendency amongst the British to blame the government for everything. This culture, Howell entreated, must be reversed:

The opposite of the defeatist view that the world owes us a living and has somehow cheated us, is that we <u>can</u> help ourselves as a nation and that we can and will look after our interests. It is that the firm or the factory can and will compete rather than succumb amidst pleas of unfair oriental competition. It is that our cities can and will be revived and pulled together by the efforts of those who live within them, rather than falling back on a ceaseless liturgy of blame on central Government interlaced with demands for more money ... It is not 'someone else's' responsibility.'[34]

Howell of course said very little about the main cause of the riots: the sense of helplessness amongst the unemployed or the frustrations of the victims of police harassment. Instead he focused his attention on inflation: 'a world of stable money would be a world of stable values'; a sentiment with which Thatcher no doubt concurred.[35] Nor was Howell naive about the political consequences of policies such as home ownership and share ownership: 'The more that people become familiar with capital and profits and how the social market economy works, the weaker the political support for attacks on capital.'[36]

Willie Whitelaw, who as Home Secretary was responsible for the government's response to the riots, offered a much more straightforward solution to ill-discipline amongst Britain's youth. His perspective, though, stemmed not from a dogmatic belief in popular capitalism but probably what he had experienced during his schoolboy days at Winchester. 'Sport', i.e. enabling teenagers to 'unleash their physical energies through games rather than bricks and petrol bombs', was in Whitelaw's view one credible solution to the crisis in law and order.[37] Keith Joseph, on the other hand, was sceptical of Mount's proposed curriculum on values. He was not against the idea in principle, just not convinced that the left-wing teaching profession could be trusted to teach it. He also used the FPG as an opportunity to peddle his favoured policies of education vouchers and apprenticeships. Another of Joseph's ideas, which would only get the green light under the Conservative-led Coalition in 2010, was to enable parents to set up their own schools. Returning to his favourite subject of irresponsible parenthood, which he had first outlined in his controversial speech at Edgbaston in 1974, Joseph pondered on the problem of young single mothers who saw pregnancy as a 'means of escape' and wilfully shifted their dependency to the state. His solution was a series of government-funded 'scare films' on the realities of parenthood. Advisers at Downing Street were clearly wary; a note accompanying his paper read: 'Keith Joseph on important but sensitive ground.'[38]

Chancellor Geoffrey Howe responded with characteristic pragmatism. While he acknowledged that 'state paternalism' was the 'enemy', Howe saw it much more in terms of managing people's expectations at the time of recession rather than an ambitious desire to rid the nation of its collectivist ethos.[39] Howe, too, was the only one to recognise the inherent contradiction of a government committed to shrinking the state while implementing a centralised programme to reinvigorate values. Michael Heseltine's paper, on the other hand, simply listed his own successes, chiefly the 'Right to Buy' scheme and his ambitious plans for the regeneration of Liverpool, while Patrick Jenkin at Industry made the rather un-Thatcherite point that the prevalence of long-term unemployment was 'profoundly anti-family' and that job creation was the best way of ensuring that couples stayed together.[40]

Norman Tebbit at Employment was the only minister to remark on the profound changes occurring within British society – notably the rise of women in employment and the decline of the male breadwinner – although he took a somewhat blinkered view of the problem. On the changing make-up of Britain's workforce, Tebbit considered that the growth of women in the workplace was out

of necessity rather than aspiration and was ultimately a regressive
step that distracted women from their roles as 'mothers and home-
makers'.[41] Surprisingly, there is no evidence that Margaret Thatcher,
the ultimate career woman, ever challenged him on this point.

Tebbit was much more concerned, however, with the decline of the
male breadwinner and the void that it created, which was now being
filled by 'anti-social groups, ranging from left-wing social workers ...
to the criminal elements within whom the political extremist collabo-
rate in areas such as Toxteth'. Tebbit added that this phenomenon was
most noticeable amongst 'immigrant Caribbean families'.[42] Tebbit also
wondered whether the government's incentives should be directed at
the poor, who were apparently unlikely to be responsive, and that it
would be much more worthwhile to encourage those 'who have the
will and the dedication to restore values in their family lives'.[43] This
is, of course, what actually happened. Thatcher's policies would isolate
and disenfranchise certain sections of the poor, while providing the
conditions in which the upwardly mobile could take full advantage.

Mount took a much more positive view on the perceived problem of values amongst Britain's immigrant population, pointing out
that many ethnic minorities were 'imbued with precisely the sorts
of values which the Group is trying to encourage', citing the 'Asian
corner shop open in the evenings and at the weekends' as an example of the Protestant work ethic in operation.[44] It was agreed that
the government should 'publicise success stories of immigrants who
have made good' and encourage 'immigrant behaviour in accordance
with the philosophy of self-reliance'.[45] A cynic might see this as a
Conservative strategy to win over new voters. An optimist might see
it as a desire to counter the public denigration of immigrant communities. Nonetheless, there was a clear demarcation being made
between Asians and West Indians; the latter were believed to have
adopted the blame, dependency and defeatist culture of Britain's
white working class.

Thatcher's 'values project' demonstrated the ideological impetus at the heart of government and, more specifically, how values rather than policies were the starting point for reform. Yet the discussions also revealed a failure to recognise how British society was changing. There was no sense that deindustrialisation was something that needed addressing, and yet it arguably posed a greater threat to the body politic than 'collectivist' values. Nor was there any substantial consideration given to the globalisation of industry, trade and finance and its inevitable consequences for employment as well as consumption. More parochial and petty concerns dominated, evident in the targeting of 'left-wing' teachers, rioters, students, single mothers and immigrants, and likewise in the encouragement of Asian shop keepers and autonomously minded civil servants.

The rise of married women working was thought to be equally damaging to the family as divorce, not permissive behaviour. Solutions, ranged from encouraging couples to marry later (thereby apparently halting divorce) and tweaking the tax system to incentivise women to stay at home. The government's economic policy hinged on tackling inflation at the cost of unemployment, but this led it to make a frankly odd link between cause, consequence and solution in the realm of social policy. High inflation and recession had apparently forced mothers to go out to work, thereby weakening the motivation of the father, leading to 'latch-key' unruly children, and ultimately divorce, with the woman believing that the state would support her where her ex-husband had been unable to. Such was the Thatcher government's assessment of the dissolution of family life and morals in Britain. Under the spell of monetarism, this was how social policy in the early 1980s was discussed and enacted.

The group were, however, adamant that these plans should not be presented as a 'spiritual revival' – no doubt wary of how badly this would go down with the British public although this is exactly what it was.[46] Margaret Thatcher was enthused by these proposals; she marked all her ministers' papers with approval and was fully prepared to do the rhetorical 'sell' to the electorate. She contributed little to the formation of policy although she was said to be particularly concerned that discipline be restored. This was a virtue she believed was best exuded by the armed forces. In this post-Falklands era, the army was already for her the best demonstration of an ordered and responsible ethic and, indeed, it would become the one institution in British life upon which she felt she could always rely. The 1983 election would be fought and won on the back of her Falklands' success and also on the values and policies that emerged out of the Policy Family Group.

III. Nonconformist woman

THERE ARE MANY reasons why the Conservatives won three successive elections under Margaret Thatcher. One could point to the decline of the traditional working class, the weakness of the Labour Party leadership or the split of the anti-Conservative vote between Labour and the SDP-Liberal Alliance, but, if opinion polls are to be believed and the pollsters are correct, the main reason a significant number of Britons voted Conservative in 1983 and 1987 was down to the personality and leadership of Margaret Thatcher herself. Writing soon after the Conservatives' third election victory in 1987, political scientist Ivor Crewe concluded that there was little evidence that the British electorate had become 'suffused with Thatcherite values on either the economic or moral plane'; rather he attributed the Conservatives' electoral dominance down to the figure of Margaret Thatcher, whom the public appreciated as a leader who 'knows what needs doing'.[47] This was certainly how Thatcher's press secretary Bernard Ingham saw it. Writing to the Prime Minister of the state of her leadership in 1982, Ingham was brutally honest but hopeful: 'You are ... heartily disliked and indeed hated, though still commanding respect ... Your merit is that you appeal to [the British public's] understanding of reality.'[48] Ivor Crewe, on the other hand, attributed Thatcher's success to her 'warrior style' and the way that she was perceived to be 'setting objectives, leading from the front, confronting problems, holding her position'.[49] It hardly needs adding that these were qualities that Thatcher exuded, and ones that her rivals, Michael Foot and Neil Kinnock, clearly did not. As if to prove a point, the puppet satirical television show *Spitting Image* always portrayed Thatcher as a dominant presence in a man's suit, and, in a nod to Churchill, chomping on a cigar; Thatcher seemed an unstoppable force next to her less than impressive rivals: the ageing Michael Foot, the arrogant yet indecisive David Owen, and Neil 'the Welsh Windbag' Kinnock.

It is often remarked that the Falklands War was transformative for Margaret Thatcher's image. Up until that point she was certainly a vulnerable leader who seemed to excel in alienating everyone; in 1981 she was voted the most unpopular prime minister in history. But Thatcher emerged from victory anew; appreciated for her steely resolve and constancy; known for rolling up her sleeves and getting on with the job; a masculine figure lacking in feminine frailties. 'NOW IS THE HOUR – MAGGIE IS THE MAN' ran the headline in the *Daily Express* on the day of the 1983 election. This image was only to be reinforced by her future battles with Arthur Scargill's National Union of Mineworkers (NUM), the 'loony-left' councils and the 'wets' within her party. By the late 1980s, Thatcher appeared to morph into Liberty herself: brandishing the torch of freedom amidst the rubble of communism abroad and socialism at home and with a dogged determination 'to go on and on'. The religious aura and providential air that surrounded Margaret Thatcher was one that the public bought into, opposition leaders found impossible to counter, and historians and commentators still find remarkably difficult to dislodge. It is, of course, necessary for all political leaders to cultivate a public image, but if it is too distant from the reality, it fails to be credible. Important though the press and her supporters were in bolstering the perception of Iron Lady, much of its source and power was down to the fact that the public Margaret Thatcher was never far from the private woman.

That the sleeping patterns of the Prime Minister should become public knowledge or even the stuff of legend tells us much about the connection between Thatcher's image and authority. Perhaps it was necessary for the first female leader to be associated with a masculine tenacity, but, this aside, the idea of Margaret Thatcher working tirelessly for the nation projected a vision of moral energy, conviction and a determination 'to get things done' that was politically invaluable. Callaghan's infamous 'Crisis? What crisis?' comment made during the Winter of Discontent may have been a misquotation but its reportage generated an air of complacency that soon spiralled into election defeat. Margaret Thatcher, in contrast, was always pictured caught in the action, whether it was driving a tank, on the production line of a factory, or on a sofa with her heels kicked off attending to her red box. She became the living embodiment of the Protestant work ethic, always on the move in her characteristic speedy shuffle. But this was not just for the cameras; it is no secret that relaxation did not come easily to her. Margaret Thatcher's attitude towards holidays was much like her attitude towards sleep; it was for the idle. It is hard to imagine Thatcher ever indulging in something akin to Ted Heath's passion for yacht racing, which would take him away from Westminster for weeks on end. She was by anyone's standards a workaholic and, in contemporary parlance, could have been said to have had a poor work-life balance. She was addicted to politics, had little life outside it and, in some senses, was the first of a new breed of professional politicians that would later become the norm in Britain.

The presentation of Margaret Thatcher as the thrifty housewife is equally notorious. On this matter, perhaps more than any other, Thatcher really did practise what she preached. Even though money was never a problem once she was married, Thatcher maintained her mother's standards. Old curtains were transformed into duffle coats for the twins, her wedding dress recycled into an evening gown, and she continued to drive around in a battered second-hand car while Denis enjoyed his passion for fast, expensive vehicles. On arriving at No. 10, Thatcher insisted on paying for a new ironing board and bed linen out of her own pocket; used her old crockery and raided nearby Admiralty House for spare furniture. She also famously had the swimming pool drained at Chequers when she discovered that the heating bill was £5,000 per year. Certainly, at a time of recession, it was politically wise to demonstrate personal fiscal prudence, but it was also something that came naturally to her, unlike some of her ministers. In 1981, she berated Welsh Secretary Nicholas Edwards for his proposed £26,000 renovation of his residence in Cardiff. 'Get some other estimates' she scribbled across the page when the bill came in.[50] Edwards obediently reduced it to £12,000. Such distaste for excess, as Cecil Parkinson observed, was ingrained in her:

> Her Methodism had quite an impact on her, she didn't like show, she was quite an austere person in a way, except for sometimes her dress was a little flamboyant ... she didn't like spending money; hers or other peoples ... It was an instinct with her, living within your means, she drew heavily on her background and she was very much the product of it.[51]

Parkinson also hinted that her thriftiness was the cause of tension with her colleagues. When she demanded that the Cabinet set an example and not take a pay increase, he, along with others ministers, remembers feeling slightly aggrieved that she could afford to take such line. Thatcher had the additional benefits of Denis's salary and free accommodation at Downing Street and Chequers, while her ministers were sat round the Cabinet table stressing about how they would pay their children's education fees.

One aspect of her private character that never filtered into the public consciousness was Thatcher's personal compassion. There are many who could testify to her acts of kindness, letters of condolence or congratulations. Just before the 1979 election, a memo from Conservative HQ observed that while it was 'agreed by the electorate that Mrs. Thatcher is a highly competent and well-qualified woman. An aspect of her character about which the majority of the electorate are far less aware of is the fact that she is both warm and feeling.'[52] Margaret Thatcher's frequent hospital visits to casualties of disasters and victims of IRA terrorism were always sincere but did little to soften her image; the conviction politician did not sit well with a caring one. Moreover, all Thatcher's efforts in this regard were somewhat superseded by that other female who dominated the front pages: the 'touchy-feely' Princess Diana was the ultimate 'compassionate woman' of the 1980s.

Margaret Thatcher may have spoken openly of her faith and values but the public was less aware of her personal piety and devoutness. The habit of Sunday worship, ingrained in her since childhood, never left her. As Prime Minister, she was a member of the Methodist Parliamentary Fellowship. On weekends spent at Chequers, she would worship at the nearby Anglican parish of St Peter and St Paul in Ellesborough. According to the rector, Thatcher attended more often in her first two years of her premiership than all the previous post-war prime ministers put together. The incumbent, the Reverend David Horner, however, was always mindful not to delve into political matters in his sermons and was under strict instructions from Denis to keep it short: 'Padre, most of us know what the Sermon on the Mount is all about, we don't need you to explain it to us. Twelve minutes is your lot.'

Later in life, she and Denis regularly attended the Chapel of the Royal Military Hospital in Chelsea (founded in 1681 to care for those 'broken by age or war'), which some say was down to her enduring fondness for the military, forged in the Falklands War. Margaret Thatcher's ashes would later be buried alongside her late husband in the Royal Hospital cemetery.

Thatcher may have made the journey from Methodism to Anglicanism but she remained 'low-church' in her tastes. She always refused
Communion given that she was never confirmed into the Anglican
Church; perhaps it was the thought of having to kneel in front of a
bishop that dissuaded her. She was not a great enthusiast for contemporary worshipping forms; Jonathan Aitken remembers seeing her
looking rather perplexed during George Carey's inauguration ceremony
at Canterbury in 1990 when the congregation was instructed to shake
hands in an offering of peace.[53] Like Tony Blair, Margaret Thatcher was
a keen reader of religious works. Again, Jonathan Aitken remembers
browsing her private bookshelves in the 1970s (when he was dating
Carol Thatcher) and was surprised to find, in his words, 'more Bible
than Burke'. Unlike Blair, who has always taken a keen interest in the
early Church, those books on Thatcher's reading list were predominantly of a scriptural rather than historical nature. They included C.
S. Lewis's wartime lectures *Mere Christianity* (which Thatcher had
heard on the wireless in her youth), the collected sermons of John
Wesley, works by evangelical Stuart Blanch, the Archbishop of York,
and Roman Catholic Archbishop, Cardinal Basil Hume, as well as
books on Jewish ethics. In 1988, she read all thirty-nine books of the
Old Testament, which she would reportedly quote at length to her
civil servants. Margaret Thatcher's faith was always rooted in Scripture rather than sacraments, as her official biographer, Charles Moore
confirmed: 'She is a highly religious person in a highly English way.
What I mean by that is that she doesn't have any sense of sacraments,
liturgy, Church history, nor Catholicity, nor theology, but she is orthodox in religion without thinking.'[54]

'Her faith was quite real to her,' according to former Archbishop
of Canterbury George Carey. Drawing upon the contrast with Tony
Blair, he offered: 'Margaret's [faith] appealed to me much more than
Tony's. I couldn't see where his was going ... whereas I could see her
thinking was quite theological in many senses.'[55] Carey seemed to

suggest that while Blair's faith was an appendage, which was liable to slip, Thatcher's faith was an unshakeable, underlying core, even if he sometimes disagreed with its political manifestation. According to Bernard Ingham, Thatcher had five key qualities as leader: ideological security (she knew what she wanted to achieve); moral courage (a determination, in the words of her father, not 'to follow the herd'); constancy; an iron will to stick to the task; and, finally, she did not wish to be loved. When, on one occasion, Denis Thatcher heard Ingham give a talk on this subject, he offered a corrective: 'You should have a sixth: she has a deep religious faith.'[56]

It was not uncommon for Margaret Thatcher to turn to prayer during the testing moments of her political career. Carol Thatcher has hinted how her mother found strength in worship during the Falklands War, while Denis remarked that the conflict 'marked her soul and mine'.[57] Her assistant, Cynthia Crawford, has also recounted how on the night of the Brighton Bomb, while they were holed up in a dorm at the local police college, Margaret Thatcher had pondered 'this was the day I was not meant to see' and suggested they both kneel and recite the Lord's Prayer.[58] Later that week, Thatcher wrote to her head of communications, Harvey Thomas, confiding, 'It would have been difficult to have gone through last weekend without a very strong faith.'[59] Before joining the Conservatives, Harvey Thomas had spent fifteen years organising 'conversion' tours for Billy Graham and had been charged with bringing the same evangelical fervour to the Conservatives' election campaign in 1979. Of Margaret Thatcher's belief, Harvey was certain: 'Good, straightforward, practical evangelicalism. It was quite a driving thought in her mind.'[60] As someone who had worked for the world's most prominent evangelical organisation, one assumes that Harvey would be able to tell a believer from a doubter. In the wake of Brighton, Margaret Thatcher received several letters of condolence and support, including one from the Archbishop of Canterbury and a number of other Anglican bishops. It was a note from conservative evangelical Maurice Wood, the Bishop of Norwich, that was particularly appreciated by Margaret Thatcher, who thanked him for reminding her of the extract from Romans: 'Neither death nor life shall be able to separate us from the love of God, in Christ Jesus.'[61]

The tragic events in Brighton appear not to have stirred an inflated sense of manifest destiny in Margaret Thatcher, which some say consumed Ronald Reagan after the assassination attempt on his life in 1981, yet, undoubtedly and understandably, it was a moment when she drew on her faith to help her through one of the gravest moments of her premiership.

IV. 'Beware of false prophets'

WHETHER OUT OF a sense of propriety or indifference (or maybe both), Margaret Thatcher refused to be drawn into the internal divisions between conservatives and liberals in the Church of England. She made brief references to it in the 1970s, but as Prime Minister wisely trod a diplomatic line. On the key issue, which split conservatives and liberals – the ordination of women – Thatcher clearly sided with the liberals: 'No one ever stopped them being missionaries', she told the *Catholic Herald* in 1978, before adding: 'What you do has got to be somehow in touch with and in tune with the times, otherwise you cause friction and you mustn't cause friction if you have a positive message.'[62] Ten years later, when the Church was finally heading towards a decision, she publicly declared herself in favour but privately remained concerned about the possible consequences for the Church. Certainly, it would have seemed odd for a female prime minister to oppose female ordination, but Thatcher was always careful to distance herself from the debate. One area of ecclesiastical policy in which she did take a considerable interest, however, was in selecting her bishops.

The process of appointing Anglican bishops does not hold the same allure or mysticism of a papal conclave; there are no puffs of smoke or priests holed up under lock and key. It may operate under a similar veil of secrecy but the process is of a more pedestrian and distinctly English kind. George Carey, for example, remembers being ordered to the rather un-saintly surroundings of Pratt's Hotel, Bath, where he was handed the official letter offering him the See of Canterbury. The procedure for appointments had actually been updated in 1976 under Jim Callaghan, which had given the Church a greater say over the selection of diocesan bishops. For those of York and Canterbury, the prime minister would select a prominent lay Anglican as head of a commission made up of clerical and lay figures. The views of the diocese were taken into account, although the committee would meet in secret and eventually pass two names to the prime minister, who was free to select either candidate or reject both. On this aspect of prime ministerial patronage, Margaret Thatcher was particularly reliant on Robin Catford, her rather forceful evangelical appointments secretary. Known as 'God's talent scout', Catford would conduct lengthy tours of the diocese before producing long-winded Trollopian-esque reports on the personal characteristics and suitability of the candidates, which Thatcher would scrupulously read over. Catford's role may have been purely advisory, but his conservative evangelical bias was never in doubt. Within Lambeth Palace, he was disparagingly known as 'Cat food'.

Speculation and gossip were rife, but on only two occasions did Thatcher refuse the commission's preferred candidate: in 1981 when she appointed the High Anglican conservative Graham Leonard over the liberal John Habgood for London, and in 1987 when she rejected the openly left-wing Jim Thompson in favour of Mark Santer for the bishopric of Birmingham (who, unbeknownst to her, shared Thompson's politics). There is just one instance of outright nepotism when she awarded Philip Goodrich, the brother of an old school friend, the Bishopric of Worcester. 'You are looking for a person who propounds, expounds, explains and preaches the Christian faith,' Thatcher later said on the qualities of the bishop.[63] But despite her obvious evangelical preference, Thatcher never broke with protocol even on one occasion when Jim Callaghan reminded her that she could reject both names. Margaret Thatcher was always conscious of upsetting the Church, particularly given its frosty relations with her government, and was wary of the potential media outcry had she be seen to be delving too deeply into ecclesiastical appointments. This did not seem to bother Harold Macmillan, who in 1961 promoted his favoured candidate, the Anglo-Catholic Michael Ramsey for Canterbury, much to the displeasure of the outgoing Archbishop Fisher. 'I thought we had had enough of Martha ... and it was time for some Mary,' judged Macmillan, who refused to be bullied by Fisher on a matter he considered to be a legitimate sphere of prime ministerial influence.[64] Times had changed since the early 1960s though. With the Church now having greater autonomy over its governance, appointments and doctrine, it was deemed imprudent for prime ministers to demonstrate *too* much interest in the Established Church.

Ultimately, Margaret Thatcher exercised little influence over ecclesiastical appointments, except that is, in 1990 with the election of George Carey to Canterbury. By selecting evangelical layman Viscount Caldecotte to chair the Crown Appointments Commission, Thatcher had done her best to ensure that it would go to a low-churchman, but few expected that it would be the little-known Bishop of Bath & Wells. According to those close to her, Thatcher was, however, disappointed in Carey, who turned out not to be the evangelical she had hoped for. In 1976, the prime minister's role in ecclesiastical appointments had been reduced due to pressure from the Church. In 2007, on the initiative of Gordon Brown, it was announced that the prime minister would now go with the first-named candidate rather than select between the two. The prime minister's role was now to endorse the appointment on behalf of the Queen.

Margaret Thatcher's input into ecclesiastical affairs may have been minimal but she was head of a party that continued to take an active interest in Church matters. The first difficult moment came in 1974 when Parliament was asked to endorse the Worship and Doctrine Measure, granting the Church full control over its liturgy. Most MPs regarded it as a natural extension of powers following the establishment of the Synod, but a small, determined band of Anglican Conservatives decried this further curtailment of parliamentary authority over the Church. One MP thought it signalled the 'denationalisation of the Church of England' while Enoch Powell, in bullish form, was intent on putting up a fight: 'The only representative of that Church of England are those who created the Church of England by establishing it by law, namely, this House.' Powell's point was highly contestable; the Church of England was not the creature, nor was it the creation of Parliament.[65] Conservative Anglicans' chief worry, however, was not Parliament's diminishing authority but the reforms the Synod was likely usher in once it had complete power over its liturgy; namely the replacement of the 1662 Book of Common Prayer.

The process of modernising the Prayer Book dated back to the early 1960s, during which time the Church's liturgical commission had produced three different versions under the rather uninspiring titles of Series I, II, III. Conscious that the subject was likely to arouse feeling in Parliament and with the 1927–8 Prayer Book debacle still fresh in their minds, the Anglican leadership made sure that liturgical revisions were presented as 'alternatives' rather than actual replacements for the Book of Common Prayer. After the Worship and Doctrine Measure passed, however, the Synod was technically free to establish a new orthodoxy. Those traditional Anglicans opposed to reform mobilised to form the Prayer Book Society (PBS) a year later in 1975 and secured the support of a number of sympathetic parliamentarians to defend what they termed the 'spiritual birthright of the nation'.[66] To traditionalist Anglicans, the sweeping away of 1662 represented the most catastrophic decimation of the Church's heritage in recent history. 'When this country has lost an empire and has not found a role,' wrote one PBS member Geoffrey Sheppard, 'it is an entirely inappropriate time to obliterate the Book of Common Prayer by endless nervous variations and forfeit utterly any way of saying our public prayers in unison.'[67] Traditionalists may have spoken of the 1662 Rite as one that united the nation both past and present but this was not strictly true. Much of the 1928 Revised Prayer Book was then widely used and there was little uniformity across the Anglican parishes, let alone across successive generations.

In a strategic attempt to put as much pressure on the Church hierarchy as possible, the Prayer Book Society amassed a petition signed by an impressive list of prominent names from Britain's military, academic, legal and literary spheres, including a number of notable peers and twenty-nine MPs (three of whom were members of Thatcher's shadow Cabinet). Conservative peer Lord Sudeley, who could trace his ancestral roots back to one of the knights who had murdered Thomas à Becket, performed a similar act of defiance against spiritual authority when, in 1978, he introduced a bill in the Lords to allow each parish to hold a referendum on the use of the 1662 Prayer Book.[68] His bill was the first time since the 1919 Enabling Act that ecclesiastical legislation had been initiated in the Houses of Parliament. The then Bishop of London, Gerald Ellison, thought it an 'attack upon the whole system of Church government'.[69] The bill was shelved; the cause, however, was not.

In what was to be the fourth liturgical revision in twenty-five years, the Alternative Service Book was finally published in 1980. This time it was the Commons who led the fight with Conservative MP and heir to the Salisbury title, Viscount Cranborne, introducing a bill for the preservation of the 1662 Prayer Book, controversially calling for a

Parliamentary Select Committee to investigate its use in the parishes. Fearing the potential constitutional ramifications of the state examining Church practices, Margaret Thatcher decided to enforce the whip on this occasion, but it was to no avail, Cranborne still succeeded in gaining a 152/130 majority in favour of the bill progressing. In a diplomatic move, Runcie invited the group of PBS campaigners and MPs to lunch at Lambeth Palace with the hope of preventing further disruption. Runcie's schmoozing failed, in part because he refused to make a public declaration in defence of the retention of the 1662 Prayer Book. With Runcie dithering, Lord Sudeley once again decided to push the cause in the Lords and in a bold act wrote to every diocesan bishop demanding statistics on the use of the Prayer Book in the parishes.

What the Bishop of Derby, Cyril Bowles, called Sudeley's 'self-appointed inquisition' sent the bishops into a blind panic.[70] And yet evidence that eventually came in from the dioceses proved what the bishops had been saying all along. There was no uniformity of worship even within dioceses, let alone across England, rather the statistics pointed to a variation of 1662, 1928, Series I, II, III and the Alternative Service Book. The liturgy used was, as had always been the case, entirely dependent on the incumbent vicar. In what many considered an inappropriate ruling from an archbishop, Runcie finally gave concrete assurances that the 1662 Prayer Book would not be phased out in the parishes and, more crucially, in the theological colleges. Parliamentary pressure on this matter had been pivotal in protecting the 1662 Rite. Parliament had put up an impressive fight over the 1662 Prayer Book although what was clearly at stake was a dogged defence of the old trinity of Englishness, Anglicanism and Toryism. Runcie's conciliatory words would mark only a temporary truce in Church–state affairs.

One of the stipulations of the synodical government in 1970 was that Church Measures would require vetting by the Ecclesiastical Committee (a cross-party group comprised of MPs and peers) and ratification by Parliament. The expectation, by those in the Church at least, was that this process was a mere formality. In July 1984, the Appointments of Bishops Measure, a relatively minor piece of legislation on election procedure, reached the House. As the last piece of business of the day, the debate was sparsely attended (not one Labour MP was present), however an important cluster of aggrieved Anglican Conservatives had shown up determined to use the occasion to vent their frustrations on the newly Bishop-elect of Durham, David Jenkins, who in a recent television interview had uttered some clumsy remarks implying that the Virgin Birth, Resurrection and the miracles of Jesus had not *actually* happened. Days after the broadcast, York Minster was struck by lightning, which many took as a sign of God exhibiting his wrath on the 'unbelieving bishop' Jenkins. At 12.21 a.m. the vote was taken and lost in what was the first time that Westminster had thrown out a Church Measure since the Synod's formation. Not content, Conservative Anglicans appealed to Thatcher for Jenkins to be deselected and urged for increasing temporal influence on the Crown Appointments Commission.

Canon Colin Buchanan considered the parliamentary intrusion a 'declaration of war' on the Church, but while the bishops did not quite see it in these terms, they were certainly worried (not to mention extremely irritated) by this challenge to synodical autonomy by a handful of Conservative MPs.[71] Conservative Anglican MP William Powell took a different view, judging that parliamentary intervention was necessary in order to save Anglicanism from its 'narrow paths' and 'unwanted reforms'. Writing to a sympathetic Bishop of Peterborough, Powell insisted that the Church needed to drop its obsession with political concerns and rediscover the meaning of 'Royal Supremacy'.[72] Some Conservatives, both inside and outside the House, increasingly came to see synodical government as the source of problems within the Church. Writing in 1986, Charles Moore thought that the separate chamber completely undermined the fact that 'the Church of England is the property of the English people (and therefore looked after them by their elected representatives)'.[73] That the Church's identity and authority derived from its relationship with Parliament was a concept that few clergy took seriously, nor did they accept the argument frequently articulated by Conservative Anglican MPs that they, rather than synod representatives, spoke for the 'ordinary man in the pew'. The truth was that parliamentary prerogative assumed new relevance at a time when the Synod was increasingly divided between traditionalists and liberals. Needless to say, Anglican traditionalists certainly welcomed the MPs' intervention: 'If Parliament does not protect them no one will from those awful ecclesiastical sectarians and their trendy ways,' wrote lay Synod member Gervase Duffield in a letter of thanks to Enoch Powell.[74] The traditionalist cause was beginning to find its voice in Parliament as Synod members turned to Conservative MPs to help stem the liberal tide in the Church. In 1986 lay Synod member Kathleen Griffiths wrote to Enoch Powell suggesting a meeting between 'conservative Synod members' and MPs in order to coordinate a 'common policy' against 'ecclesiasticism'.[75]

When, in 1986, Conservative Anglican MPs demanded regular meetings with the bishops to discuss forthcoming Measures, the Bishop of Southwark refused point-blank. 'To you, who do not relish democratic argument,' wrote Conservative MP Ivor Stanbrook in a somewhat curt reply, 'it appears we are a nuisance.'[76] Labour Anglican MP Frank Field, who sat on the Ecclesiastical Committee, was convinced that the tensions between Church and Parliament were not the fault of disgruntled MPs but the result of the dismissive attitude of the Anglican leadership who, he believed, enjoyed the privileges of establishment and seats in the House of Lords, but were unwilling to countenance that this relationship should be a reciprocal one.[77] Field was right, the bishops were not prepared to allow Westminster an opinion in its affairs; this was not out of spite, but because they genuinely believed that the Church of England was not beholden to Parliament, which admittedly, was a somewhat strange position for the bishops of an Established Church.

On the surface, the parliamentary fight over ecclesiastical Measures seems like an irrelevant sideshow given the more pressing issues that the country and government faced; this is certainly how Thatcher saw it at the time. Yet the constitutional tussle between Synod and Parliament had exposed two things: firstly, the level of discontent within the Church itself between the predominant conservative (both evangelical and High Anglican) laity and its liberal leadership, which was only exacerbated by Anglican Conservative MPs in Parliament. Secondly, it revealed the increasingly bitter relationship between the Tory Party and the Church leadership on the changing character of Anglicanism. As Alfred Sherman pointedly remarked, Conservatives always considered Anglicanism as an institution rather than a system of belief; it was therefore a matter of identity and one that many Conservatives felt increasingly alienated from.[78] All talk of a constitutional gulf between the Synod and Parliament disguised their true concern: the widening cultural gulf between the Conservative Party and Anglicanism. With the Church entering the political fray on matters of social and economic concern, these tensions would only intensify.

CHAPTER FIVE

TURBULENT PRIESTS

'If we truly believe that we are all members of one Body then we have a responsibility to show that we are prepared to share our personal wealth.'
— FAITH IN THE CITY, 1985[1]

'If the incarnation were to take place today, Jesus would exercise his ministry in places like Netherley and Toxteth.'
— BISHOP DAVID SHEPPARD, 1987[2]

'If only they had stuck to religion, we all would have been better off.'
— NIGEL LAWSON, 2011[3]

I F ONE WERE to trace the beginnings of the tense relations between the Thatcher government and the Church of England, it would be the fallout over the Thanksgiving Service for the Falklands War in St Paul's Cathedral in July 1982. When Thatcher announced her decision to send a task force to the South Atlantic, the Anglican bishops had approved military action, but they were decidedly less enthusiastic about the government's proposed service in St Paul's Cathedral to celebrate victory. As it was the Dean of St Paul's who held the keys to the cathedral, so it was the Very Rev. Alan Webster, well known for his pacifist sympathies, who took charge. Webster had initially proposed that half the service be conducted in Spanish and that Pope John Paul II's sermon on reconciliation, given on his recent tour of Britain, be included in the Order of Service. In scriptural selections he hoped might impress the Prime Minister, Webster chose a bidding prayer to 'commit ourselves to be makers of peace in a divided world' and an extract from Micah: 'nation shall not lift up sword against nation, neither shall they learn war any more'.[4] On seeing the dean's plans, Defence Secretary John Nott thought the event should be abandoned altogether. The Bishop of London, Graham Leonard, was also concerned and went to see the Prime Minister. 'Even when the form of Service had been agreed,' ran the memo in expectation of the meeting, 'there was no guarantee that the Dean of St Paul's would follow it. On past form, he might well insert changes or additions at the last minute.'[5] No. 10 agreed to put pressure on the Archbishop of Canterbury to rein in the dean.

In what might be interpreted as state-orchestrated Christianity, the Ministry of Defence and No. 10 challenged the dean on every aspect of the service from the choice of hymns to the selection of readers. They consented to the involvement of the Moderator of the General Assembly of the Church of Scotland, Mrs Rosalind Goodfellow, reportedly a 'robust person of no pacifist leanings', yet there were some misgivings over the President of the Methodist Conference, Rev. Kenneth Greet, who had recently voiced anti-Falklands sentiments in The Guardian. Contrary to popular opinion, Thatcher was sensitive to accusations that she was politicising the war and was thus keen for her own role in the service to be limited. She did not wish to read a lesson, believing with some justification that it would be 'misinterpreted and leave a bad taste'.[6] All agreed that there should be a place for Catholic Cardinal

Basil Hume, which in itself was an innovative step; Britain's Catholic leaders had only recently been accorded a prominent role at national religious occasions. Hume, however, had legitimate concerns about the proposed title, 'Liberation of the Falklands' given that 'liberation' meant something quite different in Catholic theology. The Dean of St Paul's had favoured 'a service of reconciliation', which the Ministry of Defence vetoed and eventually 'thanksgiving' was the title on which all were agreed. After much to-ing and fro-ing, the service was finally settled, although No. 10 had not thought it necessary to probe or censor the Archbishop of Canterbury on his sermon.

Would the nation's spiritual leader reflect the sense of national jubilation and reunite the historic trinity of patriotism, militarism and Christianity? 'War', Archbishop Runcie declared from the pulpit of the parish of the empire, 'is a sign of human failure.'[7] Lest he be misunderstood, Runcie was clear to differentiate between the armed forces engaged in combat and those 'armchair warriors' at home whom he reprimanded for indulging in a distasteful enthusiasm for war.[8] In a sermon that veered sensibly between sentiments of patriotic hope, peace and reconciliation, Runcie also sounded warnings about the international arms trade and nuclear rearmament (the purchase of Trident had just been agreed). In front of a congregation that included the Cabinet, the Prime Minister and the Queen, it was nonetheless to the military personnel that Runcie directed his message. It was a sermon that could only have been delivered by a soldier of the Scots Guards who knew what it meant to be under active fire. In seeking to pour water on the raging fires of Tory nationalism, Runcie was well aware that he risked incurring the wrath of the diehards. And so he did. Returning to the Commons terrace bar after the service, Denis Thatcher fed the loitering hacks a titbit that the 'boss was livid'. But it was one of Thatcher's backbenchers, hothead right-winger Julian Amery, who gave them the quote they wanted, lambasting Runcie's sermon as symptomatic of the 'pacifist, liberal wet establishment', which was out of touch with the mood of the country.[9]

Up until that moment, great expectations had been pinned on the war-hero archbishop, whom it was hoped might inject some much-needed oomph into Christianity. After his Falklands moment, however, Runcie became a sitting target for the right-wing press and Tory back-benchers. Mood over content was what had counted and there was little doubt that the archbishop's sermon struck a discordant chord against Tory triumphalism. The government obviously thought so and hastily organised a victory parade through the City of London two months later. Speaking at the Guildhall after the procession, Margaret Thatcher uttered sentiments which her archbishop had been unwilling to do: 'The Falklands campaign was one of the most brilliant achievements of modern times – a triumph of endeavour and skill of planning and imagination.' Thatcher then drew on the words of eighteenth-century Anglican priest, Sydney Smith: 'I have boundless confidence in the British character … I believe more heroes will spring up in the hour of danger than all the military nations of ancient and modern Europe have ever produced.' She signed off, 'Today we know that is true.'[10]

'Meringue to her roast beef': Margaret Thatcher and her 'wet' Archbishop

I. The 'conscience of the nation'

THE BISHOPS IN charge of the Church of England in the 1980s were predominantly (but by no means all) Anglo-Catholic liberals, ecumenical in outlook and centrist in politics. Most were drawn from the middle-to-upper class, had served in the army – either in the war or through national service – and had attended either Oxford or Cambridge. For this generation of clergy, there were normally three main routes up the ecclesiastical ladder: a don's life; the challenges of ministry in exotic parts of the Anglican Communion (usually former colonies in Africa); or the harsh realities of an inner-city parish. At the helm was Robert Runcie who, as principal of Cuddesdon theological college during the 1960s, had transformed the college into a hub of liberal Anglo-Catholic influence, nurturing the careers of many who would later serve under him as archbishop. Runcie was accused of indecisiveness, but while it was true he was not a zealous reformer, he preferred considered options rather than hasty judgements in both ecclesiastics and in politics. This was undoubtedly a drawback in the world of media, which demanded instant opinions, and in a Church that was full of tensions. Runcie may not have been as openly partisan as some of his bishops, but this did not mean that he was not a political animal. Runcie always favoured the subtle approach; his strength was his gift for diplomacy, whether it was holding the Church of England together or mopping up after his politically outspoken bishops.

England cricketer and evangelical, David Sheppard, Bishop of Liverpool from 1975, was the archetypal man of the establishment who had had a smooth ride from Sherborne to Cambridge. He envisioned his ministry, which he first performed in the urban parishes of London, as demonstrating a Christian 'preference for the poor', although a more suitable label for Sheppard's approach would be 'patrician evangelicalism'. One of his lasting achievements in Liverpool was his close partnership with the Catholic archbishop, Derek Worlock, and it is largely down to their

efforts that this city did not become another Belfast in the 1980s. Bishop
Stanley Booth-Clibborn arrived at Manchester via Sheffield and Kenya
(where he witnessed the Mau Mau uprising first-hand) and would become
a leading proponent against poverty, although as bishop he was never very
good at drawing a line between showing spiritual concern and showing
his support for the Labour Party. At Birmingham was Liberal Anglican
Hugh Montefiore, bishop from 1978 to 1987. Born into one of the most
eminent Jewish families in England (he was the great-great nephew of
Victorian Jewish leader Sir Moses Montefiore), Montefiore converted to
Christianity after seeing a vision of Christ while a teenage pupil at Rugby
School. After Oxford, he joined the Royal Artillery and saw action in
India before entering the priesthood. Montefiore never lost his capacity
for controversy and as Bishop of Birmingham was a leading proponent
for female ordination, an early crusader for environmental issues and an
openly Liberal Party supporter. Another bishop with a knack for making
the headlines for all the wrong reasons was David Jenkins, the Bishop of
Durham, whose liberal Anglicanism had been nurtured at Oxford, the
World Council of Churches in Geneva and the theological department at
Leeds University. Jenkins, though, failed to grasp the fact that what passed
for honest intellectual enquiry in theological or ecclesiastical circles had
the potential to cause consternation when voiced in public. John Habgood, Archbishop of York from 1983, was a much more cautious man. His
early training as a scientist had instilled a sense of rationality and complexity of thought, which he applied in his ministry. Liturgical reform was his
passion and he had provided much of the impetus behind the modernisation of the 1662 Prayer Book. As Bishop of Truro, the Anglo-Catholic
Graham Leonard had made few ripples, but when he was elevated to the
bishopric of London in 1981 he became the leading conservative Anglo-
Catholic bishop and a magnet for disaffected Anglicans and those slighted
under Runcie's patronage.

In the 1980s, the presence of twenty-six bishops in the House of Lords
acted as a reassuring nod to the continual Christian character of the British

Parliament and its legal code. David Sheppard, however, was sceptical of his purpose in the chamber, confessing in a letter to the Bishop of Birmingham in 1983 that 'it is difficult to know how much notice anyone takes of what one says'.[11] Partly down to poor mobilisation but also because of competing pressures on their time, the bishops' bench was rarely instrumental in deciding the fate of legislation. The British Nationality Act of 1981 (the final death-nail to immigration from the Commonwealth) and the abolition of the Inner London Education Authority in 1985 (when the Bishop of Leonard of London led a rebellion in the Lords), were the only two occasions when the Lords Spiritual proved pivotal. The voting patterns of the bishops' bench are, however, revealing. Between 1979 and 1990, only 27 per cent of the bishops' votes were in support of the government. The Archbishop of Canterbury voted on a ratio of 6:1 against, while the Archbishop of York opposed the government on every occasion he entered the division lobby.[12] Of greater importance, however, was their work behind the scenes lobbying on behalf of all Christian denominations and any other group – charities, the poverty lobby, public sector unions or local councils – that aligned with the Church of England's interests. The bishops cut distinctive figures in the second chamber not least because they were one of the few groups in the Lords who could claim to have an active constituency.

This generation were more likely to be openly critical than to whisper their views behind shielded cloisters, and enjoyed more exposure and publicity than their predecessors as a result. The Church still had the capacity to set the agenda. A controversial sermon would make front-page news. Synod debates, like those of Parliament, were reported verbatim in the press, while the religious correspondent of *The Times* acted as the de facto correspondent of the Church of England. Much of this reportage was negative of course, especially in the right-wing tabloids where 'bishop bashing' became an almost daily feature. Much like the Prime Minister's reportedly frosty relationship with the Queen, the press indulged in any hint of a friction between Thatcher and the old guard, particularly the Church. Runcie tried to enforce some PR control by employing John Lyttle, formerly of the Social Democratic Party, to head up public relations at Lambeth Palace, but given that bishops considered themselves autonomous beings with a free rein from Lambeth Palace, these efforts proved to be largely in vain.

In the 1980s, the BBC still fulfilled its Reithian obligations in delivering its set quota of Christian programming. When, in 1978, a Sikh presented Radio 4's *Thought for the Day* it provoked a barrage of criticism and the precedent was not soon repeated. The BBC's religious broadcasting department was still considered to be the 'Church of England at the microphone' and remained in the safe hands of the Anglican priests in charge.[13] What was discernible was a new understanding that Christianity was something newsworthy, as coverage of the General Synod as well as religious affairs across the globe, including the rise of liberation theology in South America and Islamic Fundamentalism in the Middle East, now featured alongside the regular broadcasting of worship.

Congregational numbers may have been on the wane and but weekly parish attendances still gave the Church a bigger audience than most Sunday newspapers, especially in the Conservative heartlands. Moreover, it had resources that most pressure groups spend years and millions of pounds trying to acquire: a recognisable brand, extensive land, royal patronage, connections with the corridors of power and the media, a professional staff (many of whom came from the ranks of the civil service), its own think-tank (the Board for Social Responsibility), an extensive local network and an army of volunteers at the grassroots.[14] And yet, any claims that it was a 'national' Church or that the Synod was representative of society was highly dubious to say the least. A staggering 71 per cent of its House of Laity had attended London, Oxford or Cambridge universities (compared with only 44 per cent of parliamentary candidates in the October 1974 general election). Nonetheless, the local parish remained the centre of the nation's pastoral activities and Christians still made up the majority of Britain's charity workers with over 70 per cent of volunteers claiming a godly motivation. Its network of parishes across the land was one that no other institution had, and as Archbishop Runcie legitimately pointed out during a Lords debate on the Brixton riots in 1981, the clergy, unlike other public servants such as policemen, doctors and social workers, did at least live where they served. It was easy to reel out a long list of the failures of the Church, particularly in the secular urban enclaves, and yet when seen in a civic rather than a spiritual light, the Church could legitimately claim (and often did) that its local clergy were better informed and more intimately connected with their communities than the impersonal and bureaucratic mechanisms of state.

Archbishop William Temple once observed that the Church 'is the only institution that exists primarily for the benefit of those who are not its members' and in an era of declining observance, Anglican clergymen came to rely on this definition even more. Back in the 1970s, many feared that the distinction between committed worshippers and nominal members was so acute that Anglicanism was in danger of becoming another congregational sect rather than fulfilling its proper role as the territorial Church of the land. Over the following decade, the Church hierarchy rediscovered its responsibility to the unchurched mass, which, in essence, meant clinging to a vague and contestable notion of folk and residual Christianity as the main rationale for the Established Church. In his 1983 work *Church and Nation in a Secular Age*, Archbishop of York John Habgood challenged the view that rising secularism rendered Christianity redundant, arguing forcefully that the Church of England (and indeed all churches) remained key 'struts and beams' of social harmony and the means through which 'social values' were 'generated and transmitted'.[15] That such sentiments were being voiced at a time of political and social division upheaval was no accident but, importantly, this understanding of the Church's role was largely accepted in an era when multiculturalism was still in its infancy and the term 'multi-faith' had not yet garnered currency.

Some radical Anglicans, though, were unconvinced and many came to see disestablishment as the only way forward if the Church was to fulfil its social prophecy: 'Today the myth of a national Church, the religious arm of the nation, is blatant nonsense,' wrote Christian socialist Fr Kenneth Leech, before posing a legitimate question: 'Is not the Church's entanglement with the structures and value system of the ruling class a major obstacle to its influence being taken seriously?'[16]

Most, though, still spoke confidently of Britain as a Christian country and the Church of England as its chief spiritual representative. Delivering *Thought for the Day* on the wedding day of Prince Charles and Lady Diana Spencer in 1981, the Archbishop Stuart Blanch of York asserted:

> ...for the greater part we remain, if we are anything, a Christian nation – Christian by instinct if not by conviction. If we have any standards, if we have any spiritual aspirations they are Christian aspirations, if there is a name that still evokes some responses in our hearts, it is the name of Christ.[17]

Secularists and some Anglicans routinely challenged these assumptions but, encouragingly, there was statistical evidence for the continuation of residual Christian faith amongst the populace, what sociologist Grace Davie called the 'believing without belonging' phenomenon. The European Values System Study of 1981 revealed that three-quarters of the British sample still pledged a belief in God while half admitted to praying regularly, even though only one-fifth were weekly worshippers. Sociologist A. H. Halsey, the man behind the survey, offered a reassuring assessment:

> With respect to honouring their parents and injunctions against murder, adultery, theft, envy and lust they [the British] out-do the Scandinavians, Northern Europeans and Latins in virtuous declaration. In short ... the British are to be seen and see themselves as a relatively unchurched, nationalistic, optimistic, satisfied, conservative, and moralistic people.[18]

When *The Times* religious affairs editor Clifford Longley wrote to Robert Runcie informing him that Roman Catholics now outnumbered Anglicans in terms of weekly worship, Runcie confidently dismissed its significance: 'The ebb and flow of belief and unbelief is not readily translated into statistical bedrock.'[19] According to Archbishop Blanch, it was not secularism that was the real obstacle, but ecclesiastical introspection: 'The fields are ripe for harvest if we can only get out into the fields and not spend all our time mending the barns or oiling the machinery,' he said in a spirited plea to the Synod in 1982.[20] Many considered that political engagement was one way of reaping that harvest. Clifford Longley, though, probably judged the public's relationship with Anglicanism more accurately when he wrote in 1976: 'The church is a place to stay away from, but on which they secretly depend, just as a rebelling adolescent needs to know his parents are still there.'[21]

II. Blessed are the poor

CONTRARY TO POPULAR belief, the Conservative government did not foresee nor did it plan for the sharp rise in unemployment, which by January 1982 had reached the symbolic mark of three million. The government was not ignorant or dismissive of its political impact, particularly Margaret Thatcher, who had to face off serious threats of rebellion from within her Cabinet. The Treasury continued on its economic path of tackling inflation while the Department of Employment, in a marked consistency with post-war policy, piled funds into the state's jobs quango, the Manpower Services Commission (MSC). As Secretary of State for Employment from September 1981, Norman Tebbit's first action was to sack the MSC's long-serving chairman Richard O'Brien and replace him with some fresh Thatcherite blood. Businessman and philanthropist Lord Young was a director of the

Centre for Policy Studies, but it was his involvement in youth training that Tebbit believed made him the ideal candidate to head up the
MSC. Young's goal was to specifically target unemployed youth, who
he rightly presumed were a more malleable and mobile workforce
than the long-term unemployed. His method, though, was to massively increase the role of the voluntary sector and compel unemployed
youth to undertake state-funded voluntary roles; an initiative, which
many pointed out, was a corruption of the voluntary ethic. This did
not prevent charities and Christian groups (still the leading form of
non-statutory welfare provision) from helping the government con-
tend with what many considered to be the biggest crisis in the body
politic since the Depression.

MSC funds were initially channelled into establishing a mobilising
group, Church Action with the Unemployed, which aimed, in its own
words, to entreat the laity to extend their Christian obligation 'beyond
mowing the Church lawn and arranging the flowers' to running gov-
ernment-sponsored job schemes for the unemployed.[22] Demonstrating
a commitment and energy not seen since the formation of the welfare state, Christians worked alongside trade unions, local councils and
charities in establishing resource centres, training and business coopera-
tives for the unemployed. The British Youth-for Christ organisation, an
evangelical group founded by Billy Graham in 1946, led over sixty-three
youth resource centres across the UK. Some church groups even acted as
managing agents for the government's Community Programme such as
the Bristol Churches Group, which oversaw a £1.5 million budget and
twenty-one different schemes. In Hampshire, Industrial Mission priests
in alliance with local trade union representatives set up an advice centre run by the unemployed themselves. It encountered problems when
it launched a 'take up your benefit rights' campaign which, unsurprisingly, was challenged by the local Conservative council, and the MSC
subsequently withdrew its funding.

Christian involvement was not an entirely selfless act; churchmen were enthused by the evangelical potential and the practical advantage of having an army of unemployed volunteers at their disposal. Many an organ was fixed and a leaky parish roof patched up in the name of Thatcher's job-creation schemes. Initial enthusiasm, however, soon turned into resentment as the laity soon found that they were ill-equipped and ill-trained to deal with the administration of large funds and the pressure of government expectations. Some questioned whether the churches should be acting as 'managing agents' for a government committed to piecemeal measures and pursuing an economic doctrine that put inflation ahead of jobs. Giles Ecclestone, head of the Church of England's Board for Social Responsibility, wondered whether the role of the Church was 'not so much to take over the Samaritan role from statutory agents, as to question a system which puts so many people into the ditch'.[23]

'I believe that the volunteer movement is at the heart of all our social welfare provision,' Margaret Thatcher had told the Women's Royal Voluntary Service in 1981, in a speech which heralded her government's commitment to re-balancing the welfare system in favour of the voluntary sector.[24] And yet, Thatcher's contention that the third sector could significantly replace government responsibilities, or even that there was a clear division between the two, betrayed a willing miscalculation of how the modern charity sector actually operated. From its dip in the post-war years, the third sector had evolved into a fully professionalised service with paid personnel and, with a large number of local authority contracts going to non-profit organisations from the mid-1970s, its fate was now inextricably tied to the state. In 1981, in a Lords debate on proposed cuts to public services, the Bishop of Liverpool put forward the alternative case on behalf of all those involved in the third sector: 'Voluntary organisations, important as they are, cannot carry the main load of caring for the neediest ... The belief that the community as a whole has that responsibility expresses an important moral principle in our country.'[25] In the era of small state thinking, the Church found itself in the rather paradoxical position of defending state services against its own efforts in the voluntary sector. Over the course of the decade, through a steady drip feed of pamphlets, sermons and speeches, the Church consistently opposed contractions in public spending and the privatisation of state services while upholding the welfare state as an institutionalised demonstration of the Christian duty to one's fellow man.

The decline of Britain's Victorian industries and the shrinking of its associated workforce was a situation that Thatcher inherited rather than caused; unemployment had started to rise in the mid-'70s while its true origins could be dated back to the inter-war period, if not further. And yet, one of the features of Britain's experience of deindustrialisation in the 1980s was an unwillingness to acknowledge that it was actually taking place, let alone make effective contingency plans for those communities centred on those key industries. The debate hinged rather narrowly on monetarism versus Keynesianism and a war of words between a Labour Party that blamed the government and the government that blamed the union as the unemployed were instructed to get on their bikes.

In his 1983 book, *Bias to the Poor,* Bishop David Sheppard offered an analysis based on what he had witnessed on his own patch in Liverpool. Sheppard accepted that the post-war concept of the state as the supplier of jobs was over, but also understood that in an era when traditional industries were crumbling, more and more women were entering the workplace and, with the additional pressures of technological development and the globalisation of production, it was highly unlikely that Britain would ever return to the full employment of the post-war years. This was something that the government refused to admit, with Thatcher pledging that unemployment would fall as soon as inflation had been tackled and Britain's 'industrial spirit' had been revived. Sheppard, however, wondered whether individuals could be expected to 'get on their bike' and find work when it was blatantly clear that the individual, particularly the low-skilled male worker, could no longer be said to be in control of his means of production. During the Depression, William Temple had spoken of the 'dignity of work' in his Keynesian-inspired plea for the state to supply jobs; forty years later, Sheppard wrote of an alternative 'life-ethic', calling for a different employment policy and redefinition of the Protestant work ethic in line with the new post-industrial reality. Sheppard was short on solutions but at least he had highlighted the problem. Even though unemployment declined in the late 1980s, even in 1990 it was still running at 7.5 per cent, with 9.6 per cent the average across the decade (between 1950 and 1970, in contrast, unemployment never once rose above 3 per cent). Successive governments in the 1990s and 2000s would mask this problem by fiddling the statistics, chiefly by shifting the middle-aged long-term unemployed onto incapacity benefits, as Britain became a nation of dual-wage earners, part-time workers and households solely reliant on benefits. In 1993, those on incapacity benefits stood at three million, exactly the same number that had been on the dole approximately a decade earlier.[26] A high unemployment rate proved not to be a short-term by-product of a national economy in transition but a lasting feature of a neo-liberal economy.

By 1983, the number of those in receipt of supplementary benefit – the government's own poverty measure – was an estimated 8.6 million, which represented a rise of 60 per cent in just four years. But it was the widespread riots during the long summer of 1981 which thrust social deprivation and unemployment into the spotlight. Lord Scarman had been appointed to look into the specific case of Brixton, but as his investigation was restricted to police relations with Britain's Afro-Caribbean community, it only lightly touched on the underlying tensions such as youth unemployment, which in Brixton was estimated to be over 60 per cent. Archbishop Runcie had seen the raging fires in South London from the tower at Lambeth Palace and at once set to the task of convening a meeting between Brixton's Christian leaders (who had been crucial in restoring police–community relations) and his friend from the Guards, Home Secretary Willie Whitelaw. Meanwhile in Toxteth, Liverpool, Bishop David Sheppard and Catholic Archbishop Derek Worlock in a practical move raised the funds for a legal advice centre to address local grievances against the police. Writing in the aftermath of the riots, Worlock confided to one of his colleagues that his was 'almost the only non-political voice which can be raised at the moment and people appear to be listening'.[27] One who certainly was listening was Margaret Thatcher, who, at Worlock's suggestion, appointed a minister with special responsibility for Merseyside.[28] In this role, Michael Heseltine would later lean on Worlock and Sheppard for advice as the two religious leaders became crucial brokers in Heseltine's Merseyside Task Force, designed to regenerate the city.

Some wondered though whether the Church of England could or should be doing more. In May 1981, director of Christian Action and urban priest Eric James wrote a scathing letter to *The Times* in which he accused the Church of 'retreating to suburbia' and abandoning those places where it was needed most.[29] A sympathetic David Sheppard convinced Runcie to gather together a group of experts and practitioners to investigate the state of the nation's cities. In what must have been a calculated move, Runcie also appointed the recently ex-head of the Manpower Services Commission, Sir Richard O'Brien, as its chairman. Following in the well-trodden footsteps of Joseph Rowntree and Charles Booth, the archbishop's 'blue-chip' commission went 'slumming', staying in over thirty towns and cities across England over a two-year period. The result, *Faith in the City*, published in December 1985, would prove to be one of the most incisive and important critiques of Thatcher's Britain. It laid bare, in stark and shocking terms the 'two nations' that existed in Britain: that of the 'shabby streets, neglected houses, sordid demolition sites of the inner city ... obscured by the busy shopping precincts of mass consumption'.[30] In heavily politicised sentiments, *Faith in the City* also set out what it considered to be the role of the Church:

It must question all economic philosophies, not least those which, when put into practice, have contributed to the blighting of whole districts, which do not offer the hope of amelioration, and which perpetuate the human misery and despair to which we have referred. The situation requires the Church to question from its own particular standpoint the *morality* of these economic philosophies.[31]

In naive hope the commission issued twenty-three policy recommendations to the government, most of which were a rehashing of post-war policies and involved greater public investment. Importantly, the commissioners did not hide behind their closeted walls of piety and were equally scathing of the Church's own failures. The report called for the establishment of a fund to redirect resources to the inner cities, improved training for urban ministers and a commission for Black Anglican concerns to address the endemic problem of alienated Afro-Caribbean Anglicans in what was to be the first systematic attempt to confront structural racism within the Church. After its decline of the 1960s, the Church of England could have easily retreated into its strongholds in suburbia; *Faith in the City* ensured that the Anglican urban parishes actually underwent a revival over the next thirty years.

To the surprise of the Archbishop of Canterbury, the report caused a stir when it was eventually published, largely because an undisclosed Cabinet member leaked it to the press, slamming it with the inflammatory label of 'pure Marxist theology'.[32] The revolutionary tag was of course a political tactic to frighten parishioners; it backfired and only resulted in more people actually reading it. The truth was that neither *Faith in the City* nor any other statement by the Church in the 1980s owed any great debt to liberation theology, rather the report drew on what had always been the Church's default belief in community and communality, which the commission confidently proclaimed were in line with 'basic Christian principles of justice and compassion' and shared by 'the great majority of the people of Britain'.[33] This was a thread of thought whose lineage could be traced back to William Temple: one that positioned the well-being of the poor as central to national harmony and prosperity.

The commissioners measured the scale of social deprivation not in terms of nutrition or income, as had been the way of Beveridge and Rowntree, but offered a structural and interrelated concept of poverty; one that positioned the underprivileged in the context of the affluent. This was important, not least because Margaret Thatcher consistently denied that 'primary' poverty existed in the UK and tended to put such circumstances down to either 'bad budgeting' or a 'personality defect'.[34] The legacy of Tawney's *Equality* was clearly evident in *Faith in the City* but so too was modern sociological understandings on social exclusion; indeed A. H. Halsey and Ray Pahl, both experts in this field, had served as members of the commission. In the words of commission adviser, Rev. John Atherton, *Faith in the City* was a challenge to Thatcherite individualism and self-help by helping to explain why 'Etons and Harley Streets will always mean Liverpool 8s and Grunwicks'.[35]

Despite this, there was no denying the essentially paternalistic tone of the report with the 'poor' the subject of the piece rather than the intended audience: 'By any standards theirs is a wretched condition which none of us would wish to tolerate for ourselves or to see inflicted on others,' the commission insisted.[36] There was little sense that the 'poor' could be initiators of their own emancipation, although the commissioners thankfully avoided a tone of moralistic condemnation as favoured by their Victorian predecessors. It was, however, easy to dismiss *Faith in the City*, as many did, as yet another episode in the long history of elite spectatorship.

The Labour Party leadership welcomed *Faith in the City* as an opportunity to embarrass the government, but Neil Kinnock was never likely to take policy instruction from the Established Church. Norman Willis, head of the Trade Union Congress, advised all trade union members to read it, although most left-wing activists found the report's consensual tone too moderate to merit serious consideration. Unsurprisingly, Conservative minister John Gummer dismissed it as misguided, ignorant and reflective of the Church's tendency to prioritise societal ills above its true evangelical purpose: '[It] is the word of God which the Church of England should be bringing to our God-forsaken inner cities not soggy chunks of stale politics that read as if they have been scavenged from the Socialist Party's dustbin.'[37] The most positive press review came from the *Financial Times* and interest from City leaders would eventually prompt the Dean of St Paul's to establish a *Faith in the City* group in which financiers and businessmen were taken on visits to deprived areas. The response from Anglican congregations was inevitably mixed; those who had been slogging away in the inner cities felt a genuine sense of validation while those of a Tory persuasion were distinctly uncomfortable with its anti-Conservative tone. Others objected not to its politics but to the vague theological basis underscoring it. As Frank Field pointedly observed, the report had begun not with an extract from the Bible but a quote from a government White Paper.

Nonetheless, *Faith in the City*'s detailed portrait of a sinking society, descending under the weight of unemployment, social dilapidation and fragmentation was hard to counter or rebuke. It made all Thatcherite talk of 'get on your bike' seem frankly out of touch with reality: what about those who did not even have bikes, the report rightly questioned. It challenged the New Right's critique of dependency culture by juxtaposing the Thatcherite ideal of individual freedom next to the reality: the sense of powerlessness amongst the disenfranchised poor. More pointedly, neo-liberalism was not simply denounced as unworkable or wrong, but morally reprehensible and unchristian. *Faith in the City*, therefore, was important in fuelling the growing public perception of Thatcherism as a doctrine that entirely prioritised profit over human need; a view that particularly rankled Margaret Thatcher.

The Church's unequivocal opposition was clear, as David Jenkins succinctly put it in 1982: 'Poverty is morally offensive as well as divinely offensive … it is not one of the unfortunate incidents on the way until we get somewhere else.'[38] Compared to the simplistic protestations by politicians, the facile slogans of the press and the profit motives of the boardroom, the Established Church appeared to be saying something worthwhile that demanded a response. *Faith in the City* did not provide a political blueprint, but, in the words of Frank Field, it did force 'the ruling class to consider that even if there was not an alternative, attempts should be made to find one'.[39]

The Conservative and Labour parties may have abandoned the values and policies that had defined the post-war settlement, but the Established Church was clearly prepared to mount a defence. Quite why the Church so readily embraced this role can partly be explained by its historic involvement in the formation of the welfare state. This was not simply a distant legacy, but a personal attachment; many of those clergy who assumed the leadership of the Church in the 1980s had developed their faith and political outlook in the era of Butler, Beveridge, Temple and Tawney. Indeed, David Jenkins has stated that hearing William Temple preach at the Royal Albert Hall was one of the defining moments in the formation of his faith. The world of corporatism, full employment, the NHS and the welfare state was not only a political environment in which the Anglican leaders felt comfortable, but one which their forebears had helped create. This was why the Board for Social Responsibility published *Not Just for the Poor: Christian Perspectives on the Welfare State* in 1986, which amounted to a Christian vindication of Beveridge's original vision. It was also why the Church forcefully opposed the government's Social Security Act of 1985 on the grounds that it reintroduced Victorian notions of 'deserving' and 'undeserving' poor that the welfare state had been designed to remove.

In the face of Margaret Thatcher's ideological onslaught on state welfarism, Anglicans were pushed into reasserting the case – which many believed had been fought and won forty years previously – that a redistributive state was the fairest, most humane and closer to the Christian ideal than the Victorian vision of charity, philanthropy and self-help. The Bishop of Durham certainly framed the battle in these historical terms. Speaking out against the government's proposed privatisation of health services in 1989, he questioned: 'Much has gone wrong, but were the undertaking and intentions in themselves wrong? Was the *message* false, the message, that is, that we as citizens acknowledge together some responsibility for one another?'[40] The bishop christened the NHS, along with state education, social security benefits and pensions, as 'practical sacraments', representative, he contended, 'of the sort of society we desire to be'.[41]

Not all Anglicans were convinced though. Jonathan Redden, a lay Synod member and surgeon from Sheffield, thought the Church's position not only politically rigid, but theologically unsound in the way that it lauded the NHS and other public services as 'an extension of the Kingdom of God, whose constitution is written on tablets of stone'.[42] The Church could certainly be accused of peddling an out-of-date consensus and policies. For all its honourable intentions, it could not escape criticisms from both the left and the right that it was predominantly an upper-middle-class institution in both composition and outlook, and that its attitude towards the underprivileged was essentially an age-old paternalistic one. What churchmen called the theology of Christian compassion, Thatcher would dismiss with equal fervour as upper-middle-class guilt.

The Ten Commandments according to Margaret Thatcher. The Church of England is forced into repudiating the Gospel of Thatcherism with their own tablets of stone.

III. '*Guardian* readers preaching to *Telegraph* readers'

IN THE SPRING of 1983, Bishop David Sheppard was invited to deliver the BBC's prestigious Dimbleby Lecture. Determined not to waste this golden opportunity of preaching to the masses, Sheppard envisaged his speech as a 'state of the nation' address and wasted no time in setting out why Thatcherite individualism contravened the corporate ethic of Christianity. What made his speech controversial, however, was at whom he pointed the finger. According to Sheppard, it was not the government but the middle classes who, through their own self-interest, ignorance and willing compliance, were to blame for the plight of places such as Liverpool. In its editorial the next morning, the *Daily Telegraph* predictably leapt to the defence of Middle England: 'Christ died for them, too: and this Easter it would be good to hear Bishop Sheppard say so.'[43]

But David Sheppard, more than any of his contemporaries, understood that if Thatcherite individualism was to be countered, the chief battleground was not Parliament, nor was it in places such as Toxteth, but Tory-voting middle-class constituencies – crucially those areas where the Church still had some influence. This had in fact been the main motivation behind *Faith in the City*, as Sheppard confirmed in a letter to the Chief Rabbi: '[It] is rightly aimed at suburban Britons, who all too easily seem to blame those who have been left behind.'[44] The hope (however misguided) was that if the Church could mount the right form of priestly pressure, it could undermine Thatcherite appeals to self-interest and reignite a sense of Christian compassion amongst the middle classes. 'Those of us who know the reality of poverty in Britain today,' David Sheppard later declared, 'owe it to the rich and comfortable – our brothers and sisters – to tell them about the actual experience of people, who belong to the same body, the same marching regiment, the same nation.'[45] Canon Eric James, of the pressure group Christian Action, was more direct in his assessment, seeing its mission as challenging the entrenched 'white middle-class mentality' that prevailed in Britain's 'BUPA areas'.[46] If this class-specific approach was in any doubt, it was made blatantly apparent in Sheppard's own favourite phrase, to 'remember the poor', which as Joe Hasler, a church community worker from Liverpool pointed out, the poor themselves did not need reminding of.[47]

Age-old class tensions had reared their ugly head once more in Thatcher's Britain as the working class were posited as either a threat to social stability or a drain on the nation's resources and naturally in direct opposition to middle-class interests and prosperity. With the Thatcher government encouraging the 'opting out' of public health-care, pensions, education and housing under the banner of individual freedom, the perception in the Church at least was that the buttresses holding the British social democratic system together were gradually being eroded. Sheppard was articulating a fear, then widespread, that if some sort of balance was not restored and the middle classes kept on board, the whole structure would crumble.

This, though, was an airbrushed view of post-war history. To a degree, the social democratic consensus had been sold to the middle class on the twin pillars of collective altruism and personal gain. They ben-efited from the expansion in public housing, pensions, free education, health and welfare as much, if not more than any other section of British society, but the system also relied on their compliance given that the tax burden fell unduly on them. Middle-class discontent did not begin with the election of Margaret Thatcher but could be traced back to the 1950s and had clearly reached a point of crisis in the mid-1970s. That this had sharpened into animosity towards the poor was proven in a European-wide survey from 1976, which revealed that Britons were far less sympathetic towards those at the bottom of the social scale than their European counterparts, with 43 per cent of UK respondents believing that the poor were responsible for their own circumstances (compared with a European average of 24 per cent).[48]

The Church, like many others, tended to position Margaret Thatcher incorrectly as the cause rather a consequence of a gradual change in middle-class values in Britain since the Second World War.

Nonetheless, every sermon, speech and Church pamphlet was geared towards reigniting public altruism out of a genuine fear that the middle classes, like the Conservative parliamentary party, had lost faith in the collective idea of the nation. Education may have been the method but it was conceived as a divine cause; namely, the salvation of Britain's Christian social democratic values. The Church drummed up all sorts of imaginative and novel ways to appeal to Anglicans and a broader non-religious audience, whom they termed 'men of goodwill'. One particularly inspired example came from the Christian Unemployment Group in Yorkshire, which created a board game, 'The 24 Steps'. Described as a 'lived experience', participants would move through each stage of a family's struggle with unemployment including the selling of the car, relationship breakdown, even interrogation from the Department of Health and Social Security. The game reportedly aimed to 'cut through the lies, the myths, the sheer ignorance of so many'.[49] Rev. Donald Reeves of St James's in Piccadilly opted for a more direct approach; 'an immersion scheme' in which he dumped willing parishioners in London for two days without any money. Lest there be any doubt of the political slant of the Church's 'educational' material, it is worth considering this piece from the York diocesan newsletter which encouraged parishioners to consider the following questions:

> Am I by conviction an individualist (stand on your own two feet) or a corporate person (let's share the burden)?
> Who is the poorest person I know?
> How did I measure that poverty?

The parishioners of York were instructed to speak to 'one who is deprived' in order to understand who was 'benefiting from our prosperous economy'.[50] This sort of politicised education (which Sheppard termed 'fostering dialogue') had long been established practice within the churches, especially in promoting causes in the developing world, but on the domestic front, the Church was clearly treading a fine line between what was deemed legitimate Christian concern and what could be construed as politicalised campaigning.

The publication of *Faith in the City* elevated this conscious-raising activity to new heights as Runcie instructed that the report be debated in every parish in the land. *Faith in the City* officers were positioned in each diocese and a shortened version of the report was produced, which soon sold over 60,000 copies. *Faith in the City* awareness days were run by the Mothers' Union while the City of Hull had their own *Faith in the City* group led by the Evangelical Coalition for Urban Mission. A professional theatre company was also commissioned to perform a play, *Up the Wall*, 'designed to promote interest in the inner city issues and to stimulate giving'. The production received a glowing review from the Bishop of Oxford, who thought it a 'superb drama … containing the right mixture of humour and challenge'.[51] One wonders, though, if it achieved anything more than providing work for unemployed actors.

What the Thatcher government refused to do through the taxation system, the Church was determined to enact through the parish collection box as a result of the establishment of its Church Urban Fund (CUF). The prelates led the way, producing the *Bishop's Cookbook*, a collection of recipes that included the Bishop of Aba's Nigerian Spinach Soup and the Bishop of Dover's wife's 'Never Fail' Sponge Cake, which raised over £20,000 for the fund. Winchester proved an interesting test case for the local operations of the fund. This diocese in the south-west, which had the lowest unemployment rate in the country (4 per cent), comparatively high levels of church attendance, and was then a stronghold for the Conservative Party, exemplified David Sheppard's notion of 'comfortable Britain'. Initially, the Winchester laity rallied to the cause; Lady Prideaux raised funds by selling her hand-made red church kneelers, while clergy wife, Mrs Virginia Sutherland, organised an open day for visitors to view her 'English Vicarage Garden'.[52] By 1988, however, with only £20,000 generated, local clergyman Michael Robinson concluded that the CUF had failed to capture the imagination of the Winchester laity. This he put down to suspicions about the laity's political slant with its overemphasis on 'social and community projects' and 'too little on the saving of souls'.[53] The letters pages of the *Winchester Churchman* also revealed the laity's alternative priorities: opposition to female ordination and the modernisation of the Prayer Book. In seeking to heal a divided nation, the bishops were in danger of aggravating the wounds of a divided Church.

'[The] average Anglican preaching today is rather like *Guardian* readers talking to *Telegraph* readers' wrote one Anglican priest to the *Yorkshire Post* in an observation which perfectly encapsulated the breach between the shepherds and their flock in the Church of England.[54] For the majority of those who filled the pews every Sunday, the label of 'Tory Party at Prayer' still meant something. An estimated 62 per cent of Anglicans considered themselves Conservatives while this political bias was also evident in the Synod, with approximately 55 per cent of lay members being Tory supporters in contrast to 27 per cent in the House of Clergy.[55] ¶ For a significant section of the Anglican laity – those middle-class, Anglican Tories residing in 'comfortable Britain' – the breach between their church and party felt distinctly personal. It appeared as if their religious and political loyalties were now in direct conflict. Lord Chancellor, Lord Hailsham, wrote to Runcie in 1983 as a 'distinguished member of the laity' informing him of the disaffection amongst the pews, something of which Runcie was well aware. Hailsham did not hold back, however: 'We are put off by bishops, priests, and committees who appear to us to be advocating policies and practices at once profoundly repugnant to our deepest beliefs and common sense.'[56]

¶   The Catholic Church, of course, could be said to suffer from the opposite problem: predominantly Labour-voting congregations led by Conservative-voting men of the cloth.

This, however, was precisely what the bishops aimed to do. During the 1983 election, for example, the Bishop of Winchester, John Taylor, appealed to his laity in his diocesan newsletter to seriously consider which of the party manifestos came 'nearest to what is morally right and just' and reminded his flock that they 'should never be blindly loyal to the party they have always voted for in the past'.[57]

Soon after the publication of *Faith in the City*, in a heated debate with Norman Tebbit, David Sheppard appeared to utter the unutterable on national television: that it was impossible to be a Christian and vote Tory.[58] What had been inferred in the report was now an unequivocal statement by a senior bishop of the Church of England. 'I am a Tory, but not a so-called "wet" Tory,' complained one parishioner in a letter to Sheppard soon afterwards, 'so that must make me right-wing, and apparently, in your eyes I am no longer Christian.'[59]

Frustrated Conservatives may have casually dismissed the bishops as a bunch of 'socialists', but as Runcie made clear in a letter to Neil Kinnock, the Church of England hierarchy claimed little solidarity or intimacy with the modern Labour Party.[60] This was in part because of the leftward direction that Labour had taken under Michael Foot. If Harold Wilson had been right that the party owed more to Methodism than to Marx in the 1960s then the opposite was true in the early '80s. At the annual R. H. Tawney lecture in 1981 (the year that the Social Democratic Party splintered from the Labour Party and Tony Benn fought an infamously close fight with Denis Healey over the deputy leadership), Frank Field made a spirited plea to his party to remember its ethical origins. Evoking Tawney's axiom that 'morality was superior to dogma', Field correctly observed that it was the Christian ethos of the party that had been the source and strength of the Labour Party throughout the twentieth century.[61] At the time, though, Tawney was out of vogue within the left and the party was not yet ready to heed Field's advice.

The troubles within the left of course predated Thatcherism and can be traced back to the late 1960s with the birth of a more militant trade union movement and a self-conscious New Left intelligentsia, which collectively pulled the party leftwards as the right lost ground and eventually power under Callaghan. So it was that the Church came to see itself as filling the centrist void – deliberately positioning itself between dogmatic socialism on the left and dogmatic neo-liberalism on the right.

The Church's intervention in the battle between the government and the city council in Liverpool proved to be a case in point. With the red flag flying from City Hall, the Labour-run council was just the kind of municipal socialism that Thatcher and the right-wing press loved to hate.[62] Tensions had come to a head when the council refused to set a rate, and when it finally produced a budget with a significant deficit, the district auditors decided to take it to court. With the coffers completely empty of funds, the city's leadership took the bold and miscalculated step of delivering redundancy notices to 31,000 of its workforce via hired taxis round the city: a political stunt that cost the council the support of the Labour Party, the unions and eventually the city's religious leaders. Worlock and Sheppard had initially endorsed the council's high spending budget and led the negotiations with the Secretary of State, Patrick Jenkin, to broker a deal, believing, with some justification, that they were more likely to receive a sympathetic hearing from Whitehall than from the councillors themselves. The redundancy fiasco had, however, convinced Worlock and Sheppard of the need to open up communications with the Labour leadership and thus engaged in secret meetings with Neil Kinnock and shadow Environment Secretary, Jack Cunningham on how best to deal with the Militants in Liverpool. Significantly, on the day that Kinnock was due to address the Labour Party conference, Worlock and Sheppard published a joint piece in *The Times*, laying the blame on the intransigency of both the council and the government. Later that day, the Labour leader delivered an almost identical

message to delegates in Bournemouth, singling out the militant councillors for prioritising 'rigid dogma' over the well-being and employment
of its workers. It proved be a symbolic turning point in Kinnock's war
with the radicals in his party.

"As we've taken up politics because we don't know anything about God
any more, can we mediate between you and Mr Kinnock?"

*The Church of England in its self-appointed role as political negotiator between
the right and the left in Britain*

Deputy council leader Derek Hatton later criticised the religious leaders
for cowardly siding with the government when the negotiations came to
a head. Patrick Jenkin, who had unlike Thatcher been prepared to show
some leniency towards the council, was however much more appreciative of Sheppard and Worlock's position, confiding in a private letter to
the Archbishop of Liverpool that 'the way your clergy and congregations
are able to work together should be an inspiration to the politicians, an
inspiration to which perhaps too few of us are ready to pay heed'.[63] Jenkin was not the only one to remark on the sharp difference between the
ecumenism amongst the churches and the polarities between political
parties in this period.

The Church had to wait ten years before it could forge a close

relationship with the Labour Party; in the 1980s however, the Church
of England acquired the label of 'SDP at prayer'. The link was an obvious one for in tone and outlook the Church and SDP shared a great
deal in common: both claimed to be inheritors of consensus politics, both projected themselves above class or sectional interests and
both promoted a *via media* between the free market and state socialism, which, if the early polls are to be believed, was also in line with
the majority of the British public. The fact that the SDP named its
think-tank the Tawney Society – much to the ire of Labour activists
– indicated a desire on the part of the SDP to fashion itself as the true
inheritor of the ethical and progressive tradition in Britain. Its manifesto, with pioneering policies on environmentalism and international
aid, obviously appealed to liberal Christians, while the religious bias
amongst its leadership was also clearly evident, with Roman Catholic Shirley Williams, Anglican David Owen and Church of Scotland
David Steel leading what would later become the SDP-Alliance with
the Liberals. Ivor Crewe likened the SDP to a 'well-heeled suburban
church congregation' who 'seemed to think that all one had to do to
solve the world's problems was to think the right thoughts and occa-
sionally write out a modest cheque'. This was indeed how a significant
number of suburban Anglican congregations thought in the 1980s.[64]

Conscious that Christian leaders might prove a useful ally, Shirley
Williams approached a number of prelates in 1981 in a hope that
they might come out publicly in support of the Council for Social
Democracy (the precursor for the SDP). Most prelates declined the
invitation, conscious that it would be politically imprudent to do so,
although the Bishop of Manchester offered more specific reasons for
his refusal. Writing to Williams, the bishop thought that it was 'too
middle class and too intellectual to make a real grassroots appeal' and
rightly predicted that the establishment of a third party would split
the anti-Conservative vote. The bishop, though sympathetic to the
cause, was unconvinced that it was the answer: 'I am torn in two on

this one ... I agree with you on virtually every point so far ... but I still have hopes of a redemption in the Labour party.'[65] 'I completely understand,' wrote Williams in reply, 'though I have grave doubts about whether the Labour party can be saved now or indeed whether many people even seriously want to save it.'[66]

IV. Voice of reason in the age of conviction

WHEN THE MINERS' Strike was announced in March 1984, the Thatcher government deliberately adopted a hands-free approach, presenting it as an internal dispute between National Coal Board (NCB), led by Ian MacGregor, and Arthur Scargill's National Union of Mineworkers (NUM). Behind the scenes, of course, the government closely monitored every aspect of the dispute, from the energy stocks to police presence and media management, while trying to incentivise the miners back to work through bonuses as well as the removal of benefits for strikers. Scargill kept an equally close hand on the negotiations although his chronic mismanagement ensured that he lost the support of the TUC, Labour Party and, eventually, his own second-in-command at the NUM, Mick McGahey. Scargill's catastrophic error of not holding a national ballot reinforced Thatcher's claims that the unions were inherently undemocratic, while also severely hampering the Labour Party's support. Nothing revealed the divisions within the labour movement more than the Miners' Strike; the resilient pits in Yorkshire, Kent, Durham and Scotland held firm while in Nottinghamshire and Derbyshire miners could be seen waving 'Adolf Scargill' banners on their way back to work.

Historically, the Church of England could make no claims on the mining areas of Britain but during the strike of 1984–5 it would prove to be one of the few voices of reason amidst a destructive chorus of dogmatism on both sides. The Church of England's intervention contrasted with the comparative silence of the Nonconformist churches, once the moral heartbeat of the mining villages. Their relative absence from what was the labour movement's greatest struggle for a generation was a sure sign that the link between the pit and the chapel was no more. That the decline of Nonconformity directly paralleled the rise of union militancy was symbolised in the figure of Arthur Scargill himself. A product of a Primitive Methodist mother and a communist father, it was political ideology rather than theology that provided men of Scargill's generation with the answers.

During the strike, the local support from the churches for the miners' cause varied and was largely dependent on the political views of the incumbent clergy. When a call for funds for mining families was put to the congregations in the village of Easington in Co. Durham, the appeal amassed just £72 from the Methodist chapel and a pitiful £5 from the local Anglican parish. The local Catholic Church raised the most, contributing £711, but this was a tiny sum compared to the funds flooding in from solidarity groups in the south and from abroad. In Durham City, all the local churches ignored letters inviting them to participate in the non-political, non-affiliated charity, the Durham Miners' Family Aid. Nearby in Coxhoe, it was a similar story, and made all the worse when the local Methodist minister appeared on the radio urging the miners to return to work. Examples such as these could be contrasted with good deeds from individuals such as Anglican Rev. Peter Holland in Seaham, Co. Durham, who opened the doors of his church hall for a soup kitchen and the local women's support group; after the strike he was given £100 from the group to rewire the church hall.[67]

Officials in Church House, London, seized on such efforts, which they considered would be 'most readily appreciated' by the public and conveyed 'the feeling that church leaders are aware of the local pains and problems'. It concluded, rather optimistically, that the Church was now 'welcomed by people and groups who hitherto would have had little time for it'.[68] In fact, local demonstrations of Christian solidarity with the miners' cause had been patchy to say the least.

During the first six months of the strike, ecclesiastical leaders refrained from publicly commenting on the dispute. This policy of enforced silence, however, became increasingly hard to sustain over the summer of 1984, as negotiations reached stalemate, Thatcher cast the striking miners as the 'enemy within', and violence erupted at pits between picketers and policemen, most notably and fatally at Orgreave Colliery in South Yorkshire. That September, David Jenkins was elected to the Bishopric of Durham, the fourth highest position in the Church of England, and in a blatant break with ecclesiastical convention, decided to use the occasion of his enthronement ceremony to reflect on the matter most pressing for his diocese: 'The miners must not be defeated ... They are desperate for their communities and this desperation forces them to action.' Mindful to present the strike as one not about union power or higher wages but the defence of community, Jenkins then referenced the one word missing from both MacGregor's and Scargill's vocabulary – compromise – and posited the blame squarely at the government for failing to coordinate a settlement between the NCB and NUM. The only solution, Jenkins proposed, was for the NCB Chairman, Ian MacGregor, whom he incorrectly and clumsily described as an 'elderly imported American', to resign.[69]

The congregation erupted into a spontaneous applause after Jenkins sat down and the sermon was reprinted in its entirety in the local newspaper the next day. Jenkins's intervention was a long way from that of his predecessor, Hensley Henson, during the General Strike of 1926. Then the angry pitmen of Durham had tried to throw a man they believed to be the bishop into the River Wear because of the prelate's vociferous anti-unionist stance. Over the following months, Jenkins met with local union leaders, visited communities and joined in protest marches. For those who had no time for Scargill and had lost all hope of a dignified settlement, Jenkins was a welcome presence. The bishop followed his sermon with an open letter to Energy Secretary Peter Walker, accusing the government of making a 'virtue of confrontation' and demonstrating little understanding of 'what a community is and what a country is'.[70] Jenkins merely claimed that he was fulfilling his duty of taking the Gospel into the real world but his trenchant words riled the government: 'The Bishop of Durham is plain Mr Jenkins when he gives me his political views' preached John Gummer (then Chairman of the Conservative Party) from the pulpit of the University Church in Cambridge that November.[71] Peter Walker tried a different tack responding in a public letter not with anger but a hint of mockery: 'I was surprised to hear that in a Christian's view there was something wrong with being elderly or American. And I hope all Christians will look very carefully at those who organise mob violence.'[72]

Jenkins's intervention had the effect of propelling a reluctant Church into the centre of the conflict as journalists stationed themselves outside Auckland Castle, ready for the bishop's next uncensored statement. Robert Runcie, who was reportedly appalled by Jenkins's tone, hastily issued a letter of apology to MacGregor on his bishop's behalf. But Runcie too let it be known that he considered Jenkins' intervention a legitimate act of Christian prophecy: 'You can no more preach in Durham without mentioning the miners' strike that you can preach in South Africa without reference to Apartheid,' said Bishop Ronald Gordon, head of Runcie's personal staff.[73] A week later the Archbishop of Canterbury was pictured visiting the Creswell colliery near Derbyshire and in a sermon in Derby Cathedral, using carefully chosen words, Runcie reiterated Jenkins's call for a settlement while also resolutely condemning the violence at the picket lines. For Runcie, it was not a question of engaging with the intricacies of the dispute but offering some pertinent words on the damaging ramifications for the body politic. As he later explained in an interview with *The Times*, published on the eve of the Conservative Party conference, it was the 'abuse, the cheap imputation of the worst possible motives, treating people as scum in speech, all this pumping vituperation', which had escalated the industrial dispute into violence.[74] Here Runcie was clearly passing comment on Thatcher's denigration of the miners as the 'enemy within', while also using the government's handling of the strike as an illustration of its values; namely the prizing of economic efficiency over social harmony. Neil Kinnock, mindful to distance himself from Scargill and the violence at the pits, had taken a similar line, but his hands were tied in a way that the archbishop's were not. In a battle in which there was apparently no middle ground, the Church was inevitably positioned as siding with the unions. *The Economist* wryly mooted that this was possibly because churchmen could sympathise with an institution that was also suffering from a depleting membership. Some even made the pertinent point that the Church's systematic closure of parishes was much like MacGregor's planned reorganisation of the mining industry: Anglicanism, like coal, was yet another nationalised industry going to the dogs.

The Church's position, however, was a classic and instinctive Anglican reassertion of the centre ground, much like Archbishop Randall Davidson's botched intervention in 1926. This was the doctrine of 'keeping everyone on board', softening animosities between warring factions, particularly classes. With Thatcher content to allow the undemocratic intransigency of the NUM to dominate the legitimacy of the strike, it was the Church which broadened the discussion to what was really at stake; the impact of deindustrialisation on communities. This may have been out of Anglican distaste for extremity rather than genuine solidarity or expertise, but, as Jenkins explained in his enthronement sermon, this concept had a sound biblical basis. 'Mutually worked out compromise is the essence both of true godliness and of true humanity. Anyone who rejects compromise as a matter of policy, programme or conviction is putting himself or herself in the place of God.'[75] Here Jenkins was not only dismissing the conviction politics of the right and left but also making an explicit link between consensual political values and liberal Christianity. As if to reinforce his point, Jenkins added: 'We have no right to expect a church which will guarantee us infallible comfort' or 'a Bible which will assure us of certain truth'.[76] Politics, like theology, he pertained, should not be based on uncompromising dogma but on continual negotiation. This was the liberal basis of his faith, hence his questioning of the historical validity of the Bible, and also at the root of his politics.

More important than any of this, though, was the fact that the Church was articulating what the majority of the British people felt. The year-long strike, with its intransigency, violence, and even death, in the words of historian Richard Vinen, 'all seemed un-English'. The public were undoubtedly sympathetic to Thatcher's attempts to curtail union power, but at the same time were equally uncomfortable with the harsh tactics being deployed.[77] A Mori poll by the *Sunday Times* at the height of the strike revealed that nearly 90 per cent considered that Thatcher was doing a 'bad job' managing the dispute, while another by the *Evening Standard* showed that even 49 per cent of Conservative voters disagreed with the government's approach (Thatcher personally had an eight-point lead over Kinnock in the polls). The country hardly needed reminding of how damaging the dispute was, yet where the Church proved to be credible was as a non-partisan voice calling for reconciliation in a lengthy battle largely defined by hard-line positions and unsympathetic personalities. It was a call that was particularly welcomed by those on the moderate left. 'Their lamps shin[e] brightly with an innocence that is both sobering and inspiring in a world grown cynical under the pressure of so much claptrap from so many other quarters,' wrote Geoffrey Goodman, industrial editor of the *Daily Mirror*, who had himself attempted to negotiate a settlement along with his boss, newspaper magnate Robert Maxwell.[78]

Recognising the importance of public opinion and frustrated by Scargill's continued attempts to scupper negotiations, Norman Willis, the

General Secretary of the TUC, established the Miners' Hardship Fund in November 1984. The aim, which was separate from the Miners' Solidarity Fund, was to support families in the run up to Christmas and, no doubt, to generate public sympathy not with the miners, but the mining communities. For this explicit purpose, Willis turned to two Christian leaders who had no mining connections but who symbolised unity: David Sheppard and Derek Worlock, along with Moderator of the Free Churches Council, Howard Williams, former union man, Mr George Lowthian and Labour leader in the House of Lords, Lord Cledwyn of Penrhos. In its first three months, the Miners' Hardship Fund raised over £900,000, with one parishioner writing to Worlock informing him that he had sold his shares in the recently privatised British Telecom and donated the proceeds to the fund: a symbolic, albeit minor victory for the churches in their battle against Thatcherite values.[79]

In late 1984, with the NUM's position significantly weakened and with miners drifting back to work, an increasingly desperate Scargill reached out to the Christian leaders, issuing a statement welcoming their help in negotiating a settlement. That November, an ecumenical delegation made up of Archbishop Habgood, Derek Worlock and the Bishop of Lincoln, Simon Phipps, met with NUM representatives in the rather grand surroundings of Bishopthorpe Palace, York. At the press conference after the meeting, the delegation put the onus on the NCB, hinting that a negotiation was possible if the government and MacGregor were willing. In a private letter to Worlock, however, Peter Walker warned that the Church leaders risked being pawns in Scargill's games:

> Whilst not a member of your church, I endeavour to take a Christian approach to this problem. I am very concerned when I see not just your church but my church being used by a person who is not only in total disagreement with the Christian faith, but is in close association with governments of powers passionately opposed to the Christian faith and who has certainly used methods which any Christian should condemn.[80]

The religious delegation, though, pressed ahead and over the next three months senior church representatives from all denominations in Wales, Scotland and England, met with the NUM and eventually Walker himself, in a concerted effort to succeed where the NUM, TUC and the Labour Party had all failed. In the end, it was to no avail. The miners trickled back to work as all lost hope for a settlement being reached.

It has been estimated that the Miners' Strike cost the state £6 billion, with the police bill amounting to £200 million alone. For a government supposedly committed to reducing public expenditure, the fact that such sums were spent without question indicates the level of determination of the Thatcher government in defeating the most powerful union in Britain. Many interpretations have been imprinted onto the Miners' Strike. For the left, it was a triumphant tragedy, a time when old solidarities were destroyed and new ones forged; for the right, Thatcher's unrelenting and resounding victory against the over-powerful and undemocratic union movement remains her greatest triumph. For the Church though, the Miners' Strike was a moral fight about the nation's values: between community and capital; dogmatism and compromise; harmony and conflict. 'Their solidarity and endurance, have helped the rest of the nation to see that materialism is not the only motivating force in people's lives' wrote the Bishop of Lincoln in pointed words at the end of the strike.[81] Reflecting years later, David Jenkins concluded that the social consequences of economic policies was not a 'wet' question, but a necessary one in order to formulate a proper assessment of the 'structural deficiency or inefficiency' of the government's agenda.[82] Anyone who had witnessed not only the social but also the economic costs of those communities that had been built on mines, could not fail to agree.

•   •   •

'WHEN GOVERNMENTS START attacking the consensus,' wrote *Guardian* journalist Hugo Young in 1984, 'other people – its custodians, if you like – start behaving differently as well ... When government has ceased to be a healer and becomes for its own good reasons, a fighter, others begin to fight back accordingly.'[83] Young had highlighted the motivation and political position of the Church as one of the main custodians of consensus. But it was not alone – the SDP Alliance, some beleaguered One-nation Tories, the liberal press and (as much as it could get away with) the BBC and even the monarchy – would also assume this mantle during the Thatcher years. But of all of these, it was the Established Church – despite its clumsy interventions, patrician tone and outdated thinking – which proved to be the most forceful enunciators of the centrist position. 'The effect may be not to stir the conscience but to start a fashion,' wrote Clifford Longley in *The Times* at the height of the Miners' Strike, 'the time may be soon when it is fashionable to be "wet". If it does happen the Church of England could reasonably claim to have started it.'[84]

Broadly speaking, the Church of England's socio-political values had been forged in the Second World War and engendered a sort of patrician decency; a sense of 'this will not do'. This ethos had remained largely intact despite flirtations with 1960s radicalism, which meant that its leadership at least were disinclined to see politics and indeed all aspects of national life, in adversarial terms. It might be said that this had been the Anglican way of doing things since its inception. As the historian Brian Harrison has noted, the Elizabethan religious settlement, in pursuing a doctrinal middle road between Catholicism and Puritanism, 'set the tone' for Anglicanism 'by exemplifying the *via media*'.[85] This tradition continued into the twentieth century, whereby the Church of England bishops consistently acted as prominent articulators of these values, particularly in respect to class relations. Individual Anglicans may have held strong partisan convictions but in tone and content the Church of England remained very much tied to its *via media* tradition. The Church of

England had succeeded in exposing some of the moral failings within Thatcherism; Thatcherites, however, were equally determined to disclose similar failings within Anglicanism.

CHAPTER SIX

LEAD US NOT INTO TEMPTATION

*'It is hard to conceive of a more emotive mix than one
that combines questions about the legitimate use of the Bible
and the proper use of one's genitals.'*
— DAVID JENKINS, BISHOP OF DURHAM, 2002[1]

*'[Margaret Thatcher] is trapped between her belief that individuals must
be free to make their own choices and her equal belief that she must do
something about it when those choices are in her view wrong. In the end,
the mother of the nation washes her hands of any responsibility.'*
— MELANIE PHILLIPS, 1990[2]

*'The trouble is that the Church of England has to do its pastoral work in
the full glare of publicity. How much better are those who do it in secret
and preferably in Latin!'*
— ARCHBISHOP ROBERT RUNCIE, 1983[3]

ON MATTERS OF private morality and the family, never was the divide between what Thatcher preached and what she put into practice so stark. Despite ministers' protestations against the permissive age, the Conservative government did very little to reverse the legislative reforms of the 1960s and, in some cases, actually travelled further down the liberalising road. In this, they were simply continuing what Parliament had always done: reforming the law in accordance with changing public opinion and behaviour. Private morality did become more closely aligned with party politics in the 1980s (a characteristic of the left as much as it was the right), but Margaret Thatcher never showed any great desire to patrol the nation's bedrooms. If anything, she was personally naive when it came to sexual morality (particularly on the indiscretions and activities of some of her political allies) and pragmatic on the need for legislative change. Ultimately, she regarded such matters as a distraction from her main priorities and, like constitutional reform, a political minefield best avoided.

Thatcher could have chosen to put a hardliner such as Norman Tebbit in the Home Office, but instead went with liberal figures such as Willie Whitelaw and Douglas Hurd. Her backbenchers, egged on by a reinvigorated moral lobby and an increasingly moralistic right-wing press, showed no such restraint, and along with MPs and peers of all political shades campaigned for a tightening of existing laws on abortion, obscenity and homosexuality. If there was a whiff of a moral revival in the 1980s it was not because the Conservative government was engaged in some moral offensive, but precisely because it was not. The moral lobby's relationship with the Conservative government – much like its engagement with the Established Church in the 1970s – would be one of frustration and unfulfilled promise.

I. The Liberal march forward

MARGARET THATCHER HAD been a consistent advocate for capital punishment although she had always classified it as a law and order issue rather than a moral one, forwarding the spurious argument that it acted as a necessary deterrent. It was under her initiative that the Conservative Party pledged to review the existing capital punishment in its manifesto in 1979. When the debate was held a year later, a reluctant Home Secretary, Willie Whitelaw, let it be known that he would not support abolition and delivered a forceful defence of his position in the Commons. The free vote was lost by 119 votes in what was probably the last time that the issue would ever be brought before the House. A law banning corporal punishment in state schools was included in the government's 1986 Education Act; but it had been Education Secretary, Kenneth Baker, who had been the impetus rather than the Prime Minister, who had always voted for its retention.

In 1969 when the Divorce Reform Act was passed there was genuine hope that the time lapse of three years in which a petition could be made would help prevent permanent separation. This was not what happened for the divorce rate rose in the 1970s and soon there were demands from the legal profession to shorten the time so as to prevent an unnecessary prolonging of the procedure for families.[4] In 1984, the government introduced the Matrimonial Causes Act, which reduced the necessary time for finalising divorce from three years to one. It was a free vote but no more than thirty-two Labour MPs and four Liberals voted in each of the divisions. It was a different mood on the Conservative benches as some MPs vocalised what admittedly now felt like outdated arguments, namely that Parliament, as a Christian institution, should uphold the sanctity of marriage. 'This debate is about marriage and God's interpretation of it,' complained Harry Greenway

MP in frustration, 'not about man's legal interpretation of marriage, because it is a gift of God.'[5]

There was no way that the 1984 Act could be construed as anything but a relaxation in the divorce laws. The divorce rate did decrease by 6 per cent between 1986 and 1990 – although this was largely due to fewer people getting married. Speaking in 1977, Thatcher admitted the limitations of politicians in this sphere but also the need for fair and just laws: 'What can I do about the rising rate of marital breakdown? What am I expected to do? Go into the houses? To say that if you are living a violent, drunken life you may not divorce?'[6] In 1969, the Wilson government had taken great care to consult the bishops' bench; fifteen years later, the Thatcher government felt little need. The bishops of Birmingham and London led the opposition to the bill in the second chamber but it was a little too late and to no avail. The fact that the Church was reduced to commenting on the sidelines was a sure sign of the growing separation between secular law and Christian morality in Britain. When, much later, John Major's government introduced the Family Law Reform Bill in 1996, allowing for 'quickie' divorces, the opposition from the 'party of the family' was still strong but only one Conservative, Edward Leigh MP, made reference to the fact that Britain, as a 'Judeo-Christian' county, might consider the religious implications of the bill.[7] Even the bishops seemed to give up on the idea that the divorce law could or should be compatible with a Christian view of marriage and were even less inclined to promote reconciliation through counselling. The law assumed a greater responsibility on the part of the individual, chiefly women, who were no longer beholden to Christian standards, public shame, or a restrictive legal code.

•   •   •

IN OCTOBER 1983, Catholic mother and campaigner Victoria Gillick submitted a million-strong petition to the Commons calling for the prevention of doctors prescribing contraception to underage girls without parental consent. Gillick's proposal of chastity as the solution to curbing underage sex may not have been shared by all her supporters, but her campaign of parental rights over doctors was endorsed by over 200 MPs, many Christian groups as well as Islamic and Jewish representatives, along with notable figures in the press and a credible section of the British public. Gillick's campaign was the cause of much agitation within the Department of Health, especially when, in December 1984, she won her case in the Court of Appeal, which ruled that existing NHS guidelines were unlawful. The trouble was that Gillick presented her case in distinctly right-wing terms: a critique of secular humanist culture, the reining-in of permissive behaviour and the prerogative of parents over the professional class. Led by the pragmatic Kenneth Clarke, the Department of Health challenged the Court of Appeal's ruling, eventually winning its case in the House of Lords. Gillick may have ultimately lost the fight but her efforts had cast a revealing light on political moralising: 'The Tory Government had played such an abominably duplicitous trick on us all … It was all electioneering humbug!' was Gillick's cynical conclusion on the Conservative government's commitment to family values.[8]

In the ten years since the passing of the Abortion Act, the number of legal terminations carried out had more than trebled. Pro-life lobbyists complained that the restrictive law had gone beyond its original intention and made the unsubstantiated claim that women were now casually using abortion as a form of contraception. Pro-life groups LIFE and the Society for the Protection of the Unborn Child (SPUC) had fought without success for tighter restrictions in the 1970s, although with the election of a leader proclaiming a Christian motivation, there was genuine optimism that reform could be on its way. As issues such as abortion rarely make it into party political manifestos in Britain, the only way they can reach the legislative chamber is through a Private Members' Bill, which can be carried so far but ultimately fails without government backing. In 1979, Scottish Conservative MP John Corrie used this privilege to introduce a bill to reduce the legal time limit for abortion from twenty-eight to twenty weeks. It received considerable support in its second reading (242 votes to ninety-eight) although it would prove to be one of many attempts that had to be abandoned owing to the government's unwillingness to grant the issue sufficient parliamentary time. Sensing renewed enthusiasm for their cause, however, pro-life groups marshalled support within the House and in the election of 1983 fielded their own pro-life candidates and endorsed pro-life MPs – whether Conservative, Liberal or Labour.

The leading advocate for abortion reform came not from the Tory benches, but from the Liberals, in the form of Catholic MP David Alton, who resigned as Chief Whip of his party in order to devote himself to the cause. When Alton proposed his eighteen-week restriction, the bill passed its second reading with a majority of 296–251, despite a forceful showing from pro-choice MPs. Thatcher was mindful of the strong feeling within the House but let it be known that while she would not support Alton's bill (nor allow it parliamentary time), she would consider a proposal backed by the British Medical Association and the bishops, of twenty-four weeks. Alton was incandescent, casting Thatcher as 'an immovable object who has almost single-handedly prevented parliament from considering the abortion issue further'.[9] The Prime Minister's tactic had been to offer tepid support to a compromise measure, while essentially kicking the issue into the parliamentary long grass by not granting Alton's bill adequate time.

That there was an eventual reduction in the number of weeks permissible for an abortion was largely down to progress in science rather than the efforts of the pro-life lobby. In 1982, developments in neonatal medicine and embryology research had led the government to appoint philosopher Mary Warnock to head a commission into possible legislation in this area. Arguably, this position would have once gone to a churchman and even though Professor A. O. Dyson, a theologian at

Manchester University, also served on the commission, the scientific and ethical (rather than Christian) bias was clearly evident. When the Human Fertilisation and Embryology Bill of 1989 was finally brought before the House, an amendment of twenty-four weeks, along the lines previously agreed by the bishop, medical profession and endorsed by the Prime Minister, was tagged on to the legislation. The time limit had been reduced but the Act had also removed any restriction to abortion if there was any threat to the life or mental well-being of the woman or evidence of extreme abnormality to the foetus. It satisfied neither pro-lifers nor the pro-choice lobby but it did represent a consensus; one that was triggered not by a changing moral climate in politics, or intervention by Christians, but chiefly due to developments in science.

II. Let's talk about sex

'IT WAS A wonderful thing to have a Prime Minister utter those marvellous words of St Francis before the whole world – already one senses a lifting of the spirit!' wrote Mary Whitehouse to Thatcher soon after her Conservative election victory.[10] In the late 1970s, Whitehouse had aligned herself much more closely to the Conservatives, while putting the blame for Britain's moral slide on what she termed the 'colour supplement living' promoted by the left-wing 'lilac establishment'. In turn, the Conservative Party had cosied up to Whitehouse and her associates. Yet, once in power, the Conservatives clearly had less need of such affiliation and, although ministers would still grant Whitehouse an audience, they took little interest in her campaign against obscenity and, when pressed, pursued a policy of pragmatism rather than regulation.

When, in 1980, philosopher Bernard Williams published his review of the existing obscenity laws, Whitehouse was understandably disappointed. Williams had concluded that pornography and violent material were not harmful to the individual and advocated a move away from words such as 'obscene' and 'indecent'; instead the test for restricting such material should be whether it caused offence to 'reasonable people'. Whitehouse expressed her faith that the Prime Minister would push for further regulations 'because she is a woman, and especially because she is a mother'.[11] Thatcher and her government however showed little interest although it did back Conservative MP Timothy Sainsbury's Private Members' Bill to regulate sex shops and ban explicit window displays, which became the Indecent Displays Act of 1981. Whitehouse felt let down: the Act was an even more watered-down version of what had been recommended in the Williams Report. The legislation was to have little impact and probably only resulted in customers feeling less awkward when frequenting those establishments, which were now devoid of lewd window displays.

'Cosmetic measures' was how Whitehouse privately judged the government's action on obscenity, scribbling 'Moral Falklands – if she would only give the same lead' over Margaret Thatcher's polite correspondence in 1983.[12] But in many ways, Whitehouse was fighting an old battle. The contents of the Williams Report reflected the fact that the definition of obscenity had changed from the old notion of shock and disgust to the potentially more serious offence of depravity. It had less to do with public morals and much more to do with the damaging effect that indecent material was considered to have on the mental health of the individual – a sure sign that psychologists rather than moral campaigners or churchmen were now exerting a greater influence over the debate. Implicit within this was a switch from a notion of public morality to a focus on the 'vulnerable child'. This had been the thinking behind Parliament's Protection of Children Act of 1978, which outlawed the indecent photography of children (interestingly, in light of recent allegations, it also established corporate responsibility for such offences).

Writers, directors and producers remained paranoid about the threat to artistic license but they need not have been. The fact was that there was less concern about the written word, i.e. those things that had dominated the 'anti-filth' campaigns of the 1960s and 1970s and greater emphasis on imagery. This was largely because of the increasingly explicit and edgy content in films and the invention of home video entertainment. In 1982 Whitehouse brought a private prosecution against *The Romans in Britain*, a play then being staged at the publicly funded National Theatre, which featured a simulated homosexual rape scene as a rather crude metaphor for colonialism. In the end, Whitehouse was forced to withdraw her case because the prosecution could not firmly establish whether the act was simulated or real; it was to be last time she would pursue her obscenity crusade through the courts. Those in the theatres, TV studios and publishing houses may have spoken of a new Puritan age, but the fact was that the Conservative climate proved as great a stimulant to artistic output as any substance in the 1960s. There was no serious threat or suppression of material and, if anything, the disapproval and consternation from figures such as Whitehouse only reinforced artists' and writers' sense of radical credentials against the right-wing tide.

A pledge to ban 'video nasties'– those films of a violent and sexual nature – had been included in the Conservative manifesto in 1983 and was eventually translated into law in the Video Recordings Act the following year, with support from all parties. Mary Whitehouse could claim most of the credit for this; she had hosted showings of the damaging material at the Conservative Party conference and during the election had organised a caravan tour of the marginal constituencies to draw public attention to the issue. Whitehouse, however, was again disappointed. She had wanted full censorship rather than what Parliament had voted on, which was a classification system for home videos along the same lines as cinema films and regulated by the British Board of Film Classification. The Video Recordings Act was a reaction to a perceived moral panic: not one person would be jailed for illegally providing such material, while prosecutions (in the form of fines) averaged just 2,000 cases over the next ten years. The Act was actually declared void by the EU as the European Commission had not been notified of its passing. In the end, it was not successful in preventing the availability of such material and the media continued to highlight the psychological damage and availability of such content, particularly in the wake of the Jamie Bulger murder case in 1993.

Whitehouse did not relinquish her battle with the nation's public broadcaster, even when the emergence of a new commercial channel, the self-consciously subversive Channel 4, became a new target for her energies. In 1988, she could claim some success with her campaign for TV regulation when the government established the Broadcasting Standards Council. It was a questionable victory, however, given that the government's licensing of satellite television two years later weakened the concept of regulation and, in the new era of multiple channels, the debate moved on from filth to one about quality and TV-overload for children.

In Whitehouse's view, the Standards Council was too weak to be effective and she eventually came to the conclusion that the Thatcher government was a less than reliable ally in her moral crusade. Perhaps reluctant to alienate her supporters in and outside the House, Whitehouse refused to admit that the government's promotion of individual liberty was completely at odds with her fight for increasing moral regulation.

Meanwhile, shrewd observers contrasted the laxity with which the government dealt with obscenity with the aggressiveness with which it pursued politically sensitive material, such as the tell-all MI5 *Spycatcher* book by Peter Wright, which it unsuccessfully tried to ban in 1987, and, likewise, the ITV show *Death on the Rock* the following year, about the SAS shooting of IRA members in Gibraltar (which some say was the reason Thames Television later lost the London ITV franchise). When the government was willing (i.e. when its reputation was at stake), it was fully prepared to act as a forceful repressive machine.

It is one of the paradoxes of the Church in the 1980s – a fact that the moral lobby would frequently point out – that Anglican leaders seemed more comfortable and spoke with greater certainty on social and economic matters than they did about personal morality. In a letter to a parishioner explaining why he had not publicly supported the Festival of Light's campaign against pornography, David Sheppard offered a somewhat cagey defence:

> The Church's record in disapproving of things connected with sex is such that I do not believe we are very well listened to in that area. When we have taken up some of the other great human issues, which might be a little more to our disadvantage, we might be better heard in that field. I am thinking of matters like unemployment and educational opportunity for those at a disadvantage, housing, race relations, the deprived urban areas.[13]

Sheppard put the onus on the laity, who in his view were 'heard much more clearly than church leaders'. On the one hand Sheppard was right. From the 1960s denunciations of individual sin had tended to fall on deaf ears, whereas a recognition of social sins were much more likely to ingratiate the Church to the general public. For Whitehouse, however, it amounted to a wilful abdication of responsibility and a failure to uphold the moral standards of the Gospel. In 1987 she wrote to Sheppard reprimanding him for not condemning moral depravity with the same earnestness with which he spoke out against social deprivation. Sheppard's response to Whitehouse was again less than convincing: 'I have tried always to speak only about subjects that I can find time to be properly briefed about and which I can sustain.'[14] Sheppard was not alone in this; many of his fellow bishops took the same view. The Church did not talk about sex not out of a considered theological position or because they had not, in Sheppard's words, been 'properly briefed', but because it was thought to generate bad PR and likely to be ignored. In short, Whitehouse was right, the shift of emphasis from individual to social sin was a consequence of the Church's attempt to adapt itself to the modern age. In a lengthy rebuke, Whitehouse insisted that individual and social sins were in fact intertwined:

> It always seems to me, if I may say so, that the attack upon the quality of character and of culture which is implicit in the pornography of violence and of sex, does much to destroy those very personal characteristics which enable people to be outgoing and selflessly caring – the very qualities which are surely essential if we are going to deal effectively with those other issues which concern you.[15]

Whitehouse may have criticised Sheppard for being selective and political in his advocacy, but it was a charge she was equally guilty of. She, like Thatcher, happily tarnished the left with the 'permissiveness' tag and targeted publicly funded institutions, such as the BBC, local government and the National Theatre. The moral lobby fuelled the right-wing notion that collectivism, liberalism and moral breakdown were inextricably linked, while they were noticeably silent on the pernicious forces of consumerism, the free market and a culture of individualism, which arguably were as much to blame. Whitehouse always maintained that lewd imagery gave rise to sex crimes and yet the NVLA and other Christian moralists demonstrated little solidarity with Labour MP Clare Short's parliamentary bill to ban *The Sun*'s 'Page Three Girl', which touched on remarkably similar ground. And when *The Sun* launched its 'Save our Sizzlers' [SOS] campaign, it was Conservative MP and Synod member Peter Bruinvels, a man who liked to berate the Church for its moral laxity, who offered his wholehearted support to its Page Three 'beauties', who he said were 'pure harmless fun' that 'brightens up every man's day'.[16] Unsurprisingly, Claire Short's campaign did not win over many converts on the right, chiefly because she linked her cause not to declining morals but to the culture of patriarchy and sexual violence against women. She was dismissed as either a censorious spoilsport or a militant feminist, and indeed faced as much vitriol from the right as Whitehouse faced from the liberal left. An alliance between feminists and moralists was never likely, especially as the former tended to view organisations such as the NVLA as reinforcing the very structures and values that oppressed women. In the 1980s, however, a much more dangerous phenomenon emerged, one that would eventually break all the taboos surrounding the public discussion of sex.

In 1985, the chaplain of Chelmsford prison, Rev. Gregory Richards, was found to be one of the first victims to die of AIDS. The prison was put in full quarantine; no one was let in and definitely no one was let out. An autopsy was not carried out on Gregory Richards's body as it was deemed too risky. The media, however, conducted a full post-mortem into the priest's double life as a homosexual and hunted down his former lovers: 'If any of them have the disease there is nothing anyone can do to save them,' said a spokesperson for the jail. When Richards's death was announced, the local radio station was flooded with calls from concerned worshippers who had taken wine from the priest's chalice. Holy Communion did not necessarily bring eternal life, but apparently potential death.

It is easy to forget the panic that greeted the discovery of the HIV/ AIDS virus in the early 1980s. The few known facts quickly became clouded in a murky stigmatisation of the disease as the 'gay plague' or the 'permissive pandemic'. It was later classified as a retrovirus contracted through blood, meaning that haemophiliacs and heterosexuals were as much at risk as heroin addicts and homosexuals. Three decades on it is clear that those most vulnerable are not 'deviants' at all, but, as with all diseases throughout history, those without proper access to sanitation, healthcare and education. In the early '80s, though, it was commonplace for people such as Alfred Sherman to dismiss HIV sufferers as 'undesirable minorities … mainly sodomites and drug-abusers,

[and] women who voluntarily associate with this sexual underworld', or for the Chief Constable of the Manchester Police, James Anderton, known as 'God's Copper', to dismiss HIV sufferers as 'swirling in a cesspool of their own making'.[17] Anderton's comments were widely condemned but he was not forced to retract them. Margaret Thatcher, an admirer of Anderton, did everything she could to keep him in his job and later awarded him a knighthood just before she left Downing Street.

The AIDS crisis was never that far from the Conservative Party. Nicholas Eden MP (son of former Prime Minister Anthony Eden), who had served as a minister under Thatcher, was one of the earliest public figures to die from the disease, although at the time it was reported that he had suffered from pneumonia. The government, however, was slow to respond to the AIDS crisis and was only forced out of its inertia by worrying predictions on the extent of the problem. One report that arrived on the Health Secretary's desk came from the British High Commissioner in Zambia, who estimated that one in five in that country had contracted the disease. AIDS was no longer a minor concern; everyone was at risk.

AIDS was one issue that Margaret Thatcher was happy to delegate. She rarely mentioned the topic in interviews and appeared distinctly uncomfortable when forced to answer questions on it. She did however take the unprecedented step of setting up a special committee to be spearheaded by Health Secretary Norman Fowler and Leader of the House of Lords Viscount Whitelaw, who Fowler later said approached the matter 'like he was running a VD campaign in the army'.[18] In another unprecedented move, the government tabled a full day's debate in Parliament in November 1986 and prepared a public awareness campaign, which would be ground-breaking in its scale and content. However, the government was conscious that it was on sensitive ground. Long protracted meetings with medical professionals and civil servants were held in Whitehall over the appropriate semantics for various sexual positions. Norman Fowler was bemused that oral sex would need to be referenced: 'Do we know how many people *do* this sort of thing?' he reportedly enquired.[19] When the campaign was finally launched, it proved too much for Lord Chancellor Lord Hailsham, who conveyed his disapproval in a letter to Whitelaw: 'I am convinced that there must be some limit to vulgarity! Could they not use literate "sexual intercourse"? If that is thought to be too narrow, then why not "sexual relations" or "physical practices", but not "sex" or, worse, "having sex"!'[20] Nor was Margaret Thatcher overly enthused when she saw the campaign posters, and suggested that they be placed in public lavatories rather than as full-page spreads in newspapers. Thatcher was not being unnecessarily prudish, but reflecting an apprehension that many shared: could Britons stomach all this open talk about sex?

The mastermind behind the campaign was advertising guru Sammy Harari, who clearly had a better instinct for what the British could tolerate: chastity would be hard to sell, but fear would not. Everyone over thirty can still remember actor John Hurt's chilling warning to us all not to 'die of ignorance' against a volcanic scene as the word AIDS is chiselled into a headstone and lilies slumped on a tomb. The government's campaign was not exclusively directed at the homosexual community but also at women and married couples, as well as travelling businessmen seeking pleasures after office hours. Advertisements were matched with a leaflet through every post-box, a week-long series of TV programmes and, in a bold move, the opening of needle exchanges (one of the reasons why the figures on heroin abuse rose so dramatically in the 1980s). The government also dished out a threefold rise in monies for the hospice charity, the Terence Higgins Trust. The employment of Sammy Harari was a triumphant example of government outsourcing and a rare demonstration of the advertising world contributing to the public good.

The Church, like the government, initially dragged its feet over AIDS. As is so often the case, the initial impetus came not from the leadership but from the grassroots, and the inspiration from abroad, in this case, America. The rector of St Botolph's Church, Aldgate, Rev. Malcolm Johnson, took it upon himself to go on a tour of the US talking to ministers who worked with AIDS victims. On his return he coordinated a conference of clergy at King's College, London, chaired by the Bishop of Edinburgh, who admitted afterwards that until that moment he had assumed that 'rimming and frottage' were a firm of West Country solicitors.[21] Robert Runcie later headed out on a fact-finding mission to San Francisco, while the Bishop of California came to Britain to advise the Bishop of London. Christian Aid worker and Synod lay member Barnaby Miln soon became the leading Anglican spokesperson on AIDS, organising an awareness day and red ribbon symbol, which was later adopted by the World Health Organization. Miln, though, had a knack for upsetting traditional Anglicans. He was openly gay (his partner was Derek Pattinson, the Secretary General of the Synod) and he did not hold back from reminding the Church that its credibility on AIDS was compromised by its own ambiguous position on homosexuality.

The bishops both reassured worshippers and urged Christian compassion. Writing in his diocesan newsletter in 1987, David Sheppard reminded his laity that it was the Christian approach to deal with people 'where they are, not where we might like them to be'.[22] He too highlighted the example of Africa, where the Church's outspokenness against homosexuality had not halted the spread of the disease. Any fears about drinking from the chalice were made clear in an information leaflet circulated to the parishes, although communicants at King's College Chapel in Cambridge were allowed to dip the bread into the wine. The Venerable Basil March, Archdeacon of Northampton, helpfully suggested that all brides and grooms might like to take an HIV test before marriage: 'It would be a little like having a car MOT,' he reassuringly clarified.[23] Inevitably, there were some Christians predisposed to a more condemnatory attitude. Rev. Robert Simpson from

Humberside informed *The Sun* that he thought homosexuals should be banned from taking Holy Communion, adding that should his eighteen-year-old son develop AIDS, he would take him to a mountain and shoot him. 'Sometimes I think he would like to shoot me whether I had AIDS or not,' was his son's nonchalant reply.[24]

The General Synod held a debate on AIDS in 1987 and, rather than fuelling the hysteria, it showed the Church at its most measured. Runcie asserted that it was a pastoral rather than a moral concern; the bedside of a dying man was not a place to grapple with the theology of sexuality, he said. Few Anglicans believed that chastity was the answer while many drew upon biblical comparisons with leprosy to legitimise AIDS as a case of human suffering rather than God's wrath. The Catholic Church tried a different tack: encouraging abstinence. 'You deserve to know that you can live and love with real immunity from AIDS,' read the instruction from the Catholic bishops, 'it means standing out against many attitudes and much pressure from others.'[25] The Vatican hosted a conference with over 1,000 delegates from over eighty-six countries, although no AIDS organisations were invited and with addresses such as 'Is AIDS a divine punishment?' few were convinced that it would lead to constructive action, especially given the Catholic Church's position on condom use. By far the most outspoken and critical religious leader in Britain was the Chief Rabbi. Of the government's awareness campaign the normally pro-Conservative Chief Rabbi was forceful in his condemnation: 'It is like sending people into a contaminated atmosphere, but providing them with gas masks and protective clothing.'[26]

The government's AIDS campaign, however, was arguably one of Thatcher's greatest achievements; 95 per cent of people polled agreed that the government had taken the right approach to the crisis. By this calculation it was the most popular initiative that Margaret Thatcher ever enacted. This was in stark contrast to America, where gay protestors resorted to heckling Ronald Reagan at a rally in New Orleans out

of sheer frustration at the level of condemnation and inaction. The
success of the British government's campaign is borne out in the statistics. New diagnoses of HIV, which were 3,000 in 1985, were down a
third within three years and remained relatively low compared to the
rest of Europe and the US. The encouragement of condom use also had
the knock-on effect of triggering an overall drop of STDs from 50,000
in 1985 to 18,000 in 1988, and by the mid-1990s this had declined to
an all-time twentieth-century low.[27]

It is hard to imagine that Margaret Thatcher ever claimed her crown
as a pioneering and influential leader in the fight against venereal disease, but there is much truth in it. Crudely speaking, Thatcher was
much more successful in bringing down STD rates than she ever was in
bringing down state expenditure. Moreover, this had been achieved not
through restriction but education, nor through moralism but through
medicine combined with a large dose of that old reliable political tactic: fear. AIDS changed the way that the state and the public talked
about sex. The ban of advertisements for condoms was lifted and oral
sex was mentioned on TV for the first time. Britain's sexual revolution had been nudged a little further in the liberal direction as a result.

III. Politicised morality

JUST WHEN IT appeared that the Conservative government was encouraging a new culture of sexual openness, it passed a bill that sought directly
to curb it. Section 28 of the Local Government Act, which outlawed
the promotion of homosexuality in schools, was one of those pieces of
legislation that didn't mean anything legally (no successful prosecutions
were ever made), but would aquire monumental symbolic significance.
Section 28 would be a galvanising moment for the homosexual community in a similar way that the publication of Salman Rushdie's *Satanic
Verses* would later be for Britain's Muslim community.

The source of the initial hysteria was a series of children's books normalising homosexual relationships (*Jenny Lives with Eric and Martin* being the most notorious), which were apparently corrupting the schoolchildren in the Labour-held boroughs of Haringey and Ealing. There was no evidence that any child had actually read these titles or that a single school had used the material (they had been found in a public library), but, importantly, journalists at the *Daily Mail* had. Hacks had been sent out on dirt-digging tours of Labour councils to find mud that would stick; homosexuality and the innocent child proved to be a particularly potent mix. Newspaper scare stories quickly snowballed into a parliamentary campaign led by Conservative backbenchers against the supposed glamorisation of homosexuality.

After an initial attempt in which the necessary forty MPs were not present to pass it, an amendment banning the promotion of homosexuality in schools was successfully tagged onto the Local Government Act in 1988. The whole premise of the clause was farcical; it only applied to local councils and not to schools, and, with the government about to grant head teachers autonomy in matters of sex education, Section 28 was pretty much redundant as soon as it was passed. What was meant by promoting homosexuality was not entirely clear either, as one teacher legitimately questioned: 'Am I encouraging [homosexuality] if I do not make clear that all homosexuals will rot in hell fire?'[28] An additional clause had been inserted so as not to compromise the government's AIDS education programme, which further muddied the waters; arguably nothing had done more to make homosexuality mainstream than the AIDS campaign.

The Cabinet was divided but Thatcher endorsed the proposals, both before the 1987 election and even more forcefully afterwards, at the Conservative Party conference that year, when she repeated scare stories of children being taught 'that they have an inalienable right to be gay'. It would not happen under her watch, Thatcher pledged, as the Tory faithful clapped in hysterical jubilation. Yet Margaret Thatcher was not personally committed to Section 28; had it not gathered pace so close to an election she might not have supported it and, had it failed, she would probably have done nothing to salvage it. It was, however, a convenient sop to her Conservative backbenchers: 'a piece of red meat' to satisfy the 'wolves', according to one commentator.[29] Section 28 also pushed some key Thatcherite buttons: the rights of parents; the apparent promotion of 'deviancy' at ratepayers' expense; and supposed mismanagement of public funds; all key messages that would also conveniently discredit the Labour Party.

In March 1987, just before the election, Labour's press secretary, Patricia Hewitt wrote privately to MP Frank Dobson confirming that the 'gays and lesbians issue is costing us dear amongst the pensioners'.[30] The Labour Party was worried. Neil Kinnock had just rid the party of its radical elements and had no desire to address the 'gay and lesbians issue'. Arguably more of a problem for the left than it was for the right, homosexual rights exposed the contrasting outlooks and priorities between old working-class voters and the new liberal left. The head of the Labour Campaign for Gay Rights, for example, remembers being instructed by one ex-Labour MP that she should concentrate on 'building the New Jerusalem and not Sodom and Gomorrah'.[31] These tensions over homosexuality had first been exposed in the Bermondsey by-election in 1983 when Michael Foot and the outgoing Labour MP, Bob Mellish, had been unforthcoming in their support for the new candidate Peter Tatchell (who consistently refused to answer questions on his sexuality), as Liberal Simon Hughes pressed to victory with his overtly homophobic 'straight choice' campaign. When the debate on Section 28 reached the Commons after the election, shadow Local Government minister Jack Cunningham clarified that it was not the duty of the local authority to 'promote homosexuality' and nor was it Labour policy either.[32] It was only after mounting pressure within his party that Neil Kinnock forcefully came out against it, which he tactfully framed as an unfair attack on the civil rights of a minority.

As a piece of legislation, Section 28 was not worth the parliamentary roll it was written on; as a political ploy to discredit the Labour Party, it was invaluable. History, though, is often a series of unintended consequences, and Section 28 was no different. Nothing did more to promote homosexuality than passing a law *banning the promotion of homosexuality* and nothing made homosexuality more of a public issue than a law seeking to privatise it. It laid down the gauntlet to the gay community, who responded with due wrath. It marked the end of a quiet but tolerated minority and the beginnings of a sustained campaign for full equality. Nineteen eighty-seven would be the last time that homosexuality would be used as a political pawn by the mainstream parties at election time. From the late 1980s, homosexual pressure groups concentrated their efforts on unmasking prejudice within the media, harassment and inaction at the hands of the police, and the hypocrisy within the Established Church.

When Section 28 was announced, the Church issued a memorandum for Anglican schools advising that heterosexuality must be taught as the 'norm' and that any 'attempts by extremists to persuade [children] that homosexuality is preferable' must be challenged. It tempered this by advising teachers to avoid words that 'make homosexuals feel inferior' for 'the aim should be to help pupils accept themselves for who they are'.[33] In the Parliamentary debate, however, more than one Conservative seemed to imply that a bill on homosexuality would not be necessary if the Church had provided a lead. 'I am not entirely sure that the Church of England is unanimous in its opposition to sin, nor am I entirely sure that it is unanimous in its definition of sin,' remarked Tory peer Baroness Blatch.[34] Anglican ambiguity was confirmed when the Lords Spiritual entered the division lobby with two bishops supporting the clause and four voting against. Speaking in opposition to Section 28, the Archbishop of York positioned it as a matter of civil liberties, while the Bishop of Manchester labelled it as an infringement on local government autonomy. These positions, although perfectly rational, hardly reassured traditional Anglicans, and it was left to lay Catholic peer and moral campaigner, Lord Longford, to forward the unequivocal view that homosexuality was forbidden in Christian teaching.

Section 28 had revealed the extent to which the political debate in Britain was still conceptualised around the idea of the traditional family, and the ease with which those outside this 'norm' were cast as deviants. Of greater interest from the Conservative government's perspective were not homosexuals but single mothers, who would come to symbolise the Thatcherite notion of the amoral citizen dependent on the state. Single mothers made up 14 per cent of families in 1986, a rise of 6 per cent since 1971.[35] In 1988, American sociologist Charles Murray added academic clarity to an idea already ingrained in Conservative circles when he spoke at the party conference on the causal link between single mothers, spiralling crime and state expenditure. Echoing sentiments which Keith Joseph had vocalised back in the 1970s, Murray maintained that the state, by financially supporting lone-parenthood, had in effect contributed to the destruction of the family and turned single-motherhood into an ambition for young teenagers, leading to the ballooning social security budget and the breakdown in law and order. The title of Charles Murray's 1990 pamphlet for the Institute of Economic Affairs, *The Emerging British Underclass*, hinted at the class-bias of his analysis, even though a significant proportion of single mothers (whether divorced, widowed or unmarried) were middle class. What Murray called the 'freeing' of single mothers from an over-reliance on the state would later translate into a policy of getting them into work; very few seemed to point out that long-term male unemployment was then a greater drain on the public purse and one of the chief causes of familial breakdown. Moreover, it was difficult to see how more women working was a solution: female employment had increased by 77 per cent since 1961 and by the 1980s Britain had the highest female-employment activity rate in Europe.

All the hot air over single motherhood revealed the secularisation rather than the moralisation of the debate about the family in Thatcher's Britain. Whereas once the preoccupation had been on the moral implications of pregnancy out of wedlock, it was now on its economic cost. The perceived 'failure' of these women was not that they had engaged in immoral behaviour but that they demonstrated the ultimate act of irresponsibility by seeking support from the state for their child. Wayward fathers were also to be targeted, tracked down by the Child Support Agency (established under John Major) and sold to the electorate on the potent rationale that the taxpayer should not pay for the father's wilful irresponsibility. The Conservative government may not have been authoritarian in its regulation of sexual morality, but it was increasingly prepared to police the breakdown of the family when it came at a cost to the state. A comment from Adrian Rogers, of the pressure group the Conservative Family Campaign, was telling of this new economic focus: 'Moral problems are political problems because of the amount of money we spend on them.'[36]

The minister often wheeled out to push the case for traditional morality was 'Thatcher's Rottweiler' Norman Tebbit. In a speech to the Conservative Political Centre in 1985 on the 'permissive society', Tebbit made clear that at its source was 'the economic failure and personal irresponsibility engendered by the socialist state'.[37] An assortment of associated progressive ideas – secularism, collectivism, feminism, the rise of the professional class – were also blamed in a right-wing analysis which was characterised by lazy historical generalisations about a pre-1960s golden era of the family and exaggerations about its contemporary decline. As *Daily Mail* journalist Mary Kenny countered: 'The individual and the libertarian values are in conflict with the family much more than those of a socialist ethic.'[38] Ironically, the expansion of choice and freedom in the economic sphere had the effect of accelerating these values in the social and moral sphere. With a society orientated towards consumption, so greater sexual liberation and the loosening of traditional societal associations was an inevitable by-product. As historian Mark Garnett has surmised: 'A context was developing in which Conservative supporters ... could enjoy the benefits of the permissive society, while blaming their political opponents for its perceived success.'[39]

As much as the 'permissive' tag was used to tarnish the Labour Party and the SDP Alliance, it was even more effective as a line of attack against the Established Church. 'When the authority of those institutions [the churches] is undermined because they haven't been forthright, it is then that people turn too much to the State,' so said Margaret Thatcher in 1987 in a speech which seemed to place the blame for a dependency culture on the moral laxity of the Church.[40] The *Daily Mail* editorial the next morning praised the Prime Minister's moral leadership, which it contrasted with the Church's supposed 'pussy-footing' over AIDS.[41] For MP John Gummer, the answer was simple, the Church needed to rediscover 'the theology of judgement'.[42] The following year Home Secretary Douglas Hurd delivered this message to the General Synod, in which he entreated the Church to preach individual responsibility as an effective bulwark against crime and social breakdown. Archbishop Habgood was unimpressed, though: 'I doubt whether young people are led into crime because they haven't heard enough sermons about morality from bishops.'[43]

Needless to say, the bishops did not welcome ministers telling them what role the Church should perform in society and yet Tory protestations about the Church's ambiguous moral leadership posed a legitimate question. Should the Church, as traditionalists advocated, adhere to a strict and uncompromising line and risk upsetting its liberal members and being ignored by the general populace, or should it, as liberals proposed, attempt to offer a Christian perspective on contemporary morality, in all its complexity, but be accused of compromising the Gospel? As is the Anglican way, the Church tied itself up in knots as it tried to carve out a middle line. When, in 1983, Cecil Parkinson's affair with his secretary, Sarah Keays, became public knowledge, Lambeth

Palace received more letters on this than on any other issue (far more than on Runcie's controversial Falklands sermon the year before), with most of the opinion that Parkinson should not be allowed to remain in office. Margaret Thatcher had reportedly been reluctant to sack her favourite minister, whom she had earmarked for the Foreign Office; she made him Trade and Industry Secretary and it was only later, when it was revealed that Keays was carrying Parkinson's child, that he resigned. Officials at Lambeth Palace thought it wise to draft a response affirming that adultery was wrong but that Christianity was a merciful religion: 'Christians do not kick a man when he is down.'[44] Runcie also wrote a personal letter of support to Parkinson. Conscious that the Church should be seen to be defending Christian standards, the Bishop of Birmingham penned a piece for the *News of the World*, but chose his words carefully: 'If [the Parkinson affair] makes us look again at what is happening in this country, it will have done some real good.'[45] Any accusations that the Church did not speak out about morality were of course exaggerated; the problem was that when it did, it was often ignored by the press and possibly even by the Tory Party, especially when the message was one that they did not want to hear.

In 1984, the same year that the government pushed through legislation relaxing divorce regulations, the Church's Board for Social Responsibility produced *Foreword to Marriage*, aimed at prospective couples and designed to inflect modern approaches to sex within a Christian perspective. The pamphlet acknowledged sex as a pleasurable activity and not just for procreation, although couples were advised to seek a joint health check and virgins to consider an easing of their hymen before their wedding night. Husbands were encouraged to give their wives 'gentle reassurance' in the bedroom, being advised that equality in pleasure should be the aim but rarely the result: 'like most other human activities [sex] can have its hilarious moments'.[46] Much more controversial were the references to homosexuality, which was not condemned outright as wives were warned not to be surprised if their husbands admitted to youthful dalliances with men. Conservative Anglicans were predictably unimpressed with *Foreword*, especially as it seemed to condone sex outside marriage; nor did they have much faith in the Bishop of Birmingham, who chaired the board: 'What people do in their own bedrooms is between them and God' was the bishop's favourite retort to any questions on sexual morality.[47] *Foreword into Marriage* was the Church's attempt at a frank and open discussion about sex but one wonders how many couples actually read it or whether they found it of use. In this post-feminist and *Cosmopolitan* era, its discussions about sex, and indeed its assumptions about women appeared a little quaint. The fact was that more and more couples were looking to the state rather than to the Church to endorse their unions let alone their activities behind closed doors.

IV. Beneath the vestments

MARGARET THATCHER MAY have criticised the bishops for failing to provide moral leadership, but a far more serious and fractious development for Anglican traditionalists was that secular notions of morality and equality were seeping into the Church itself. The surge in second marriages in the 1980s lent credibility to an already well-established argument for the Church to consent to the marrying of divorcees, with many believing it a necessary move if the Church of England wished to fulfil its role as the Established Church. In the recognition that enforcing uniformity on this matter was likely to prompt a revolt, Lambeth Palace referred the matter to a diocesan vote, which thirty-two rejected and twelve accepted. Bishops therefore could consent to clergy remarrying divorcees, but no clergyman would be forced to marry a couple against their will. In this case, the Church conceded that individual conscience should play a part, but no such resolution was possible over the next issue on the Church's agenda: whether to allow remarried or divorced men to enter the priesthood. This issue split both the Synod and Parliament's Ecclesiastical Committee, the latter, in an unprecedented move, calling for a conference with the legislative committee of the Synod to solve the issue. When the Measure finally reached the House of Commons, admittedly late in the day and with a handful of frustrated Anglican Conservatives present, it was marginally defeated by fifty-one votes to forty-five. Seven months later, the necessary powers within the Church and Parliament made sure that the Measure passed, although according to a disgruntled John Gummer, it did so only on the 'strength of votes from atheists and agnostics'.[48]

In a letter to the Bishop of Stepney, Jim Thomson, in 1979, David Sheppard privately acknowledged the difficulty that homosexuality posed for the Church and for him personally:

> I have personally determined not to be involved more publicly than I need about this matter. I hope that it is not cowardice … I genuinely believe that there is a danger that a subject like this would be used by many of the more orthodox Christians as a reason for not listening to things that I believe I am meant to say about some of the other great human issues.[49]

Sheppard was not the only one to deliberately shy away from the homosexuality debate within the Church. When he had first arrived at Lambeth Palace, Runcie had refused to add a foreword in support of the British Council of Churches liberal report *Sexuality and Christian Insights*. He publicly instructed his bishops not to ordain openly gay priests but that was as far as Runcie was prepared to go. In 1983 Rev. Giles Ecclestone of the Board for Social Responsibility, spelt out the dilemma facing Anglicans: 'If the Church simply joins one or other of these pressure groups it contributes to the continuing process of protection, splitting and polarising of attitudes. How can it remain open while refusing to ignore the genuine issues?"[50] This was a question that the Church hierarchy seemed reluctant to face, but their indecisiveness became increasingly impossible to sustain, with gay Christians on one side and traditionalists on the other both urging for clarity. Some, though, were appalled to see that gay activism had gained credibility in the Church. Writing in the *Evening Standard* in 1984, Max Hastings considered that 'homosexuality is a misfortune that deserves every social sympathy. But it is contemptible to behold prominent members of the Church of England encouraging its exponents within the Church to "come out"'.[51]

In November 1987, the House of Bishops published *Sexuality and the Church* but it was a cautious document. It offered tentative support to homosexual Christians but made clear that it would not be tolerated amongst the clergy. A line was drawn between homosexuality in society and homosexuality within the priesthood and therefore ultimately between the morals of the nation and standards within the Church. Arguably, this was a theologically unsound distinction for it implied that an individual's homosexuality was an entirely different matter should the lay Christian seek an ordained role in the Church. When the report reached the Synod, however, the debate was co-opted by a group of conservatives who managed to pass a resolution affirming that sexual relationships should be conducted within marriage and that homosexuals should be called upon to repent. The Church was beginning to contradict itself.

A year later, the Bishop of London took the bold step of expelling the Gay Christian Movement from its headquarters in St Botolph's Church in East London. Run by two openly gay clergymen, it had started life as a counselling service for gay men and lesbians but had gradually evolved into the main pressure group for gay Christians. The Bishop of London successfully won his case in the ecclesiastical court but it was an unfortunate saga that caused much bitterness and showed the Church in an unflattering light. As the Bishop of Durham wrote much later, the problem was not that there was a division over homosexuality but the lengths that the Church went to brush over these divisions: 'The presiding principle was deemed to be that the Church of England had to be kept together … our fudge only postponed the inevitable showdown.'[52] Nor did the intervention from evangelical Tory MPs help matters. The Church's muddle over homosexuality became the main reference point for those Tories who wished to characterise the Church as lacking moral direction. Not that any of this concerned Margaret Thatcher, but it did certainly enhanced the growing divide between the party and the Church.

By far the most contentious issue to preoccupy the Synod was the proposal to allow women to enter the priesthood. The campaign for female ordination had been quietly gathering pace for fifty years or more and gained increasing momentum with the acceptance of female priests in other parts of the Anglican Communion, notably in America. In what was to prove a galvanising moment for both advocates and opposers, in 1975 the General Synod passed a resolution affirming that there was 'no fundamental objection' to women becoming ordained. The Movement for the Ordination of Women was established in 1979, in part to ensure that the Synod stuck to its word while traditionalists – both Anglo-Catholics and evangelicals – fearing that the Measure would be steamrolled through, combined forces to form an anti-ordination faction in the Synod. By the next time synodical elections came around (with many candidates campaigning on a pro- or anti-ordination ticket), positions in the Synod had hardened to such an extent that the issue would take over a decade to resolve. The House of Laity was divided, although the largest opposition came unsurprisingly from the House of Clergy. Most members of the House of Bishops were in favour but were aware that it would take time and required careful negotiation.

When, in 1987, the Synod consented to female deacons (which

allowed women to undergo the same training as men and to conduct
baptisms, weddings, and funerals, although not the Eucharist), reformers saw it as a natural stepping-stone to full ordination. Traditionalists,
on the other hand, considered female deacons, given the references
in the Bible and their role in the early Church, an entirely different
order. Runcie hoped, rather than believed, that the Measure would
satisfy those pushing for change. The Movement for the Ordination of
Women pressed ahead, encouraged by the growing legitimacy of their
cause, which now counted members of the House of Lords, judges,
bishops and theologians as well as a number of laity amongst its supporters. As for traditionalists, they too could point to a notable level
of support in Parliament (including some such as John Gummer who
also sat on the Synod). Anglican liberals accused traditionalists of
being misogynistic and out of touch with the modern world; traditionalists in turn accused liberals of wilfully sabotaging the notion of the
universal Catholic Church in pursuit of the secular cause of equality.

In retrospect, what is striking about the debate over female ordination in the 1980s is not the legitimacy or pedantry of either side, but
the level of vitriol and disagreement. Anglicanism's gift had always been
its ability to incorporate those of differing opinions and yet by the end
of the decade, many began to talk in all seriousness of the break-up of
the Church of England. Runcie's ultimate prerogative was to prevent
a schism; he had no wish to preside over the division of the Church of
England and believed that patience rather than haste was the best means
of achieving this, although it was precisely this lack of clear direction
that allowed factionalism to fester and positions to harden. In the end,
the Church would have to face the issue one way or another. Runcie
had begun his career as archbishop as an opponent of female ordination, fearing that it threatened any eventual union with Rome, but he
soon came to accept the way that the Church was heading, although
he made sure that he would not be the one to steer it through.

In 1987, the Church would experience one of the bleakest episodes in its modern history, one that would ultimately illustrate, in a rather tragic way, the cracks within Anglicanism. It was established custom that *Crockford's Clerical Directory*, a reference book listing Anglican clergy, featured an anonymous preface by a priest. For the 1987 edition, the task was assigned to distinguished Church historian and prominent Anglo-Catholic, Rev. Gareth Bennett. Runcie had come to rely on him (as well as others) as a speechwriter although Bennett had grown frustrated with the archbishop, believing that Runcie had deliberately thwarted his career.

Bennett's preface, which was published unedited significantly just a week after the Synod had voted to allow women to become deacons, was a candid and damning attack on what Bennett considered to be the 'liberal' mafia running the Church of England who were marginalising those with different views and jeopardising the comprehensiveness of Anglicanism as a result. More worrying, though, was Bennett's contention that Anglicanism was suffering from a crisis of identity. Those features, which had kept the disparate factions together – the Church–state relationship; the Book of Common Prayer; its priesthood; and finally, its conservative theological tradition – were gradually being eroded. Rather than correctly seeing this as a long-term phenomenon, Bennett heaped all the blame on the Archbishop of Canterbury as someone predisposed 'to put off all questions until someone else makes a decision for him'.[53] Bennett also singled out David Jenkins as a 'minor Anglican disaster' and attacked the sentimentalism and misguided priorities of *Faith in the City*. Bennett's rather fatalistic conclusion was that the Church was theologically and politically in the quagmire.

Just before it was published, Runcie's chaplain, Graham James, passed it on to his boss with the accompanying note: 'Odd piece … he's just as confused as the rest of us about the nature of the Anglican Church.'[54] Bennett's vituperative tone and personal attacks on Runcie ensured that the preface would not go unnoticed. The national press soon picked up the story and engaged in a witch-hunt to uncover the identity of the anonymous author. The Archbishop of York rallied to Runcie's defence and denounced the preface as 'scurrilous' while conservative Anglicans publicly came out in support of Bennett's critique.[55] The appearance of the unedited preface in an official publication of the Church of England had been an error in judgement not only by Bennett but also by those at Church House who had commissioned it. Fearful that his name was about to be revealed, Bennett committed suicide at his home in Oxford. As David Jenkins sensibly remarked in his autobiography: 'Too much absorption in church affairs is a damaging thing and total absorption in church affairs is devastating.' So it proved in the 1980s.[56]

CHAPTER SEVEN

GOD OR MAMMON?

*'The Church keeps saying we must relieve poverty and when
we do, they say we're making everybody materialistic.'*
— MARGARET THATCHER, 1988[1]

*'Without a vigorous challenge, it would have developed no
rationale other than expediency. In truth, it is the challenges
of the Anglican bishops, notably the Bishop of Durham but also
the Bishop of Liverpool, which have shaped Thatcherism.'*
— SIMON LEE AND PETER STANFORD, 1990[2]

O N THE 15 April 1986, after nine long hours of heated debate, Margaret Thatcher suffered her one and only parliamentary defeat as Prime Minister. This was not over the more contentious issues of trade union reform or the privatisation of state industries, but a seemingly straightforward bill to loosen shop-opening hours on Sundays in England and Wales. The government had boldly opted for a policy of complete deregulation and imposed the party whip on a matter historically considered one of individual conscience, but not even the shrewdest political commentators predicted that over seventy Conservative MPs would rebel and overturn the Prime Minister's majority.

When the bill was introduced, the government heralded deregulation as a populist and libertarian move in the name of 'consumer choice'. But Thatcher soon faced accusations of hypocrisy; given that the bill seemed at odds with her so-called 'Victorian values'. 'Is she, as the Head of the Government going to besmirch her father's memory,' asked former Methodist preacher and Labour MP Ron Lewis at Prime Minister's Questions, 'by bringing in legislation that will help to consign the sanctity of the Sabbath day to the scrapheap?' In a rather awkward response, Thatcher highlighted the possible benefits for employment.[3]

Meanwhile, those outside Westminster – churches, trade unions and evangelical organisations – were busy forming themselves into a coalition called the 'Keep Sunday Special' campaign (KSS), which within months had amassed a petition of over one million signatories. The KSS specifically targeted their campaign in the Conservative strongholds, putting pressure on conscience-ridden MPs who were aware that a general election was looming.[4] Chairman of the 1922 Committee Cranley Onslow found himself on the receiving end of a barrage of abuse from his constituents. 'The government pays lip service to God but its real god is money,' complained one, a charge, that in respect to the Shops Bill, Onslow felt unable to counter.[5] Douglas Hurd, who as Home Secretary was responsible for pushing it through, knew it was looking bad for the government when at his local parish the Sunday before the crucial vote, the vicar led the congregation in prayers for the defeat of the bill.

In Parliament, the government went to great lengths to dismiss the opposition as puritanical Sabbatarians at odds with the will of the people. Viscount Cranborne, the man behind the Prayer Book Protection Bill in 1981, accused the 'canting bishops' of predisposing 'to tell us what we should do', and in a rather desperate bid to woo his fellow

Conservatives, compared the Church's defence of the Sabbath to the 'sort of spirit which the Labour Party introduced for the first time in its paternalistic legislation in 1945, and which this Government has done so much to repeal'.[6] Meanwhile, Douglas Hurd, in an effort to appease Christian opposition drew on the example of Scotland, which did not have any restrictions on Sunday trading but had a higher attendance of religious worship than England. Yet, as the Bishop of Birmingham pointed out in the Lords, 'There never has been any law in Scotland against Sunday trading because it was never conceived possible that any shop in Scotland would open.'[7] Speaking in support of the bill, Lord Simon of Glaisdale, in a nod to free-market economist Lionel Robbins, spoke of the supposed harmony between consumerism and democracy:

> There every day is a general election. Every shop is a polling booth. Every penny laid down on the counter or at the till is a vote for various candidates that are produced for the favour of the shopper. That is a day-to-day immediate democracy … why should we restrain it?[8]

Such talk sounded worryingly libertarian to many Conservatives. Those who opposed to the bill spoke not of Sabbatarianism but in defence of what they called 'the traditional English Sunday'; a romantic and admittedly vague notion which did not seem to have a great deal to do with religion. But their nostalgic defence of roast beef lunches and family trips to the countryside, however, concealed their real concern, namely that deregulation completely contravened those values and institutions upon which Conservatism was supposed to be based: the social order, family and Christianity. 'Conservatives are not libertarians,' Anglican Tory MP Ivor Stanbrook reminded his fellow backbenchers in an impassioned outburst. 'We are not devotees of the free market to the extreme, certainly not to the extreme that involves conflict with a deeply rooted institution in the life of the British people and a part of our Christian heritage.'[9] The small matter on whether to allow shopping on a Sunday had escalated into a crisis about the nature of Conservatism under Thatcher. Just before the crucial vote, a ghost from the Conservative past appeared in his self-appointed role as the party's conscience. Harold Macmillan, at the grand age of ninety-one and in his final performance in the Lords, forewarned that the bill was another step 'in the gradual secularisation of our people' and, even more profoundly, represented an abandonment of the party's principles. New Conservatism was not Conservatism at all, he said, but an amalgamation of 'the worst elements of the liberal Victorian tradition', which by his definition was a toxic mix of laissez-faire economics and Victorian moralism.[10] After Macmillan's speech, Margaret Thatcher reportedly had his portrait removed from her study in No. 10.

More than any other issue during the 1980s, Sunday trading exposed the internal contradictions within Thatcherism: the championing of economic and individual freedom on the one hand and the preservation of community, family and faith on the other. When faced with the choice between social conservatism and libertarianism, Margaret Thatcher seemed prepared to prioritise the latter, but many of her MPs were unable to follow their leader into the division lobby. Realising that this was a matter on which she had unwisely tested the loyalty of her backbenchers, Thatcher abandoned the bill and it was to be another eight years, in altogether different circumstances, that a Conservative government under John Major would cautiously steer through limited deregulation of Sunday trading.

The Shops Bill was just one instance of the Prime Minister's wobbling authority in the mid-1980s, with the Westland fiasco in 1985 further evidence that Margaret Thatcher's authority was on the wane. As the 1987 election approached there was a genuine belief amongst reformers that the public had grown weary of the Conservative government and that a Labour victory might be possible. The campaign of 1987 would turn out to be a very different battle to the election of 1983 when the 'Falklands factor' had conveniently masked the holes in the economy and halted the rise of the centrist option, the SDP. In 1987, the Thatcher government could confidently claim that Britain was prospering but it now had to confront the charge that neo-liberal economics was a zero-sum game in which the wealth of one came at the expense of the other.

The debate switched from one concerning the unemployment figures and a miscalculated monetarist strategy to the growth of materialist values, the unfettered market and the widening gap between rich and poor. Unemployment and poverty continued to persist, especially in the north of England, Wales and Scotland, yet opposers were now disposed to link this situation with the prosperous south in order to highlight the moral paradox that came with free-market inspired affluence. The Labour Party regained their appetite for power and edged much closer to the Church's position, using moral rectitude rather than fiscal imprudence as the chief way to attack the Tories. Two moves in 1986 – the explosion of Militants and the integration of the Christian Socialist Movement into the Labour Party – symbolised this shift. They dusted off their copies of Tawney's *Equality* and rediscovered their ethical drive.

Writing in the *Daily Mirror*, Walter Schwarz dubbed 1987 the 'moral election': 'Plenty of politicians and pundits will be arguing that Thatcherism doesn't work … the churches can do better, with more effect, just by pointing out that Thatcherism is wrong.'[11] During the campaign, the Christian vote was deemed significant, perhaps for the first time since the Edwardian period. Three MPs from the main parties contributed to a collection of essays *Which Way Should Christians Vote?* in a bid to tag biblical legitimation to their cause and lure the Christian electorate. The British Council of Churches organised local hustings, although Conservative Central Office advised prospective Tory candidates to stay away from what they predicted would be hostile occasions.

The BBC, too, feared that its religious output might compromise the Corporation's impartiality. Head of Religious Broadcasting, David Winter, was warned by executives not to allow 'some lefty bishop' to rant on Radio 4's *Thought for the Day*. According to Winter, every sermon was scrutinised, each speaker was cautioned and all content 'kept so scrupulously to genuinely religious topics that someone unkindly remarked that if they kept this up people might think it was a Christian programme'.[12] The Kensington & Chelsea Conservative Association also waded in, writing to the Bishop of Stepney to advise him not to make partisan statements that risked alienating the Church's only loyal adherents. This did not stop David Sheppard, days before polling day, from issuing a public appeal to 'comfortable Britain' to think beyond their own sectional interests (i.e. not to vote Conservative).

All of this was in vain of course. The Conservatives may have had their percentage reduced but they still managed to gain the support of over half of the middle classes, as well as 36 per cent of the working-class vote.[13] In the wake of the result, many left-wing campaigners and activists were now resigned to the fact that the Tories, third term would ensure that Thatcherite values would be permanently imprinted onto the political and psychological landscape of the nation. In a rather morbid assessment, poverty campaigner Paul Whiteley judged that there was 'no longer the same willingness to listen to reformers that existed amongst "middle England"' in the 1960s and that the left needed to deploy the Thatcherite tactic of appealing to 'self-interest' rather than 'moral indignation'.[14] For liberal Anglicans it represented something equally as profound but potentially more serious from their perspective: the collapse of Christian values. In a paper for the Church's Board for Social Responsibility, Dr Michael Bayley considered that Britain had undergone a 'sea change' in national values with the 'solidarity' of the post-war years having been replaced with the 'nineteenth-century ethic of individualism'. This transition, Bayley forewarned, had serious ramifications for the Church and Christian faith in Britain, for, as the 'communal and broadly Christian values had been taken out of the political structure', religion was now only a matter for the private sphere.[15] The idea that nine years of Thatcher at the helm could reverse nearly a millennia of Christianity in Britain was a tad apocalyptic, to say the least, but Bayley's sentiments reveal the extent to which Anglicans invested in the ideals of social democracy as the chief guarantor of a Christian social order.

I. The Christian basis of the market: late-Thatcherite theology

THE SUNDAY TRADING debacle had questioned Margaret Thatcher's integrity and it bothered her – not too much, but it did. Despite her bullish defence in public, Margaret Thatcher was privately concerned that her government was becoming associated with a culture of greed, libertarianism and selfishness, not because of the negative press this generated but rather because it ran contrary to her own moral understanding of her political values. Thatcher's Christian vision, which she had clearly articulated in the first years of her premiership, needed reaffirming. It was not enough that the market was seen as efficient; Thatcher wished to assert its moral superiority over any other alternative. In her third term, Thatcher returned to her Bible and, specifically, turned to the head of her policy unit, Brian Griffiths.

Born into a Welsh Baptist family and later a convert to Anglicanism, Brian Griffiths had been academic adviser to the Bank of England when he had caught the attention of Margaret Thatcher with his lectures on 'Morality and the Marketplace'. She soon made him her special adviser and eventually head of her policy unit in 1986. Nicknamed 'the prof', Griffiths was held in high esteem by Margaret Thatcher even if his piety and zealousness tended to alienate others in No. 10. 'I used to despair of that chap,' Bernard Ingham later admitted.[16] Griffiths had a secure understanding of the Christian integrity of the market, which he set out in a series of published works in the early 1980s, critiquing not only Keynesianism and Marxism but also the neo-liberalism of Hayek and Friedman. It was Griffiths's view that as libertarianism and Marxism were both products of the secular humanist Enlightenment, they both lacked the moral legitimacy of Christianity. More pointedly, Griffiths challenged Friedman, Hayek and those at the IEA for their over-emphasis on personal freedom, and even Adam Smith's contention that self-interest, when commercially encouraged, could contribute to the common good. Griffiths agreed that individual freedom was the desired goal, but he believed that it needed to be contained by a Christian sense of social responsibility, otherwise it was liable to give rise to injustice and exploitation. Griffiths's answer lay not in monetarism, which he considered 'mechanistic', nor in a social welfare system, for which he believed there was no biblical basis, but in a social market economy guided by three basic principles rooted in Scripture. Firstly, that the Bible legitimised the right to private property and market transaction. Secondly, that there was a clear distinction between creating wealth, which was a blessing and a godly pursuit, and the worship of wealth, which was a sin. For this, Griffiths not only referenced Scripture, but also John Wesley's message in his 'Use of Money' sermon: 'Earn all you can, save all you can and give all you can.' Thirdly, Griffiths argued that the Bible did not promote an abstract notion of equality, only instructed that the relief of poverty was a fundamental Christian endeavour.

Griffiths was not simply forwarding an ethical case for capitalism, but an explicitly Christian one. (He was as guilty as Christian socialists of cherry-picking from the Bible and he was teasingly vague on the notion of debt, usury and how these key principles operated within the globalised financial services market.) Nor was his call for freedom with responsibility altogether coherent. Griffiths seemed to suggest that if secular humanism was cast aside and Christianity was allowed to flourish, then responsible capitalism, led by responsible capitalists, would prevail. Needless to say, Griffiths's model was not readily applicable to the secular pluralist society that Britain was fast becoming.

And yet for Margaret Thatcher, Griffiths's ideas were enticing. In the first part, the social market economy was the reality: Britain had a market-led economy and a welfare state for its inactive members; unlike libertarians, Margaret Thatcher never believed in the abolition of the welfare state. On the point of freedom with responsibility, she was much closer to Griffiths than Hayek, but she was also attracted to Griffiths's distinction between the creation and the worship of wealth. Unlike Adam Smith, Friedman or Hayek, Griffiths purported that capitalism did not simply encourage selfishness but enabled individual virtue to flourish – a view with which Thatcher readily concurred.

It is perhaps down to Griffiths's influence, then, that, in 1988, Margaret Thatcher started reading the Old Testament and returned to the sermons of John Wesley. Griffiths was a much more attractive prospect than, say, Rev. Edward Norman, who, although critical of Christian socialism, refused to be drawn into positively endorsing the alternative. Margaret Thatcher always preferred men who gave her answers, not just critiques. Another theologian from whom Thatcher took inspiration was American Catholic theologian Michael Novak. In his highly influential work *The Spirit of Democratic Capitalism*, first published in 1982, Novak argued that capitalism did not threaten the predominance of spirituality, rather it complemented it. In his 1976 essay 'A Closet Capitalist Confesses', in which he set out his conversion, Novak explained: 'Capitalism, accepting human sinfulness, rubs sinner against sinner, making even dry wood yield a spark of grace.'[17] This was quite different from the position of Lord Harris, who believed that the market was neutral and provided whatever humans desired: 'from prayer books and communion wine to pornography and hard liquor'.[18]

When Novak was invited to Downing Street, Thatcher proudly presented him with her annotated copy of *The Spirit of Democratic Capitalism*, while she also later made explicit reference to his influence in her memoirs. What appealed to Thatcher was Novak's contention that the democratic capitalist system was not just an economic system but also a moral one, which encouraged both individual virtue and, crucially, mutual cooperation. As historian Gertrude Himmelfarb has correctly pointed out, Thatcher was not an 'individualist' who held an 'atomised view of the autonomous self as the alternative to statist collectivism'; she stressed the social responsibility that came with individual freedom.[19] Whereas Friedman and Hayek were libertarians, Griffiths and Novak pushed forward a Christian notion of capitalism that incorporated both the individual and the social responsibility, in effect to rescue the market from hard-nosed capitalist ideology.

By the late 1980s Thatcher was confident that she had the theological and philosophical armoury to fight any accusations that she had given rise to a culture of greed and so it was that in 1988, she ventured once more into the pulpit. It would turn out to be the most controversial speech she ever made.

'It was an unmitigated disaster and she should never have done it,' was how Charles Powell remembers Margaret Thatcher's address to the Church of Scotland's General Assembly in May 1988.[20] Her advisers must have anticipated that the Kirk would be a tough audience, given the Conservatives' dismal electoral performance north of the border in 1987, which had left the party with just ten MPs. In those pre-devolved days, the Church of Scotland was not only the source of Scottish religious identity but also of nationalist sentiment, which, after its setbacks in the 1970s, was once more in the ascendant, capitalising on the resentment towards high unemployment, the early-introduction of the poll tax and the southward direction of most of the profits of North Sea oil. 'Frankly, even if she had read from a telephone directory, they would have taken objection,' recorded Thatcher's former Scottish Secretary Malcolm Rifkind.[21]

Dressed in a resplendent Tory blue suit with matching hat, Margaret Thatcher looked like a convict in the dock as she faced the packed gallery of professors, elders and presbyters. Griffiths's fingerprints were all over the script but so too were the Prime Minister's, in an address which was composed as a theological defence of

Thatcherism. Quoting the phrase 'Christianity is about spiritual redemption, not social reform', Thatcher went on to elaborate: 'We must not profess the Christian faith and go to Church simply because we want social reforms and benefits or a better standard of behaviour – but because we accept the sanctity of life, the responsibility that comes with freedom.'[22]

Convict in the dock: Margaret Thatcher offers a spirited defence of the Christian basis of her political philosophy. The audience, however, are left unconvinced

Margaret Thatcher set out the tenets of her theology on the sanctity of the individual, God-given liberty and the Protestant work ethic and how they applied to the temporal sphere. She controversially offered the words of St Paul: 'If a man will not work he shall not eat' as proof that 'abundance rather than poverty' had a biblical basis while making a careful distinction between the creation of wealth and the worship of money. By focusing on the creation rather than the consequences of wealth, Thatcher was of course conveniently dodging the main criticisms of capitalism. Devoid of personal reflections and romantic evocations of her Nonconformist upbringing, this speech differed from Thatcher's earlier public proclamations of her faith. It was more theological and definitely more political. For critic Jonathan Raban, the speech was a potent summation of the ethos behind Thatcherism:

If Britain under Mrs Thatcher's government feels like a nation in the throes of a zealous and puritan Reformation, its old priests on the run, its icons smashed, its centres of learning under siege, its history rewritten in the mould of a stiff new orthodoxy, then this address supplies a text, a Proclamation, from which the engine of Reform derives a lot of its continuing energy.[23]

In her claims of the Christian nature of the market and individual freedom, Thatcher was not saying anything new – what was different was the time and context in which she was saying it. The fact was that Margaret Thatcher's protestations on the Christian basis of the free economy, or her attacks on atheistic Marxism were now much less palatable than they had been a decade earlier, given that the neo-liberal experiment was now in full swing and the communist threat was beginning to wane.

A politician lecturing on the *real* meaning of Christianity to a religious gathering was politically bold, preaching this message to the Scottish General Assembly was political suicide. It had been written by a Welsh Baptist-turned-Anglican, was delivered by an English Methodist-turned-Anglican to a gathering of Scottish Presbyterians, and thus the potential of wandering into cultural insensitivities was there from the start. The fact that Thatcher ended up quoting from the Anglican rather than the Scottish hymnody did not help matters either; religious ministers tend to notice such slips. To the shipbuilders of the Clyde, the redundant miners and the Glaswegian poor, the message seemed callous and cold.

Writing to *The Scotsman* afterwards, one woman suggested that Mark 4:25 was the most appropriate scriptural explanation for Thatcherism: 'Whoever has, to him will be given more and whoever does not have, even what he has will be taken away from him.' From that moment, Scottish political identity, both its socialist and nationalist mutations, would position itself in direct opposition to Thatcherite individualism, as Scots became convinced that only self-governance would save them from this alien creed. It did not matter if Scotland was the home of the Enlightenment and Smith's *Wealth of Nations* (a point Thatcher repeatedly made); this was no longer how the nation wished to view itself.

Margaret Thatcher was despised in Scotland as much as that other English conqueror Oliver Cromwell, who incidentally had made a similar plea to the General Assembly against its support for Charles I: 'I beseech you, in the bowels of Christ, think it possible you may be mistaken.' Then, the Scots' reply had been emphatic: 'Would you have us to be sceptics in our religion?' The response in 1988 was much the same. On finishing her speech, the Prime Minister was handed a copy of *Just Sharing: A Christian Approach to the Distribution of Wealth, Income and Benefits*, a report by the Church of Scotland that advocated heavy taxation of the rich and a revived Beveridge Report for the poor, by Moderator Dr James Whyte. The muffled chuckles were soon drowned out by courteous applause.

The Church of England's Board of Social Responsibility issued an open letter in which it begrudgingly thanked the Prime Minister for 'giving time and thought to matters of Christian faith' before putting a red pen to her entire speech. In rather sexist and patronising remarks, the Anglican Bishop of St Andrews slammed Thatcher's 'unsophisticated' theology, which he thought came across as 'the laywoman's use of the Bible with a vengeance'.[24] The Catholic Cardinal Hume chose not to make a public statement: 'I already have to deal with one leader who thinks they're infallible,' he remarked to his aides.

The address caused such a monumental row that Thatcher understandably went off talking about her faith in public. She did, however, support an initiative by Michael Alison (then chairman of Parliament's Christian Fellowship and Second Church Estates Commissioner) of a dialogue between Christians and Conservatives, which resulted in a collection of essays: *Are Christianity and Conservatism Compatible?* (The answer, unsurprisingly, was the affirmative).[25] And in an unexpected stroke in November 1988, the Prime Minister summoned seven selected Anglican prelates to a private meeting at Chequers. Runcie had been reluctant, but fearing that any slight would further sour relations agreed to drive up to Chequers with a carload of his bishops. The prelates were ushered into the drawing room and lined up like body dummies in a shooting range ready for the Prime Minister to take a pop. She first honed in on the Bishop of Oxford, Richard Harries who remembers:

> I came across the room and she held out her hand to greet me and she said, 'Ah, yes, the Bishop of Oxford. I listen to you on the radio. Sometimes I agree with you and sometimes you make me mad.'
>
> And then she asked me what I would like to drink and I said unthinkingly, 'I think I'll have some Perrier water, please.'
>
> 'We only serve British water here,' she replied.
>
> At lunch, Runcie took charge and began chronicling the problems his clergy faced in the inner cities. 'Well, Archbishop, I don't think it's quite like that,' she retorted. Thatcher then launched into a speech on the harmony between Christianity and individual liberty. Mid-way through the Bishop of Chester, a rather polite, unassuming evangelical, piped up: 'I'm afraid you misunderstand, Prime Minister. Christianity is not about freedom, it is about love.' The interjection barely interrupted her flow. Although the meeting ended in joint prayer, it had not been a meeting of minds.[26]

II. Is there a Gospel for the rich?

THE CHURCH MAY have spent most of the 1980s clinging to outdated political consensus, but what, if anything, did it have to say on the new market economy and the Thatcher boom? In short, not a lot that was positive. 'To return to the ethics of nineteenth-century entrepreneurial individualism', declared the Bishop of Durham in the Hibbert Lecture broadcast on BBC's Radio 4 in 1985, 'is either nostalgic nonsense or else a firm declaration that individual selfishness and organised greed are the only motivations for human behaviour.'[27] Even in the height of the Lawson boom, his views clearly had not changed. In a radio interview broadcast on Easter Sunday, Jenkins offered an unequivocal statement that the government's social and economic policies were 'wicked' and a year later, denounced the government's proposals to introduce an 'internal market' into the NHS, as 'sheer fraud'.[28]

In 1988 Margaret Thatcher pledged that a 'wealthy nation would be a giving nation' and in the Budget of that year Chancellor Lawson committed to this pledge by lowering the high income tax rate from 60 per cent to 40 per cent and cutting the basic rate. Initiatives such as the Payroll-Giving Scheme also gave credibility to the Conservatives' new idea of the 'active citizen', which Margaret Thatcher hoped would counter any accusations that she had bred a nation of materialistic yuppies. 'For every Pharisee our system produces, you will find at least three Good Samaritans,' Thatcher enthused at the Conservative Party conference in 1989.[29]

But the Church was sceptical and for good reason. The culture of charitable giving had certainly changed in the '80s although this had little to do with Lawson's tweaking of the tax system. In the first instance, causes became more visible as national organisations increasingly looked to professional agencies for their advertising campaigns; these budgets leapt eight-fold from 1977 to 1989. Meanwhile, those public institutions and organisations that had seen their public budgets cut now employed a great deal of energy into attracting wealthy donors and corporate sponsorship.[30] Charities became more politicised too. Taking their lead from secular pressure-group politics, Christian organisations soon added lobbying and engagement to existing remedial work and fundraising. Many believed that if the Thatcher government really wanted to help charities, it could do so by making charitable donations exempt from tax and reforming the existing Charities Act, which allowed for the advancement of religion and the relief of poverty but forbade political campaigning.

The government was never likely to consent on the latter, even though its policies had been one of the main reasons why charities devoted so much of their energy in the political sphere.

Britons now channelled their monies into national, media-driven, celebrity-endorsed causes such as Band Aid or Children In Need rather than into local or smaller charities; although even in this, there was evidence of 'donor fatigue' by the end of the decade. A survey conducted by the Charities Aid Foundation in 1989 revealed that those who gave the most were committed Christians – as had always been the case – although these donors came not from the prosperous south but were disproportionately located in Northern Ireland, Scotland and the north of England, i.e. those areas which had benefited least from the Thatcher boom.

Responding to Lawson's Budget of 1988, religious leaders in Manchester organised a campaign to persuade the public to donate their extra income to the NHS. As the Bishop of Manchester explained in a lengthy letter to the *Church Times*, individual giving was not 'morally superior to action in the political field, which is absolutely vital – and often far more effective'. Drawing on the Hunger Marchers' slogan from the 1930s, he concluded, 'Damn your charity, we want justice.'[31] David Sheppard put it even more decisively in a speech to his Diocesan Synod the following year: 'Charity,' he affirmed, 'is discriminate and dictated by preferences or prejudices, whereas indiscriminate contribution through taxation is a greater example of collective giving and "belonging to one body".'[32] In an age when marathon telethon charity appeals could generate £24 million in twenty-four hours (equal to the annual budget of a local authority), it was the Anglican bishops who spoke of the limitations of giving and proclaimed the spiritual superiority of progressive taxation over charity.[33] To Conservatives, though, Sheppard's characterisation of donating as a demonstration of 'private prejudices' was yet further confirmation that Church leaders were reading from a different Gospel.

Competition, profit and interest were dirty words to churchmen, which they tended to dismiss outright as encouraging human sin, possessive individualism and debasing relationships and values in society. This portrayal of wealth, materialism and the market as an unsavoury and ungodly business was hardly a novel position for Christians. Throughout the nineteenth and twentieth centuries, the Church had offered no effective retort to Adam Smith's positive notion of the 'natural order' as Christians withdrew into speaking about the ill effects of industrialisation and the market rather than offering a framework in which economic forces should operate.[34] Martin Wiener, in his highly influential book *English Culture and the Decline of the Industrial Spirit: 1850–1980*, which traced the hostility to industrialisation and wealth creation amongst the English literary elite from the mid-nineteenth century, singled out Tawney and Temple in particular as reflective of what he called the 'moralistic and anti-materialistic radicalism' predominant within Christianity.[35]* Anglicans, though, had embraced this tradition with fresh intensity in the era of neo-liberalism and the growth of multinational corporations and the globalisation of the financial markets. Like their predecessors, modern Christians were much more willing to talk about the challenges of being poor rather than rich and of the redistribution of wealth rather than its creation. The problem was that Anglicans appeared to speak as if they wished global finance could simply be undone, rather than actually engage with what was fast becoming Britain's most important sector. This did not go unnoticed by the Director General of the Institute of Directors, Peter Morgan, who in a speech in 1990 echoed Wiener's critique of the 'anti-industrial spirit' in Britain and pinpointed the contemporary Church as one of its main offenders:

> The enterprise culture is an alien concept for the established church. It takes no pleasure in wealth creation ... They hope that the '80s will prove to have been a nasty one-off experience which can be set aside in the '90s. In the meantime they have deployed all the propaganda methods at their disposal – the classroom, the pulpit, the press, the stage and

broadcasting channels – to characterise the '80s as a decade of greed, to brand the successful as materialistic, and to denigrate individualism. For them the distribution of wealth is a noble activity – creating wealth is mucky and squalid.[36]

When Margaret Thatcher and others criticised the Church for its anti-materialist and anti-industrial spirit, they did so with some justification. The Church had very little to say that was constructive on the acquisition of money, while Christians engaged in business tended to be cast as either 'corrupt or naive'.[37] Professions, lifestyles and choices were divided into those that encouraged altruism and social duty and those characterised by selfishness and a lack of integrity. There was no sense that a merchant banker could have the same calling as a teacher or a doctor or, perhaps more importantly, that chaplains should be positioned in banks as they were in prisons, hospitals or schools (which in hindsight might have been a good idea).[38] No Church leader took seriously Home Office Minister John Patten's call in 1989 for the Church of England to conceive a theology 'appropriate for the climate of success that we have in Britain in the late 1980s'.[39] This is perhaps understandable, but nor did they listen to affluent Anglicans' frequent complaints that the Church was ignoring their spiritual concerns: 'May I remind the Synod that ... the Gospel is for rich and poor?' reprimanded one lay member during the debate over the urban poverty report *Faith in the City*.[40] For Rev. Malcolm Grundy, this question was central to the future of the Church and its prophecy: 'If the principal Christian denominations cannot affirm the ways in which most people in this country earn their living, then is there any surprise that God is seen as an optional interest on the edge of life?'[41]

Too often the dialogue between economists and theologians resulted in what Rev. John Atherton called 'the dialogue of the deaf'. Christian Conservatives and neo-liberals tended to dismiss Christian social commentary as either 'socialist' or 'outdated' while church leaders and

theologians failed to acknowledge that their criticisms of capitalism were
to a large degree part of the reality of living in an advanced Western
economy. Some attempt at dialogue was orchestrated by the Church's
Board for Social Responsibility in 1986, which brought together Brian
Griffiths, Lord Harris and theologian John Atherton. Harris, clearly in
no mood for compromise, dismissed clerics such as David Sheppard, for
propagating a 'socialist testament', while remarking that the Church's
failure to engage with the market was down to a misappropriation of
blame on the system rather than the individual: 'How can the fat man
in the restaurant blame his own obesity on the waiter?'[42] Harris thought
that the Church had a legitimate role in elevating individual human
conduct, but nothing of any value to say on the economic system with
which the individual engaged. John Atherton was prepared to admit
some of the shortcomings within Christian theology on economics, but
pointed to the flaws of Griffiths's own concept of a Christian social market, particularly on inequality, which Atherton maintained was contrary
to the Christian notion of fellowship. The problem was an unwillingness
on either side to concede on two crucial points: Christian theologians
seemed unprepared to admit that laissez-faire capitalism had historically
raised thousands out of poverty and was now the reality, while economic
liberals seemed reluctant to admit that the capitalist system had a ruthless ability to marginalise people out of the market place. It was indeed
a 'dialogue of the deaf'.

In an essay written in 1985, political philosopher and Anglican
Raymond Plant was sceptical about what was precisely 'theological'
about the Church's prophecy, which, in his view, amounted to a simplistic reinforcement of more powerful and complex political theories:

> It is not clear what the Church is adding, for example, to a theory of
> redistributative justice of its own, and one is left with the despair of feel-
> ing that one is looking for the odd bit of theological backing for one's
> political preferences which are held on quite other grounds.[43]

This was a critique that probably Enoch Powell, Maurice Cowling, Margaret Thatcher or even Hensley Henson would have agreed. Plant's contention was that whereas the New Right thinking had an 'internal coherence', the Christian social thought countering it was theologically and politically weak.[44] This was a point that Archbishop Runcie was eventually to concede. In his last Synod as Primate, Runcie admitted that although the Church had been 'saying important things' in the 1980s, it could be accused of 'framing them in the sort of collectivist language which has been thought to be discredited ... I cannot emphasise and agree with that enough.'[45] The Methodists came to a similar conclusion. At a meeting on the ethics of wealth creation in 1991, John Kennedy spoke plainly: 'We bring embarrassingly little to modern debate, and tend to struggle behind it, adjusting our alleged insights, pumping up our supposed visions, and rewriting our tradition in ways that might have made Stalin blush.'[46]

One of the deficiencies of social Anglicanism in the 1980s was its refusal to accept that those on the right were also arguing from a legitimate biblical basis. Christian Conservative commentators were indeed right when they spoke of the intolerance of liberal Anglicanism. It was this tendency to project theo-political values as undeniable biblical truths, while at the same time completely dismissing alternative political theologies, which so incensed Margaret Thatcher, Conservative Anglican voters and the wider traditional Anglican movement in the 1980s. The New Right could be criticised for being overly optimistic and complacent about the free market and unwilling to pay due attention on the need for constraints and regulation, but the Church could be equally criticised for not recognising the positive benefits of competition and the free economy. For all this talk about the morality of capitalism, the question that neither the Church nor the New Right sufficiently addressed was whether the answer for regulating the free market lay at an individual, corporate or state level: a glaring oversight, which would later become all too apparent.

III. Shalom, Prime Minister!

RELATIONS BETWEEN THE Church of England and the Conservative Party may have soured in the '80s, but there was also evidence that a new religious–political alliance had forged between the Conservative Party and British Jewry. Between 1955 and 1980 there had been only two Jewish Conservative MPs (both with inherited titles) but by 1987 this had increased to sixteen, far more than on the Labour benches. Outside the parliamentary party, there was a notable Jewish presence at the Centre for Policy Studies, with the likes of Alfred Sherman, Keith Joseph, Lord Young and retail businessman Stanley Kalms. In fact, Joseph was anxious that the CPS might be cast as a Jewish pressure group, which was one of the reasons why he appointed millionaire Nigel Vinson as its treasurer. The presence of Nigel Lawson, Michael Howard, Leon Brittan and David Young filling the top posts prompted Harold Macmillan to famously declare that there were more 'Estonians than Etonians' in the Cabinet, while Tory journalist Peregrine Worsthorne went so far as to dub Judaism as the 'New Creed of Thatcherite Britain'.[47] Margaret Thatcher never hid her admiration for the Jewish community (necessary given that her constituency in Finchley had a significant Jewish population), yet this new alliance was not simply down to prime ministerial favouritism or political expediency, rather it was a consequence of the social and political evolution of British Jewry in the post-war period. In short, the answer was economic rather than religious.

A small but influential band of Anglo-Jewish elites had always aligned themselves with the Conservative Party but the Jewish immigrants who came to Britain via Eastern Europe and Russia at the turn of the twentieth century were disproportionately low-skilled workers who initially aligned themselves to the Liberal Party and subsequently Labour in the wake of the former's demise. The Conservative Party, with its associations with hierarchy, establishment and privilege, was never likely to attract working-class Jewish support, especially given the suspicion that anti-Semitism always lurked beneath the surface. The 1905 Aliens Act (a law chiefly to restrict Jewish immigration) and Moseley's Black Shirts were not too distant memories while the widespread riots in 1947 that followed the murder of two British soldiers by Zionist paramilitaries in Palestine demonstrated how easily anti-Semitism could still be aroused.

As a child, Keith Joseph's Jewishness was felt to be enough of a social barrier that his father, one-time Lord Mayor of London, made the conscious decision not to give him a bar mitzvah. This shift from a culture of suspicion and alienation to top ministerial rank in the Conservative Party is not to be underestimated and was as radical a development as the election of a female leader.

Not without evidence did Margaret Thatcher herald the Jewish community as the embodiment of her 'upwardly mobile' values. In one generation, Anglo-Jews rose from working-class tradesmen of the East End slums to professional middle-class men of the suburbs. In the late '80s, Jewish Labour MP Leo Abse penned a scathing attack of what he termed the 'yuppie Jew' with their materialistic values and self-serving charitable endeavours: 'the only battles that can command their attention are the takeover struggles of the company boardrooms', he wrote.[48] Abse's accusation that British Jewry had become dislocated from its traditional identity, roots and left-wing politics (in Abse's mind all interchangeable things) concealed his actual frustration at what was now a fact: the Jewish vote had turned blue. But Anglo-Jewish embourgeoisement was not the only reason for its distancing from the left. Important, too, was the increasingly anti-Israeli position of the Labour Party in the wake of the Six Day War in 1967 and, moreover, Jewish unwillingness to associate itself with the restrictive model of multiculturalism, which had become Labour's default position by the 1970s. The lumping together of minorities' interest was problematic for all concerned, but especially for British Jewry, which had evolved out of an earlier understanding of assimilation rather than difference. 'To show sympathy to the Black community may be a principle,' wrote the *Jewish Tribune* in 1978 at the height of National Front fervour, 'but is this principle so pure and important that it is worth jeopardising the security of the Jewish public?'[49]

In January 1978, Margaret Thatcher broke with the bi-partisan consensus on immigration and, in a direct follow-up to Enoch Powell's 'Rivers of Blood' speech, legitimised popular anguish in a television interview by making it clear that a vote for the Conservatives would mean tighter restrictions. Thatcher attracted wide criticism for her inflammatory use of the term 'swamped' but she leapt ahead in the polls. Weeks later, in the crucial by-election in Ilford North, Keith Joseph delivered a targeted message to Jewish constituents, urging them to support the party's policy on immigration. The Conservatives won the seat with support from the Jewish community (an 11.2 per cent rise in support) having been crucial. A year later, in the 1979 general election, the Tories experienced their biggest swing in precisely those outer north London seats where the Jewish community resided.

Margaret Thatcher's seat of Finchley then had the largest Jewish contingency in Britain, representing approximately 20 per cent of residents. Thatcher had proved herself adept at winning the Jewish vote from her very first campaign in 1959, when she faced down a challenge from the Liberals who were then capitalising on accusations of anti-Semitism at the local Tory-dominated golf club. Never one to take her seat for granted, Margaret Thatcher continued to nurture links with her Jewish constituents. She frequently addressed synagogues, was on first-name terms with the local rabbis and was president of her local branch of the Anglo-Israel Friendship League. One young Finchley resident and enthusiastic politics student, Jonathan Sacks, the future

Chief Rabbi, went to interview his local MP for his school project on Proportional Representation. Thatcher immediately questioned his motives. 'You're not a Liberal are you?' was her initial salvo.[50]

Margaret Thatcher once remarked that 'Israel is not a Sparta, but an Athens'.[51] It has been said that not since Winston Churchill had the Conservatives elected a leader more committed to the State of Israel. Thatcher first visited in 1965 and was apparently impressed with what she saw: 'They don't pay people for being idle in Israel,' she told the Anglo-Israel Friendship League on her return.[52] She visited again in 1972 where she had an audience with Israeli Prime Minister Golda Meir. Clearly keen to be associated with Meir (incidentally, the first female leader to be given the title the 'Iron Lady') Thatcher described the meeting as 'one tough nut visiting another tough nut'.[53]

Thatcher was one of the few British politicians to openly endorse Israel's controversial new borders after the Six Day War, and in what would be the only time that she rebelled against Edward Heath, opposed her government's policy of neutrality during the Yom Kippur War in 1973 and, along with Keith Joseph, publicly spoke out against Heath's refusal to provide Israel with military support. When she became leader in 1975, Thatcher's pro-Israel sympathies were pronounced enough to raise concerns amongst Foreign Office diplomats. One embassy official in Jordan related his fears that Thatcher might be perceived as 'prisoner of the Zionists' by the Arab world and advised her to sever all links with the 'Conservative Friends of Israel' (the parliamentary group of which she had been a founder) and even consider swapping Finchley for the safe Tory seat of Westminster.[54] In these days of heightened tensions in the Middle East, where the politics of oil and the Cold War were proving a toxic combination, the new Leader of the Opposition, with little experience in diplomacy, was being instructed to tread a careful line.

As Prime Minister, Thatcher's relationship with Israel was inevitably more complicated, given that it tended to be curtailed by Foreign Office pragmatism and American leadership. Admiring of its democracy as a bulwark against Soviet influence in the Middle East, she was extremely vocal in her support for the persecuted Soviet Jews (so too was Ronald Reagan) and, in 1986, became the first serving Prime Minister to visit Israel. But she was not an uncritical friend. She publicly opposed Israel's war with Lebanon in 1982 (she controversially compared it to the Argentinian invasion of the Falklands) and the following year objected to former Irgun fighter Eliyahu Lankin's appointment as Israeli ambassador to the UK because of his terrorist past. She always supported a settlement with the Palestinians, and could be partly credited for persuading Reagan to enter into diplomatic talks with the PLO in the final years of his administration.

Much more striking than Thatcher's relationship with Israel was her identification with the Jewish faith. Frequently, Thatcher would allude to the shared characteristics between the Methodism of her youth and Jewish values of family, self-help and hard work. She would repeatedly refer to what she termed 'Judaeo-Christian values', which she applied to anything from capitalism and democracy to British culture. This was a relatively modern phrase (more widely used in America than in Britain), referring to the shared characteristics of the two Testaments, but its modern usage more accurately reflected the collaborative spirit of the post-Holocaust age. According to Thatcher, though, it had a more specific meaning. Explaining her specific understanding in her memoirs, she noted that her 'whole political philosophy' was based on 'Judaeo-Christian values', with the Old Testament providing the 'history of the law' and the New Testament the 'history of mercy'.[55] Doctrinal unity aside, Thatcher certainly felt a personal affinity with a group that was socially mobile and not part of the establishment. It is true to say that anti-Semitism has always been less evident amongst Nonconformists than other Christian denominations, possibly because both historically had been marked as outsiders in British society. But Thatcher's linkage with Judaism was to a large degree down to one man, the Chief Rabbi, Immanuel Jakobovits, whom Peregrine Worsthorne

considered, the 'spiritual leader of Thatcherite Britain'.[56] As Chief
Rabbi of the United Hebrew Congregations of the Commonwealth,
Jakobovits had a higher public profile than any of his predecessors
although casting him as representative of the whole of British Jewry
is, of course, rather like saying that the Pope is representative of the
Christian Church. Certainly, there was a degree of personal rapport
between Margaret Thatcher and Jakobovits, but it was his critical
response to *Faith in the City* that most endeared him to the Prime
Minister. In his pamphlet *From Doom to Hope*, published in 1986,
the Chief Rabbi posited that 'cheap labour' was 'more dignified than
a free dole' and that community responsibility was morally superior
to collective taxation and state aid.[57] He also gave a necessary nod to
self-discipline, hard work and the acquisition of wealth, while at the
same time lambasted union militancy and a dependency culture as a
denial of responsibility. Margaret Thatcher was clearly delighted with
this endorsement and swiftly elevated him to the House of Lords. He
was the first Chief Rabbi to be granted such an honour, which was a
milestone in itself, although Thatcher probably hoped that his presence would prove an effective antidote to the Anglican bishops in the
chamber. (Jakobovits in fact always sat on the cross benches.)

Jakobovits's sentiments may have succeeded in impressing the Prime
Minister, but they provoked consternation from those within the Jewish community, who neither shared his politics nor his interpretation
of Jewish law. Factionalism within Judaism, it must be said, is as bad,
if not worse, than it is within Anglicanism. Rabbi Dan Cohn-Sherbok
criticised the Chief Rabbi for his reductive take on Jewish ethics, arguing with equal force that Torah was one of liberation and social justice
with the prophets the conscience arousers of their day. Jonathan Sacks,
however, pointed to the fact that Judaism, unlike Christianity, did not
hold to a notion of the nobility of poverty or paternalism but rather
the shame of poverty and the self-esteem that comes from prosperity.

On the occasion of Jakobovits's retirement in 1991, Thatcher heaped praise on a man whose twenty-four years of leadership had been characterised by an 'unyielding commitment to principle, a refusal to seek easy popularity at the expense of integrity and a fearless statement of values symbolised not just in the life of the Jewish people but of lasting relevance and general application to the modern world'.[58] Tellingly, Margaret Thatcher never lavished such praise on any of her Anglican bishops.

IV. One nation under one God?

IN THE 1980s, the concept of 'Christian Britain' still held currency, though this was now spoken of in terms of heritage and values rather than active worship and faith. Thatcher, in her unashamedly spiritually patriotic flourishes would speak of a nation 'founded on biblical principles' that of 'the acknowledgement of the Almighty, a sense of tolerance, of moral absolutes and a positive view of work'.[59] The truth was, however, that Britain was at the crossroads of its religious identity, neither exclusively Christian, nor fully secular and certainly not 'multi-faith'. Two developments in the late 1980s – the reform of religious education provision and the publication of Salman Rushdie's novel *The Satanic Verses* – would force the government and the Established Church to consider where Britain stood in relation to its Christian past and its multi-faith future.

The 1988 Education Act, which still holds the record for being the longest-debated bill in Parliament, was one of the most controversial pieces of legislation to be passed by the Conservative government. Sold on the notion of extending parental choice and improving standards, it was arguably a centralising measure, which established the National Curriculum and permitted schools to financially 'opt out' of their local education authority. The stipulations regarding RE and the daily act of communal worship had originally been set out in the 1944 Education

Act as the only mandatory subject and part of a school's day. R. A. Butler had implemented this, partly to appease the bishops' fears about Church schools integrating into the state system. The negotiations over religious education forty years later would be a very different, but no less fractious, battle.

No one, especially not the Church, seriously considered that preserving religious education (RE) would halt the decline of Christianity in Britain, although it was appreciated that in an age when children were unlikely to receive religious instruction in the home or in church, school might be the only place where the next generation would encounter the Christian faith. Right-wing educationalists were sceptical of the credibility of RE, but for different reasons. Their main concern was that left-wing teachers were deliberately flouting the 1944 regulations and were indoctrinating children in a multicultural and multi-faith curriculum (what Mary Whitehouse called 'a Cook's Tour of World Religions'), giving rise to a generation who were biblically illiterate and morally ambivalent.[60] Such accusations were no doubt exaggerated and yet few could deny that the teaching of RE had undergone profound change since Butler's Act.

In the 1940s, when 'religion' had been the default word for Christianity, the word Christian was not made explicit. This had allowed for flexibility in the classroom and as Britain became more pluralised and secular in the 1970s, so religious teaching began reflect these changes.

Birmingham council's religious syllabus in 1975 was one such example, yet it caused a stir not for its inclusion of other faiths but for its incorporation of what was termed 'other world views' such as humanism and communism. Birmingham was the exception rather than the rule, however. Much more notable was the move from a prescriptive approach to a more inclusive teaching of religion: symbolised in the renaming of 'Religious Instruction' to 'Religious Education'. But, for right-wing educationalists, RE (much like sex education) became the litmus test that exposed the left-wing leanings of the teaching profession and the spiritual and moral ill-health of Britain's youth. In a pamphlet entitled *The Crisis of Religious Education*, cross-bench peer and educationalist Baroness Cox encapsulated the fears of many when she forewarned that Britain was in danger of 'selling' its 'spiritual birth right for a mess of secular pottage'. In sentiments she hoped might convince the Education Secretary, Kenneth Baker, Cox pointed to the teaching of those ideologies in schools, which denied 'human freedom, human responsibility and the reality of sin'. In a coded appeal to the government, Cox maintained that Christian teaching was necessary for the revival of the nation's 'entrepreneurial spirit'.[61]

Kenneth Baker was already knee-deep in a fight with councils and teachers over the right to opt out, and the contents of the curriculum, and was in no mood for a tussle with right-wing Christian groups and the Church over the provision of RE. Baker, himself a devout Anglican, initially showed little interest in RE and was more concerned with making sure that the education policy reflected the Thatcherite goal of creating a generation fully equipped for the free-market economy, with City Technology Colleges his pet project. Hence, when the proposals for the National Curriculum were announced, RE was not included: 'they must recover their position themselves. I can't do it for them,' Baker told *The Times*.[62]

Baker's difficulty was that the inclusion of RE in the newly centralised curriculum would mean that its content, like other subjects, would have to be decided by a secular body, the National Curriculum Council, which was far from ideal and a ruling that the churches were unlikely to agree to. And yet, as opposers rightly argued, its complete omission would inevitably lead to a demotion of its prime place in schools. Religious representatives, however, carried considerable weight within the Department of Education, especially the determined and redoubtable Graham Leonard, the Bishop of London, who, in his role as head of the Church's Board of Education, eventually managed to carve out a worthy compromise with Baker whereby RE would be included as part of the compulsory curriculum but accorded special status. RE content would be in the hands of local syllabus bodies made up of representatives from all faiths but dominated by an Anglican presence. The Church of England rightly considered this a victory for the preservation of RE, Christianity and all faiths in schools.

Right-wing educationalists, however, were not content to leave the responsibility of RE to local syllabus bodies; a fact which reveals as much about their faith in local autonomy as it does about the Church of England. Baroness Cox, backed up with an impressive band of Tory heavyweights, whom Leonard dubbed the 'Tribe' and which included ex-party chairman Lord Thorneycroft and former Prime Minister Alec Douglas-Home, proposed an amendment to the bill stipulating that teaching should be predominantly Christian. Margaret Thatcher had reportedly been briefed by Brian Griffiths to support the Cox amendment and chose the occasion of her sermon to the Church of Scotland to publicly endorse it.

While Leonard was not opposed in principle to Cox's amendment, he did consider it as an unwelcome intrusion onto the Church's terrain and a subversion of the proper consultation process. Those in Lambeth Palace saw it slightly differently, with Runcie's assistant, John Lyttle, concerned that it put the Church in a dilemma between appeasing 'Christian dogmatics' and recognising 'multi-faith Britain'.[63] While Cox and her followers tended to associate 'multi-faith' unfavourably with secular left-wing multiculturalism, there was evidence that some within the Church were beginning to see an alliance of all faiths as the most effective bulwark against secularism. Recognising the multi-faith nature of Britain, be it in education or in any sphere, was now considered to be one of the Church of England's prime duties. It was beginning to look though as if the bishops might *oppose* an amendment that *strengthened* Christianity. Pressure mounted on the Bishop of London, not only from Cox and her supporters, but also from the Synod. 'If we are not careful,' wrote one lay member in a letter to Leonard, '"Karma" and "Koran" will be as, or more, familiar than "Messiah" and "epistle".'[64]

Thatcher pressed the Bishop of London to broker a compromise on which all could agree. This Leonard duly did and, crucially, gained the support of leading Catholic peer Duke of Norfolk, Methodist Lord Soper and the Chief Rabbi, Lord Jakobovits. Leonard's amendment, which had been based on the regulations then in place for religious broadcasting, stipulated that RE teaching and the daily act of worship should reflect the fact that 'the religious traditions in Great Britain are in the main Christian, whilst taking into account the teaching and practices of other principal religions represented in Great Britain'. Leonard's amendment was not wildly different from what had previously been proposed by Cox, but, crucially, it had come at the initiative of the Established Church and had the full support of other faiths. The Islamic community were perhaps the least enthusiastic, despite reassurances that the curriculum would be modified in Muslim-populated areas. Their chief grievance, however, was not over religious education but the Tory government's persistent refusal to allow Islamic state schools: a privilege that had long been granted to Britain's other religious minorities.

'A government which has done its best to ignore the problems of falling school rolls now appears set to try and halt falling church rolls,' was how *The Guardian* saw the new RE stipulations.[65] But this was neither true nor was it the outcome. Like Section 28, the religious aspects of the 1988 Education Act had very little to do with what was appropriate for the classroom: an Ofsted report conducted five years later revealed that few schools actually adhered to the law, especially the daily act of Christian worship. Rather, it was the legislative outcome of a debate chiefly between Conservatives and the Church as to how best to maintain Britain's Christian identity. When confronted with the choice of either completely secularising curriculum content, adopting a pluralist approach or reasserting the primacy of Christianity, Parliament chose the latter, albeit with certain caveats. It too showed the continuing influence of the Established Church in the sphere of education although Roman Catholics were equal in their opposition to the bill, particularly on the parental influence in school governance. More profoundly, the 1988 Act had revealed that the main obstacle was not secularism, but the accommodation of other faiths, and was thus an indication of much bigger problems to come.

When viewed alongside the other demonstrators of the 1980s – Brixton rioters of 1981, the colliery picketers of 1984–5 or the poll-tax rebels in Trafalgar Square in 1990 – the book-burners outside Bradford Town Hall in 1989 burning their copies of Salman Rushdie's *Satanic Verses* in protest appeared wildly out of context. Nor did they appear to share much in common with campaigners such as Mary Whitehouse's NVLA, who were also engaged in a fight against religious offence. The widespread outrage and violence sparked by the publication of Salman Rushdie's novel in 1988, not just in Britain but also across the world, felt like an aberration, with the religious hysteria on display seemed out of sync with the modern age. In these pre-9/11 days no one had yet realised that it would be Islam rather than communism which would become the battleground for Western culture. The book burning, which incidentally had to be re-staged for the press photographers, was obviously an offence to liberal sensitivities, but it was Ayatollah Khomeini's fatwa that ultimately escalated what was a legitimate grievance into mass hysteria on both sides.

Up until the publication of the *Satanic Verses* controversy, Britain's second largest religious minority had been a largely silent, ill-organised force. If the furore surrounding the publication had any lasting consequence, it was in the way in which it mobilised the Muslim community in the public sphere. While some chose illegitimate and even violent tactics to get the book banned, the UK Action Committee on Islamic Affairs (UKACIA), in part out of a desire to contain the more radical elements, pursued legal means. It soon found, though, that they had little means of legal redress other than to take the route paved by Mary Whitehouse a decade earlier – to push to have Rushdie tried under the Blasphemy Act. After a lengthy legal process, the UKACIA lost a high-court ruling, which affirmed that the existing Blasphemy Act only protected the Anglican faith. Although few recognised it at the time, UKACIA's failed legal bid cast an exposing light on Britain's model of secular multiculturalism. Sociologist Tariq Modood has correctly judged that the Rushdie affair was a crucial turning point, in that it put the spotlight on long-held Muslim grievances and revealed the failures of the existing multicultural legislation. In demographic terms, Britain had become a multi-faith nation in the early 1970s, and yet it was not until the late 1980s that the religious (rather than racial) dimensions of this social change were addressed. As Modood has argued, diversity and legislative protection policy up until that point had been conceptualised around a racial (and secular) framework, underscored by a white/black dualism, which completely overlooked the notion of religious identity.[66] Secular multiculturalism, therefore, could (and indeed did) co-exist quite happily alongside the continual prioritisation of Christianity in law. The shortcomings of this situation were blatantly exposed by the Rushdie affair, for it revealed the lack of legal redress for the nation's second largest religious minority, the limitations of multiculturalism and the problems concerning the privileged place for Christianity on the statute book in a secular plural nation.

In seeking to try Rushdie for blasphemy, the UK Action Committee on Islamic Affairs had sought legitimate means through the courts but had found that they had few forms of redress or even alliances in the political or legal sphere. The Home Secretary, Douglas Hurd, consistently refused pleas for an extension of the Blasphemy Act to include non-Christian faiths. This was not out of any commitment to the existing law but because Hurd considered the Rushdie case as one concerning freedom of expression and foresaw the potential legal difficulties in establishing the appropriate boundaries for religious offence.[67] These were perfectly rational reasons, although subsequent utterances by Hurd and his junior minister, John Patten, questioning the loyalty and 'Britishness' of the Muslim community, also suggested that the Home Office saw the problem as Muslim unwillingness to assimilate into British society. The Labour Party meanwhile was divided: those MPs with constituencies in Muslim areas understandably advocated the right to protest, but the majority fell into line with liberal opinion in defending the author.

The debate over changes in the blasphemy law had been debated long before Rushdie had even begun the first draft of his novel. In the early '80s an Ecclesiastical Committee headed by the Bishop of London had recommended to the Law Commission that the common law offence of blasphemy should be abolished and replaced with a law of religious offence protecting all religions. Calls for reform had largely been inspired by Whitehouse's successful case against *Gay News* – the first prosecution for blasphemy for fifty years – which had left the Anglican hierarchy more than a little embarrassed and the Law Commission pressing for change. The Church's proposals aimed to scrap the idea of blasphemy in respect of God and to legislate on 'religious offence' in order to protect believers; legalisation they justified as necessary in a plural society. The Law Commission instead advocated that the Blasphemy Act be abolished and not replaced. The government, however, failed to initiate any changes as the Blasphemy Act remained intact. It was to prove a fatal mistake.

When the furore erupted, Archbishop Runcie recognised that the book was unlikely to be banned but thought it wise to legitimise Muslim complaints. The Church of England's aim was to stand shoulder-to-shoulder with Islamic leaders, which it did chiefly by setting up an Anglican–Muslim consultation party to consider a reformulation of the Blasphemy Act.[68] Andrew Brown of *The Independent* was unimpressed and mocked the Church's naivety: 'There is no better and more effective way of disarming a potential book-burner than to take him to tea at Lambeth Palace and draw him into endless Anglican conversation.'[69] Brown's comments, though, were a little unfair. The fact was that Muslim groups welcomed the archbishop's invitation especially at a time when the press, the political and legal establishment

and secular intelligentsia were so hostile. The same was true in Brad-
·ford, where the local bishop, Robert Williamson, while condemning
the tactics of the protestors and the legitimacy of the fatwa, struck
a cohesive chord by bringing religious leaders and police together to
help ease tensions.

The Rushdie controversy came to be seen as one of British liberal
values versus an uncompromising and un-British Islamic fundamentalism, but this concealed what was actually happening; a growing
dualism between the sacred and the secular in a plural democracy.
This was only reinforced when the Chief Rabbi, inter-faith forums and
the Roman Catholics also backed the right of religious offence. The
Satanic Verses controversy directly challenged both liberal tolerance
and Christian privilege, but it became less about the latter and more
about the former as the debate developed into one about the rights
and recognition of the sacred in a secular liberal country.

The Church's new position, as *primus inter pares* on a multi-faith
platform, had the effect of reinforcing rather than undermining the
notion of establishment. As Bishop John Habgood explained in a letter to *The Independent* in the wake of the Rushdie affair, the Church
of England was necessary precisely because it acted as a protector
and enabler of religious pluralism within the nation.[70] The rationale
behind establishment was being reconfigured once more; the Church
of England was no longer the spiritual head of a nominally Christian
nation (as Habgood had argued in the early 1980s), but the chief
religious representative in a secular plural society. There were obvious problems and contradictions with this position, especially as it
rested on a notion of Anglican dominance, but rather surprisingly
it was not challenged by other faiths. The Islamic cause for equality
before the law did not start with disestablishment as previous struggles by religious minorities had done. The main obstacle to Islamic
integration was secularism not Christianity, for in the words of Tariq
Modood:

The minimal nature of the Anglican establishment, its relative openness
to other denominations and faiths seeking public space and the fact that
its very existence is an ongoing acknowledgement of the public character of religion are all reasons why it may seem far less intimidating to
minority faiths than a triumphal secularism.[71]

For this reason, Muslims leaders had not called for the abolition but for
the extension of the Blasphemy Act, as the UK Action Committee on
Islamic Affairs put it: 'Abolition would mean negative equalisation.'[72]
Muslims did not seek to undermine all religions by the removal of the
Blasphemy Act, but equal recognition of all faiths through the extension of it; sentiments with which Anglicans broadly agreed. Somewhat
paradoxically, it was now non-Anglicans who were the most eloquent
articulators of establishment religion. None more so than Jonathan
Sacks, then Chief Rabbi-elect, who in his 1990 Reith Lectures, *The
Persistence of Faith*, advocated that in an age of pluralism and division, the Established Church expressed a desire and fulfilled a need
for shared values that was supported by all faiths.

Nevertheless, familiar voices of disquiet could be heard within the
Church of England from those who saw inter-faith dialogue as further
evidence of the secularisation of Anglicanism. Some conservative
Christians saw the Rushdie controversy in slightly different terms,
contrasting the Muslim reaction to Rushdie's book with the muted
response from British Christians to the Martin Scorsese biopic *The
Last Temptation of Christ*, which had been released the same month
as Rushdie's novel. Traditionalist Anglican Rev. Peter Mullen wondered whether the whole Rushdie affair revealed not the intolerance
within Islam but the paucity of sacredness within English Christianity:

Up until fairly recently in England, Christian classic texts were known
by heart in large chunks. In the Muslim faith, children still learn the
Holy Koran in its original language: these words are written not just in

the refined intellect, but in the heart … the words are truly made flesh, incarnated.[73]

Contrasting expressions of faith in the 1980s: the Ayatollah Khomeini and the Church of England's 'unbelieving bishop', the Bishop of Durham

Soon alliances were formed between conservative Anglicans, Catholics, Jews and Muslims. Catholic campaigner Victoria Gillick, for example, was surprised to find that her crusade against contraception had more support from non-Christian faiths than the mainstream Christian denominations. Just as liberal Catholics, Jews, Muslims and Anglicans were engaging in fruitful dialogue, likewise conservative factions within different faiths began to realise that they too had more in common with each other than with liberals within their own faith.

· · ·

THE 1980S WITNESSED three great challenges to England's Christian culture; a fight for the preservation of the Sabbath, an opportunity to abolish or extend the Blasphemy Act and the debate over the Christian content in classrooms. In the cases of blasphemy and

Sunday trading the law remained unchanged and in the case of education it was actually reinforced. Yet this strengthening of the various aspects of Christian culture and law concealed the fact that Britain was a nation in transition. It was a defence born not out of confidence in the nation's Christian identity, but out of a concern for it. A Christian-centric RE curriculum had been fought for in the name of heritage rather than evangelism; the cause against Sunday trading had been fought to protect the 'traditional English Sunday' rather than to preserve worship; and despite calls for reform, the Blasphemy Act was retained not because it was actually believed to be necessary, but out of an unwillingness to extend it to other faiths. What might be called the 'heritage' argument amounted to a post-modern, post-secular preservation of Christianity, one which tacitly recognised its decline as a belief system, but reflected a desire to sustain this tradition rather than fully adapt to the alternative. It might be added that in all three cases, neither Margaret Thatcher nor her ministers were the ones standing up for the preservation of Christian culture; and on Sunday trading, were the ones actually seeking to undermine it.

For a large part of the 1980s, the debate between Margaret Thatcher's government and the Established Church had hinged on the rights and wrongs of capitalism. Any future divide between sacred and temporal power in Britain would largely concern the accommodation of faith in Britain's secular plural society.

CHAPTER EIGHT

HOLY WARRIORS
AND BLESSED
PEACEMAKERS

'My guess is that within a hundred years a non-Marxist government
will be the exception. The Red Flag will fly over most of the globe ...
What should be the reactions of those who hold to the symbol
of the Cross? Hostility or co-operation?'
– RT. REV. MERVYN STOCKWOOD, 1978[1]

'Surely, as free and creative nations, we have the better opportunities and
the more convincing arguments ... Why don't we use them? "Ideological
aggression" simply means that the communists are waging a verbal war
against us. Right – so should we against them.'
– MARGARET THATCHER, 1983[2]

'Men have forgotten God; that's why this has all happened.'
– ALEKSANDR SOLZHENITSYN, 1983[3]

'FOR HER IT was about moral values or it was about nothing,' according to George Urban, the Prime Minister's speechwriter on foreign affairs.[4] There was undoubtedly a moralistic fervour underscoring Thatcher's denouncements of communism, but ultimately the Prime Minister was a mistress of realpolitik in her dealings with the Soviet bloc and, indeed, in all areas of her diplomacy. When it came to tying up the loose ends of empire for example, the Falklands campaign turned out to be the exception rather than the rule. Above all, pragmatism guided the Conservative government's carefully judged settlement of black-majority rule in independent Zimbabwe with Marxist leader Robert Mugabe as its newly elected head. Pragmatism also ruled when it came to the hand-over of Hong Kong to communist China, which Thatcher signed, albeit reluctantly, with few stipulations.

Thatcher's foreign policy has been raked over again and again by historians, but one aspect that is often overlooked is the part that religion played both as a motivation and as a factor in the personalities and policies of 1980s diplomacy. A religious motivation was clearly evident amongst the three key Western leaders – President Reagan, Pope John Paul II and Margaret Thatcher – who all confidently proclaimed that the fight against atheistic communism was a religious one. It was also true, but in a very different way, for the Church of England. Anglicanism had a global reach and network which rivalled that of the Foreign Office which, in certain circumstances, meant that the Church was able to wield influence in places where diplomats could not. Archbishop Runcie's Falklands sermon in 1982, however, had proved that the Church was not willing to endorse any form of Tory nationalism, while it was also clear that it did not fully subscribe to Thatcher's crusading rhetoric on the Cold War. Christians were busy promoting an alternative view on Britain's priorities and place in global politics: leading the fight against poverty in the developing world; marching against nuclear rearmament and pressuring the government to impose sanctions on South Africa.

I. Sacred cause

THE COLD WAR was, first and foremost, an ideological conflict fought predominantly between Moscow and Washington and conditioned as much by domestic concerns as by the battle for global dominance. It was also one in which religion had, from its inception, been a central feature. For the chief protagonists involved, the Cold War was 'one of history's great religious wars, a global conflict between the god-fearing and the godless' in the words of historian Dianne Kirby.[5] In the USSR, religious persecution gathered apace after a lull during the Second World War, and while it was not as aggressive as it had been during the great purges of the 1920s, the suppression of religion was still considered as important as any other state initiative in order to ensure the strength and longevity of the communist cause. In the West, anti-communist posturing was often accompanied with a fanatical tone and biblical endorsement.

As early as 1947, President Truman had made overtures to Pope Pius XII, seeking to forge a united Christian front against communist ideology. This gave rise to a unity of purpose between the Vatican and Washington, which, despite some wobbles, was to last until the end of the Cold War. Truman appropriated Christianity (and co-opted the churches) as part of his plan to elevate the Cold War from a strategic conflict about East/West rivalry to one about ideology. Later, in 1956, President Eisenhower adopted 'In God we Trust' as the official motto of the United States. Displayed on all paper currency, there was no stronger indication of the harmony between the dollar and the cross. American evangelical fervour sat comfortably with Cold War paranoia and was best summed up by leading evangelist and pastor to presidents, Billy Graham: 'When communism conquers a nation, it makes every man a slave; when Christianity conquers a nation, it makes every man a king.'[6]

The Catholic Church had always viewed communism as more of a problem than fascism, which partly explains why Mussolini was able to nuzzle his way into the bosom of the Vatican in the 1930s. The rise of the communist party in Italy after the Second World War, however, was greeted with a wave of paranoia within the Church, and although the party never won a majority, its presence did prompt the Holy See in 1949 to publicly rule that no Catholic should belong, associate or promote communism in any form. This remained the Vatican's hard line until Pope John XXIII, in the wake of the Cuban Missile Crisis, issued *Pacem in Terris* in 1963, which was unequivocal in its rejection of nuclear war as a just act and called for negotiation between nations towards disarmament. Coinciding as this did with the meeting of the second Vatican Council, to which Catholics from the Eastern bloc countries were invited (including Karol Wojtyla, the future Pope John Paul II), it aimed at a consensual approach to guarantee the protection of its churches behind the Iron Curtain.

Britain's post-war leaders were not as bold as their American counterparts, although Winston Churchill, the great articulator of the cause, certainly was not averse to speaking of the threat that communism posed to Western civilisation and Christianity. The same was true for Ernest Bevin, Labour's Foreign Secretary between 1945 and 1951, who considered ramping up the Christian rhetoric an effective way of convincing the Americans that there was a difference between socialism in Britain and communism in the East.[7] In the early years of the Cold War, the Foreign Office was acutely aware of the influence of the churches at home and of their network of contacts abroad, particularly the Church of England with its close ties with the Russian Orthodox Church and the Episcopal Church in America. The Anglican Council on Foreign Relations established a working relationship with the Foreign Office and even had a Whitehall diplomat on its board.

During the early years of the Cold War, the Anglican hierarchy dutifully reinforced the state view of the Soviet aggressor, taking the opportunity of the 1948 Lambeth Conference to issue a forceful condemnation of Marxist ideology. In 1950, Archbishop Fisher established a committee to ascertain the appropriate position of the Church of England on East–West relations, which the Foreign Office ensured was appropriately briefed. Lambeth Palace also monitored those members affiliated with the Society of Socialist Clergy and Ministers. This was no McCarthy-like witch-hunt, rather the Church's approach was to subtly restrict the influence of communist sympathisers and noisy pacifists through lack of preferment. One clergyman who caused a headache for both the Foreign Office and Lambeth Palace was the Very Rev. Hewlett Johnson, known as the 'Red Dean' of Canterbury (who when abroad was often mistaken for the archbishop). A famous apologist of Soviet communism and holder of the Stalin peace prize, Johnson had been under MI5 surveillance since 1917 and had been banned from delivering sermons to troops during the Second World War. The Foreign Office tried to prevent his visit to Eastern Europe in 1947 and it was no coincidence that the Archbishop of York, Cyril Garbett, was sent on an official tour shortly afterwards. What is surprising, though, is not that men such as Hewlett Johnson existed, but that they were allowed to operate so freely.[8]

If the Fisher years saw the Church operating in semi-compliance with the state then it would become more of a critical friend under the leadership of Archbishop Ramsey. Nuclear weapons, from their inception, had been an issue that Anglicans had agonised over and had come to separate conclusions about, but this division became even more acute following the formation of the Campaign for Nuclear Disarmament, founded in 1958, with Canon John Collins of St Paul's as chairman. Many praised the emotionalism and the passion of CND, but those at the top were never attracted by the idealism of a unilateral policy. 'I'm glad that the bulk of the clergy don't spend their time organising a campaign for unilateral nuclear disarmament. I'm sure that there are more important things for them to be doing,' Archbishop Ramsey told *The Economist* in 1964.[9]

The Church of England's official position had not altered since Britain acquired its nuclear capability in the 1950s. No clergyman was likely to declare the use of such weaponry as a just act of war, but most confidently endorsed Britain's status as a nuclear power, which they defended on the not-so-strictly Christian grounds that Britain could be trusted to act responsibly whereas other nations could not. Over an issue on which theological judgement was clouded, most Anglicans adhered to the political consensus.

After the close call of the Cuban Missile Crisis, there followed a calming of tensions in East–West relations, culminating in the signing of the Helsinki Accords in 1975. On the one hand, détente was successful in halting the momentum towards a third world war, but tensions prevailed as the Soviets and the Americans clearly differed in their definitions of what was meant by a policy of accommodation. In the West, a retreat from aggressive posturing was coupled with a new emphasis on shaming the Soviets on their human rights abuses, particularly the persecution of believers. Anyone who read Aleksandr Solzhenitsyn's moving memoir The Gulag Archipelago (published in the West in 1973), with its vivid first-hand accounts of the atrocities and terror in the Soviet prison camps, could not fail to be swayed by the dark portrait it painted of life in the Soviet Union. Those in Washington and London certainly recognised the political capital that such testimonies afforded, particularly as a rebuke to Soviet sympathisers at home.

In the East, religious organisations were still closely monitored as governments executed a twin policy of repression of churches and an ideological affront against Christianity. But it varied from country to country, with Russia being the most aggressive and East Germany the most relaxed. In Poland, the state adopted a heavy hand over the Catholic Church, particularly on the patronage of clergy and bishops, while the youth were subject to scientific materialism lessons in an effort to dislodge the tight grip of Catholicism amongst the populace. In Romania, party officials regulated publications and buildings and sat on church selection boards, often removing those priests who made a nuisance of themselves. Under such circumstances, it is a little wonder there emerged a generation of religious 'yes' men behind the Iron Curtain.[10]

For some in the West, détente was an acknowledgement that communism was a lasting reality and thus needed to be understood. One man who aimed to do just that for a Christian audience was the Bishop of Southwark, Mervyn Stockwood, in his 1978 work *The Cross and the Sickle*, which included a supporting foreword by his former student, the then Foreign Secretary David Owen. Recounting his own tours of Eastern Europe in the 1950s and again in the 1970s, Stockwood praised Romania's Nicolae Ceauşescu as a man of 'exceptional ability and industry' and considered Russia 'a stable society', which was 'gradually reaping some benefits after years of hard work'.[11] If only Christians would go to communist countries themselves, Stockwood reassuringly wrote, 'prejudices would evaporate'.[12] The most striking aspect of the Bishop of Southwark's testimony was not his flattering account of communist rule or his fusing of Christianity with the proletarian struggle but his moral relativism. Russians, he insisted, simply had a different concept of human rights to the West, particularly on freedom of speech.

As Stockwood was composing these words, however, the mood was changing. That same year, Edward Norman delivered his BBC Reith Lectures, *Christianity and the World*, forwarding the intellectual and spiritual case against the politicisation of Christianity and specifically the accommodation of Marxist ideas. A year later, the Soviets invaded Afghanistan, which signalled the reigniting of the Cold War, and by 1980 there were three leaders in place – Margaret Thatcher, Ronald Reagan and Pope John Paul II – determined to turn the policy of détente on its head.[13]

II. The crusade

NO ONE WHO knew anything about the newly elected President, Pope and Prime Minister could have been surprised by their virulent anti-communism. All three had been remarkably consistent in their position well before they assumed office. Reagan's hostility could be dated back to the

1950s when as President of the Screen Actors Guild he had unmasked 'un-American' activities in Hollywood. He had fought the 1980 presidential election on an anti-détente ticket, capitalising on Americans yearning for some gun-slinging hard talk after years of soft diplomacy (which Jimmy Carter's bungle over the Iran hostage crisis only reinforced).

Ronald Reagan's Christian faith, much like Margaret Thatcher's, though, is hard to pin down. From his days as Governor of California, Reagan had mastered the language of conservative evangelicals preaching a message of revival and salvation from the pernicious forces of humanism and hedonism, all of which stood him in good stead as President.[14] As to his personal faith, he was known to pray regularly but was not an active churchgoer and appears not to have objected to his wife's insistence that they consult an astrologer over all his actions and appointments. It was, apparently, the other great female figure in his life, his mother, who inspired his Christian faith. Nelle Reagan was a committed member of the Disciples of Christ Church in Illinois and would conduct church readings, run Bible study classes and, it was said, even perform healings, while the young Ronald was himself a Sunday school teacher and had led prayer meetings.[15] Reagan eulogised his mother in the same way that Thatcher eulogised her father and yet, importantly, the Bible-based tutelage that Reagan received at the Disciples of Christ Church in Illinois was not a world away from that experienced by Margaret Thatcher at Finkin Street Methodist Church in Grantham.

In 1975, speaking to the Anglo-British Pilgrim Society in London, not long before Reagan would first bid for the White House, he set out what he considered to be the choice facing the world: 'Either we continue the concept that man is a unique being capable of determining his own destiny with dignity and God-given inalienable rights ... or we admit we are faceless ciphers in a godless collectivist ant heap.'[16] His critics may have dismissed his understanding as simplistic while admirers may have praised his assured principles, nonetheless there was little doubt that Reagan's world-view was shaped and articulated in Christian terms.

As Archbishop of Kraków, Karol Wojtyla was one of many priests to defy the communist regime in Poland, but this was done not through open hostility, rather with subtle negotiation. Wojtyla's experience of living under communist repression made him pessimistic of détente and especially of theologians' enthusiasm for using Marxism as a learning tool for Christian ethics.[17]

Margaret Thatcher had made her position on communism clear long before she delivered the speech in 1976, which would famously earn her the title of 'Iron Lady' by the Soviet Defence Ministry's paper, the *Red Star*. In 1950, on the eve of the Korean War, in a New Year message to her Dartford constituents, Margaret Roberts had channelled her best Churchillian rhetoric: 'We believe in the freedom of the democratic way of life. Communism seizes power by force, not by free choice of the people. We must firstly *believe* in the Western way of life and serve it steadfastly.'[18] Almost immediately on becoming Conservative leader, Margaret Thatcher established herself as a sceptic of détente and critical of the 'gullible disarmers' who naively followed such a course.[19] 'I am also for *attente* … for not letting down our guard; for keeping our powder dry,' she told the Pilgrims of the United States in New York in September 1975, barely a month after the Helsinki Accords had been signed.[20] She reinforced this message back home a year later in her infamous 'Iron Lady' speech at Kensington Town Hall: 'They [Soviets] put guns before butter, while we put just about everything before guns.'[21]

Quite why Thatcher was determined to present herself as a hawk so early on in her leadership may have been because she was a novice in foreign policy; talking tough afforded the new female Conservative leader some much needed gravitas. But she was also articulating an opinion she had long held. Like most, Thatcher did not foresee the impending collapse of the Soviet Union, but unlike most, she was prepared to talk as if it should (and could) one day be a reality.

If one were to compare the contributions of this Western trio – the President, the Pope and the Prime Minister – Margaret Thatcher was the least important in helping to bringing the Cold War to an end. She could however claim credit as a conciliator rather than as an aggressor in initiating a dialogue with Mikhail Gorbachev and opening up diplomatic links with faint-hearted members of the Warsaw Pact (Thatcher was the first Western Cold War leader to touch down on Ukrainian, Hungarian and Siberian soil). Nor should Thatcher's contribution to the propaganda offensive be underestimated either. Early on in her premiership, her speechwriter and expert on Eastern Europe, George Urban had pressed on her the need to adopt a tone of 'moral outrage rather than cool reason'.[22] Urban's view, one with which Thatcher readily concurred, was that the West in the 1970s had lacked the self-confidence of the Soviets and had been shy in asserting its values, particularly on democracy and freedom. Urban's idea of an ideological counter-offensive certainly appealed to Thatcher; she had always dismissed the notion that there was any moral equivalence between the USSR and the West. More than any British leader since Churchill, Thatcher was willing to elevate the Cold War into one about ideas and values. 'I'm perfectly prepared to fight that battle,' Thatcher said in enthusing tones to Urban. 'We've got all the truth on our side and all the right arguments.'[23] In 1983, still basking in her Falklands triumph, Margaret Thatcher used the occasion of her acceptance speech for the Winston Churchill Foundation Award in Washington, to assert the Cold War as one chiefly of ideas not weapons:

> 'You in the West,' said an Hungarian poet, 'have a special duty because you are free. That freedom is both a blessing and a burden. For it makes you spiritually responsible for the whole of humanity.' He was right. For if we do not keep alive the flame of freedom that flame will go out, and every noble ideal will die with it. It is not by force of weapons but by force of ideas that we seek to spread liberty to the worlds oppressed.[24]

On this occasion, Thatcher had specific reason for revving up the ideological war rather than the arms race, for Reagan had recently announced the Strategic Defence Initiative, of which Thatcher was privately sceptical.[25]

Margaret Thatcher's linguistic style though always went down better with the Americans than it did back home. Labour's shadow Foreign Secretary Denis Healey thought Thatcher 'an ignorant and opinionated demagogue', while *The Guardian* served up a fearful assessment: 'There is not just Churchill in her rhetoric; there is Harry before Agincourt, even Richard the Lionheart, setting out for the Holy War with Saladin.'[26]

Thatcher's crusading language was all well and good, but even she realised that it was not a serious diplomatic strategy. In the early 1980s, the hope in the West was that communism would be defeated from within. Encouraging dissent movements within the Eastern bloc had always been Western policy but this was pursued with pressing urgency with the rise of Solidarity in Poland. Led by pious electrician Lech Wałęsa, Solidarity was an independent trade union federation, which had a membership of ten million (a quarter of the population) and used civil resistance methods to advance the cause of workers' rights against the state. Poland, though, represented a unique case. Never fully communist (the rural peasants were still landholders), its identity had formed against centuries of successive foreign creeds and occupation, and, more specifically, as a bastion of Roman Catholicism in Eastern Europe made all the more resonant with the recent election of a Polish-born Pope. The huge crowds that greeted Pope John Paul II on his visit to his homeland in 1979 had been greeted with panic in Moscow and excitement in Washington.

Solidarity drew much of its inspiration, symbolism and leadership from the Catholic Church. It was in essence a Catholic social movement, which is one of the main reasons why Arthur Scargill publicly came out against it. At the dock of Gdansk, the home of the movement, murals of the Virgin Mary and John Paul II were set against the backdrop of Solidarity's colours of red and white. Polish Catholic leaders stood shoulder-to-shoulder with workers in a unity that partly reflected the strength of ties between Polish nationalism and Catholicism but also the weakening authority of the crumbling communist state. Pope John Paul II knew all too well of the sustained interrogation and abuse that the Roman Catholic Church suffered in his homeland. For this and for many other reasons, Solidarity was a social resistance movement to which the Vatican willingly lent its support – both financial and verbal – unlike to those priests fighting for social justice in other parts of the world.

Many in the West, especially Ronald Reagan, were convinced that religion might prove to be the Soviet Union's 'Achilles heel' and there was genuine hope that Poland's Christian-inspired resistance movement could pave the way.[27] In a sign of support, Washington substantially increased investment in their propaganda service, Radio Free Europe, which also regularly broadcast Mass. It also channelled funds to Solidarity, although admittedly these were paltry sums compared to the funding sent to the Mujahideen to help their fight against the Soviets in Afghanistan. When the Polish government, weakened by food shortages, strikes and protests, declared martial law in 1981, Reagan, in a unilateral move took the bold step of imposing sanctions on the whole of the Eastern Bloc.

As Britain's closest ally in the East, and with substantial investments in Poland, the Foreign Office wished to tread a cautious line with respect to Solidarity. Thatcher, though, always gave her uncompromising support to a movement she believed to be the perfect showcase of revolt against communist tyranny. She was copied into all telegrams from the British embassy in Warsaw and studiously scribbled all over them. Reagan's move on sanctions, however, put Thatcher in an impossible situation; it put at risk millions of pounds of business and jobs at a time when the British economy was in dire straits. Reagan had, in effect, used the situation in Poland as an opportunity to attempt to economically freeze out the Russians through industrial sanctions; his specific aim was to halt the production of the Siberian gas line – the export of American grain, for example, was not halted. The problem from Thatcher's perspective, and shared by her European allies who also had substantial economic interests at stake, was that American policy threatened to harm the European economy as much as that of the Soviet Union. After a year, a compromise was eventually reached with Washington, but the whole episode had revealed the contradictions, self-interest and above all pragmatism rather than Christian solidarity that governed the politics of the Cold War.

The Polish government limped on, outlawing Solidarity in 1982 and combining this with the more fearful tactics of tanks, bullets and beatings, including the murder of the outspoken priest Father Jerzy Popieluszko, who was killed by the secret police in 1984. His funeral attracted over 250,000 mourners and his grave soon became a shrine, to which Pope John Paul, Reagan and Thatcher would later pay homage. By the time that Thatcher visited Poland in 1988, the government had been forced to change its tack. The shipyard of Gdansk, the home of Solidarity, was being closed down in the name of 'economic efficiency'; a tactic of curtailing union power with which Margaret Thatcher herself was intimately familiar.

On the day that the British Prime Minister arrived, however, the rusting dockyards were overrun with cheering crowds, men clinging onto cranes waving their arms and Solidarity flags, even anti-Scargill placards. 'I knew I had to come and feel the spirit of Poland for myself,' Thatcher said, purposefully dressed in a green (Aquascutum) coat, the colour of hope in Poland. The workers had come out in force, but it was not the British Prime Minister they were shouting for, but Solidarity, in the hope that such images beamed round the world would finally shame the Polish government into submission.

After her reception at Gdansk, Margaret Thatcher attended a service at St Brygida's, the spiritual HQ of Solidarity, which had also acted as a sanctuary for leaders of the movement. The congregation applauded as Thatcher entered and spontaneously burst into a rendition of 'Give us back free Poland'. As she listened intently, tears could clearly be seen in Thatcher's eyes. Over lunch, she advised union leader Wałęsa that popularity without a plan of action was pointless. Wałęsa immediately interjected: 'If you have a free society under the rule of law, it produces both dignity of the individual and prosperity.' Thatcher could not contain herself: 'Stop, Stop, Mr Wałęsa, this is music to my ears, wonderful, your government should hear this.' Wałęsa gently raised a finger to the chandelier directly above the dining table, 'Do not worry, Mrs Thatcher, they are hearing every word.'[28]

As Thatcher was whisked out of Gdansk in a small boat, the shipyard cranes bowed in salute.[29] Two months later, Solidarity was recognised as an independent labour union and in the subsequent elections of 1989, won nearly all the seats in the Polish Parliament. In a small but significant way, Margaret Thatcher had played a part by recognising Polish resistance to communist tyranny. It was no surprise that Lech Wałęsa could later be found amongst the congregation on the occasion of Margaret Thatcher's funeral in 2013.

III. By papal decree

IF ONE WERE to take a long-term view, John Paul II's tour of Britain in 1982 was the most significant diplomatic event of the 1980s. In terms of historic symbolism, the first visit by a reigning Pope since the Reformation certainly trounced Thatcher's tête-à-tête with Gorbachev and her infamous speech against European federalism in Bruges. That the visit is not traditionally seen in this light is perhaps because it signified the cessation rather than the beginning of something, but that end was no small feat: the 450-year-old conflict between Canterbury and Rome.

Archbishop Runcie had first broached the idea of a visit when he had met Pope John Paul II in Accra in 1980, but it was Cardinal Hume, as head of the Roman Catholic Church, who issued the formal invitation given that it was to be a pastoral rather than a state visit. Personal meetings between the head of the Catholic Church and the head of the Anglican Communion dated back to the 1960s when Archbishop Fisher was the first to break with history and call on Pope John XXIII in Rome, although it had not been an official welcome and the Vatican pointedly insisted on referring to the archbishop as 'Dr Fisher'. By the time that Paul VI welcomed his successor, Archbishop Ramsey, the second Vatican Council had issued its decree on ecumenism and the stage was set for the announcement of the Anglican Roman Catholic International Commission (ARCIC) which aimed at putting ecumenical dialogue on a solid footing and settling the theological divisions between the churches. The meeting did not run entirely smoothly though; Ian Paisley and his band of protestors had been on the same plane as the archbishop and proceeded to stage a demonstration in their 'Archbishop Ramsey traitor to Protestant Britain' shirts at the airport.

A further nudge towards re-approachment came in 1977 when Archbishop Coggan and Paul VI signed a joint declaration on unity but as yet no pope had set foot on British soil. Runcie was very keen for John Paul II's visit to go ahead; he saw it as a necessary seal of approval for ARCIC, whose report, published in 1981, seemed to pave the way for closer union, if not full communion, between the two churches. Runcie also wished to see the Pope publicly demonstrate respect for Anglicanism, which he felt was not always accorded due status in Rome, and he hoped that John Paul II might revoke the 1896 papal bull nullifying Anglican orders. Runcie later admitted that he had doubts about John Paul II, particularly his conservatism on sexual matters and women in the church, which Runcie considered stemmed from the 'Mediterranean male conservative' atmosphere of the Vatican. The divisions were felt to be so extreme that some in Lambeth feared that the visit would reveal divisions rather than harmony between Catholicism and Anglicanism.[30]

The concerns in Whitehall were quite different. Here the priority was to get the protocol and arrangements correct, especially with regard to the Queen in her role as Supreme Governor of the Church of England. The outbreak of the Falklands conflict weeks before the Pope's arrival would eventually force Margaret Thatcher to withdraw entirely from the visit, but, even before this, when the initial arrangements were being made, the Pope appeared distinctly reluctant to meet Britain's state representatives. Buckingham Palace's proposal for a luncheon was reduced to a half-hour call, while the Thatcher's suggestion of a gathering at Downing Street was also rejected. Even before the Falklands War had been declared, Thatcher had decided against attending the proposed service at Canterbury Cathedral for fear that the papal tour was becoming too politicised.[31] Runcie, however, urged her to reconsider and, in an attempt at flattery, added that her presence was crucial in order to 'put the Pope in context'.[32] Runcie was keen for the British state to be as visible as possible; he consciously wanted to avoid the event being turned into a celebratory papal road show. The fact was, though, that both Church and state were entirely at the will of the Vatican: '[They are] effectively presenting us with a *fait accompli*,' wrote Mr Vereker of No. 10 in frustration at Rome's handling of the PR for the visit.[33]

The Catholic Church had agreed to cover costs, although the bill for policing and security – necessary given the recent assassination attempt on the Pope – would have to be met by the Home Office. Thatcher was warned to keep a close eye on the coffers. 'I have no doubt especially as the Roman Catholics in this country are, apparently, so short of money, there will be further requests of one kind or another for public expenditure,' wrote a civil servant in the Home Office.[34] Another administrative headache was trying to find an appropriate venue for the Pope's scheduled Mass near London, which was expected to attract one million people. Epsom Downs Racecourse was suggested but soon rejected, not for of its association with gambling but because it would clash with one of the most important days in the racing calendar. 'Nobody in their senses would alter the date of the Derby!' cautioned a Miss E. Chaplin of the Protocol and Conference Department.[35] Richmond Park was proposed as an alternative but, as Michael Heseltine pointed out, the Pope's visit would take place precisely when the park's deer would be dropping their young, while it was also feared that the crowd would likely cause damage to the nearby golf course.[36] Wembley Stadium was eventually chosen, but the fact that officials and ministers spent their time fretting about the possible consequences for the Derby, Richmond's deer and the local golfing fraternity revealed the level of paranoia in Whitehall over an event for which there was no precedent.

When the visit was formally announced, Ian Paisley, unsurprisingly, wrote a letter of protest to Margaret Thatcher pointing out the illogicality of welcoming a religious leader who considered the Church of England a blasphemous inception. 'Best to be brief, rather than pursue all Dr Paisley's hares,' wrote Colin Peterson, who drafted the Prime Minister's response.[37]

Meanwhile, Enoch Powell, then an Ulster Unionist MP, used an address to the East Grinstead Young Conservatives Association to press home some obscure points of historical fact: 'Either the Pope's authority is not universal or the Church of England is not the Catholic and Apostolic Church in this land.'[38] Thatcher's parliamentary private secretary, Ian Gow, sent a copy of the text to No. 10 with the accompanying note: 'JEP, whose brain I revere, really is off course here.'[39]

Paisley's and Powell's concerns could not easily be dismissed though. Anti-Catholicism may not have been as endemic as it had once been but it was still evident, particularly in Liverpool and Glasgow where the Pope was due to visit. Runcie himself had been on the receiving end of such abuse weeks before the visit, when anti-papal protestors had hijacked a service he was giving in Liverpool. As a pre-emptive move, Bishop David Sheppard met representatives from the Orange Order to seek assurances that they would not cause undue disruption. Clergy and

MPs' postbags revealed enough discontent for Downing Street to draft a standard response to ensure a consistent line on a sensitive issue. Even some within the Church of England were uneasy. Writing to Runcie, the Bishop of Birmingham confided that he was reluctant to 'dance attendance on the Pope' for fear that it compromised the oath that all diocesan bishops have to swear before the Queen: 'no foreign potentate or prelate hath any jurisdiction in this realm of England'.[40] Letters of opposition were one thing, but the real concern was the likelihood of any violence. Police intelligence concluded that protests by Paisley and his supporters were to be expected but that terrorist attacks from Northern Irish paramilitaries were not. The People's Opposition to Papal Edicts (POPE), consisting of women's and gay liberation groups and humanist societies were also not thought to pose much of a threat.[41] (Tellingly, when Pope Benedict XVI visited the UK in 2010, the loudest protests came from atheists and gay activists. It was Richard Dawkins and Peter Tatchell rather than 'non-popery' Protestants who in 21st-century Britain led the charge against Rome.)

In the end, it was not anti-popery protests that nearly sabotaged the event but the fact that Margaret Thatcher went to war with a Catholic country weeks before the Pope was due to arrive. A determined Cardinal Hume immediately flew to Rome to plead with John Paul II not to cancel, although he combined this with a subtle warning that the decision would be construed as a comment on the Falklands War and might fan the flames of anti-Catholicism in Britain.[42] The government agreed to stay away, although it remained wary of what the Pope might say, sending a note of advice to Cardinal Hume for John Paul II to 'stick to general principles ... the need for peace, freedom and a just and lasting solution to the problem in the South Atlantic'.[43] This he did. By the time that the Pope touched down at Gatwick, though, the Argentinians had already surrendered at Goose Green.

Few could deny the symbolic importance of the ecumenical service at Canterbury Cathedral, when Pope John Paul II and the Archbishop of Canterbury led a joint service in the home of English Christianity. Runcie would subsequently meet the Pope on several occasions, nurturing a bond that soon went beyond the ceremonial, becoming a working relationship that was historic in its own right.

In Runcie's view, in many ways the Pope's presence north of the border and his meeting with the Moderator of the Church of Scotland was equally significant as his visit to Canterbury, especially given the level of sectarianism within Scottish society. The fact that the Pope's tour took place at all demonstrated the dilution of the nation's Protestant identity, yet its success reflected the enduring strength of Christianity in Britain. It also signalled the fact that Roman Catholicism had finally achieved its place at the centre of British public life.

IV. Just war in a nuclear age

MARGARET THATCHER NEVER wavered in her belief that nuclear weapons were a guarantor of peace and stability rather than a route to war. On entering No. 10, she immediately set to the task of finalising a deal with the Americans, which had been initiated by her predecessor: negotiating the replacement of the Polaris system with Trident. Some may have considered that, given Britain's dire economic situation, such a move was a bit like a family purchasing the latest car when they could not afford their mortgage, but for Thatcher it ensured Britain's independence and a prominent seat at the international table; two things on which it was impossible to put a price. In this and in her later commitment to allow the US to stage cruise missiles on British soil, Thatcher was merely continuing what had been the post-war status quo pursued by both Labour and Conservative governments.[44] What made it politically sensitive was the resurgence of the anti-nuclear movement both within and outside Parliament between 1980 and 1983. CND, having experienced a lull in the 1970s, underwent a renaissance with its membership increasing to 90,000 national members and additional 250,000 in its local branches. CND had always been a broad movement comprising of churches, unions and left-wing activists, but in the 1980s its Christian character (in its leadership at least) was more prominent than ever before, with Catholic priest Father Bruce Kent as its head and Anglican priest Paul Oestreicher, its Vice-Chairman. At this point, CND demonstrations could attract well over 250,000 protestors; a fact that has led historian James Hinton to reflect that it was 'one of the largest political organisations in Britain and probably the largest peace movement in the world'.[45] CND may have attracted the numbers but it was the Greenham Common Women's Peace Protest, stationed at an RAF camp in Berkshire – home to the US Cruise Missiles – that dominated the headlines. The women protestors, who tended to be caricatured by the right-wing press as hippy communist lesbians, surpassed the moderate men of the cloth as symbols of the movement.

In public, Margaret Thatcher casually dismissed unilateralists and peace demonstrators as fantasists while positioning herself as the ardent realist. And yet, as a meeting of the Lord President's Council in November 1982 reveals, the Conservatives were concerned that the public consensus on Britain's defence policy, which had remained intact since the 1950s, seemed to be 'in danger'.[46] In particular, it was floating voters – those who would normally endorse Conservative defence proposals – that seemed to be drifting towards a position of unilateralism. Margaret Thatcher's tactic was to appoint the self-assured Michael Heseltine at the Ministry of Defence, with the explicit purpose of fighting a propaganda war against CND and setting public opinion back on course. One of Heseltine's first initiatives was to establish the Defence Secretariat 19 whose aim, he told the Commons, was to explain the 'facts' to the public about its nuclear deterrent and defence policy, although as Heseltine later admitted in his memoirs, it principally involved a change of tone and language; 'Trident' was dropped in favour of 'Britain's independent deterrent', while unilateralists were dismissed as 'one-sided disarmers'. Another tactic was to portray the anti-nuclear movement as more left-wing than it actually was. The press fulfilled this function by running scare stories about Soviet funding and Marxist infiltration, which the government hoped might put off moderate sympathisers. The portrait of CND supporters as communist-funded radicals could not have been further from the truth, of course, as the following observations of a CND demo in June 1982, produced by the Conservative Research Department (CRD), proved: rather than incendiary Marxists, the researcher from the CRD observed that it was a 'rather folksy, relaxed atmosphere', and amongst the 150,000-strong crowd were mostly women and families, religious groups, along with 'miscellaneous gay, feminists and punks ... archetypal *Guardian*-reading parents eating their nut cutlet picnics under the trees while the children watched a Punch (President Reagan) and Judy (Mrs Thatcher) sideshow.'[47]

The fact that such a report was commissioned, not least by party chairman Cecil Parkinson, revealed the Conservative Party's overriding fear that defence, and especially the nuclear issue, was likely to play a pivotal part in the 1983 election. This was made all the more urgent when the Labour Party adopted an unequivocal policy of unilateral disarmament. Labour's policy had not been conceived out of naive hope but was a policy that the party genuinely believed was in tune with popular sentiment – polls at the time suggested that approximately 30 per cent of Britons were in favour of full disarmament.

The Church of England's 'The Church and the Bomb' report, which had taken nearly three years to compose, would probably have been ignored had it not been published just as the debate about Britain's nuclear policy was coming to a head. To the surprise of most bishops and the government, the committee advocated the phasing out of Britain's nuclear deterrent, in effect an endorsement of unilateral disarmament. Just as the Labour Party had departed from the defence status quo, so it seemed the Established Church (a much more worrying prospect from a Conservative's point of view) appeared to be following suit. Conservatives, aided by the right-wing press, did their best to rubbish the report and, in a rare act of solidarity with the government, so did the senior clergy. The pro-Conservative Bishop of Norwich made the point to *The Times* that there were 'no uni-lateralists in the Kremlin', while Richard Harries, the future Bishop of Oxford and leading advocate of multi-lateralism, offered a more focused assessment, remarking that the report contained 'no discussion of the role of power in human affairs and no theology of power'.[48] In February 1983, four months before the election, the General Synod held a five-hour-long debate on the report which was relayed live on BBC2; a sure sign of its considered importance and something not yet possible in the camera-shy Houses of Parliament.

In a move that indicated the seriousness with which the govern-ment considered the Church's influence, the Ministry of Defence sent out propaganda literature to every Synod member before the debate.[49] When the report's policy of unilateralism was put forward, it was effectively quashed in a unifying act of prelate pressure. Gra-ham Leonard of London, who as Chairman of the Board for Social Responsibility had actually commissioned the report, played a signifi-cant procedural role in undermining it. Likewise Runcie, to whom the Synod has always showed due reverence, while the Archbishop of York played the 'declinist card', forewarning what disarmament would mean for Britain's status as a world power.

The weight of the bishops, particularly of Runcie, drowned out the loud chorus of unilateralists in both the Houses of Clergy and Laity. In the end, the Synod passed a resolution that Britain should not pursue a 'first strike' policy but should maintain its nuclear capabilities. This was successfully carried, although not wholly convincingly, by 275 to 222. The debate (and for that matter the result) revealed the Church not as Christian idealists but concerned pragmatists, although US observ-ers could not help but remark on the lack of theological insight and the latent anti-Americanism of some of the contributions. No doubt the government was relieved. Months before the election, the Synod had firmly rejected the Labour line as unrealistic. The Synod's resolution was not an explicit endorsement of government policy but the debate was an important moment in halting the popular swing towards disarmament.

V. Spiritual struggle: South Africa

FOR CHRISTIAN SOCIAL activists of the 1980s, there was one issue in international affairs on which there could be no moral ambivalence or compromise: South Africa. Anglicans had been involved in the struggle against apartheid since the late 1940s, both within and outside South Africa, with such figures as Anglican priest Michael Scott and Canon John Collins of St Paul's legitimising the cause at home and gathering support from the press, Church hierarchy and the secular left. Through Christian Action, Collins managed to establish a fund for those engaged in resisting apartheid in South Africa; Christian Aid soon followed suit by redirecting its funds from war-torn Europe into providing legal aid and support for families of imprisoned ANC activists. The movement was bolstered by the presence of South African exiles in London, but it was another Anglican priest, Trevor Huddleston, who would become the public face of the anti-apartheid movement in Britain. Arriving in South Africa as a missionary in 1943, Huddleston spent more than a decade in the slums of Sophiatown before penning *Nought for your Comfort* in 1956, one of the first publications to unmask the realities of the apartheid system, which Huddleston unapologetically compared to Nazi Germany. Later, as Bishop of Stepney and President of the Anti-Apartheid Movement (AAM), Huddleston would play a pivotal role in legitimising the ANC, pressing the issue of sanctions to the UN and campaigning for the release of Nelson Mandela. Of Trevor Huddleston, Mandela later said: 'No white person has done more for South Africa.'

Anglicans had played no small part in supporting independence movements in Africa, but after the wave of British decolonisation in the 1960s, the anti-apartheid movement slotted into a broader set of international causes deemed worthy of Christian concern and action, including CND, opposing the war in Vietnam and addressing poverty in the developing world. The growth of 'Christian internationalism' fed off old imperial bonds and a paternalistic sense of a Christian civilised order, but it also borrowed from the language and tactics of contemporary left-wing civil rights and liberation movements. Canon John Collins was one such Christian who combined his leadership of CND with his role as part of the International Defence and Aid Fund, bringing the atrocities and inequalities in South Africa to public attention. Another prominent Anglican who also lent credibility to the anti-apartheid cause was David Sheppard, who in his cricketing days had refused to play against an all-white South African team and in 1968 was instrumental in getting campaign cricketer Basil D'Oliveira reinstated as part of the England team for its proposed tour of South Africa. The tour never went ahead but the affair had convinced anti-apartheid activists that sport was one way of bringing international shame on the Pretorian government. The sporting boycott of South Africa was eventually made official in the Gleneagles Agreement signed by the Commonwealth of Nations in 1977, but the question of trade embargoes and sanctions, which Anglicans, along with left-wing sympathisers, had been pressing for since the 1960s, would prove to be a much more complicated thing to engineer.

Britain, of course, was not the only location for anti-apartheid activity, but it was the most important international pressure movement outside South Africa, largely because the old imperial perception of London as the metropole still remained. The movement in Britain was also incredibly well organised with the formation of the Anti-Apartheid Movement (AAM); an umbrella organisation of church groups, left-wing activists, trade union supporters, local councils and a strong following of Liberal and Labour politicians. Funding from Christian organisations such as the World Council of Churches and the British Council of Churches was crucial to AAM, as was the involvement of many Christians and churches, whose advocacy of non-violent tactics was crucial in ensuring the movement's legitimacy and widespread appeal; as it was for CND.

Despite intense pressure from the AAM, successive governments refused to be drawn over the issue of sanctions to South Africa; even Archbishop Ramsey was not convinced. In a letter to Foreign Sec-retary Alec Douglas-Home in 1970, the archbishop endorsed the government's policy of 'friendly criticism' rather than 'ostracism'.[50] Neither were the World Council of Churches or the British Coun-cil of Churches sold on the case for sanctions. That the international campaign against apartheid would become crystallised around disinvest-ment was largely down to Huddleston's tireless leadership on the issue and, even more importantly, changing events in South Africa itself.

If Huddleston was a moderate face who could stir the conscience of those in Britain, then the same too could be said of his protégé, Desmond Tutu, General Secretary of the South African Council of Churches. Robert Runcie had been personally committed to raising Tutu's profile, smoothing his elevation to the bishopric to Johannesburg and finally Cape Town (the first black man to hold this office).[51] Terry Waite, Lam-beth Palace's diplomatic envoy, later said of Runcie's intervention: 'That was an example of what other people might think was intrigue, but it was good diplomacy – it had a big effect on world affairs.'[52] In this instance, Runcie's discreet exercise of his patronage certainly did more good than any public dressing down of the Conservative government's policy. In contrast to the passive patriarchs in Moscow, Christian leaders in South Africa became the leading voices of resistance to state ideology and in Desmond Tutu the opposition movement had a legitimate spokesper-son who could not simply be dismissed as a terrorist or a communist; indeed, Tutu always described communism as being as evil as apartheid and condemned violence as much as state oppression.

The key moment came in 1985 when, in response to a state of emergency being declared, 150 Christian leaders issued 'The Kai-ros Document', a damning indictment of the ideology of apartheid and one of the most eloquent and powerful theological responses to state oppression ever produced. The point was not only to cast a Christian light on the state's approach to law and order but also to cast shame on the Dutch Reformed Church, which publicly supported the status quo. 'This god [of the state] is an idol ... the very opposite of the God of the Bible ... the devil disguised as Almighty God.' The Kairos Document's influence would extend well beyond South Africa; Central American theologians published their own version, 'The Road to Damascus', in 1988 and some Anglicans even saw it as a blueprint for how they should respond to the Conservative government.

Margaret Thatcher is often cast as an apologist for apartheid, although her position on South Africa was complex, pragmatic and, some might argue, a continuation of the British government's position from the 1960s. What was deemed an acceptable policy in the 1970s, however, was considered unacceptable in the 1980s as South Africa descended into chaos and international and domestic pressure mounted. On South Africa, Margaret Thatcher quite clearly diverged from the Foreign Office and, as negotiations unfolded, South Africa proved to be one of the main sources of agitation between her and her Foreign Secretary, Geoffrey Howe. Both were of the view that dialogue rather than isolation was the best course of action, but Howe was prepared to be much more aggressive in pressurising the South African government than his prime minister. Margaret Thatcher had always been sceptical of sanctions as a tactic of diplomatic pressure (she opposed them against the Soviet Union as well as South Africa); she was, however, clear where she stood in respect to the South African regime. 'I loathe Apartheid and everything connected with it,' she had said in a speech to the National Press Club in Australia in 1979; Harold Wilson had said much the same thing, but, significantly, in an address at an anti-apartheid rally.[53] Margaret Thatcher, unlike her colleagues at the Foreign Office, tended to view the problems in South Africa through two prisms: her ideological war with communism and her opposition to terrorism.

Writing to Thatcher in 1980, South African Prime Minister Botha offered to dispel what he considered to be some of myths surrounding the apartheid system, while also position his government's ideological alignment with Western democracy: 'Whatever imperfections there may be in South African society, South Africa has a democratic, free-enterprise, Christian society and is spiritually, emotionally and ideologically committed to the democracy of the Greeks, Europeans and Americans.'[54] More pointedly, Botha made sure to position the apartheid struggle within the context of what he called the 'Soviet doctrine of world domination': 'It has taken the rape of Afghanistan to open the eyes of the West,' he added, words which Margaret Thatcher had underlined with her pen.

To a point, Botha's positioning of the internal struggles in South Africa as part of the broader conflict between communism and the capitalist democracy was legitimate, albeit not exactly in the terms he proposed. Following decolonisation, both the West and the Soviet Union had engaged in a scramble for African influence through a mixture of trade deals, aid programmes and arms sales. By the mid-1980s, the Soviet Union could count Angola, Mozambique, Congo and Benin as well as the ANC as either comrades or customers. She was not, however, naive enough to take Botha's reassurances about apartheid at face value, nor was she prepared to support the oppositional movements then gathering pace. To Thatcher, the ANC were Marxists who deployed terrorist and undemocratic tactics: a perception that was shared by most in her party. When Derek Worlock and David Sheppard were invited to speak on South Africa at a fringe meeting at the Conservative Party conference in 1989, they were shocked to find that the event had been fly-leafleted with posters claiming 'ANC equals IRA'.[55]

The case for international sanctions was brought to a head in
1985, when intense violence and disruption in South Africa forced
Botha to declare a state of emergency. Yet support for disinvestment
was not universal nor were the issues clear cut; dreamy Trotskyites
within the AAM thought that sanctions would only prolong the
capitalist revolution which they believed was a prerequisite to racial
reform in South Africa, while even some ANC members thought
sanctions a pointless path. Margaret Thatcher, always vulnerable to
the charge that she prioritised economics above all else, was, in this
case, cast as protecting British jobs over black injustices in South
Africa. Thatcher, though, was defiant. 'What is moral about that?'
was her reply when pressed by The Guardian's Hugo Young on the
ethical case for sanctions. 'Add starvation, poverty, unemployment
to the problems you have already got ... when people call that moral,
I just gasp.'[56] By this stage, though, the issue of sanctions, in a large
part due to the forcefulness of Church leaders and the AAM, had
assumed an ethical mantle on which there could be no compromise.
Anyone who took an opposing view, such as John Gummer, who, in
an address to Christians for the 1987 election claimed it '[was] not
a moral one but a matter of political judgement', was dismissed as
either a racist or a supporter of the regime.[57]

Thatcher's aim was to bring Botha back in from the diplomatic
cold and to coax him into reforms, while holding off the international pressure. This was a legitimate strategy as long as Botha was
willing to comply, but he was not. The showdown came at the Commonwealth Heads of Government Meeting in Nassau in 1985, where
Thatcher fought hard to halt economic sanctions much to the ire of
Commonwealth leaders and her foreign secretary. 'I received a good
deal of abuse, of being concerned with pennies rather than principles,'
Thatcher wrote to Botha soon afterwards.[58] Margaret Thatcher had
put her diplomatic head on the line and wanted some concessions
from Botha in return, including the release of Mandela as well as

consenting to a monitoring delegation, the Eminent Persons Group, from the Commonwealth. But Botha rejected the stipulations, which, in his words, had been issued by countries that were 'total strangers to democracy'.[59]

Meanwhile, mounting domestic pressure in the US led the Senate to pass the Comprehensive Anti-Apartheid Act in 1986. Reagan, who shared Thatcher's line on constructive engagement with the regime and about communist implications in Africa, had used his veto before going on national television to denounce the Act as 'immoral' and 'utterly repugnant'. The Republican-majority Senate, though, overrode it in what was the first time in the twentieth century that it had overturned a presidential veto on foreign policy.

Thatcher was beginning to look like a lone voice standing up for a corrupt and crumbling regime. She was dismayed by Botha's intransigency but she had perhaps overestimated her own powers of persuasion. Botha was no Gorbachev and certainly not the man to enact change in South Africa.[60] While Margaret Thatcher was not a supporter of apartheid, she could certainly be accused of not condemning it with the same moral certitude she denounced communism. This may have been out of diplomatic pragmatism but it was also true that she did not equate the two on the same moral plane; both Desmond Tutu and Lech Wałęsa were beneficiaries of the Nobel Peace Prize, but Margaret Thatcher never showed the same admiration for the former as she did for the latter. For those Christians involved in the AAM, on the other hand, there was no compromise to be had or grey area to be considered. The South African regime was condemned outright as un-Christian and disinvestment the only possible leverage to bring the apartheid system to its knees. For some Conservatives, though, the Church's uncompromising stance on South Africa was yet further evidence of its tendency to wrap left-wing causes in a Christian guise

Given the Anglican leadership on sanctions, it was thus more than a little embarrassing when the Church of England's own economic entanglements in South Africa were revealed. The Church Commissioners, who oversaw its investments and crucially its pension fund, had over £1 million in companies that operated in South Africa, including Leyland, ICI and General Electric. Midland Bank, in which the Church had £600,000 worth of shares, also had loan arrangements with the Pretorian government. The Church, somewhat legitimately, was accused of both condemning and profiting from organisations with interests in South Africa. Even if the Commissioners dissociated from companies with substantive investments in South Africa, this was not a solution: what of those companies with subsidiaries? Of the 146 British companies in which the Church was involved, sixty-seven had some direct or indirect investment in South Africa.[61] In 1990, the Bishop of Oxford, Richard Harries, decided to take the Church Commissioners to court to ensure that its investment portfolio was in accordance with the Church's teaching. The case hinged not on what was deemed a legitimate Christian investment, which is of course a slippery concept (changing attitudes towards smoking had proved that), but on the precise relationship of the Commissioners to the Church.[62] The court ruled that the Commissioners' policy was sound and yet the whole debacle marred the Church's spiritual struggle against apartheid. The issue had also shone a light on the complexities of the modern global investment system and the near-impossibility of having a 'clean, ethical' policy.

As important as the AAM and the Church were in opposing apartheid, it was internal events within South Africa as well as the end of the Cold War (specifically the settlement of Namibia and Angola in 1989) that ensured the regime's demise. Important, too, had been the resilience of the US Congress in passing the Comprehensive Anti-Apartheid Act, which had prompted a flight of international capital out of South Africa (which was always more important than trade) and seriously destabilised the South African economy. Within Britain the anti-apartheid cause demonstrated the left in a rare moment of unity in the 1980s while Anglicans, both behind the scenes and as the public face, were crucial in transforming the cause into a broad-based movement. The British government may not have bowed to pressure in this instance, but the AAM would prove to be the blueprint for transnational mass movements in this new era of global politics.

When Nelson Mandela and Margaret Thatcher both passed away in 2013, it really did feel as though the curtain had finally fallen on the twentieth century. But while Thatcher was the subject of division, Mandela was universally mourned. All grieved for a global icon who had once been dubbed a terrorist but was now lauded as the world's benevolent grandfather. While Mandela was raised on a plinth, Thatcher underwent repeated decapitation. Both leaders could be said to have been politicians of integrity, but, while there was no question over the legitimacy of Mandela's cause, Thatcher's crusade remains mired in moral ambiguity. Perhaps it was because Thatcher stood for humanity as it is – individualistic, self-interested and parochial, whereas Mandela stood for what it aspires to be: a figure the embodied courage, justice and reconciliation. The future doctrine of humanitarian interventionism would adopt the language, lessons and methods from the anti-apartheid cause in South Africa; it is little wonder that Mandela is the figure who all modern leaders aspire to emulate.

VI. Feeding the multitude

THATCHER WOULD OFTEN speak of international aid in the same derogatory terms as the domestic welfare system, as encouraging an unhealthy relationship of economic dependency. 'If a person can't afford to keep himself he can't afford to keep his neighbour' was Thatcher's response to a question on Britain's aid budget to the *Catholic Herald* in 1978.[63] Thatcher certainly subscribed to the maxim that 'charity starts at home', explaining in a letter to the Bishop of

Warrington in 1979 that the government's priority was to get Britain's own finances in order first, which it duly did by cutting the aid budget by £50 million.[64] Thatcher was not the first prime minister to cut Britain's aid budget, the Wilson government had reduced it in 1976, the year of the IMF bailout, the difference was that Thatcher framed her case of trade over aid as a moral one. Tellingly, she never felt the need to set out the ethical justification for Britain's arms trade, which expanded exponentially under her watch. On the matter of trade, Margaret Thatcher also seemed unprepared to concede the distinctly 'unfree' and unfair of nature of the existing trade arrangements between developed and developing countries. A point that pop-star-turned-charity campaigner Bob Geldof cornered her on in a brief exchange at the *Daily Star* awards in 1985:

> *Geldof*: I mean at the moment you've got a problem with the butter mountain and you don't know how to dispose of it, you sell it to the Russians is the cheapest way.
>
> *Thatcher*: I'm sorry but butter doesn't do very much good in Africa as you know, it's grain.
>
> *Geldof*: Well butter oil actually does, it's one of the major—
>
> *Thatcher*: Butter oil if you can, if you can get down—
>
> *Geldof*: Well, it is a by-product of butter.
>
> *Thatcher*: Well, look, a lot is going, a lot of surplus food is going, but don't forget —
>
> *Geldof*: But Prime Minister there are millions dying and that's a terrible thing.
>
> *Thatcher*: Indeed.[65]

International attention had been shifting towards the developing world well before Geldof took up the cause. The Brandt Report published by the World Bank in 1980 and chaired by the former socialist Chancellor of West Germany, Willy Brandt, sought to address the economic disparity between the northern and southern hemispheres. The report did not drastically diverge from established academic thinking, but it had the effect of pushing international development to the forefront of the agenda of both domestic governments and global organisations, especially the United Nations. Margaret Thatcher, unsurprisingly, was not sympathetic to the report, which in her view positioned the West as exploiters and capitalism as an exploitative system. Brian Griffiths came to the same conclusion, writing in 1981, that he considered it an attempt to impose a 'global welfare state based on an automatic system of taxation'.[66] Edward Heath (who had served on the Brandt commission), in a rare moment of contact with Margaret Thatcher, wrote to her with some advice for a forthcoming conference in Mexico, which was convened to discuss the report – Thatcher did not follow her former boss's guidance.[67] The fact was that Thatcher was more likely to concur with Anthony Parsons, the UK's representative at the UN, who in his valedictory dispatch on the 'bizarre world' of the United Nations concluded that its 'central premise' of 'North/South dialogue' had 'degenerated into a sea of meaningless words' with aid programmes that were 'top heavy and slow moving'. Nor did Parsons think it was an area in which the Soviet Union took much interest (and by implication nor should the West). According to Parsons, the UN role required 'resistance to stupefying boredom' and the 'patience of Job'.[68]

For the churches and Christian organisations that had been campaigning on poverty in the developing world for the last twenty years, the Brandt Report was welcomed. Like *Faith in the City*, its findings were distributed to the parishes through a study pack complete with cassette tape (narrated by Edward Heath) and a trading game. For those in the pews, the cause of international aid was a less contentious issue than domestic poverty given that it was less overtly political and was thus more easily categorised as a legitimate sphere of Christian concern.

Given the success and growth of organisations such as Christian Aid and CAFOD since the 1960s, it was perhaps easy to accuse Christians of 'abandoning faith in the next world for certainties about the third world'. John Gummer was certainly of the view that humanitarianism had replaced evangelicalism as Christians' *raison d'être* even though his government were guilty of encouraging this phenomenon. Christian Aid, for example, saw its income rise from £5.5 million in 1979 to £28 million in 1989, largely due to it receiving government support for the first time.[69] Gummer could be accused of making a facile point, but in some senses the charge was a fair one. Over the course of thirty years, Christian relief organisations had become noticeably less evangelical, began to hire non-Christians, and engaged in political lobbying as well as professional advertising. These organisations, both secular and Christian, were certainly beneficiaries of the growing public consciousness about poverty in the developing world in the 1980s, but this had very little to do with secularisation or politicisation; it was chiefly down to a new phenomenon in contemporary culture: the humanitarian celebrity.

Gone were the days when coked up pop stars threw TV sets out of hotel windows; the ageing rockers of the '80s were now to be seen on TV, banging their fists on the table in moral earnestness, pleading to viewers 'Give me the F***ING MONEY!' Live Aid in 1985 was not the beginnings of the VIP crusade against global poverty; this perhaps could be dated back to George Harrison's concert for famine relief in Bangladesh in 1971. But it was only in the 1980s, with the emergence of Live Aid as well as Children in Need and Comic Relief, that such causes significantly galvanised both the press and public. Ironically, Live Aid had all the markings of a Thatcherite parable: the uniting of the Anglo-American world, capitalism contributing to the greater good, and one man determined to enact change against an establishment that did not want to know. Geldof later admitted a degree of affinity with Thatcher: 'She lashed out with her handbag at every institution she saw; the monarchy, the old Tory Party, the old Labour Party, the trade unions. She was a punk.'[70] Although Thatcher may never have realised it, Bob Geldof was a living embodiment of her idealised vision of the individual: a Good Samaritan who refused to pass by on the other side.

Few could have predicted that what started as a Christmas single and a pop concert would give rise to a culture of international humanitarianism, which over ten years would prove as much a magnet for popular appeal as any Thatcherite call to self-interest. No longer were such causes confined to a minority group of left-wing or Christian activists, but, with the help of a show-business-obsessed media, was a cause that was able to arouse an impressive amount of national outrage and united action. The British public raised more money than the government for the Ethiopian famine relief with the Treasury actually profiting from the VAT receipts from the Christmas charity single. In the long term, celebrities would become much more successful in rattling the nation's conscience than either clergymen or politicians. In the aftermath of the Miners' Strike, *The Times* observed that Live Aid 'felt like the healing of our own nation'.[71] The comparison was a logical one, for these endeavours did inspire a new type of solidarity, which had very little to do with old politics, ideology or religion but satisfied the British yearning for unity and community in a fractured age and made that much more attractive with a sprinkling of stardust. Clergymen may have been chosen as the figureheads of the Miners' Hardship Fund in 1984, but it would be celebrities who would subsequently take up the cross.

Conservatives had not yet cottoned on to the strength of popular feeling and political potential that such causes afforded, but Labour and the Alliance had. In 1987 Labour pledged to double the aid budget within five years and create a special department for overseas aid. Live Aid, it has been said, was much more influential than the Miners' Strike in the formulation of Tony Blair's socialism and as Prime Minister he would prove himself particularly able at tapping into this new celebrity-driven, humanitarian-inspired solidarity. By the late noughties, largely as a result of public pressure, the maintenance of Britain's international aid budget would become the one issue on which there would be cross-party consensus.

VII. Dog-collar diplomacy

RELATIONS BETWEEN THE Foreign Office and the Church continued to operate along the same lines as they had done at the start of
the Cold War in the 1950s: as an exchange of information rather than
of pressure. A FCO diplomat continued to sit on the Church's International Affairs committee, while all bishops received FCO briefings
before their foreign visits. Archbishop Runcie himself was in regular contact with the Head of the Soviet Department in the Foreign
Office, partly because of his close relations with the Russian Orthodox
Church (he had chaired the Anglican-Orthodox Commission in the
1970s). Nor did the Foreign Office object when Runcie sent envoys to
the international gathering of religious leaders at the Moscow Peace
Conference, unlike in the US where the State Department reportedly
urged the Catholic bishops not to go and even the Vice President personally tried to dissuade Billy Graham from attending.

The same year, a delegation from the Church of England toured the
churches in Eastern Europe, which included a trip to Zagorsk, the home
of the Russian Orthodoxy and a stay in the British embassy in Moscow ('my bathroom is like the Booking hall at St Pancras Station and
the water flowed as slowly as the tickets do there', observed one of the
party).[72] It appears not to have been a serious diplomatic mission rather
a nosing around to check the pulse of Christianity behind the Iron Curtain. Reporting on the healthy state of the Russian Orthodox Church,
Rev. Paul Oestreicher noted with some surprise: 'There is no sign of a
dying church here' with congregational numbers more considerable
'than would be found in English parish churches – or even Cathedrals
– on a week-day evening'.[73]

When, in 1980, Cardinal Laszlo Lekai of Hungary visited England,
the Foreign Office, Church of England and the Catholic Church all
went out of their way to make him feel welcome. Lekai was an important figure within Eastern European Catholicism who was credited

with preserving the Catholic Church in his native land (his predecessor had had to run his ministry from the US embassy after the 1956 Hungarian uprising); but many considered that Lekai had gone too far in supporting the state. Within Hungary, he was satirically known as the 'peace priest'. On his visit to London, Lekai was treated to some of the finer things in the 'free world'; a lunch at the Athenaeum Club, tea at St Paul's, a day at the Henley Regatta and, finally, a pilgrimage to Thomas à Becket's tomb at Canterbury. (Perhaps it was hoped that Cardinal Lekai might be inspired by Becket's example.)

Runcie was always mindful to tread a fine line between cordiality and criticism with the Russian patriarchs. When he publicly came out in support of the government's proposed boycott the Moscow Olympics in 1980, it was misconstrued in Russia: 'What you said was no doubt seen in Moscow as support for the Conservative line, just as the Patriarch has to voice support for Soviet foreign policy,' noted one of his staff.[74] The concept of an Established Church that was openly critical of the state was not something that made much sense to the subservient patriarchs of the Russian Orthodox Church.

As the Archbishop of Canterbury's diplomatic envoy, Terry Waite's chief responsibility was as ambassador to the Anglican Communion, but it was not long before he veered off his official job description and became consumed by the more dangerous and exciting world of hostage negotiation. In the days when hostage crises in the Middle East were not a media show and negotiators had not yet realised the power of domestic public pressure, Terry Waite was to prove himself an extremely able man behind the scenes.

Since the 1979 Revolution, all clergy in the Anglican diocese of Iran had been either killed, imprisoned or exiled. The bishop had had his house broken into and his son had been murdered. His secretary, Miss Waddell, had failed to get an exit visa and had been ambushed in a hotel where she had been gagged, blindfolded and detained along with two missionaries and one English businessman. Tehran radio had reported that the government had unmasked a plot to overthrow the revolution, involving the Church of England, with Miss Waddell allegedly a spy backed by the CIA. After weeks of silence, Tehran agreed to enter negotiations about the prisoners, but only in exchange for two Iranian students then imprisoned in Britain. The Foreign Office, though, was in no position to respond. Anglo-Iranian relations, which had weakened since the revolution, had completely frozen in the wake of the Iranian embassy siege in May 1980, which Tehran claimed had been deliberately staged by the UK and US governments. Unable to call on the Foreign Office for help, Terry Waite turned to Archbishop Capucci, the Vatican's negotiator in the Middle East who was then playing a key role in the ongoing US-Iranian hostage crisis and was known to have the sympathetic ear of Ayatollah Khomeini. Capucci was a hero in the Middle East after serving twelve years in prison for smuggling arms to the PLO (they had been found in the back of his Mercedes limousine), with the governments of Egypt, Iraq, Libya and Syria all issuing stamps celebrating the archbishop. Capucci arrived in London in October 1980, where he was hosted by the Bishop of London, given full use of the Archbishop of Canterbury's car and, with the agreement of the Foreign Office, allowed to visit the Iranian students being detained in Wormwood Scrubs. Runcie also handed Capucci documents refuting any conspiracy claims and a personal letter from himself to Ayatollah Khomeini reassuring him of the Anglican prisoners' innocence. Four months later, to the Foreign Office's surprise, the Iranian captives were released in a move that demonstrated not only the diplomatic skills of the archbishop's envoy but also the level of trust and cooperation that existed between the Vatican and Lambeth Palace.[75]

Waite's next success came in negotiating the release of British citizens being held in Libya. Foreign Office relations with Libya at this point were as bad if not worse than they had been with Iran especially following the Libyan embassy siege in 1984, in which policewoman Yvonne Fletcher had been killed. So when it came to the capturing of four British nationals by the Libyan government, the Foreign Office turned to Terry Waite for help. In what must have been a bizarre scene, Waite spent the Christmas of 1984 in a Bedouin tent with Colonel Gaddafi. Waite's first smart move was to greet Gaddafi in Arabic; his second was to present the leader, who had a high regard of his own intellectual capabilities, with a book on the relationship between Greek and Arabic thought. Gaddafi treated his guest and the prisoners to a carol service and later insisted on phoning the Archbishop of Canterbury to wish him a Merry Christmas. Waite's combination of flattery and 'soft' diplomacy had worked; months later the prisoners were released.

It was not long before Waite's negotiating skills became of great interest to the Americans, who contacted him, via the Presbyterian Church of America, to help with the release of American captives in the Middle East. Robert Runcie, conscious of the need to rein in Waite, urged him to return to prepare for the forthcoming Lambeth Conference. Runcie had been warned by Cabinet Secretary Sir Robert Armstrong not to get too involved with the Americans, but Waite was adamant that he could do some good.

Waite was later to become implicated in selling arms for hostages as part of the US Iran-Contra affair. He always insisted that he did not know about the arms to Iran and that the Americans had double-crossed him by negotiating with Hezbollah. Waite was captured in Beirut and held in chains for five years with no word from his captors as to whether he was alive or dead. The only way that Lambeth Palace knew anything of his situation was through a Kurdish man whom Runcie's PA used to meet at Victoria Station for information. Runcie kept a vigil and candle burning continually in the years that Waite was held in captivity.

Theories and rumours are still rife as to why Waite was released when he was, with some even suggesting that it had been Iran rather than the Libyans who had been responsible for the Lockerbie bombing of Pan Am Flight 103, but that the American and British were content to allow Libyans to be blamed to ease tensions with Iran. Days after

Libyan intelligence officers were charged with the Lockerbie bombing, Waite and his fellow prisoners were released.[76] Reflecting on Waite's role, Runcie later said: 'Of course it was totally absorbing to him, but if he was going to be an international negotiator, he oughtn't [have been] on my staff.'[77]

•   •   •

IN 1990, AS the Iron Curtain was being ripped down across Europe, Thatcher used the occasion of what would be her final party conference speech to declare that the 'secular creed' of socialism had 'utterly failed' and that the moral case for a free capitalist society reigned supreme: 'Ours is a creed which travels and endures. Its truths are written in the human heart. It is the faith which once more has given life to Britain and offers hope to the world.'[78] According to Thatcher the victory of capitalism over communism was not an economic, or even diplomatic, success but a moral victory. Capitalism was presented as the natural order, one from which both Britain and Eastern Europe had temporarily diverted, but had been steered back onto the right path once more. Thatcher seemed to present the outcome of the Cold War as an act of divine providence, with herself as a victorious Christian warrior; a portrayal which her subsequent memoirs and lecture tour did much to cement. Delivering a speech to the Polish Senate in 1991, Margaret Thatcher declared: 'it is not just that capitalism works. It is not just that capitalism is morally right. What we have to recognise and proclaim with the most intense conviction is that capitalism works *because* it is morally right.'[79]

CHAPTER NINE

EXODUS NATION

*'The Church has "come down in the world" like an aristocrat
in a revolution. In twentieth-century terms, it finds itself in a
buyers', not a sellers' market ... It is no longer for the Christians
to dictate terms, but rather to see how and where they fit in to
a world that no longer gives them a prime place.'*
— MONICA FURLONG, 2000[1]

*'A society has not ceased to be Christian until it
has become positively something else.'*
— T. S. ELIOT, *CHRISTIANITY AND CULTURE,* 1940[2]

IN 1941, WILLIAM Temple had claimed that 'all the great political questions of our day are primarily theological' and this still
rung true forty years later as Christianity continued to be an
important means and prism through which political decisions were
conceived, communicated and assessed. Reformulating Temple's statement slightly, it might be said that all the great theological questions

were primarily political given the level of partisan squabbling that surrounded much of the ecclesiastical debates of the 1980s.[3] The Thatcher years were marked by a cross-fertilisation between religious and political conservatism on the one hand and liberal Anglicanism and progressive politics on the other. In the end, the New Right posed a theological challenge to liberal Anglicanism just as liberal Anglicanism posed a political challenge to the New Right. This debate may have been uniquely focused around the politics of late-twentieth-century Britain, yet these contrasting doctrinal positions had a much longer history. Emerging in embryonic form in the nineteenth century, this division had become clearly evident by the 1940s and, for this reason, it could be argued that much of the script and sentiments that would determine the conflict between the Church and the Tory government in the 1980s, had already been penned by William Temple in his *Christianity and Social Order* and preached by Alderman Roberts from the pulpit of Finkin Street Church some forty years earlier. Throughout the century the division between reformists and reactionaries within the Church loosely paralleled the progressive and conservative boundaries within politics and shaped both Christianity and politics accordingly. This dualism intensified rather than dissipated following the collapse of worship in the 1960s. The war of words between the New Right and liberal Anglicans in the 1980s represented the final breath of this theo-political tradition.

In his *Case for Conservatism*, Lord Hailsham considered that when a politician turned to religion for legitimising purposes, it was the 'end of honest politics'.[4] But as tempting as it is to dismissive Margaret Thatcher's appeal to an individualistic Christianity as a debasement of both Scripture and politics, it is important to appreciate not only its sincere origins but also its context. Britain saw the rise of a religiously flavoured political conservatism in the 1970s, which tagged itself (somewhat clumsily) onto classical liberal economics. The mood that underscored all the anger about trade union militancy, rising inflation and national self-doubt was a paranoia about the decline of traditional middle-class (Christian) values prompted by secularisation. It was no accident that those such as Mary Whitehouse, Maurice Cowling, Enoch Powell and John Gummer, saw *secular* liberalism as the enemy, not just liberalism or socialism.

Both Britain and the US experienced a Christian Conservative movement in the late-twentieth century, which intertwined a moralistic with a capitalistic agenda and engaged in a cultural and economic war of words with secular progressive liberals. That the Christian Right in Britain was to prove less pervasive and powerful than that in America was largely down to the fact that the British were more secular. Yet one need only to name check Maurice Cowling, Enoch Powell, Mary Whitehouse and Margaret Thatcher to realise that the Christian Conservative movement in the UK was not part of an international phenomenon but very much rooted in the ideas, prejudices and tastes of Englishness. It was inextricably tied to the religious culture of England (rather than Britain) and in particular, to the historic bond between Toryism and Anglicanism. The revision of the 1662 Prayer Book incited more anger and mobilised greater opposition than the reform of the Abortion Act, for example. While American political culture still fed off its Puritan roots, the age-old fight concerning Anglican uniformity continued to be the source of conflict within England. Contrasting religious histories and cultures, therefore, are as crucial as congregational figures in explaining the varying fortunes and character of UK and US Christian conservatism.

Thatcherism represented the casting aside of One-nation Toryism and the birth of a new brand of Conservatism, which was marked by its radical evangelical fervour and individualistic message, and which even Margaret Thatcher admitted owed more to nineteenth-century liberalism than Tory tradition. This switch was of course symbolised in the changing class make-up of the party, as the grammar-school boys seized the baton from the gentleman squires. The Thatcher years symbolised not just the end of the post-war consensus, but, as Stephen Haseler noted, the final death nail to the culture of paternalism, which was a long-established tradition in British politics that incorporated different Christian traditions, was ingrained in the welfare state and guided all three parties and class relations.[5] By destroying paternalism, Thatcher succeeded in making Britain more egalitarian in an American sense, but she also created a nation more sharply divided into winners and losers.

Paradoxically, while politics in the 1980s was characterised by conviction, polarisation and fundamental truths, Christianity on the other hand was associated with ambiguity, compassion and dialogue. To put it bluntly, politics had replaced religion as the sphere of certainty. As tempting as it is to view Anglicanism's twentieth century as one of increasing radicalism, one need only compare the words espoused by some of the clergy in the 1880s with those in the 1980s to realise that this was not so. Its intervention and influence in the 1980s although limited was important and demonstrated that even in more secular times, the Church still retained authority as custodians of consensus and moral judgement. Paradoxically, despite its spirited defence of the welfare state, the Church actually benefited from growing disillusionment towards bureaucratic centralism as it enhanced its role and sought its legitimacy from its pastoral support within civil society. The Church's foray into politics, however, exacerbated existing tensions within its organisation. The nature and purpose of the Church's prophecy emerged as one of the chief dividing lines between liberals and traditionalists as prelates struggled with the difficult balancing act of leading both the Church and those outside it. At the heart of this tension was a fundamental dilemma concerning the role of the national Church in a secular age: should the Church exist for the benefit of those who are not members of it?

The divide between the Church and the Tory Party, although both political and theological, was also historical, hinging as it did

on two conflicting religious narratives of modern British history.
Thatcher, on the one hand, crudely characterised the post-war
years as a period of individual and national moral decay, which
she unfavourably contrasted with those values which had sustained
the Victorian era; that of self-help, moral restraint and laissez-faire
capitalism. Anglican leaders, in contrast, tended to portray the
nineteenth century as a time when the Industrial Revolution and
imperialism had been borne on the backs of the nation's powerless
citizens while it was only in the mid-twentieth century with the
formation of the welfare state that the nation had transformed into
a compassionate Christian society.

Both Thatcherism and liberal Anglicanism were rooted in providential narratives of the political history of England, which betrayed
divergent understandings of the meaning and characteristics of
Englishness and of the nature of Christianity itself. But both were
essentially flawed, given that they rested on an increasingly outdated idea that Britain was still a Christian country. Developments
over subsequent decades would eventually render both these positions untenable and the conflict between the Church and the Tory
Party largely irrelevant, as a new configuration of the relationship
between religion and politics in Britain would prompt a reordering
of the nation's spiritual identity.

I. The death of public Anglicanism

PUBLIC ANGLICANISM, THAT is, an understanding of the Established
Church as a moderate, non-partisan voice in the political realm, first
obtained currency at the beginning of the twentieth century and was
resuscitated with some success in the 1980s. Once Margaret Thatcher
left office, however, much of the motivation behind this prophecy dissipated. In the 1990s, the Board for Social Responsibility was notably

more muted, the Synod became consumed by ecclesiastical affairs, and even the new generation of bishops seemed unwilling to rock the political boat as their predecessors had done. John Major's premiership signalled an immediate change in tone from Thatcher as the affable former bank manager pledged to create a 'nation at ease with itself'. At the 1992 election, the churches of Manchester issued yet another appeal to voters, which was distinctly anti-Tory in tone, although the Suffragan Bishop of Salford wondered whether they had highlighted the right cause: 'Would it have been better under Labour? ...we may need to recognise that only in the Lord will there be built a kingdom of justice, love and peace.'[6]

If Runcie's time at Lambeth would be remembered for the Church's run-ins with the Thatcher government, then his successor's period in office would be defined by a preoccupation with internal ecclesiastical affairs. Archbishop George Carey was to have a tough ride at Canterbury between 1991 and 2002. Some critics would say, not without a hint of snobbery, that the son of a hospital porter from the East End – the first archbishop for centuries not to have been to either Oxford or Cambridge – was not quite up to the job; his foes even joked that he was Margaret Thatcher's revenge on the Church of England. Yet these assessments do not take into account the disastrous situation Carey was confronted with. In what was one of the most scandalous examples of financial ineptitude ever demonstrated by a leading British institution, in 1992 it was revealed that the Church Commissioners, through reckless speculation in the property market, had managed to wipe off £500 million of the Church's assets. It turned out that the commissioners had been indulging in exactly the type of casino-capitalism that clergymen had exhausted so much energy denouncing in the 1980s. The shadowy figure behind the Church's investment portfolio was the First Church Estates Commissioner, Sir Douglas Lovelock, whose rationale was to invest and *keep on investing* through the securement of loans, which rose from £4.7 million to £518 million in a matter of years. At one point the Church had £60 million ventured in the US and £40 million in Japan as well as a considerable amount in the UK.[7] When the property recession hit in the early 1990s, the Church's assets were doomed. What was striking is that hardly anyone seemed to be aware of what was about to unfold, not even the Second Church Estates Commissioner and parliamentary representative on the committee, Michael Alison MP. After all its warnings to the government on the dangers of the market, no one had thought to subject the Church's finances to the same scrutiny, especially not the General Synod, which was guilty of spending most of the funds. An independent inquiry later found that 'reckless property investments, unethical conduct, massive borrowings of hundreds of millions of pounds and a level of administrative incompetence' had characterised the Commissioners' dealings.[8] Much to the Church's embarrassment, the Archbishop of Canterbury was called to give evidence before a Parliamentary Select Committee, but Lovelock himself was never held to account.[9]

The ripples of this disaster would be felt over the next ten years as the Church effectively drew up the drawbridge and got its house in order. Archbishop Carey was accused of being a bureaucratic bore, yet he had little choice but to regain some control over an organisation facing financial ruin. Parishes were closed, the number of priests reduced from 12,000 to 8,000 and even the Commissioners' annual £1 million donation to the Church Urban Fund ceased.[10] The Archbishop's Council formed in 1999 was essentially a centralising measure, which took power from the Synod, Commissioners and pretty much every other semi-autonomous part of the Church. Meanwhile, the Church became even more reliant on contributions from its congregations and thus ever more accountable to its loyal adherents.

A period of exhausting introspection and division plagued the Church of England, similar to that which had paralysed the Labour Party the previous decade. In earlier times, the battles for the identity of Anglicanism had centred on liturgy and worship, yet by the 1990s it had become entirely fixed on who was qualified to lead the flock. On the subject of female ordination, never was there a matter to arouse such passions within the Church but generate so little interest amongst the public. 'Vicars in Knickers' was the The Sun's infamous headline when the Measure finally passed in November 1992. Soon, though, the story became about the impending schism within Anglicanism rather than the decision itself, with the Church increasingly perceived not as a progressive institution, as liberals had hoped, but that of a broken family, ripping itself apart and unaware of the outside world that it was meant to serve. David Jenkins lambasted the 'medieval' and 'neurotic' opinions of those opposed to female ordination, whose arguments he thought were 'tinged with misogyny'.[11] Traditionalist Francis Brown, chairman of the Anglo-Catholic group Ecclesia, fought back with equal aggression when the vote was announced: 'The Church of England will soon be no more than a rotting carcass.'[12]

If ordaining female priests, as traditionalists argued, robbed the Church of England of its place in the universal Catholic Church, then the divisions that engulfed Anglicanism over the issue also robbed it of any pretensions of being a national Church. The admittance of women into the priesthood was no Reformation moment, but had definite parallels with the nineteenth-century Oxford Movement: the last time a wave of Anglicans flocked to the Tiber in protest to the liberal dilution of Anglicanism. The exodus, though, was less than some feared – four bishops and approximately 300 clergy – and far less than in Cardinal Newman's day. Numerically speaking, this was a loss that the Church could afford, especially given that female priests would within twenty years make up the majority of new ordinands. The compromise of appointing 'flying bishops' to administer those parishes unwilling to accept the new reality was a temporary measure rather than a permanent solution, given that the decision over female bishops inevitably loomed on the horizon.

Carey's successor, Rowan Williams, assumed his role in 2002 and was immediately handed the unenviable task of keeping together not just the Church of England but the whole of the Anglican Communion

over an issue that was to prove even more fractious than female ordination. In 1998, the Lambeth Conference had passed what had seemed
an unequivocal resolution affirming heterosexual relationships as the
norm and prohibiting the blessing of same sex unions or the ordination
of those in a same gender relationship. Bishops had long been ordaining gay priests under a hushed policy of 'don't ask, don't tell' but the
matter was brought to a head in 2003 when, in defiance of Anglican
teaching, the American Episcopal Church consecrated openly gay
Gene Robinson as the Bishop of New Hampshire.

The Archbishop of Canterbury, Rowan Williams, was soon to be
confronted with a similar scenario much closer to home when Jeffrey
John, a homosexual priest in a celibate relationship, was selected as
the Bishop of Reading. The Bishop of Oxford, who had forwarded
John, must have been aware of the likely outcry. Trying to coerce the
Church in this public way, however, was not the Anglican way of doing
things and it was only a matter of time before John withdrew his name.

Williams's decision to elevate the subject to Communion level was
designed to keep everyone on board but it was also a convenient delay-
ing tactic. Anglicans dedicated years to formulating what was called
the 'Anglican Communion Covenant', but as it did not commit to a
policy on homosexuality, only prevented branches of the Communion
from acting alone, it failed to address the matter in hand. It also showed
Canterbury desperately trying to cling on to its prime place when the
numeric strength of other parts of the Communion, particularly in
Africa, now weighed heavily against it. Unveiled in 2010, the agreement satisfied neither liberals nor the conservatives and completely
contravened the autonomous basis of the Anglican Communion. It
was quietly shelved.

Williams, who probably commanded greater respect in the Church
than any of his predecessors, was no manager of men. His subtle call
for 'dialogues' rather than resolution on the pressing subject of women
bishops failed to convince even his keenest advocates. This was in

contrast to his successor Archbishop Justin Welby, a former oil executive, who eventually achieved the necessary majority in the Synod
not through persuasion but tactics, by hastening the legislative time-
table, filling the relevant committees with senior women, and having
one-to-one meetings with both supporters and opponents. But more
important than any shrewd maneuvering by the archbishop was the
public and parliamentary outcry following the initial rejection by
the Synod. When it finally passed in July 2014 it was greeted with little fanfare; the perception amongst a broadly disinterested public was
not jubilation, rather 'what took you so long?'

Like the Falklands War in 1982, so Labour's controversial war in Iraq
in 2003 proved to be a galvanising moment for the Church. Rowan Williams was one of the leading critics of the war although he saved his most
damning attack for the memorial service in 2009, delivering a sermon
that made Runcie's Falklands' speech appear rather tame in comparison. Unlike 1982, however, it was people demonstrating on the streets
rather than sermons in pulpits which became the lasting emblem of the
hostility towards military engagement in the Middle East.

While George Carey had made faint disapproving noises about
divorce and homosexuality, his successor did not see much point. 'I
just wonder a bit whether, you know,' Williams told the The Guardian
in 2006, 'when an archbishop condemns something, suddenly in the
bedsits of north London, somebody says, "Oh, I shouldn't be having
premarital sex."'[13] Robert Runcie and David Sheppard had taken a similar view, yet the difference now was that hardly anyone challenged it;
the successors to Whitehouse and Gillick were nowhere to be heard.
Condemnatory language was no longer part of the clergy's vocabulary
as they came to accept the rapid pace at which societal attitudes were
changing, particularly on homosexuality; a matter over which not only
the Church but also Parliament and the press appeared to be constantly
playing catch-up. When the Act allowing gay marriage was passed in
2014, it exposed the gulf that now existed between secular law and the

teachings of the Established Church. In the 1960s, Parliament had been committed to framing the reforming legislation on homosexuality in accordance with what was deemed acceptable to the Church of England. In 2014, the government made sure to consult and consider the Church and other faiths, although this was only to ensure that an appropriate sub-clause was agreed exempting them from the law of the land.

Christians may have been pioneers in the environmental movement, yet as the matter assumed greater urgency and prominence, far greater attention was paid to scientists, environmental campaign groups and the international lobby movement. Few considered that the churches might have something distinct to say about the moral dilemmas concerning human's stewardship of the earth. This was in stark contrast to nuclear weaponry, which had once been discussed in the same apocalyptic terms.

One matter where the Christian laity certainly made their mark was leading the Make Poverty History and Jubilee 2000 campaigns. Surpassing the Live Aid campaign of 1985, this time around the goal was not public donations but structural changes, by pressuring nations of the G8 to cancel their debts to the developing world. Christians may have made up a significant number of the foot soldiers, yet it was only able to generate public support and ultimately achieve political success with celebrity endorsement.

Rowan Williams, a former member of the Labour Party and CND supporter, was arguably the most left-wing archbishop to occupy Lambeth Palace since William Temple. He was essentially paternalistic in his politics, but his view of capitalism was uncompromising. 'Every transaction in the developed economies of the West can be interpreted as an act of aggression against the economic losers in the worldwide game,' he wrote in 2002.[14] But just at the time when Britain was crying out for some moral direction in the wake of the 2008 financial crash, the archbishop seemed incapable of providing it. This was not because he was devoid of ideas, passion or boldness, but because Williams, unlike Temple, lacked that crucial ability to convey a comprehensive message to the un-churched mass. When the Church did attempt to question the moral practices of the financial world – as it did over the proliferation credit loan companies – the Church Commissioners yet again proved an embarrassment. In 2013, Archbishop Welby was forced to retract his bold pledge to 'sink' leading credit-lending firm Wonga when it was revealed that the Commissioners had investments in the company. The Church seem to specialise in such PR disasters, never more so than in 2010 when the anti-capitalist movement Occupy set up camp outside St Paul's. The Canon of the Cathedral, Giles Fraser resigned in opposition to the proposed use of force to evict the protestors, while the Bishop of London in a last-ditch compromise tried to lure them with a promise of a debate under Wren's dome. The Church was again caught in a conflict of interest, in this case, between a spiritual desire to demonstrate solidarity with the anti-capitalist protestors and a financial need to keep the tourists trickling through its cathedral doors. No one thought of staging a 24-hour evangelical rally outside the cathedral to convert the campers; it might have salvaged some credibility and undoubtedly would have compelled the occupiers to move along.

One positive change has been the growth of the Church's work in urban communities: a development that can be largely put down to *Faith in the City*. Despite its blackening by the Tory government, the report was treated seriously by those in Whitehall and, as a result, the Home Office set up a consultative group – the 'Inner Cities Religious Council' – which soon involved all faith groups. A tale of conflict was replaced with one of increasing cooperation as churches became more adept at applying for central and local government funds and the state ever more appreciative of their role. The Church Urban Fund continued and over the next ten years dished out over £30 million worth of grants to local projects, although its message became noticeably less politicised. This culture of collaboration continued under New Labour with all faith groups seen as vital agencies for fostering, something now dubbed 'social capital'. It has acquired new energy in this era of austerity, with parishes the location for food banks and credit unions, but the problems that were there in the 1980s still persist; fears about the loss of autonomy, bureaucratic obstructions and the dilemma of colluding with a government committed to a contraction in public funds.

It is generally considered good practice for the position of Archbishop of Canterbury to alternate between an evangelical and an Anglo-Catholic. The election of Justin Welby in 2013, though, symbolised something more specific: the rise of a new generation of upper-class English evangelicals taking the reins. A product of Eton and Cambridge, Welby was part of a cluster based at the Holy Trinity Brompton in London, home to the renowned Alpha Course; one of the rare evangelical success stories of the so-called 'decade of evangelicalism' of the 1990s. Much like the South Bank clergy before them, this group now yield considerable influence within the Church of England, but unlike their 1960s counterparts, they consider the social nature of the Christian faith in much broader terms, as both a Gospel for the rich and the poor. While Rowan Williams was famously arrested at a CND demonstration in the 1980s, Justin Welby, on the other hand, spent the decade negotiating contracts around the world as an executive for Enterprise Oil. With Archbishop Welby now serving on the Parliamentary Commission on Banking Standards, it might that his election finally represents a post-Thatcherite era for Anglicanism.

A statement by the Archbishop of Canterbury still has the potential to rile the government and make the headlines, but the bishops as a group certainly do not hold the same position in public life they once did. Apart from those at Canterbury and York, most Britons would be hard pressed to single out any other Anglican prelate by face or name; this was not the case in the 1980s. It is also unlikely that a Church report would have the same impact today as *Faith in the City* did thirty years ago, given the preponderance of think tanks publishing social investigations and commentary on a weekly basis. As coverage of religion has become more diverse, coverage of the Church of England has narrowed, with the media only interested when Anglicanism is in knots over sexual morality, faced with financial embarrassment, or at loggerheads with itself or the government. It is now commonplace for the political class to laud 'localism' as the solution to a host of problems, be it social fragmentation, bureaucratic centralism or the current disillusionment with institutions. The Church of England, like most faith organisations, represents one of the few public bodies that can truly claim to embody this principle, yet it is precisely its culture of autonomy which makes the Church of England such a messy and complicated business; orthodoxy across all spheres is impossible to enforce and leadership hard to get right. There is some truth in the claim that being Archbishop of Canterbury is as difficult a job as that of the England football manager; expectations are high and critique of their tactics and record are always forthcoming.

The Church maintains its prime place at the centre of Britain's ceremonial life, most recently witnessed in the celebration of the Duke and Duchess of Cambridge's wedding, the 2014 commemorations for the centenary of the First World War and, of course, the tempered and respectful funeral service for Britain's first female prime minister. The nation exceeds at spiritual pageantry and surely one of its chief successes has been the smooth integration of all faiths into national occasions and ceremonies over the last thirty years. The real test of this commitment, however, will undoubtedly come at the coronation of the next monarch.

The Church of England's constitutional position remains remarkably intact. Canon law is still an official part of the law of the land and must be ratified by Parliament. The Lords Spiritual managed to survive New Labour's cull of the second chamber and still deliver the morning prayers in Parliament and, while the Synod has complete control over its own affairs, Westminster has supreme authority should it ever wish to exercise it. Writing in the 1990s, Catholic historian Adrian Hastings considered that establishment makes 'less and less clear sense'.[15]

In truth, establishment has not made sense for a long time but it says much about the Church and its position that disestablishment has not been a serious political contention since the early twentieth century. What has been challenged is the Church of England's role as 'the conscience of the nation'. This was always a flawed concept but is now highly questionable. When, in 2001, the census revealed that over 70 per cent of Britons identified themselves as 'Christian', it was greeted with surprise and confusion by the press, politicians and most clergy, who were doubtful of its significance or sincerity. Ten years later in 2011, the figure had dropped to 59 per cent, while those claiming no religion had increased from 15 to 25 per cent. Britons are certainly becoming more irreligious rather than atheistic or agnostic, but the real question is whether the Church of England remains, as Clifford Longley put it in 1976, the 'place to stay away from, but on which they secretly depend, just as a rebelling adolescent needs to know his parents are still there'.[16]

II. The death of Tory Anglicanism

THE HISTORIC BOND between the Church of England and the Conservative Party had begun to dissolve in the inter-war period, but it was only from the late 1960s, as the Church moved to the left and the party took a sharp turn to the right, that this divergence became glaringly apparent and prompted a bitter fight over the ownership of the Church, politics and doctrine. When the Ordination of Women Measure reached the House of Commons for approval in 1993, however, only nineteen members (two-thirds Tories) voted against it. During the debate, there were notable contributions from Tory Anglicans in favour, the familiar but irrelevant call from Tony Benn for disestablishment, and strident Labour women praising it as a step towards equality, but most MPs were of the view that it was entirely a matter for the Church to decide. For some Anglican Tories, though, the admittance of women into the priesthood would be the trigger that would prompt their move to Rome. In her comprehensive critique, Ann Widdecombe complained that the Anglican leadership had been seduced by the spirit of the age and on female ordination had wilfully capitulated to secular feminist thought. Responding to a question from Labour MP Clare Short as to why she felt so much resentment, Widdecombe remarked bitterly: 'It is utter disbelief at what has been going on, that we have not only managed to consecrate bishops who do not believe in the resurrection and the virgin birth, but that we cannot get our moral message across. Yes, I am very angry.'[17] Widdecombe eventually came to the conclusion that only the Roman Catholic Church had the necessary authority, conviction and self-assurance to oppose the evils of the permissive society.[18]

John Gummer also spoke in opposition but from a position of regretful alienation rather indignation. In his view the Measure compromised 'the whole basis of the Elizabethan settlement', which had 'sought to create a Church of the nation in which everybody, except those who were at the extreme ends, could worship together'.[19] Gummer seemed to contradict himself, though, by proposing an inclusive concept of the congregation but an exclusive concept of who should be ministering them. He too would later convert to Rome.

Outside Parliament, another convert, journalist Charles Moore also laid the blame on the Church and specifically its obsession with politics, which he considered was 'indistinguishable from those of a reasonably decent, mildly Left-wing agnostic'.[20] Moore's sentiments reflected the way in which Tories tended to heap the responsibility on the Church and not admit that Conservatism itself had fundamentally altered too. Writing after his conversion, Moore portrayed Anglicanism as a disrupted and disordered community destroyed by modernity and unnecessary change:

I felt as someone feels who has lived in the neighbourhood all his life, and notices it going downhill. There are small niggles – more noise, more satellite dishes, more litter, ruder neighbours. Then there are worse things – demolition of buildings he loves, the tearing up of a park, the closing of a library, the spread of crime. At first he is determined to stay. But eventually something snaps … I feel rather like a man standing among packing cases and looking, for the last time, at the bare boards of his old home.[21]

According to Catholic convert William Oddie the move away from Anglicanism involved a transformation of 'one's entire historical consciousness'.[22] Anglican Conservatism had rested on a Protestant reading of the nation's story. How one viewed key episodes in England's past, such as the Reformation and, crucially, the Glorious Revolution of 1688, was central to Conservative identity. Becoming a Catholic, therefore, demanded a rewriting of this narrative. Foreseeing the potential ramifications of this as early as 1987, journalist T. E. Utley had described the process in pretty bleak terms: 'I shall have to become a ghetto Christian. This is a tragic thing for a man who is, not only by intellectual conviction but to the marrow of his being, an Anglican, one who loathes the idea of belonging to a sect which separates itself from English life.'[23]

And yet, the increasing prominence and respectability of Roman Catholicism by the 1990s meant, in fact, that the leap did not feel such a great one. Those converts to Catholicism did not feel like 'ghetto Christians' although Charles Moore admitted that in some sense it involved a certain renouncement of Englishness: 'Even I could see that a religion which was *merely* English could not possibly have been what Christ intended.'[24] With the conversion of these prominent figures to Rome, so one of the remaining threads of Anglican Conservatism died with them. No longer would the Conservative cause be linked or even associated with Anglicanism, or even Christianity, in the way that it had been. Anglicanism, once closely bound to Conservatism and Englishness, ceased to be a core component of either. These high-profile conversions had, however, the effect of further raising the profile of a distinctly English right-wing Catholicism.

In 1983, Catholic MP Chris Patten wrote that 'to describe Conservatism without mentioning Christianity would be like describing a barometer without referring to the mercury'.[25] Yet by the 1990s, there were fewer and fewer who would make this case. Thatcher certainly spelt out the Christian basis of neo-Conservatism yet while her successors adopted the economic message, they seemed to disregard the theology underpinning it. Those Conservative MPs elected in the 1980s may have been 'Thatcherite' in outlook, but they came from a much wider base, both socially and religiously. Those who had led the Anglican Conservative faction in the 1970s and '80s, the likes of Bernard Braine, Peter Bruinvels, Peter Mills, John Stokes, Ivor Stanbrook and Enoch Powell, had all left Parliament by the early 1990s, only to be replaced by a younger cohort of Conservative MPs for whom Anglicanism or even Christianity was not a core component of their political DNA.

If the Conservative brand had, as many people say, become 'toxic', this was partly down to the relentless challenge it had faced on its moral foundations and integrity from its former conscience, the Church of England, whose criticisms, unlike those from the left, cut much closer to the bone. The subsequent development of 'compassionate Conservatism' reflected a desire to soften the edges of Thatcherite ideology. In 1990, less than one month after Thatcher had left office, the Conservative Christian Fellowship (CCF) was founded by future *Times* columnist Tim Montgomerie, and others, out of a desire to rectify the broken link between the party and Christian denominations. That party activists felt the need to establish such an organisation was a sure sign that the breach between the Church of England and the Tory Party was complete. This new incarnation was not only non-denominational – signalling the growing number of Catholics and Nonconformists within the party – but also aimed at courting the Christian vote. The CCF seemed almost designed to answer that key question that had preyed on Conservatives consciences throughout the Thatcher period: could a Christian vote Conservative? The CCF, however, does not forward the Thatcherite gospel of individualism, but seeks to unify the party of both Macmillan and Thatcher by promoting a much more consensual and cohesive Conservatism.

The ambition of unifying the party of Macmillan and Thatcher was certainly Cameron's goal when he became leader; a commitment to a small state and individual enterprise combined with a paternalistic vision of the welfare state. But, tellingly, Cameron's vision was articulated in secular rather than Christian language. Indeed, one of the reasons why there was such confusion surrounding his concept of the 'Big Society' was because it was conceived in a secular framework; odd, given that it chiefly relied on faith groups for its implementation. David Cameron once said that his faith was a bit like the 'reception of Magic FM in the Chilterns: it sort of comes and goes'.[26] So it came as a great surprise to many, especially Anglicans, when, in 2014, Cameron penned a piece for the *Church Times* entitled: 'My faith in the Church of England'.[27] In a piece that read like a local squire writing in a parish newsletter, Cameron gave bland assurances that Britain was still a Christian country, praised faith as something that entreats people to 'make a difference' and reminded sceptics of the generous financial support that his government had given towards the nation's decaying cathedrals. The contrast with Thatcher's dogmatic assertions could not have been more stark, yet Cameron's letter is just the type of polite endorsement that the Established Church likes to receive from the state. Further evidence of such tokenism was the initiative of Education Secretary Michael Gove to issue a bound copy of the King James Bible to every primary school to coincide with its 400-year anniversary. The Bibles gathered dust in school libraries as teachers were unsure what precisely to do with them: 'It hasn't actually been opened. I've offered it as a drama prop, in case someone fancies wandering around dressed as a vicar with a Bible under their arm,' was the response from one head teacher from Barnsley.[28] The Secretary of State for Work and Pensions, Iain Duncan Smith, can be singled out as one of the few Conservative ministers whose faith has directly translated into policy and action. After his failed stint as leader of the party, Duncan Smith became a keen student of Catholic social teaching and, in 2004, set up the Centre for Social Justice, which would later act as the source of inspiration for many of the Conservative-led coalition's social and welfare policies. Although, it is precisely because Duncan Smith claims a Christian motivation that he has faced more criticism from the churches than any other minister.

Christianity remains an important thread within the Conservative Party even if it does not always sit well with Cameron's socially liberal, metropolitan and tolerant rebranding of Conservatism. Outside the party, there remains a religious right-wing lobby – largely evangelical in flavour – which still views the secular multicultural left as the enemy, although the fight for the preservation of Britain's Christian heritage has been complicated by a new target: Islam.

The Christian Right in Britain is generally speaking left-of-centre politically. There are, in fact, very few who dare forward the Christian case for the free economy with the scriptural force and certainty that Margaret Thatcher did thirty years ago; a silence, which in itself reflects both the secularisation of British politics and the current denigration of capitalism.

The connection between Conservatism and Anglicanism is still evident at the grassroots although David Cameron's commitment to gay marriage has meant that many now consider that it is their party rather than their Church that is betraying its moral principles. This disaffection with the moral direction of the Conservative Party is something that UKIP's Nigel Farage has seized upon in a quest to broaden his party's appeal beyond euroscepticism. In UKIP, the old Thatcher cries of moral and national degeneration are finding their voice once more.

III. A brief re-encounter with Christian socialism

REFLECTING ON THE problems in the 1980s, Tony Blair once conceded that 'the Left got into trouble when its basic values became divorced from ... ethical socialism [and] Christian socialism'.[29] Blair wrote this in 1996 just at the time when he was seeking to present Labour as a credible force when there were clear political gains to be made in renouncing the ideological purity of the 1980s and pronouncing the party's Christian/ ethical heritage. Yet, as is widely recognised, Blair himself was a man of profound faith who had undergone conversion while at Oxford and whose Christian social understanding was never in doubt, even if he was discouraged by his PR men from openly talking about it. 'Religion was more important to him than anyone I had ever met outside the priesthood,' Cherie Blair later wrote of her husband.[30] Like his predecessor, John Smith, Tony Blair self-consciously sought to reignite the Christian socialist roots of the labour movement as a way of repositioning the party back onto the centre ground. Having won the symbolic battle over Clause IV, Blair set out his definition of New Labour at the party conference in 1995:

> Socialism to me was never about nationalisation or the power of the state. It is a moral purpose to life, a set of values, a belief in society, in co-operation. It is how I try to live my life: the simple truths. I am worth no more than any other man, I am my brother's keeper, I will not walk by on the other side. We aren't simply people set in isolation from each other, face to face with eternity, but members of the same family, the same community, the same human race. This is my socialism. And the irony of our long years in opposition is that those values are shared by the vast majority of the British people.[31]

In tone and language, the New Labour project seemed remarkably similar to the Church's position during the Thatcher years. Blair even made an explicit connection between the Church's leadership on social issues in the 1980s and the priorities of New Labour. 'The essential challenge posed by *Faith in the City* remains unanswered,' Blair posited in an article for *The Guardian* in 1996, a decade after the report had been published, 'Do we have the confidence and the ideas as a nation to achieve prosperity with fairness in the next century?'[32] The mid-1990s saw a growing closeness between Christian leaders and the Labour Party. Shadow ministers held regular meetings with a group of bishops, while David Sheppard was invited to sit on the committee of the Institute of Public Policy Research's Commission for Social Justice. The report, published in 1994, directly drew on *Faith in the City* and would eventually act as the foundation for New Labour's 'social exclusion' agenda once in office.[33] Sheppard actually turned down the offer, fearing that such an association would align him too closely with the party, although he would later sit on the Labour benches – as would other retired Anglican bishops who were granted ex-officio seats in the House of Lords.

Blair the Christian socialist, as we know, would later transform into Blair the Crusader. Any Christian ethos behind the New Labour project was quietly shelved as the domestic overspill from the War on Terror forced the government to face up to the complications of governing Britain's multi-faith society. Few were surprised when Blair the closet Catholic converted to Rome when he left office; the real question that many wanted to have answered was how Blair was able to reconcile his Christian faith with his political actions. Gordon Brown was the son of the Manse from Kirkcaldy and, like Thatcher, indulged in rose-tinted recollections of his minister father, although he never sought any biblical endorsement for his politics and only offered vague references to his 'moral compass'. Ed Miliband is the first non-Christian Labour leader since Neil Kinnock, although he describes himself, somewhat confusingly, as someone who does not believe in God but does have 'faith'.[34] There is little evidence that the current Labour Party shows much interest in Christian socialism although there are signs that its 'responsible capitalism' agenda draws some inspiration from Catholic social teaching. In seeking to hark back to a pre-statist tradition of socialism, it is hardly surprising that those on the left have bypassed Anglican theology and looked to the Catholic notion of the common good.

IV. The birth of multi-faith Britain

IN THE 1980s the debate on religion and politics in Britain hinged on where Christianity stood in respect of the market and the state. In the 2000s it was an altogether different issue: how religious extremism threatened Britain's secular values of liberty, tolerance and democracy. Here, after all, has been the great change since the Thatcher years: the tussle over Protestant England has been replaced with a debate, long overdue, about the nature of multi-faith Britain. But this was not triggered by a positive desire to integrate ostracised believers within British society, but a panic measure to address the threat of home-grown Islamic fundamentalism in the wake of the War of Terror. For Britain's Muslims it has resulted in mixed fortunes; greater legal recognition and presence in British public life has been matched with the inevitable disadvantages of living under a culture of heightened Islamophobia. Although it may come as no consolation, it is a process and a struggle with which Britain's Nonconformists, Catholics and Jews are intimately familiar.

One of the inevitable consequences of this has been the dominance of the radical fringe in the public discussion of religion. The moderate majority of believers are frequently drowned out by the aggressive and provocative shouts of fundamentalists, be they militant atheists, Islamic extremists or Conservative evangelicals. These developments have reordered how religion is dealt with by the ruling elite and the media. While politicians speak less about their personal faith, they now speak much more about religion. While the notion of Britain's Christian heritage still retains currency, no longer do politicians (or churchmen) make wide-ranging assertions about the relationship between Christian and political values as Margaret Thatcher once did. The focus has inevitably turned to a much trickier subject: the individual rights of the believer in a liberal secular democracy. Religious organisations are invited to make a contribution to civil society but it is on condition that they operate within the rules of tolerance and pluralism, which some faith organisations have found problematic, especially in respect to homosexuality. Meanwhile, some speak of a new phenomenon of 'Christianophobia'. Many cite the multi-faith re-marketing of Christian festivals and the fact that the hijab receives greater protection than the crucifix as evidence not of the erosion of faith, but a hostility to Christian culture, although there is some confusion over whether it is secularism or pluralism (or both) which is to blame.

Since the *Satanic Verses* controversy, the Church of England has, at both a local and national level, proved pivotal in smoothing the way for Britain to become a multi-faith society. Arguably, inter-faith cooperation rather than secular multiculturalism has been a greater aid to integration. With respect to the Church of England, this openness has not been an entirely selfless act, for in seeking to align with other faiths it has in effect reinforced its own position. The Church of England has effectively become the spiritual head of a multi-faith society, but there are limits, it seems, as to how far the Church is allowed to go.

Archbishop Williams sparked public outrage in 2008 when, in a speech to the Royal Courts of Justice, he proposed that a partial implementation of Sharia Law in the UK was 'unavoidable'.[35] Williams's nuanced argument (he referenced the precedent of Orthodox Jewish law courts) was lost in a media storm as Christians and secularists united in their criticism. Even those who did not support *The Sun*'s call for him to resign were appalled by the fact that the leading Christian voice in Britain seemed to be endorsing an extension of Muslim law. Williams's speech, however, was entirely in keeping with the position that the Church of England has carved out for itself since the *Satanic Verses* controversy; as the mediating voice between secular liberals and those of faith in Britain. Like ecumenism, inter-faithism is criticised for its tokenistic pleasantries and lack of challenging dialogue. Indeed David Sheppard once argued that its texture should be like that of a 'chunky stew' rather than a blended soup. The most fruitful inter-faith initiatives can be found at a local level between churches, chapels, mosques and synagogues. In this, faiths working together have done much to dissolve some of the tensions caused by the exaggerated and poisonous rhetoric that dominates public debate.

In 1940, T. S. Eliot wrote that a 'society has not ceased to be Christian until it has become positively something else'. The last quarter of the twentieth century saw Protestant England draw her last breath; the first decade of the twenty-first finally saw the long-awaited birth of multi-faith Britain.

CHAPTER TEN

REAP WHAT YOU SOW

*'I am sure I will have been wrong about quite a lot of things
because there is a lot of timing in politics ... but I do not believe
I will have been wrong about the fundamental things.'*
– MARGARET THATCHER, 1986[1]

*'If she kicked away the crutches, it wasn't for pleasure
or profit – but because she genuinely believed that everyone
had the ability to walk without them.'*
– JULIE BURCHILL, 2004[2]

*'She thought like the Grocer's Daughter ... she couldn't
understand the culture she had created.'*
– HARVEY THOMAS, 2010[3]

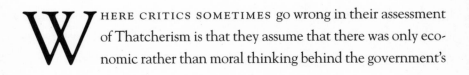 HERE CRITICS SOMETIMES go wrong in their assessment
of Thatcherism is that they assume that there was only eco-
nomic rather than moral thinking behind the government's

policies. Where its admirers often go wrong is that they do not admit that there was a fundamental discrepancy between Margaret Thatcher's intentions and the actual outcomes. Thatcher never pledged to solve inequality, rather she contended that some sort of 'gap' was necessary in order for wealth to trickle down. What she did promise was a reinvigoration of individual freedom, with social responsibility the inevitable by-product. Yet Thatcherism gave rise to a society that in the end showed little willingness to live by those Nonconformist virtues that Thatcher so fervently proselyted. Britain became a nation addicted to credit rather than thrift, one that prioritised individual gain over societal responsibility and prized moral freedom over rectitude. In truth, capitalism, or perhaps, more accurately the British public's relationship with capitalism, failed to live up to the Christian vision that Thatcher espoused. The market proved to be a dysfunctional system and the people rather dysfunctional with it. While there is little point in measuring neo-liberalism against left-wing theories of redistribution in which Margaret Thatcher did not believe, perhaps one fertile course is to judge neo-liberalism against Margaret Thatcher's own values, or perhaps her father's.

I. Naive faith

MARGARET THATCHER'S STATED ambition 'to turn every man into a capitalist' was certainly achieved, but, in the end, 'capitalist man' was not someone she herself recognised nor admired.[4] In public, she would explain the huge rise in bankers' wage packets as an inevitable by-product of the City's roaring success. In private, however, she reportedly use to rage against the bankers; why did they not follow the example of the army, she would cry, which was in her view the perfect model of leadership, responsibility and duty to one's fellow man.[5] New Labour's Peter Mandelson may have proclaimed that he was 'intensely relaxed about people getting filthy rich', but Margaret Thatcher never was.[6] Geoffrey Howe has recalled that Thatcher was always distinctly uncomfortable with the excesses of capitalism, which he admitted was never something that concerned him.[7] Nor did it bother his successor at the Treasury, Nigel Lawson, or a number of other notable worshippers of the market who, unlike Thatcher, did not have the same faith in its moral potential.

Thatcher's portrait of capitalism was often one where companies were small, privately owned and operated along much the same lines as the grocer's shop in which she had served as a child. Alfred Roberts behind the counter rather than the yuppie on the trading floor was always the predominant image of market transaction in her mind. There was little reference to, let alone justification for, the system that her government created and would later become the norm. A situation where the nation's homes and household budgets were intertwined with a global financial services sector that made up an ever-growing percentage of Britain's GDP, but which was increasingly internationally owned and in the hands of speculators, who were chiefly concerned with short-term gain and distant from the deals and lives they were gambling on.

One aspect of Margaret Thatcher's character, which is rarely commented on, was her naivety, especially when it came to economics. According to Carol Thatcher, for example, the interconnectedness of the global market used to irritate her mother:

> She would listen to the radio first thing in the morning and hear that the Far East markets had fallen and sigh, knowing that when the Stock Exchange opened, London would toboggan after them, followed by New York five hours later. One morning, totally exasperated as always when faced with something she was powerless to do anything about, she said: 'I really think everyone should be on Greenwich Mean Time – it would stop all this.'
>
> 'That's splendid, Mum, you've just condemned half the globe to living in the dark.'[8]

Margaret Thatcher did not believe in regulating the market then; only the time zone it operated in. More pointedly, for someone nurtured in a household where thrift was considered a godly virtue and an ingrained personal habit, Margaret Thatcher could not fathom why so many Britons struggled with debt. Her former head of communications, Harvey Thomas had recalled Thatcher's response to the housing recession of the late-1980s: 'I really don't understand this negative equity, because surely when young people are trying to buy a house they look at their income, they assess what they can afford, they assess what is the likelihood of potential problems. Surely?' To which the answer is 'no' when a mortgage lender on commission offers you a high percentage loan on a property that is twice the size that you dreamed of or can actually afford. Harvey Thomas reflected:

> She thought like the Grocer's Daughter ... she couldn't understand the culture she had created ... Her weakness was her naivety because she had faith in people. It never occurred to her that when you get money you want more. Greed never came into her vocabulary in that sense.[9]

Greed was certainly a charge that Thatcher aggressively refuted. When, in 1988, Thatcher was asked for her opinion of *Wall Street*'s Gordon Gekko's famous 'greed is good' mantra she leapt on it straight away, dismissing avarice as one of the seven deadly sins, before adding: 'What is good is to have sufficient self-reliance and responsibility, to want to do things for your own family, for your old folk, meet your obligations to your community.'[10] Thatcher refused to believe that she had bred a society of workaholic consumers who rarely saw their relations, but that she had merely given a leg up to those secure 2.4 units who were now able to enjoy the fruits of their labour without state interference. Thatcherism according to Thatcher, then, was the politics of aspiration and responsibility not materialism and greed, as she explained to the *Manchester Evening Times* in 1987:

Is it greedy to want a better house for your family and your children, to want better furniture, to want a good kitchen, to want nice fitted cupboards in your bedroom? Is it greedy to want to have enough over out of your earnings, yes, to let your children go on an overseas tour with the school, to see what it is like in other countries? To be able to show them sometimes the theatre; to be able to take them to London to see things; to be able to take them to the Lake District? Is it greedy to want to put some savings by for your old age? Is it greedy to want to have enough to give your parents a treat when it comes to their silver wedding? Greedy! Crackers![11]

Margaret Thatcher would always confront the charge of ruthless metropolitan individualistic avarice by recasting it as the legitimate needs and desires of the provincial hard-working family. This was certainly the reality for some, but not for all. If, as Margaret Thatcher once said, 'Marxism should be judged by its fruits', then so, too, must neo-liberalism be – and over the entire period from the 1980s to the financial crash of 2008. The Thatcher years heralded a new economic consensus, which over the following thirty years would radically reformulate the individual's relationship with money, the market, and the state. To put it crudely, during the Keynesian years the state had been expected to provide the conditions in which the majority of people had access to a home and were able to exercise their *producer power* (i.e. jobs). During the years of the neo-liberal consensus the government was now expected to establish conditions in which people could *buy* a house and exercise their *consumer power*.

II. The individual: freedom with responsibility?

THE MAJORITY OF Britons undoubtedly felt richer at the end of the 1980s than they had at the start. This, however, was not down to

rising wages, which actually lagged during the decade due to competition from emerging economies and the growing flexibility of the
UK employment market. The monthly income of middle-earners
increased by an average of 56 per cent between 1978 and 2006, even
though Britain's GDP increased by 108 per cent over the same period.
The medical, financial, legal and administrative class did experience
a steady rise, although those at the lower end, such as truck drivers
and factory packers, saw an actual decrease in real terms. The rise in
living standards in the 1980s was largely due to the expansion of personal debt, which would prove to be the most important economic
development of the decade, and was arguably more significant than
either the collapse of the unions or the privatisation of industry in
reshaping the British psyche and its economy.

'Popular capitalism' was the term and opening up the market to the
people was the aim, be it through shares, private pensions, mortgages or
forms of consumer credit. At the Lord Mayor's Banquet to the City in
1986, Thatcher rightly heralded this as a historic and democratic shift:
'The great reform of the last century was to make more and more people
voters. The great reform of our time is to make more and more
people owners. Popular capitalism is a crusade: a crusade to enfranchise the
many in the economic life of Britain.'[12] By the end of the decade, the mar-
ketisation of assets and savings as well as the democratisation of debt was
in full swing and while undoubtedly liberating in one sense, these opportunities were certainly not risk free as people's wealth, savings and home
became inextricably linked to a volatile and globalised financial sector.

Land has always been a prized commodity in Britain and the trend
towards homeownership was well established long before Margaret
Thatcher came to power. Nonetheless, Thatcher did oversee a monumental change in this regard; not only in increasing the number of homeowners
but, more crucially, changing attitudes towards homeownership, which
became the desired norm for most Britons rather than the privileged few.
The 'Right to Buy' scheme for council tenants opened up this opportunity

to those who had previously not thought home ownership possible, while the easing of lending restrictions on building societies and banks increased competition from which many inevitably benefited. As banks merged and spread the risk of their investments in the international market place, so they were able to fund large percentage mortgages and satisfy an increasingly property-hungry British public. The government was fulfilling its promise of creating a 'property-owning democracy' (and hopefully a nation of Tory-voters), an ever-increasing pool entered the housing market and the mortgage lenders were more than happy to offer a service which ensured their profits reach record heights.

As the government stopped building houses and more people entered the market so prices rose, fuelling an even greater desire for what seemed to be a guaranteed investment. The values of homes increased one and a half times the rate of inflation in the 1980s, two and half times in the 1990s, and six times the rate in the 2000s; two-thirds of UK homes were now owned, to the value of £1,000 billion.[13] But there was a clear generational disparity emerging too. At the end of the 1980s, 40 per cent of twenty to 24-year-olds were homeowners, but by 2006 this figure had dropped by half to just 20 per cent.[14] The house-buying boom of the 1980s would have negative consequences for the next generation, who now put greater faith in inheriting property from their parents than buying it for themselves.

Unsurprisingly, this phenomenon had a knock-on effect on interest rates, which would come to dominate national fiscal policy and be weighed heavily in favour of the spender rather than the saver as Britons became a nation of DIY'ers and NIMBY obsessives, determined to deploy whatever means possible to increase or at least maintain the price of their home. During the slump of the 1970s, house prices had not fallen, only stalled. The early '90s would see the first 'house-price' recession with the value of some properties falling by 10 per cent in a year as negative equity disproportionately hit younger borrowers and those at the lower end of the market.

As ex-council properties were sold on and the state relinquished its responsibility of matching this by building new homes, the private rental sector increased in importance. Letting became a legitimate entrepreneurial activity and was considered a more secure retirement package than private pensions. This was something that the Thatcher government willingly encouraged; it retained mortgage interest tax relief for buy-to-let landlords while it removed it for first-time buyers. Since 1996, one million Britons have bought properties exclusively to rent; the same number of council homes purchased in the height of the 'Right to Buy' boom of the 1980s.[15]

The growth in banking credit facilities had expanded in the affluent 1960s, fuelled by competitive wages and full employment, but it accelerated in the 1980s under quite different conditions. Total consumer credit in the UK more than doubled in the 1980s, from nearly £21 billion in 1981 to £48 billion in 1989 and would spiral to unimaginable levels in the next decade.[16] Thrift was undoubtedly one of Margaret Thatcher's favourite words, which she applied to both the personal and governmental sphere. When first canvassing in Finchley in 1959, she had referenced Abraham Lincoln's phrase: 'You cannot bring about prosperity by discouraging thrift.'[17] There is little doubt that Thatcher not only adhered to the economic concept but also its moral worth. Yet during her period in office, it became devoid of meaning and pretty much fell out of the English lexicon. The notion of deferred gratification, that is, the principle of saving for something before consuming it, became an alien concept for Britain's 'grab now, pay later' society. Credit was no longer something to be ashamed of, or morally reprehensible or even irresponsible: now you showed your lack of aspiration if you did not live your life on the 'never-never'.

Nowhere was this more apparent than in the proliferation of credit and store cards. The number of credit cards nearly tripled over the decade from 11.6 million card-holders in 1980 to 29.8 million in 1990, while credit doubled as a percentage of consumer expenditure from

8 per cent in 1979 to 15 per cent in 1989 and rose exponentially during the 2000s.[18] The nation's credit cards were not just being swiped for one-off purchases, but for everyday consumables, in effect, to bolster wages. The amount paid out on essentials such as fuel, health and food remained relatively stable in the 1980s, while spending on travel, recreation, entertainment, tobacco, alcohol and dining rocketed; a trend that also paralleled Britain's shift from a manufacturing to a service economy. The cash tills on the high street became the key test for measuring the buoyancy of the British economy, surpassing the balance of payments, unemployment figures and even Thatcher's beloved inflation levels.

Women had always been recognised for their consumer power as keepers of the household budget, but in the '80s advertisers cottoned-on to the potential of the new generation of women, who were better educated, had more disposable income and greater access to credit than ever before. The stereotypical image of the female consumer transformed from the thrifty housewife putting money aside for a rainy day to those stiletto-heeled cash cows on spending binges because they were 'worth it'. Whereas once women had faced discrimination from banks, particularly in the form of loans, they now had full equality in the economic sphere, but this did not necessarily bring greater security. By 2012, the number of women declaring bankruptcy was equal to that of men for the first time.

Between 1984 and 1993 the number of bankruptcies more than tripled but as it became more commonplace so there was no longer the same stigma associated with it, even more so when, in 2002, the Labour government relaxed restrictions and reduced bankruptcy status from six years to twelve months.[19] A declaration of bankruptcy rather than paying off the debt became the most effective and efficient way of absolving oneself from the problem, which only further encouraged a culture of fiscal irresponsibility. Between 1980 and 1989, the percentage of households with at least one non-mortgage credit arrangement grew from 50 per cent to 75 per cent.[20] In 1981, personal debt was 45 per cent of the national income, but by 2007 it was 160 per cent, which represented a three-and-a-half-fold increase.[21] A more worrying development, though, was the blurring of the distinction between mortgage and non-mortgage forms of finance. As house prices rose, so people naturally borrowed against their key asset: their home.

Given the stagnation of wages in low-skilled jobs and the large numbers of those claiming benefits, it is hardly surprising that the credit trend trickled down the social scale. But while middle-earners could apply to respectable banks and stores, those with a bad credit-rating or without a bank account (still 15 per cent in 1993 and one of the highest in northern Europe) turned to companies or loan sharks who asked few questions. The biggest rise in credit was precisely in these low-income groups; in 1980 22 per cent of low-income households were using credit but by 1989 it had more than trebled to 69 per cent.[22] A report by the Policy Studies Institute in 1992 revealed that 50 per cent of these loans were not going on luxury items but everyday essentials.[23]

In truth, the origins of this problem lay in the 1974 Consumer Credit Act, which removed all restrictions on loans and put regulatory power in the hands of the newly formed Office of Fair Trading. But it was the Thatcher government's constraints on the benefits system that meant that loan companies increasingly became the go-to option for Britain's poor. The introduction of the Social Fund in 1988, which replaced the existing grant with a loan (with repayment taken directly from the individual's benefit packet), also encouraged this normalisation of debt amongst the poorest members of society. As the New Economics Foundation report of 2002 into debt recognised, what the taxpayer was providing in terms of benefits, the lender was often taking away – with interest. Low-income households were not only funding their household budgets on debt, but were paying more for the privilege. While the top income group paid 60p a week on every £100 of debt, the poorest paid £1. This disparity is put into sharp focus when seen in terms of interest, which was often well in excess of 100 or 200 per cent. In 1989, it was estimated that 500,000 had obtained loans through moneylenders, although in the mid-1990s a more accurate calculation put the figure at three million.[24] In his speech as president of Rotary in 1936, Alfred Roberts had labelled debt as the 'curse of mankind' and it is doubtful that even Margaret Thatcher considered this expansion of debt as part of her plan to 'set the people free'.[25]

In the 1980s, traditional forms of credit, such as the mail-order catalogue, the pawnbrokers and even door-to-door loan sharks were inched out of the market by slightly more respectable licensed moneylenders and payday loan companies, such as the Australian-owned Cash Converters and hire purchase outlet Japanese-owned Bright-House. Not only was there a proliferation of high-interest lenders incentivising the poor to spend rather than save but these companies had a greater presence in deprived areas than most high-street banks. This phenomenon could hardly be characterised as a positive trickling-down of wealth and opportunity, especially as the profits of these loan companies were lining the pockets of shareholders. In 2014, the sub-prime lending market was estimated to be worth over £16 billion – approximately the same amount that the government spends on housing benefit.

If the 1960s was the age of the affluent worker, then the 1980s was the period of the credit consumer as class-consciousness in Britain became more and more identified with consumption rather than production. Despite egalitarian promises of the market place, neo-liberal economics did not destroy old class bonds; only redefined them. The derogatory label of 'chavs', which gained currency in the noughties, was symbolic of this shift towards a new consumer-driven class identity, reflecting, as it did, middle-class snobbishness about working-class spending habits: did you shop at John Lewis or Primark? Holiday in Marbella or Provence? Was your Burberry fake or real? Britain finally became unhinged from its Christian moorings as consumerism became the central source of values and social respectability. Advertising slogans and jingles were drummed into consumers like psalms, while shopping complexes dominated the urban landscape like modern-day cathedrals. Often built on former industrial sites, these shopping malls also symbolised the triumph of Britain's retail sector over its manufacturing past. Ironically, it was the Church of England who funded one of the first of these, contributing £130 million to the construction of the Metrocentre near Gateshead. Opening in 1986, it boasted over 300 shops and, under stipulations set by the Church, its own place of worship, the 'Oasis of Peace Chapel'.[26] Soon more than half of the Church Commissioners' investments were in supermarkets and retail. Church leaders defended this record, arguing that the Church was contributing to urban regeneration, but it was also indirectly financing and encouraging what would later become Britons' favourite Sunday activity.

When the financial crash occurred in 2008, many blamed the bankers; others blamed the Labour government; there were very few, and certainly not the Church, who dared to call it a crisis in individual morality and the public's own fiscal irresponsibility. While David Cameron and Chancellor George Osborne have spoken at length about paying off the 'nation's credit card', they have consciously avoided entreating individuals to pay off their own. Personal debt is a subject that politicians dare not broach for two reasons: Britain's economy (and therefore economic revival) is largely dependent on people spending and the British electorate will not tolerate being lectured on how they should spend their money. In 2011, David Cameron hastily omitted a reference to the subject in his party conference speech, realising that it would provoke an unfavourable reaction. In that year, personal debt stood at £15 trillion (a little more than the country's GDP) with forecasters predicting that it will reach £21 trillion by 2015.[27] Meanwhile, Britain's savings have fallen below zero.[28] It is now a political vote-winner, in Britain, to talk of governmental thrift but political suicide to talk of personal thrift; that is the true political legacy of Thatcherite economics. If 'popular capitalism', as Margaret Thatcher once said, was a 'crusade to enfranchise the many in the economic life of Britain' then this was certainly achieved.[29] But what in boom times was sold as freedom, in bust felt remarkably like oppression.

III. The moral market?

IT WAS NOT so long ago that the financial district of London was known for its 'gentlemanly capitalism', when the power lay in reliable hands of the 'old-boy network' with hand-shake deals agreed over long, liquid lunches and all was safely encased within the reassuringly sturdy walls of the City. In the 1980s, this was to give way to a more egalitarian, global and depersonalised culture imported from America and typified by high-risk, short-term investments. Out went the 'long term relationships between banker and client, now it gave way to brief affairs' according to former City broker and author of *The Death of Gentlemanly Capitalism*, Philip Augar.[30]

The City, though, had no option but to modernise. In 1980, the Supplementary Special Deposit Scheme, known as the 'corset', which limited the amount that banks could lend, was removed. UK banking fell into line with the US as the abolition of exchange controls allowed the free movement of assets overseas and increased the link between commercial and global banking. In 1986, the 'Big Bang' signalled full deregulation. Named after the scientific theory of cosmological expansion, it meant that whereas once banking had existed in a dense controlled state, it was now continually expanding – although much like an inflated balloon it was destined to pop. Between 1997 and 2007 the UK financial services sector grew twice as fast as the economy. Minimal regulatory constraints were imposed but with the City providing a quarter of annual corporate rate receipts, the Treasury had little cause for complaint or reason to rein it in. In 1986, financial services accounted for 15.5 per cent of the UK's GDP; by 2008 it had almost doubled to 29.2 per cent.[31] The system did indeed become too big to fail.

In 1986, the country exported £2 billion worth of financial services; by 2005 this had risen to £23 billion and quickly supplanted goods and manufacturing as Britain's biggest export. The only problem was that it employed a fraction of the workforce and was largely foreign-owned. Unlike in France or Germany, where the financial services sectors were obliged to invest in long-term industrial projects, the City of London, precisely at a time when industry needed it most, did not demonstrate the same level of commitment. Instead of siphoning off the profits, the Treasury could have compelled the City to channel these funds into rebuilding Britain's industrial base in the wake of deindustrialisation. This, after all, was how banks such as the Midland Bank had operated in the Victorian era: enhancing the growing wealth of Birmingham by helping to develop industries, railways and services. Understandably, though, the banks rejected long-term investment in favour of securing loans against assets from which they stood to gain whether they succeeded or failed. The City of London embodied what became known as the 'Wimbledon effect', i.e. like the tennis tournament, with Britain always the host and rarely the winner.

Successive governments failed to adequately regulate the market, which, it soon became clear, did not encourage individual moral responsibility but the complete opposite. Scandals of fiscal mismanagement and greed blackened the City's reputation for fair-trading and sound practice. Companies that promised huge returns on pension investments were perhaps the biggest perpetrators. The Royal and Sun Alliance was fined the paltry sum of £1.35 million for failing to compensate the 13,500 victims of its botched pension scheme, while Equitable Life, which had promised a 10 per cent return on high-risk investments, managed to wipe out the capital of its 1.5 million investors. The government stepped in, offering £1.5 billion in compensation, although the actual loss was believed to have been in the range of £4.48 billion.[32] A recent study by *Which* magazine estimated that 71 per cent of the five million people with private pensions in Britain were likely to be 20 per cent less well off than if had they stayed in the state system.[33]

In the end, the market turned out not to be the benevolent 'invisible hand' that Thatcher promised, but an unruly child (as it always had been), capable of severe mood swings and liable to blow if over-excited. Thatcher's admirers (even some within New Labour) were happy to claim it as Thatcher's legacy when things were going well, but seemed to absolve her of any responsibility when it all went badly wrong. The fact was that Margaret Thatcher was responsible for loosening the reins even if she was not riding the horse when it swerved off into an uncontrollable direction. Of course, this culture was encouraged and this behaviour continued unabated under New Labour, which was content to pocket a significant share of the profits to fund its schools and hospitals; much like a gangster's wife who enjoys the lifestyle but does not question how her husband gets his money.

When out of office, Thatcher was again invited to comment on the oft-repeated accusation that her policies had given rise to a culture of materialism and fiscal irresponsibility. This time, perhaps in a more reflective mood, she drew upon the words of John Wesley: 'Do not impute to money the faults of human nature.'[34] She might as well have said: 'Do not impute to Thatcherism the faults of human nature.' It was not money, political ideology or the capitalist system that was to blame, but man. Thatcherism may have laid the foundations for a culture in which individualism and self-reliance could thrive, but, ultimately, it created a culture in which only selfishness and excess were rewarded.

During her time in Downing Street, Margaret Thatcher liked to quote John Wesley's mantra: 'Earn all you can, save all you can and give all you can', yet it was only ever the first instruction that was sufficiently encouraged. When asked by Frank Field what was her greatest regret in office, Margaret Thatcher reportedly replied, without any hesitation, that she had not taxed the rich high enough. 'I cut taxes and I thought we would get a giving society and we haven't.'[35] Even Thatcher recognised that she had not instilled a sense of responsibility that comes with greater wealth. Perhaps, on this, she was reflecting her own father's message in the pulpit, that the real danger was not poverty but affluence. She might have also looked to the words of William Temple for the answer: 'the art of government is the art of so ordering life that self-interest prompts what justice demands'.

Margaret Thatcher always avowed to a belief in the inherent virtue of man. When she said there was 'no such thing as society', it was not a negative or flippant statement but an optimistic rallying cry for individual moral responsibility to oneself and to one another. The flaw in Margaret Thatcher's theology was not that she did not believe in society, as many criticised, but that she had too much faith in man. She had forgotten the essence of Conservative philosophy: the Fall. In many ways, Thatcherism was a challenge to individual moral virtue, yet in Thatcher's Eden, when given the choice, we, of course, ate the fruit.

The ideas of thrift, responsibility and rectitude made sense to Margaret Thatcher because she had grown up in a religious environment where the boundaries on individual freedom were clear. These were constraints, however, that British society (including the young Margaret Roberts) demonstrated a remarkable determination to escape from. The irony is that despite Thatcher's pledges to re-instil Victorian values, her government ultimately accelerated their decline. As Peregrine Worsthorne has rather bluntly surmised: 'Margaret Thatcher had set out to create a country in the image of her father but ended up creating one in the image of her son.'[36]

It was not the sexual revolution of the 1960s, as Conservatives liked to claim, which ultimately undermined the Christian fabric of Britain, but the changes, struggles and upheavals of the 1980s that would eventually transform the British psyche. Margaret Thatcher's time in office may have heralded a renaissance of individual freedom, but in doing so also hastened the death of Christian Britain. In Margaret Thatcher, Britain had its last taste of Victorian Nonconformist culture, but while Britons largely accepted the economic changes, they rejected the moral conventions and expectations underpinning it. Britain was still considered to be a Christian country in 1979, yet by the end of the 1980s it had transformed into something altogether different. In her crusade to raise Albion from the ashes, Thatcher ended up destroying all that was familiar. The future was not to be conservative but consumerist, not English, but cosmopolitan, not Christian, but secular.

NOTES

PROLOGUE: GOD AND MRS THATCHER

1   Matthew Grimley, *Citizenship, Community and the Church of England: Liberal Anglican Theories of the State between the Wars* (Oxford: Clarendon, 2004), p. 204
2   Mark Bevir, *New Labour: A Critique* (London: Routledge, 2005), p. 54
3   Antonio Weiss, *The Religious Mind of Mrs Thatcher* (unpublished paper, 2011)
      http://www.margaretthatcher.org/document/112748
4   Roy Jenkins, *Churchill* (London: Macmillan, 2001), p. 49
5   Churchill College Archives, Enoch Powell Papers, Poll 3/2/1/60. Other Political subjects and Msc. Files Appointment of Bishops correspondence 84–6. Fol. 68
6   TV interview for London Weekend Television *Weekend World*, 6 January 1980
      http://www.margaretthatcher.org/document/104210
7   *Daily Telegraph*, 12 October 1984

CHAPTER ONE: 'GOD BLESS GRANTHAM'

1   Margaret Thatcher, *The Path to Power* (London: HarperCollins, 1993), p. 3
2   Charles Moore, *Margaret Thatcher, Vol. I: Not For Turning* (London: Allen Lane, 2014), p. 4
3   Speech in Finchley, 31 January 1975 http://www.margaretthatcher.org/document/102605
4   John Campbell, *The Grocer's Daughter* (London: Pimlico, 2001)
5   Radio interview for IRN, 31 January 1975
      http://www.margaretthatcher.org/document/102602
6   Private interview with author, 14 April 2011
7   Campbell, *Grocer's*, p. 3
8   Thatcher, *Path*, pp. 23–4
9   Ibid., p. 118
10 Campbell, *Grocer's*, pp. 9–10
11 Vic Hutchinson, *Memories of Youth in Wartime Grantham: A Personal Account* (Grantham, 1992), p. 16
12 *Grantham Journal*, 6 July 1936 http://www.margaretthatcher.org/document/109894
13 Thatcher, *Path*, p. 567
14 Ibid., p. 12
15 Ibid., p. 5
16 Recorded interview with Margaret Thatcher (Wesley's Chapel, 9 April 1993)
17 Stephen Koss, *Nonconformity in Modern British Politics* (London: Batsford, 1975)
18 Adrian Hastings, *A History of English Christianity* (London: SCM Press, 4th edition, 2001), p. 112
19 Thatcher, *Path*, p. 9
20 Campbell, *Grocer's*, p. 30
21 No Games in the Grantham Parks on Sundays, *Grantham Journal*, 9 July 1938
      http://www.margaretthatcher.org/document/109896

22 Sunday Games in Grantham Parks, *Grantham Journal*, 8 May 1942
    http://www.margaretthatcher.org/document/109909

23 John Munsey Turner, *Modern Methodism in England 1932–1998* (Peterborough: Epworth
    Press, 1998), p. 15

24 Margaret Thatcher (Wesley's Chapel, 9 April 1993)

25 Margaret Roberts's Catechism http://www.margaretthatcher.org/document/109910

26 Oliver Anderson, *Rotten Borough: The Real Story of Thatcher's Grantham* (London: Fourth
    Estate, 1989), p. 34

27 Thatcher, *Path*, p. 5

28 All the sermon notes are available on the Margaret Thatcher website. Churchill College,
    Cambridge
    Alfred Roberts (sermon notes a) http://www.margaretthatcher.org/document/109898
    Alfred Roberts (sermon notes b) http://www.margaretthatcher.org/document/109899
    Alfred Roberts (sermon notes c) http://www.margaretthatcher.org/document/109900
    Alfred Roberts (sermon notes d) http://www.margaretthatcher.org/document/109925

29 Weiss, *The Religious Mind*, p. 20

30 TV interview for London Weekend Television, *Weekend World* ('Victorian Values'), 16
    January 1983 http://www.margaretthatcher.org/document/105087

31 Speech to Conservative Party conference, 13 October 1989
    http://www.margaretthatcher.org/document/107789

32 Weiss, *Religious Mind*, p. 23

33 Speech to General Assembly of the Church of Scotland, 21 May 1988
    http://www.margaretthatcher.org/document/107246

34 Thatcher, *Path*, p. 21

35 Speech at Adoption Meeting, *Erith Observer*, 28 February 1949
    http://www.margaretthatcher.org/document/100821

36 Koss, *Nonconformity*, p. 177

37 Ibid., pp. 180–81

38 *Daily Mail*, 25 November 1919, quoted in Ross McKibbin, *Classes and Cultures England
    1918–1951* (Oxford: Oxford University Press, 2000), p. 44, fn. 2

39 Lincolnshire County Archives, Minutes of Grantham Chamber of Trade 1920–1933, 1 May 1928

40 Anderson, *Rotten Borough*, p. 24

41 Ibid., pp. 53–4

42 Ibid., p. 58

43 Grantham Library, Grantham Borough Council Minutes, *Report of the Housing Sub-
    Committee*, 4 February 1925, L.A., GRANTHAMBOROUGH.5/1 (I am grateful to
    Benedict Bowden for this reference)

44 *Grantham Journal*, 9 October 1937

45 Ibid., 16 November 1945

46 Ibid., 23 May 1952

47 TV Interview for Yorkshire Television *Woman to Woman*, 2 October 1985
    http://www.margaretthatcher.org/document/105830

48 Moore, *Not for Turning*, p. 132

49 Interview for *Woman's Own* ('No such thing as society'), 23 September 1987
    http://www.margaretthatcher.org/document/106689

50 Thatcher, *Path*, p. 19

51 Ibid., p. 15

52 Ibid., p. 16

53 *Grantham Journal*, 10 March 1934

54   Ibid., 19 May 1934
55   Ibid., 15 September 1934
56   Ibid., 28 January 1939
57   Ibid., 16 November 1945
58   Campbell, *Grocer's*, p. 38–9; Moore, *Not for Turning*, pp. 20–21
59   Thatcher, *Path*, p. 24
60   The National Archives, KV22779, Fol. 22
61   *Picture Post*, 18 April 1942
62   Moore, *Not for Turning*, p. 18
63   Margaret Thatcher to William Denis Kendall, 1 March 1980
          http://www.margaretthatcher.org/document/119781
64   Thatcher, *Path*, p. 8

CHAPTER TWO: THE PATH OF CONFORMITY

1   Moore, *Not for Turning*, p. 49
2   Campbell, *Grocer's*, p. 46
3   Ibid., *Path*, p. 39
4   Campbell, *Grocer's*, p. 48
5   Ibid.
6   Thatcher, *Path*, p. 39
7   Ibid., p. 40
8   Moore, *Not for Turning*, p. 57
9   Campbell, *Grocer's*, p. 50
10   Ibid., p. 63
11   Thatcher, *Path*, p. 43
12   Anthony Wedgwood Benn, private interview with author
13   Humphrey Carpenter, *Robert Runcie: The Reluctant Archbishop* (London: Hodder &
          Stoughton, paperback, 1997), p. 56
14   Ibid., p. 86; Runcie, 'The Purple, the Blue and the Red', Episode 1: Marching as to War,
          Transcript (BBC Radio 4, 1996)
15   Ibid.
16   Private interview with author
17   Carpenter, *Reluctant*, p. 40
18   Private interview with James Runcie
19   Quoted in Carpenter, *Reluctant*, pp. 76–7
20   Hastings, *English Christianity*, p. 172
21   Edward Norman, *Church and Society in England 1770–1970* (Oxford: Oxford University
          Press, 1976), p. 224
22   Ibid., pp. 301–2
23   Ibid., p. 231
24   Hastings, *English Christianity*, p. 175
25   Norman, *Church and Society*, p. 292
26   Hastings, *English Christianity*, p. 188
27   Anthony Wright, *R. H. Tawney* (Manchester: Manchester University Press, 1987)
28   Norman, *Church and Society*, Chapters 6–8
29   Ibid., p. 252
30   Ibid., p. 256
31   Ibid., p. 334

32   Correlli Barnett, *The Audit Of War: The Illusion and Reality of Britain as a Great Nation* (London: Pan, 1987), p. 120

33   Prochaska, Frank, *A Disinherited Spirit: Christianity and Social Service in Modern Britain* (Oxford: Oxford University Press, 2006), p. 152

34   Moore, *Not for Turning*, p. 67

35   Ibid., p. 104

36   Article for *Young Kent Forum* (*Two Contemporaries – Marx & Disraeli*) 1 October 1949 http://www.margaretthatcher.org/document/109511

37   *Erith Observer*, 13 February 1950 http://www.margaretthatcher.org/document/100868

38   Campbell, *Grocer's*, p. 75

39   *Dartford Chronicle*, 30 May 1951 http://www.margaretthatcher.org/document/100905

40   Ibid., 8 June 1951 http://www.margaretthatcher.org/document/100931

41   Cecil Parkinson, private interview with author; Carol Thatcher, *Below the Parapet: The Biography of Denis Thatcher* (London: HarperCollins, 1997), p. 64

42   Carol Thatcher, *Below the Parapet*, p. 64

43   Campbell, *Grocer's*, p. 74

44   Thatcher, *Path*, p. 77

45   TV Interview for Yorkshire Television *Woman to Woman*, 2 October 1985 http://www.margaretthatcher.org/document/105830

46   Edward Carpenter, *Archbishop Fisher* (Norfolk: Canterbury Press, 1991), p. 407

47   Ibid., p. 408

48   John Pollock, *The Billy Graham Story* (Michigan: Zaondervan, 2003), p. 73

49   S. J. D. Green, 'Survival and Autonomy: on the strange fortunes and peculiar legacy of ecclesiastical establishment in the modern state, *c.* 1920 to the present day' in S. J. D. Green & R. C. Whiting, (eds.), *The Boundaries of the State in Modern Britain* (Cambridge: Cambridge University Press, 1996), pp. 312, 315

50   Interview with the *Catholic Herald*, 22 December 1978, http://www.margaretthatcher.org/document/103793

51   Patricia Murray, *Margaret Thatcher* (London: W. H. Allen, 1980), p. 50

52   Speech to the Christ Church Youth Fellowship, 15 December 1963 http://www.margaretthatcher.org/document/101218

53   Dominic Sandbrook, *White Heat: A History of Britain in the Swinging Sixties* (London: Little, Brown, 2006)

54   Hugh McLeod, *The Religious Crisis of the 1960s* (Oxford: Oxford University Press, 2007), Chapter 10

55   Radio Interview for BBC Radio 4 *Woman's Hour* ('Permissive or Civilised?') 19 April 1970 http://www.margaretthatcher.org/document/101845

56   Thatcher, *Path*, p. 150

57   New Year Message, *Finchley Press*, 2 January 1970 http://www.margaretthatcher.org/document/101709

58   McLeod, *Religious Crisis*, p. 202

59   Ibid., p. 198

60   Ibid., p. 259

61   Speech to Finchley Inter-church luncheon club, 17 November 1969, *Finchley Press*, 21 November 1969 http://www.margaretthatcher.org/document/101704

62   'Those Mad Merry Vicars of England', *Life Magazine*, 29 January 1965

63   Norman, *Church*, p. 420

64   Mark Chapman, 'Theology in the Public Arena: The Case of South Bank Religion' in

Garnett, Grimley, Harris, Whyte, Williams (eds.), *Redefining Christian Britain: post 1945 Perspectives* (London: SCM Press, 2007), p. 93

65   José Miquez Bonino, *Christians and Marxists: The Mutual Challenge to Revolution* (London: Hodder & Stoughton, 1976), p. 114

66   Thatcher, *Path*, p. 163

CHAPTER THREE: THE GREAT REAWAKENING

1   Hugo Young, *One of Us*: A biography of Margaret Thatcher (London: Pan Macmillan, 3rd edition, 1993), p. 406

2   Alfred Sherman, *Paradoxes of Power Reflections on the Thatcher Interlude* (Exeter: Imprint Academic, 2005), pp. 25–6

3   Speech to the Conservative Political Centre Lecture, 'What's Wrong with Politics', 11 October 1968, http://www.margaretthatcher.org/speeches/displaydocument.asp?docid=101632

4   *The Times*, 19 January 1970

5   *The Spectator*, Nigel Fisher, *Iain Macleod* (London: Deutsch, 1973), p. 65

6   TNA, PREM 19/602, Enoch Powell, East Grinstead Young Conservatives, 5 December 1980, Fol. 130

7   CCA, POLL 1/1/30A, File 1, Fols. 63–5

8   Rex Collings (ed.); *Reflections of a Statesman: the Writings and Speeches of Enoch Powell* (London: Bellow, 1992), p. 55

9   CCA, POLL 1/4/33 *Wrestling with the Angel* File 1 of 2

10   CCA, POLL 3/2/3/2 B Correspondence 1984–6, Letters to Powell, name withheld, 21 July, 27 July 1984

11   Duncan Forrester, *Christianity and the Future of Welfare* (London: Epworth Press, 1985), pp. 96–7

12   CCA, POLL 1/4/33 *Wrestling with the Angel* File 2, Address to the parishioners meeting, St Michael and Mary, Southwark, 11 March 1973

13   Henry Kissinger in conversation with President Ford, Ford Library (NSC NSA Memcons Box 8), 8 January 1975 http://www.margaretthatcher.org/document/110510

14   *The Times*, 9 March 1970

15   Ralph Harris, 'A Gift Horse' in Rhodes Boyson (ed.), *Down with the Poor* (London: Churchill Press, 1971), p. 19

16   Nigel Lawson, Lecture to the Bow Group, 4 August 1980 http://www.margaretthatcher.org/document/109505

17   Naim Attallah (compiler), *Singular Encounters* (London: Quartet, 1990), p. 130

18   Paul Oestreicher, 'Much Ado about Norman', *Crucible*, September–December 1979, p. 129

19   A point made by Andrew Gamble, referenced in Roger King, 'The middle class in revolt?' in Roger King & Neill Nugent (eds.), *Respectable Rebels: Middle Class Campaigns in Britain in the 1970s* (Kent: Hodder & Stoughton, 1979), p. 7

20   Ibid., p. 1

21   Neill Nugent, 'The National Association for Freedom' in King & Nugent, *Respectable Rebels*, p. 82

22   John Gummer, *The Permissive Society: Fact or Fantasy?* (London: Cassell, 1971), p. 3

23   Mary Whitehouse, *Cleaning up TV From Protest to Participation* (London: Blandford Press, 1967), p. 23

24   John Capon, *And There was Light: The Story of the Nationwide Festival of Light* (London: Lutterworth, 1972), p. 5

25   Mary Whitehouse, *Whatever happened to sex?* (Hove: Weyland, 1977), p. 24

26   Michael Tracey & David Morrison, *Whitehouse* (London: Macmillan, 1979), p. 13

27   John Poulton, *Dear Archbishop* (London: Hodder & Stoughton, 1976), p. 67

28   Keith Joseph, Speech at Edgbaston, 19 October 1974
        http://www.margaretthatcher.org/document/101830

29   Andrew Denham & Mark Garnett, *Keith Joseph* (Bucks: Acumen, 2002), p. 267

30   CCA, Margaret Thatcher Archive, 2/2/1/36, Letter from Mary Whitehouse, 26 June 1978

31   Hastings, *English Christianity*, p. 609

32   Ibid., p. 603

33   Ibid., p. 602

34   Ibid., p. 603

35   Ibid.,

36   Ibid., p. 604

37   John Poulton, *Dear Archbishop*, pp. 18–9

38   Ibid., p. 85

39   Ibid., p. 30

40   Ibid., p. 94

41   Ibid., p. 154. Another wrote, 'The climate is right for any crank or madman of the extreme
        right or the extreme left to take over.' Ibid., p. 155

42   Margaret Thatcher, speech to Greater London Young Conservatives (Iain
        Macleod Memorial Lecture – 'Dimensions of Conservatism'), 4 July 1977
        http://www.margaretthatcher.org/document/103411

43   John Ranelagh, *Thatcher's People: An insider's account of the politics, the power and the
        personalities* (London: HarperCollins, 1991), p. 174

44   Keith Joseph, *Reversing the Trend: A critical re-appraisal of Conservative economic and
        social policies: seven speeches by Keith Joseph* (Chichester: Rose, 1975), Foreword

45   *Financial Times*, 22 October 1969

46   *The Sun*, 9 January 1972

47   TV Interview for Granada TV *World in Action*, 31 January 1975
        http://www.margaretthatcher.org/document/102450

48   Alfred Sherman, *Paradoxes*, p. 25

49   Ibid., p. 86

50   Jonathan Raban, *God, Man, and Mrs Thatcher: A Critique of Mrs Thatcher's Address to the
        General Assembly of the Church of Scotland* (London: Chatto & Windus, 1989), p. 28

51   Speech to Conservative Central Council, 15 March 1975
        http://www.margaretthatcher.org/document/102655

52   Quoted in Kenneth Harris, *Thatcher* (London: Weidenfeld & Nicolson, 1988), p. 109

53   Speech to the Greater London Conservatives (Iain Macleod
        Memorial Lecture – 'Dimensions of Conservatism') 4 July 1977
        http://www.margaretthatcher.org/document/103411

54   *The Times*, 5 July 1977

55   Ibid., 11 July 1977

56   Margaret Thatcher, Letters to the Editor, 18 July 1977

57   CCA, THCR 2/6/1/177, Speech at St Lawrence Jewry, comments by T. E. Utley, 24 February 1978

58   CCA, THCR 2/6/1/177, Simon Webley, Themes for a speech on the restoration of
        Christianity and Christian values in British society

59   Speech at St Lawrence Jewry ('I Believe – A speech on Christianity and Politics')
        30 March 1978
        http://www.margaretthatcher.org/document/103522

60   Alfred Sherman, *Paradoxes*, p. 92

61   *Daily Mail*, 11 October 1975

62   E. H. H. Green, *Ideologies of Conservatism* (Oxford: Oxford University Press, 2002), p. 235

63   US embassy in London to State Department, Margaret Thatcher some first impressions, 16 February 1975
      http://www.margaretthatcher.org/document/111068

64   *Daily Telegraph*, 8 May 1977

65   Letter to Ronnie Millar, 25 August 1975
      http://www.margaretthatcher.org/document/111738

66   Charles Moore, *Not for Turning*, pp. 397–400

67   Dominic Sandbrook, *Seasons in the Sun: The Battle for Britain, 1974–1979*, p. 216

68   Remarks on becoming Prime Minister, 4 May 1979
      http://www.margaretthatcher.org/document/104078

CHAPTER FOUR: THE GOSPEL ACCORDING TO MARGARET THATCHER

1   Margaret Thatcher, interview with the *Catholic Herald*, 5 December 1978
      http://www.margaretthatcher.org/document/103793

2   *Sunday Times*, 3 May 1981

3   Thatcher, *Path*, pp. 554–5

4   Speech at reopening of Wesley's House, 24 May 1981
      http://www.margaretthatcher.org/document/104656

5   CCA, THCR 1-7-24, Letter from George Thomas, 1 June 1981

6   George Urban, *Diplomacy and Disillusion at the Court of Margaret Thatcher* (London: I. B. Tauris, 1996), p. 41

7   Ronald Millar, *The View from the Wings: West End, West Coast, Westminster* (London: Weidenfeld & Nicolson), p. 283

8   Sherman, *Paradoxes*, p. 90

9   Raban, *God, Man, and Mrs Thatcher*, p. 68

10   CCA, THCR 6-2-2-24 Letter from T. E. Utley, 6 February 1980

11   Ibid., Letter from Rev. Basil Watson, 28 March 1980

12   Ibid., Note from Denis Thatcher, 16 January 1981

13   Speech at St Lawrence Jewry, 4 March 1981
      http://www.margaretthatcher.org/document/104587

14   Raban, *God, Man, and Mrs Thatcher*, p. 35

15   TV Interview for TV-AM, 30 December 1988
      http://www.margaretthatcher.org/document/107022

16   Speech to General Assembly of the Church of Scotland, 21 May, 1988
      http://www.margaretthatcher.org/document/107246

17   John Gummer, Eric S. Heffer & Alan Beith, *Faith in Politics: Which Way Should Christians Vote?* (London: SPCK, 1987), p. 9

18   Manchester Central Library, Booth-Clibborn Papers, Z Files, Section 8, Medicine and Health file, letter from parishioner (name withheld), 17 February 1981

19   Speech at St Lawrence Jewry, 4 March 1981
      http://www.margaretthatcher.org/document/104587

20   Ibid.

21   Article for *Daily Telegraph* ('The moral basis of a free society'), 16 May 1978
      http://www.margaretthatcher.org/document/103687

22   Speech to Greater London Young Conservatives (Iain Macleod

Memorial Lecture – 'Dimensions of Conservatism'), 4 July 1977
http://www.margaretthatcher.org/document/103411

23   Article for *Daily Telegraph* ('The moral basis of a free society') 16 May 1978
http://www.margaretthatcher.org/document/103687

24   Speech to Greater London Young Conservatives (Iain Macleod
Memorial Lecture – 'Dimensions of Conservatism') 4 July 1977
http://www.margaretthatcher.org/document/103411

25   Conservative Manifesto 1979 (London: Conservative Central Office, 1979), Chapter 1

26   The National Archives, PREM 19/783 Fol. 92

27   Ibid., Fol. 191

28   Ibid., Fol. 212

29   Ibid., Fol. 208

30   Ibid., Fol. 210. Mount maintained that the broadcaster should not be a government
'stooge'. The aim was to 'shake' the BBC and the ITA into 'recording their priorities'.

31   Ibid., Fol. 219

32   Ibid., Fol. 196

33   Ibid., Fol. 167

34   Ibid., Fol. 168

35   Ibid., Fol. 169

36   Ibid., Fol. 170

37   Ibid., Fol. 160

38   Ibid., Fols. 37, 151

39   Ibid., Fol. 141 ('state paternalism' was underlined by Margaret Thatcher)

40   Ibid., Fols. 108, 116

41   Ibid., Fol. 100

42   Ibid., Fol. 100

43   Ibid., Fol. 103

44   Ibid., Fol. 63

45   Ibid., Fol. 30

46   Ibid., Fol. 181

47   Ivor Crewe, 'Has the Electorate become Thatcherite?' in Robert Skidelsky (ed.),
Thatcherism (London: Chatto & Windus, 1988), p. 41

48   Bernard Ingham, Memo to Margaret Thatcher, CCA, THCR 1/12/16 Part 1, Fol. 1, 3
August 1982 http://www.margaretthatcher.org/document/122990

49   Ivor Crewe, 'Has the Electorate become Thatcherite?', p. 45

50   Edwards minute to Margaret Thatcher (proposed improvements to Edwards's Cardiff office)
28 January 1981 http://www.margaretthatcher.org/document/129901

51   Private interview with author

52   CCA, THCR 2/7/1/27. Election Planning Meeting, 15 December 1978, p. 80

53   Private interview with author

54   Private interview with author

55   Private interview with author

56   Private interview with author

57   Carol Thatcher, *Below the Parapet*, p. 67

58   Private interview with author

59   Copy of private letter provided by Harvey Thomas

60   Private interview with author

61   CCA, THCR 3/2/149, Letter from Maurice Wood, 13 October 1984; Margaret Thatcher's
reply 18 October 1984 http://www.margaretthatcher.org/document/136288

62   'The Thatcher Philosophy', *Catholic Herald*, 5 December 1978
       http://www.margaretthatcher.org/document/103793
63   Margaret Thatcher, (Wesley's Chapel, 9 April 1993)
64   D. R. Thorpe, *Supermac: The Life of Harold Macmillan* (London: Chatto & Windus), p. 450
65   *Parl. Proc.*, HC Debates, 4 December 1974, Vol. 882, Cols. 1603, 1676
66   *Poetry Review* 13, Vol. 6, No. 5, (1979), pp. 51–62
67   Ibid., p. 10
68   *Parl. Proc.*, HL Debs, 21 March 1978, Vol. 389, Cols. 1725–85
69   Ibid., Col. 1736
70   Lambeth Palace Library, Robert Runcie Papers, Runcie/Main/1983/222, Letter from Lord
       Hailsham, 18 January 1983
71   *Proceedings of the General Synod 1985*, Vol. 16, No. 1, 14 February 1985, p. 285
72   CCA, POLL 3/2/1/60, Other Political Subjects and Msc. Files, Appointments of
       Bishops correspondence, 1984–6. Copy of Letter from William Powell to Bishop of
       Peterborough, 30 July 1984
73   Moore, Charles, Gavin Stamp & A. N. Wilson, *The Church in Crisis* (London: Hodder &
       Stoughton, 1986), p. 43
74   CCA, POLL 3/2/1/60, Other Political Subjects and Msc. Files, Appointments of Bishops
       Correspondence 1984–6, Letter from Gervase Duffield, 27 July 1984
75   CCA, POLL 3/2/3/2/B, Correspondence 1984–6, Letter from Kathleen Griffiths, 7 June 1986
76   CCA, POLL 3/2/3/2/A, File 1, Copy of letter from Ivor Stanbrook to the Bishop of
       Southwark, 4 May 1987
77   Frank Field, 'The Church of England and Parliament: A Tense Partnership' in
       George Moyser (ed.), *Church and Politics Today: The Role of the Church of England in
       Contemporary Politics* (Edinburgh: T&T Clark, 1985) pp. 55–74
78   Alfred Sherman, *Paradoxes*, p. 40

CHAPTER FIVE: TURBULENT PRIESTS

1   *Faith in the City: A Call for Action by Church and Nation. The Report of the Archbishop of
       Canterbury's Commission on Urban Priority Areas* (London: Church House, 1985), p. 259
2   Liverpool City Archives, Sheppard Papers, UPA Box, *Faith in the City* file Speech to the
       Liverpool Diocesan Synod, March 1987
3   Private interview with author
4   TNA, PREM19/658, Fol. 35
5   Ibid., Fol. 22
6   Ibid., Fols. 16, 25, 35
7   *The Times*, 27 July 1982
8   Robert Runcie, *The Canterbury Tales* (Channel 4, 1996)
9   *The Times*, 27 July 1982
10   Speech at the *Salute to the Task Force* lunch, 12 October 1982
       http://www.margaretthatcher.org/document/105034
11   LCA, SP, National Issues Box, House of Lords file, letter to Hugh Montefiore, 11 April 1983
12   Andrew Partington, *Church and State: The Contribution of the Church of England Bishops to
       the House of Lords during the Thatcher Years* (Milton Keynes, 2006)
13   David Winter, *Winter's Tale: Living through an Age of Change in Church and Media* (Oxford:
       Lion, 2001), p. 76
14   D. Rogers, *Politics, Prayer and Parliament* (London: Continuum, 2000), p. 142
15   John Habgood, *Church and Nation in a Secular Age* (London: Darton, Longman and Todd), p. 63

16   Kenneth Leech, *Struggle In Babylon: Racism in the Cities and Churches in Britain* (London: Sheldon, 1988), pp. 145–6

17   York University Library, Borthwick Institute, Blanch Papers, BP1/BLA/4/6/4, Royal Wedding file, *Thought for the Day*, 29 July 1981

18   A. H. Halsey, 'On Methods and Morals' in Abrams, Mark, David Gerard & Noel Timms, *Values and Social Change in Britain* (Basingstoke: Palgrave Macmillan, 1985), p. 12

19   LPL, RP, Runcie/Main/1983/222, letter to Clifford Longley, 26 October 1983

20   *Proc. of the Gen. Synod 1982*, Vol. 13, No. 3, 11 November 1982, p. 958

21   *The Times*, 30 August 1976

22   P. Elsom and D. Porter, *4 million reasons to care: how your church can help the unemployed*, (Bromley: Marc Europe, 1985), p. 7

23   G. Ecclestone, 'Coping with Caring', *Crucible*, January–March 1985, p. 2

24   Speech to Women's Royal Voluntary Service National Conference, 19 January 1981

25   *Parl. Proc.*, HL Debs, 8 April 1981, Vol. 419, Cols. 547–8

26   Anthony Seldon, *Major: A Political Life* (London: Weidenfeld & Nicolson, 1997), p. 362

27   Liverpool Cathedral Archives, Worlock Papers, Series 13, Box X, A Toxteth Riots, Letter to Frank Judd, 11 July 1981

28   No. 10 record of conversation, Margaret Thatcher, Archbishop Worlock and Bishop of Warrington, 13 July 1981 http://www.margaretthatcher.org/document/134870

29   *The Times*, 27 May 1981

30   *Faith in the City*, p. 21

31   Ibid., p. 208

32   *Sunday Times*, 1 December 1985

33   *Faith in the City*, p. xiv

34   Interview with the *Catholic Herald*, 5 December 1978 http://www.margaretthatcher.org/document/103793

35   Atherton's statement also echoes Tawney's statement: 'What thoughtful rich people call the problem of poverty, thoughtful poor people call with equal justice a problem of riches.'

36   *Faith in the City*, p. xv

37   *Daily Mail*, 2 December 1985

38   David Jenkins, 'Christian Doctrine: The Challenge to and from Poverty' reprinted in his *God, Politics and the Future* (London: SCM Press, 1988), p. 60

39   Frank Field, *The Politics of Paradise: A Christian Approach to the Kingdom* (London: Collins, 1987), p. 69

40   David Jenkins, 'Justice, the Market and Healthcare' in *The Market and Healthcare* (Edinburgh: Centre for Theology and Public Issues, 1990), p. 2

41   Ibid., p. 7

42   *Proc. of the Gen. Synod 1989*, Vol. 20, No. 2, 11 July 1989, p. 864

43   *Daily Telegraph*, 19 April 1984

44   LCA, SP, UPA Box, *Faith in the City* file, letter to the Chief Rabbi, 4 March 1986

45   LCA, SP, Publications Box 5, Press Statements 1989–93, The Debrabant Lecture 1989, 10 May 1989, p. 6, 7

46   LPL, CAA, MS 4445, Minutes of the Council of Christian Action, 19 June 1979, Fol. 17; Minutes of the Council of Christian Action, 19 July 1986

47   Joe Hasler, 'With you always – but absent?' *Crucible*, (January–March 1987), p. 13

48   *The Perception of Poverty Europe* (Brussels: European Communities Commission, 1977)

49   'The 24 Steps', *Crucible* (July–September 1986), pp. 46–7

50   York University Library, Borthwick Institute, PC 62.12.YOR, York Diocesan Leaflet, February 1989

51   *Winchester Churchman*, No. 317, August 1989, pp. 4–5

52 Ibid., No. 304, July 1988, p. 8; No. 305, August 1988, p. 7

53 Ibid., No. 306, September 1988, p. 1

54 *Yorkshire Post*, 18 October 1983

55 *The Times*, 1 July 1988

56 LPL, RP, Runcie/Main/1983/137, Letter from Lord Hailsham, 9 February 1983, Fol. 4

57 *Winchester Churchman*, No. 243, February 1983, p. 1

58 *Daily Mirror*, 16 December 1985. David Sheppard had in fact stated that he believed
    that it was 'very difficult to find thoughtful Christians on the Right' even though the
    press incorrectly quoted him as saying that it was impossible to be a Christian and vote
    Conservative

59 LCA, SP, UPA Box, *Faith in the City* follow up envelope, No date; Ibid.; Letter from
    parishioner (name withheld), 22 December 1985

60 LPL, RP, Runcie/main/1983/161, Letter to Neil Kinnock, 29 June 1983, Fol. 4

61 Frank Field, 'Socialism and the Politics of Radical Distribution' reprinted in Ormrod (ed.),
    Fellowship, Freedom and Equality (London: CSM, 1990), p. 57

62 Militant was a Trotskyite left-wing splinter group which had no more than a couple of
    thousand members but dominated Liverpool City Council

63 LCA, WP, Series 13, Box X, B/2 Liverpool Rate Crisis 1984, Letter from Patrick Jenkin,
    8 October 1985

64 Ivor Crewe & Anthony King, *SDP: The Birth, Life and Death of the Social Democratic Party*
    (Oxford: Oxford University Press, 1995), p. 134

65 MCL, BCP, Z Files, 2/01 Politics, National File, Letter to Shirley Williams,
    3 February 1981

66 Ibid., Reply from Shirley Williams, 13 March 1981

67 Brian Jenner, *Christian Reflections on the Miners' Strike* (New City: Sheffield, 1986)

68 MCL, BCP, Z Files, Section 5, 'The mining dispute and the churches', 7 March 1985

69 Jenkins's enthronement sermon reprinted in Jenkins, *God, Politics and the Future*, p. 8

70 *The Times*, 25 September 1984, 2 October 1984

71 'Throne and Altar', John Selwyn Gummer. Copy held in MCL, BCP, M289, Z File, 2/3, 18
    November 1984

72 *The Times*, 2 October 1984

73 *Sunday Times*, 23 September 1984

74 *The Times*, 8 October 1984

75 Jenkins, *God, Politics and the Future*, p. 7

76 Ibid., pp. 5–6

77 Richard Vinen, *Thatcher's Britain* (London: Simon & Schuster, 2009), p. 176

78 *Daily Mirror*, 23 November 1984

79 MCA, WP, Series 13, Liverpool Papers, Secular Matters Box VI, A/7, Strikes: Miners'
    Hardship Fund 1985–6, anonymous letter, no date

80 MCA, WP, Series 13, VI Social Issues A/5, Strikes, Pay and Trade Unions 1979–90, VI
    A/5 Miners' strike 1984/5, Public statements, Letter from Peter Walker, 4 December
    1984

81 MCL, BCP, Z Files, Section 5, 'The mining dispute and the churches', 7 March 1985

82 David Jenkins, *Calling of the Cuckoo: Not quite an autobiography* (London: Bloomsbury,
    2002); David Jenkins, *Market Whys and Human Wherefores: Thinking about Markets,
    Politics and People* (London: Continuum, 2004), p. 50

83 *The Guardian*, 24 September 1984
    http://www.theguardian.com/politics/1984/sep/24/past.hugoyoung

84 *The Times*, 15 October 1984

85   Brian Harrison, 'The Rise, Fall and Rise of Political Consensus in Britain since 1940',
        History, Vol. 84, No. 274, (April 1999), p. 308

CHAPTER SIX: LEAD US NOT INTO TEMPTATION

1   Jenkins, *Calling of the Cuckoo*, p. 145
2   *The Guardian*, 12 October 1990
3   LPL, RP, Runcie/Main/1983/222, Letter to Clifford Longley, 8 July 1983
4   Sandbrook, *Seasons in the Sun*, p. 402
5   *Parl. Proc.*, HC Debs, 13 June 1984, Vol. 61, Col. 991
6   Interview with the *Catholic Herald*, 22 December 1978
           http://www.margaretthatcher.org/document/103793
7   *Parl. Proc.* HC Debs, 25 March 1996, Vol. 274, Cols. 783–4
8   Victoria Gillick, *A Mother's Tale* (London: Hodder & Stoughton, 1989), p. 210
9   Martin Durham, *Sex and Morality in the Thatcher Years* (Basingstoke: Macmillan, 1991), p. 28
10   University of Essex Library, NVLA, Box 59, Letter to Margaret Thatcher, 9 May 1979
11   Martin Durham, *Sex and Morality*, p. 79
12   NVLA, Box 4, Thatcher to Whitehouse, 23 February 1983
13   LCA, DS Papers, Letter from parishoner (name withheld), 15 April 1981
14   Ibid., Letter to Mary Whitehouse, 25 May 1986
15   Ibid., Letter from Mary Whitehouse, 28 May 1986
16   *The Sun*, 26 March 1986. I am grateful to Jemima Kelly for this reference
17   Simon Garfield, *The End of Innocence: Britain in the Time of AIDS* (London: Faber & Faber,
           1994), p. 113–4
18   The 1980s AIDS Campaign, BBC, 16 October 2005 http://www.bbc.co.uk/news/
           magazine-15886670
19   Simon Garfield, *The End of Innocence*, p. 118. One DHSS official said afterwards, 'I wasn't
           sure if Norman was asking because he thought that everyone else did it but him, or
           whether he thought he was the only one.' Ibid., p. 119
20   Andrew Holden, *Makers and Manners: Politics and Morality in Post-War Britain* (London:
           Politico's, 2004), p. 245
21   Simon Garfield, *The End of Innocence*, p. 161
22   LCP, DS Archive, Social issues 1, Homosexuality file Livewire, 'Love not fear' March 1987
23   Garfield, *End of Innocence*, p. 164
24   Ibid.
25   Ibid., p. 167
26   Ibid., p. 121
27   The 1980s AIDS Campaign, BBC, 16 October 2005
           http://news.bbc.co.uk/1/hi/programmes/panorama/4348096.stm
28   *The Guardian*, 12 December 1987
29   Stephen Jeffrey-Poulter, *Peers, Queers and Commons: the struggle for Gay Law Reform from
           1950 to the present* (London: Routledge, 1991), p. 234
30   Holden, *Makers*, p. 231
31   Jeffrey-Poulter, *Peers*, p. 204
32   *Parl. Proc.*, HC Debs., 15 December 1987, Vol. 124, Col. 1021
33   LPL, BSR papers, SPC 1986, Guidance for schools, 16 November 1986
34   *Parl. Proc.*, HL Debs., 11 January 1988, Vol. 491, Col. 1003
35   'Charles Murray and the Underclass: The Developing Debate', The IEA Health and
           Welfare Unit Choice in Welfare No. 33 (1996), p. 62

36 Joan Isaac, The Politics of Morality in the UK Parliamentary Affairs, Vol. 47, No. 2, April 1994, p. 183

37 Ibid., p. 6

38 Digby Anderson & Graham Dawson (eds.), *Family Portraits* (London: Social Affairs Unit), p. 68

39 Mark Garnett, *From Anger to Apathy: The British Experience since 1975* (London: Jonathan Cape, 2007), p. 277

40 *Daily Mail*, 26 October 1987

41 Ibid.

42 Gummer, 'Conserving the Family', in Michael Alison & David L. Edwards, *Christianity and Conservatism: Are Christianity and Conservatism Compatible* (Kent: Hodder & Stoughton, 1990) p. 312

43 *The Times*, 27 July 1988

44 LPL, RP, Main/1983/212 letter format from Bishop Hook, 21 October 1983

45 *News of the World*, 16 October 1983

46 *Foreword to Marriage* (London: CIO, 1984), p. 11

47 *The Purple, the Blue and the Red, Episode 2: Schisms Rent Assunder* (BBC, Radio 4, 1996)

48 John Gummer, 'Conserving the Family', p. 307

49 LCA, SP, Social Issues, Homosexuality file, Letter to the Bishop of Stepney, 16 November 1979

50 LPL, BSRP, SPC 1983, Homosexuality Agenda Item, comments by Giles Ecclestone, 8 July 1983, p. 2

51 *Evening Standard*, 27 September 1984

52 Jenkins, *Calling of the Cuckoo*, pp. 146–7

53 *Crockford's Clerical Directory 1987/8* (Oxford, 1987), p. 68

54 Carpenter, *Reluctant Archbishop*, p. 348

55 Ibid., p. 351. It was thought that Habgood's outspokenness over the Bennet affair put him out of the race to succeed Runcie at Canterbury

56 Jenkins, *Calling of the Cuckoo*, p. 148

CHAPTER SEVEN: GOD OR MAMMON?

1 Margaret Thatcher to Woodrow Wyatt, 25 September 1988, quoted in Campbell, *The Iron Lady*, p. 248

2 Simon Lee & Peter Stanford, *Believing Bishops* (London: Faber & Faber, 1990), p. 105

3 Parl. Proc., HL Debs., 25 April 1985, Vol. 77, Col. 988

4 *Keep Sunday Special* Campaign literature, October 1988, Issue 5

5 Parl. Proc., HL Debs., 25 February 1986, Vol. 471 Col. 954

6 Ibid., HL Debs., 14 April 1986, Vol. 96, Col. 643

7 Ibid., HL Debs., 2 December 1985, Vol. 468, Col. 1071

8 Ibid., HL Debs., 16 December 1985, Vol. 469, Col. 539

9 Ibid., HL Debs., 14 April 1986, Vol. 95, Col. 626

10 Ibid., HL Debs., 21 January 1986, Vol. 470, Col. 158

11 *The Guardian*, 18 May 1982

12 Winter, *Winter's Tale*, p. 154

13 Dennis Kavanagh, 'Thatcher's Third Term', *Parliamentary Affairs*, Vol. 41, No. 1, (1988)p. 6

14 Paul Whiteley, *Pressure for the Poor: the Poverty Lobby and Policy Making* (London: Methuen, 1987), pp. 146, 148

15 LPL, BSRP, SPC 1988, M/7, Michael Bayley, 'A Christian Perspective on the welfare state', 17–18 June 1988

16   Private interview with author

17   'A Closet Capitalist Confesses' printed in E. Younkins (ed.) *Three in One: Essays on Democratic Capitalism 1976–2000* (Lanham, MD: Rowman & Littlefield, 2001), p. 4

18   LPL, BSRP, Industrial Committee, 'Lord Harris, Can a Christian legitimately support a social market economy?' IC/15/86

19   *Weekly Standard*, 22 April 2013
       http://www.weeklystandard.com/articles/victorian-lady_716278.html

20   Private interview with author

21   *Thatcher and the Scots* (BBC2, 2009)

22   Speech to General Assembly of the Church of Scotland, 21 May 1988
       http://www.margaretthatcher.org/document/107246

23   Raban, *God, Man and Mrs Thatcher*, p. 68

24   *The Times*, 1 June 1988; LPL, BSRP, SP, 27 May 1988

25   Michael Alison & David L. Edwards, *Christianity and Conservatism: Are Christianity and Conservatism Compatible?* (Kent: Hodder & Stoughton, 1990)

26   Jenkins, *Calling of the Cuckoo*; Private interview with Michael Baughen; *The Purple, the Blue and the Red, Episode 2: Marching As to War* (BBC, Radio 4, 1996)

27   David Jenkins, Hibbert Lecture 1985, reprinted in David Jenkins, *God, Politics and the Future* (London: SCM Press, 1988), p. 114

28   Ronald Butt, 'The Tension of the 1980s' in Alison & Edwards (eds.), *Are Christianity and Conservatism Compatible?*, pp. 30, 32

29   Conservative Party conference, 13 October 1989
       http://www.margaretthatcher.org/document/107789

30   Geoffrey Finlayson, *Citizen, State and Social Welfare in Britain 1830–1990* (Oxford: Clarendon, 1994), p. 381

31   *Church Times*, 19 September 1988

32   LCA, SP, Additional Deposit Box I, Part II, Addresses, lectures and other papers 1989, Church Action on Poverty Lecture 1989, p. 14

33   Finlayson, *Citizen, State and Social Welfare*, p. 404

34   Stephen Green, *Serving God? Serving Mammon? Christians and the Financial Markets* (London: Marshall Pickering, 1996), p. 34

35   Martin J. Wiener, *English Culture and the Decline of the Industrial Spirit 1850–1980* (Harmondsworth: Penguin, 1981), p. 116

36   Reprinted in Stanley Booth-Clibborn, *Taxes: Burden or Blessing?* (London: Arthur James Limited, 1991), p. 58

37   Brian Griffiths, *The Creation of Wealth: A Christian's Case for Capitalism* (London: Hodder & Stoughton), p. 11

38   Green, *Serving God? Serving Mammon?*, p. 106

39   *Parl. Proc.*, HC Debs, 13 February 1989, Vol. 147, Col. 64

40   *Proc. of the Gen. Synod 1986*, 5 February 1986, Vol. 17, No. 1, p. 138

41   Malcolm Grundy, 'Can we say "Thanks to Industry"?', *Crucible*, (Jan–March 1986), p. 2

42   LPL, BSRP, IC, 'Can a Christian Legitimately Support a Social Market Economy?', IC/15/86, p. 3

43   Raymond Plant, 'The Anglican Church and the Secular State' in George Moyser (ed.), *Church and Politics Today: The Role of the Church of England in Contemporary Politics* (Edinburgh, T&T Clark, 1985), p. 329

44   LPL, BSRP, SPC, 1988, M/7, Minutes of the Social Policy Committee, 17–18 June 1988, pp. 2–3

45   *Proc. of the Gen. Synod 1990*, 7 July 1990, Vol. 21, No. 2, p. 490

46   John Rylands Library, Methodist Church papers, Division of Social Responsibility, Box 37,

Correspondence and associated papers, minutes and working papers of ethics of Wealth creation working party, 1989–1991, 31 January 1991

47   Leo Abse, *Margaret Thatcher, Daughter of Beatrice: A Politician's Psycho-biography of Margaret Thatcher* (London: Jonathan Cape, 1989), p. 198

48   Ibid., p. 207

49   Geoffrey Alderman, *London Jewry and London Politics, 1889–1986* (London: Routledge, 1989), p. 119

50   Private interview with Jonathan Sacks

51   Speech to Board of Deputies of British Jews, 15 December 1981
      http://www.margaretthatcher.org/document/104762

52   Speech to Finchley Anglo-Israel Friendship League, 24 June 1965
      http://www.margaretthatcher.org/document/101293

53   Speech to Finchley Anglo-Israel Friendship League, 10 January 1972
      http://www.margaretthatcher.org/document/102175

54   British embassy in Jordan to FCO (MT connections to Israel) 28 February 1975
      http://www.margaretthatcher.org/document/110906

55   Margaret Thatcher, *Downing Street Years* (London: HarperCollins, 1993), pp. 509–10

56   L. Abse, *Margaret, Daughter of Beatrice*, p. 198

57   Immanuel Jakobovits, *From Doom to Hope: a Jewish View on Faith in the City* (London: Office of the Chief Rabbi, 1986)

58   Speech at dinner to Lord Jakobivits, 21 February 1991
      http://www.margaretthatcher.org/document/108261

59   Speech at St Lawrence Jewry, 4 March 1981
      http://www.margaretthatcher.org/document/104587

60   Whitehouse, *Whatever Happened to Sex*, p. 25

61   *The Crisis in Religious Education* (London: Education Research Trust, 1988), p. 4

62   *The Times*, 24 November 1987

63   Guildhall Library, Graham Leonard Papers, Box 5/2, Education Reform Bill, John Lyttle, Background information and suggested amendments. No date

64   GL, GLP, Box 5/2, Education Reform Bill: Individual correspondence, 24 June 1988 (name withheld)

65   *The Guardian*, 3 September 1987

66   Tariq Modood, *Racial Equality: Colour, Culture and Justice* (London: IPPR, 1994); *Not Easy Being British: Colour, Culture and Citizenship* (Stoke-on-Trent: Runnymede Trust and Trentham, 1992)

67   Paul Weller, *Mirror For Our Times: 'The Rushdie Affair' and the Future of Multiculturalism* (London: Continuum, 2009) pp. 73–79

68   *The Independent*, 21 February 1989

69   *The Independent*, 3 August 1989, quoted in Weller, *Mirror For Our Times*, p. 86

70   *The Independent*, 3 June 1989

71   Tariq Modood, 'Minorities, Faith and Citizenship', in *Discernment: A Christian Journal for Inter-Religious Encounter*, Vol. 6, No. 2, (1992), p. 59

72   UK Action Committee on Islamic Affairs, *The Need for Reform: Muslims and the Law in Multi-Faith Britain* (London, 1993), p. 39

73   Peter Mullen, 'Satanic Asides', in Dan Cohn-Sherbok (ed.), *The Salman Rushdie Controversy in Interreligious Perspective* (Lampeter: Mellen, 1990), p. 33

CHAPTER EIGHT: HOLY WARRIORS AND BLESSED PEACEMAKERS

1   Mervyn Stockwood, *The Cross and the Sickle* (London: Foreign Affairs Publishing Co., 1978), p. 80

2   Urban, *Diplomacy and Disillusion*, p. 38

3   Aleksandr Solzhenitsyn, 'Godlessness, the First Step to the Gulag' (The Templeton
       Address, Guildhall, London, 11 May 1983), p. 1

4   Urban, *Diplomacy and Disillusion*, p. 3

5   Dianne Kirby (ed.), *Religion and the Cold War* (London: Palgrave, 2002), p. 1

6   *The Economist*, 15 October 2010 http://www.economist.com/blogs/
       democracyinamerica/2010/10/religion_and_politics

7   Dianne Kirby, 'The Church of England and the Cold War' in Stephen G. Parker & Tom
       Lawson (eds.) *God and War: The Church of England and Armed Conflict in the Twentieth
       Century* (London: Ashgate, 2012) p. 128

8   Ibid., pp. 121–145

9   Matthew Grimley, 'The Church and the Bomb: Anglicans and the Campaign for Nuclear
       Disarmament, c.1958–1984', in Parker & Lawson (eds.), *God and War*, p. 158

10   Owen Chadwick, *The Christian Church in the Cold War* (London: Penguin, 1993), Chapters
       1–5; Dianne Kirby, 'The Churches and Christianity in Cold War Europe', in Klaus Larres
       (ed.), *A Companion to Europe Since 1945* (London: Wiley-Blackwell, 2009), pp. 203–30

11   Stockwood, *The Cross and the Sickle*, p. 81

12   Ibid.

13   John O'Sullivan, *The President, the Pope and the Prime Minister* (Washington: Regnery
       Publishing, 2006)

14   Richard Aldrous, *Reagan and Thatcher: The Difficult Relationship* (New York: W. W. Norton
       & Company, Inc., 2012), Chapter 1

15   Paul Kengor, *God and Ronald Reagan: A Spiritual Life* (New York: HarperCollins, 2004),
       Chapter 1

16   Ibid., p. 141

17   O'Sullivan, *The President, the Pope and the Prime Minister*, Chapter 1

18   New Year Message, 29 December 1950, http://www.margaretthatcher.org/document/100896

19   Speech to Chelsea Conservative Association, 26 July 1975
       http://www.margaretthatcher.org/document/102750

20   Speech to Pilgrims of the United States, 16 September 1975
       http://www.margaretthatcher.org/document/102462

21   Speech at Kensington Town Hall, 19 January 1976
       http://www.margaretthatcher.org/document/102939

22   Urban, *Diplomacy and Disillusion*, p. 3

23   Ibid., p. 39

24   Speech at the Winston Churchill Foundation Award dinner, 29 December 1983,
       http://www.margaretthatcher.org/document/105450

25   Aldous, *Reagan and Thatcher*, p. 146

26   Urban, *Diplomacy and Disillusion*, pp. 53, 51

27   James Mann, *A History of the End of the Cold War: The Rebellion of the Ronald Reagan*
       (London: Penguin, 2009), Chapter 5

28   Bernard Ingham, private interview with author

29   O'Sullivan, *The President, the Pope and the Prime Minister*, p. 298

30   Carpenter, *Reluctant Archbishop*, p. 234–7

31   PREM 10/0609, Fols. 69–72, 85. The fear was that the event was becoming too political
       rather than pastoral. This was complicated by the fact that the British government had
       just upgraded its diplomatic missions with the Vatican. Fols. 107–8

32   Ibid., Fol. 59.

33   Ibid., Fol. 43

34 Ibid., Fol. 85

35 Ibid., Fol. 90

36 Ibid., Fol. 36

37 Ibid., Fol. 16

38 Ibid., Fol. 129

39 Ibid., Fol. 126

40 Carpenter, *Reluctant Archbishop*, p. 236

41 PREM 19/0609, Fols. 21–6

42 Ibid., Fols. 39–42

43 Ibid., Fols. 12, 28. MPs and junior ministers were allowed to attend the service given that they were not part of the government

44 Aldous, *Reagan and Thatcher*, p. 58

45 James Hinton, *Protest and Visions: Peace and Politics in Twentieth Century Britain* (London: Radius, 1989) p. 63

46 Lord President's Office record of conversation, 24 November 1982
http://www.margaretthatcher.org/document/122828

47 Shipley minute to Parkinson, 7 June 1982,
http://www.margaretthatcher.org/document/122776

48 Grimley, 'The Church and the Bomb' in Parker & Lawson (eds.), *God and War*, p. 161

49 Lord President's Office record of conversation, 24 November 1982
http://www.margaretthatcher.org/document/122828

50 Roger Fieldhouse, *Anti-Apartheid Movement: A History of the Movement in Britain* (London: Merlin, 2005), p. 358

51 Runcie also personally intervened in 1980 when the South African government withdrew Tutu's passport

52 Carpenter, *Reluctant Archbishop*, p. 229

53 Speech at the National Press Club, 1 July 1979
http://www.margaretthatcher.org/document/103888

54 Prime Minister PW Botha of South Africa letter to MT, 5 February 1980
http://www.margaretthatcher.org/document/119634

55 David Sheppard, *Steps Along Hope Street: My Life in Cricket, the Church and the Inner City* (London: Hodder & Stoughton, 2002), p. 281

56 *The Guardian*, 8 July 1986 http://www.margaretthatcher.org/document/106265

57 Gummer, in Gummer, Heffer & Beith, *Which Way Should Christians Vote?* (London: SPCK, 1987), p. 7

58 Margaret Thatcher to President P. W. Botha, 31 October 1985
http://www.margaretthatcher.org/document/111650

59 President P. W. Botha to Margaret Thatcher, 12 November 1985
http://www.margaretthatcher.org/document/111651

60 Margaret Thatcher did admit this in her memoirs: Thatcher, *Downing Street Years*, p. 259

61 Andrew Chandler, *The Church of England in the Twentieth Century: The Church Commissioners and the Politics of Reform, 1948–1998* (Woodbridge: Boydell, 2006) p. 304. These investments, however, were small. It was estimated that only 1 percent of Church investments were in South Africa

62 Monica Furlong, *The C of E: The State It's In: The Past and the Present* (London: SPCK, 2nd edition, 2006), p. 171

63 Interview with the *Catholic Herald*, 22 December 1978
http://www.margaretthatcher.org/document/103793

64 Letter to the Lord Bishop Suffragen of Warrington, 11 June 1979
http://www.margaretthatcher.org/document/119118

65   Remarks at *Daily Star* Gold Star Awards, 27 February 1985
       http://www.margaretthatcher.org/document/105977

66   Brian Griffiths, *Morality and the Market Place: Christian Alternatives to Capitalism and Socialism* (London: Hodder & Stoughton, 1982), p. 147

67   Letter from Ted Heath (North/South Summit, Mexico City, 1981), 20 May 1981
       http://www.margaretthatcher.org/document/128032

68   Anthony Parsons, 'Britain at the United Nations: A Valedictory Despatch', 2 July 1982,
       http://www.margaretthatcher.org/document/123110

69   Gummer, in Gummer, Heffer & Beith, *Which Way Should Christians Vote?*, p. 33

70   *Live Aid – Against All Odds* (BBC 4 documentary)

71   *The Times*, 15 July 1985

72   LPL, RP, Runcie ACP/1980/10, Visit to Eastern Europe by Anglican Clergy, Fol. 26

73   Ibid., Fol. 28

74   LPL, RP, Runcie Main/1980/136, Russian Orthodox Church, Fol. 16

75   LPL, RP, Runcie ACP/1980/12, Iran

76   *Daily Telegraph*, 15 December 2013
       http://www.telegraph.co.uk/news/uknews/10518045/Was-Terry-Waite-freed-as-part-of-secret-Lockerbie-deal-with-Iran.html

77   Carpenter, *Reluctant Archbishop*, p. 313

78   Speech to the Conservative Party Conference, 12 October 1990
       http://www.margaretthatcher.org/document/108217

79   Speech to the Polish Senate, 3 October 1991
       http://www.margaretthatcher.org/document/108285

CHAPTER NINE: EXODUS NATION

1   Furlong, *The C of E: The State It's In*, p. 191

2   T. S. Eliot, *Christianity and Culture* (New York: Harcourt, Brace & World Inc., 2nd edition, 1949), p. 10

3   Grimley, *Citizenship*, p. 204

4   Quintin Hogg, *The Case for Conservatism* (Middlesex: Penguin, 1947), p. 16

5   Stephen Haseler, *The Battle for Britain: Thatcher and the New Liberals* (London: I. B. Tauris, 1989)

6   MCL, BCP, Pre-Election Statement folder, Letter from Patrick Kelly, Bishop of Salford, no date

7   Cole Moreton, *Is God Still an Englishman? How Britain lost its faith (But found new soul)* (London: Abacus, 2010), pp. 181, 185

8   Furlong, *The C of E*, p. 173

9   Furlong, *The C of E*, pp. 172–5; Moreton, *Is God Still an Englishman?*, pp. 183–94

10   Moreton, *Is God Still an Englishman?*, p. 189; Chandler, *The Church of England in the Twentieth Century*, Chapter 15

11   Jenkins, *Calling of the Cuckoo*, pp. 148, 185

12   Moreton, *Is God Still an Englishman?*, p. 175

13   *The Guardian*, 21 March 2006

14   Dr Rowan Williams, *Writing in the Dust: After September 11* (London: Hodder & Stoughton, 2002), p. 55

15   Hastings, *English Christianity*, p. 49

16   *The Times*, 30 August 1976

17   Parl. Proc., HC Debs, 29 October 1993, Vol. 230, Col. 1122

18   Ann Widdecombe Foreword, in Dwight Longenecker (ed.), *The Path To Rome: Modern Journeys to the Catholic Church* (Bodmin: Gracewing, 1999), pp. xii–xvi

19   Parl. Proc., HC Debs, 29 October 1993, Vol. 230, Col. 1104

20   Charles Moore in Joanna Bogle (ed.), *Come On In: It's Awful* (Leominster: Gracewing, 1994), p. 28

21   Ibid., p. 32

22   Ibid., William Oddie in Bogle (ed.), *Come On In*, p. 38

23   *The Times*, 2 March 1987

24   Moore in Bogle (ed.), *Come On In*, p. 26

25   Chris Patten, *The Tory Case* (London: Longman, 1983), p. 24

26   David Cameron: Life and Times of the new UK Prime Minister, BBC, 11 May 2010
        http://news.bbc.co.uk/1/hi/8661964.stm

27   *Church Times*, 16 April 2014
        http://www.churchtimes.co.uk/articles/2014/17-april/comment/opinion/
        my-faith-in-the-church-of-england

28   *The Guardian*, 22 April 2013
        http://www.theguardian.com/education/2013/apr/22/king-james-bible-in-schools

29   *Sunday Telegraph*, 7 April 1996

30   Cherie Blair, *Speaking for Myself* (London: Sphere, 2008), p. 95

31   *The Independent*, 27 September 2006
        http://www.independent.co.uk/news/uk/politics/blair-in-his-own-words-417732.html

32   *The Guardian*, 29 January 1996; 'The Stakeholder Society: *Faith in the City* – Ten Years On' in Tony
        Blair, *New Britain: My Vision of a Young Country* (London: Fourth Estate, 1996), pp. 297–309

33   *Social Justice: Strategies for National Renewal* (London: IPPR, 1994)

34   *The Telegraph*, 12 April 2014

35   Dr Rowan Williams, Civil and Religious Law in England: a religious perspective, Royal
        Courts of Justice, 7 February 2008
        http://rowanwilliams.archbishopofcanterbury.org/articles.php/1137/
        archbishops-lecture-civil-and-religious-law-in-england-a-religious-perspective

CHAPTER TEN: REAP WHAT YOU SOW

1   Interview with *The Guardian*, 8 July 1986
        http://www.margaretthatcher.org/document/106265

2   Julie Burchill, *The Times*, 14 November 2004
        http://www.margaretthatcher.org/document/110576

3   Private interview with author

4   Speech on Europe ('Europe as I see it') 24 June 1977
        http://www.margaretthatcher.org/document/103403

5   TV interview for BBC1 *Panorama*, 8 June 1987
        http://www.margaretthatcher.org/document/106647

6   The second half of the quote is often forgotten. ' ...as long as they pay their taxes.' Mandelson
        said it to a conference of California computer executives in 1998: Andrew Rawnsley,
        Servants of the People: The Inside Story of New Labour (London: Penguin, 2001), p. 213

7   Private interview with author

8   Carol Thatcher, *Below the Parapet*, p. 247

9   Private interview with author

10   Speech to British Society of Magazine Editors, 29 July 1988
        http://www.margaretthatcher.org/document/107300

11   Interview for *Manchester Evening News*, 8 April 1987
        http://www.margaretthatcher.org/document/106792

12   Speech at Lord Mayor's Banquet, 10 November 1986
        http://www.margaretthatcher.org/document/106512

13   Matthew Hancock & Rob Wood, 'Household Secured Debt', Bank of England, 2004, pp. 291–301

14   John Bone & Karen O'Reilly, 'No place called home: the causes and social consequences of
        the UK housing "bubble"', *British Journal of Sociology*, (2010) Vol. 61, Issue 2, p. 238

15   Ibid.

16   Richard Berthoud & Elaine Kempson, *Credit and Debit: The PSI Report* (London: Policy
        Studies Institute, 1992), p. 47

17   Article for *Signpost*, 'This is your choice', 1 September 1959
        http://www.margaretthatcher.org/document/101020

18   Berthoud & Kempson, *Credit and Debit*, pp. 46–7

19   http://www.theguardian.com/news/datablog/2009/nov/06/
        bankruptcy-iva-insolvency-debt-data

20   J. Ford & K. Rowlingston, 'Low-income households and credit: exclusion, preference, and
        inclusion', *Environment and Planning A*, Vol. 28, p. 1345

21   Stewart Lansley, 'Britain's Livelihood Crisis', Trade Union Congress, 2011
        http://www.tuc.org.uk/sites/default/files/tuc-19639-fo.pdf

22   Ford & Rowlingston, 'Low-income households', p. 1345

23   Berthoud & Kempson, *Credit and Debit*

24   Henry Palmer & Pat Conaty, *Profiting from Poverty: Why Debt is Big Business in Britain*
        (London: New Economics Foundation, 2002); Ford & Rowlingston, 'Low-income
        households', p. 1350

25   Speech to Conservative Party conference, 14 Oct 1977
        http://www.margaretthatcher.org/document/103443

26   The Church sold the centre in 1995 although it retained a 10 per cent stake

27   'Household Debt in the Economic and Fiscal Outlook,' *Office for Budget Responsibility*, 21 April 2011

28   *Daily Telegraph*, 31 October 2011

29   Speech at Lord Mayor's Banquet, 10 November 1986
        http://www.margaretthatcher.org/document/106512

30   *Financial Times*, 28 September 2011

31   Richard Davies, Peter Richardson, Vaiva Katinaite & Mark Manning, 'Evolution of the
        UK banking system', Ban of England Quarterly Bulletin, 2010, pp. 321–32; Stephen
        Burgess, 'Measuring financial sector output and its contribution to the UK GDP',
        Bank of England Quarterly Bulletin, 2011 Q3, pp. 234–46; Andrew Haldane, The
        Contribution of the Financial Sector – Miracle or Mirage?, Speech to the Future of
        Finance Conference, 14 July 2010
        http://www.bis.org/review/r100716.pdf

32   Richard Roberts, *Did anyone learn anything from the Equitable Life? Lessons and learning from
        Financial Crises*, (Institute of Contemporary British History, King's College London, 2012) p. 9

33   http://www.which.co.uk/money/retirement/guides/
        contracting-out-of-state-second-pension-s2p/the-1980s/

34   TV Interview for ITN (recalls losing office), 28 June 1991
        http://www.margaretthatcher.org/document/110849

35   Private interview with author; Frank Field made a similar statement to the Commons on
        the occasion of Baroness Thatcher's death
        http://www.liverpoolecho.co.uk/news/liverpool-news/
        birkenhead-mp-frank-field-tells-3320350

36   Quoted in Charles Moore, *Margaret Thatcher & Capitalism* (2012 Adam Smith Lecture), 6
        February 2012 http://www.margaretthatcher.org/document/114620

BIBLIOGRAPHY

Interviews

Jonathan Aitken

Rt Hon. Lord Baker

Rt Rev. Michael Baughen

Rt Hon. Lord Powell of Bayswater

Rt Hon. Tony Benn

Rt Rev. Ronnie Bowlby

Rt Rev. Tom Butler

Rt Hon. Lord Carey

Humphrey Carpenter

Cynthia Crawford

Rt Hon. Frank Field

Rt Lord Gummer

Rt Hon. Lord Harries

Derek Hatton

Rt Hon Lord Howe

Rt Hon. Lord Hurd

Sir Bernard Ingham

Rt Hon. Lord Jenkin

Rt Hon. Lord Lawson

Clifford Longley

Rev. Eric James

Rt Rev. David Jenkins

Anthony Kilmister OBE

Prof. Diamaid MacCulloch

Prof. David Martin

Charles Moore

Rev. Dr Edward Norman

Sir Richard O'Brien

Rt Hon. Lord Parkinson

Rt Hon. Lord Charles Powell

Hon. James Runcie

Rt Hon. Lord Sacks

Rt Rev. Mark Santer

Dr Michael Schluter

Lady Grace Sheppard

Rt Hon. Lord Tebbit

Harvey Thomas CBE

Rt Hon. Lord Wakeham

Very Reverend Alan Webster

Rt Hon. Ann Widdecome DSG

Archive Material

NATIONAL COLLECTIONS AND PERSONAL PAPERS:

Blanch, Lord Stuart, Papers, Borthwick Institute, University of York

Booth-Clibborn, Stanley, Papers, Manchester Central Library, Manchester

Habgood, Lord John, Papers, Borthwick Institute, University of York

Leonard Papers, Bishop of London, Guildhall Library

Powell, Enoch, Papers, Churchill College, Cambridge

Runcie, Lord Robert, Papers, Lambeth Palace Library

Sheppard, Lord David, Papers, Liverpool City Archives, Liverpool

The National Archives, Kew, Richmond, Surrey

Thatcher, Margaret, Papers, Churchill College, Cambridge

Worlock, Derek, Papers, Metropolitan Cathedral Archives, Liverpool

OTHER:

Board for Social Responsibility Archive, Church of England Record's Centre, Lambeth Palace Library

British Council of Churches Archive, Lambeth Palace Library, London

Central Religious Advisory Committee Archive, BBC Written Archives Centre, Caversham Park, Reading

Christian Action Archive, Lambeth Palace Library, London

Church Action on Poverty Archive, Church Action on Poverty, Manchester

Conservative Party Archive, Bodleian, University of Oxford

Lincolnshire County Record Office

Grantham Records Office

Methodist Church Archives, John Rylands Library, University of Manchester, Manchester

Winchester Diocesan Archives, Hampshire Record Office

York Diocesan Archives, Borthwick Institute, University of York

Newspapers and Periodicals

Baptist Times	Liverpool Daily Post
Church Times	Liverpool Echo
Crucible	New Statesman
Daily Express	Poetry Review
Daily Mirror	Poverty Network
Daily Telegraph	Salisbury Review
Encounter	The Spectator
Grantham Journal	The Sun
Grantham Guardian	Sunday Express
Mail on Sunday	Sunday Telegraph
Methodist Recorder	The Times
The Guardian	Yorkshire Post
The Independent	Winchester Churchman

TV/Radio Broadcasts

The Canterbury Tales (Channel 4, 1996)

Faith in the City Commission, Centre for Contemporary British History
Witness Seminar, Recorded 5 July 2006, unpublished transcript

Live Aid: Against All Odds (BBC2, 2010)

The Purple, the Blue and the Red: 3-part series (BBC, 1996)

Thatcher and the Scots (BBC2, 2009)

Unpublished interview with Margaret Thatcher, Wesley's Chapel, 1993

Memoirs/Diaries

Baker, Kenneth, The Turbulent Years: My Life in Politics (London: Faber &
Faber, 1993)

Blair, Cherie, *Speaking for Myself* (London: Sphere, 2008)

Carey, George, *Know The Truth: A Memoir* (London: HarperCollins, 2004)

Habgood, John, *Confessions of a Conservative Liberal* (London: SPCK, 1988)

Heseltine, Michael, *Life in the Jungle: My Autobiography* (London: Hodder & Stoughton, 2000)

Hurd, Douglas, *Memoirs* (London: Abacus, 2003)

Jenkins, David, *The Calling of a Cuckoo: Not Quite an Autobiography* (London: Bloomsbury, 2002)

Millar, Ronald, *The View From the Wings: West End, West Coast, Westminster* (London: Weidenfeld & Nicolson, 1993)

Sheppard, David, *Steps Along Hope Street: My Life in Cricket, the Church and the Inner City* (London: Hodder & Stoughton, 2002)

Sherman, Alfred, *Paradoxes of Power: Reflections on the Thatcher Interlude* (Exeter: Imprint, 2005)

Tebbit, Norman, *Upwardly Mobile: An Autobiography* (London: Weidenfeld & Nicolson, 1988)

Thatcher, Margaret, *The Downing Street Years* (London: HarperCollins, 1993)

_ _, *The Path to Power* (London: HarperCollins 1995)

Urban, George, *Diplomacy and Disillusion at the Court of Margaret Thatcher* (London: I. B. Tauris, 1996)

Webster, Alan, *Reaching for Reality: Sketches from the Life of the Church* (London: SPCK, 2002)

Winter, David, *Winter's Tale. Living through an Age of Change in Church and Media* (Oxford: Lion 2001)

Official Church of England Publications

Changing Britain: Social Diversity and Moral Unity (London: Church House, 1987)

The Church and the Bomb: Nuclear Weapons and Christian Conscience (London: Hodder & Stoughton, 1982)

Faith in the City: A Call for Action by Church and Nation. The Report of the Archbishop of Canterbury's Commission on Urban Priority Areas (London: Church House, 1985)

Foreword to Marriage (London: CIO, 1984)

The Future of the Welfare State: Questions which need attention (London, Church House, 1984)

Issues in Human Sexuality (London: Church House, 1991)

It's for you: A Study guide to Faith in the City (London: Church House, 1986)

Living Faith in the City (London: Church House, 1990)

The Nature of Christian Belief (London: Church House, 1986)

Not Just for the Poor. Christian Perspectives on the Welfare State (London: Church House, 1986)

Reform of Social Security: Response of the BSR General Synod of the Church of England to DHSS Green Paper (London: Church House, 1985)

Staying in the City: Faith in the City – *Ten Years On* (London: Church House, 1995)

Contemporary Articles, Books, Pamphlets and Speeches

[No author]

The Crisis in Religious Education (London: Educational Research trust, 1988)

Law, Blasphemy and the Multi-Faith Society (London: Commission for Racial Equality, 1990)

The Market and Healthcare (Edinburgh: Centre for Theology and Public Issues, 1990)

The Need for Reform: Muslims and the Law in Multi-Faith Britain (London: UK Action Committee on Islamic Affairs, 1993)

Proceedings of 'Poverty Today', Occasional Paper No.7 (Edinburgh: New College, 1986)

Addy, T. & D. Scott, *Fatal Impacts? The MSC and Voluntary Action* (Manchester: The William Temple Foundation, 1987)

Ahern, Geoffrey & Grace Davie, *Inner City God: the Nature of Belief in the Inner City* (London: Hodder & Stoughton, 1987)

Anderson, Digby (ed.), *The Kindness that Kills: The Churches' Simplistic Response to Complex Social Issues* (London: SPCK, 1984)

Anderson, Oliver, *Rotten Borough: The Real Story of Thatcher's Grantham* (London: Fourth Estate, 1989)

Ashford, Sheena & Noel Timms, *What Europe Thinks: A Study of Western European Values* (Aldershot: Dartmouth, 1992)

Atherton, John, *The Scandal of Poverty. Priorities for the Emerging Church* (London: Mowbray, 1983)

_ _, *Faith in the Nation: A Christian Vision for Britain* (London: SPCK, 1988)

Avis, Paul, *Authority, Leadership and Conflict in the Church* (London: Mowbray, 1992)

Badham, Paul (ed.), *Religion, State and Society in Modern Britain* (Lampeter: Mellen, 1989)

Barnett, Correlli, *The Audit Of War: The Illusion and Reality of Britain as a Great Nation* (London: Pan, 1987)

Bigger, Nigel, *Theological Politics: a Critique of 'Faith in the City', the Report of the Archbishop of Canterbury's Commission on Urban Priority Areas* (Oxford: Latimer House, 1988)

Blair, Tony, *New Britain: My Vision of a Young Country* (London: Fourth Estate, 1996)

Bogle, Joanna (ed.), *Come On In, It's Awful* (Leominster: Gracewing, 1994)

Bonino, José Miguez, *Christians and Marxists: the Mutual Challenge to Revolution* (London: Hodder & Stoughton, 1976)

Booth-Clibborn, Stanley, *Taxes: Burden or Blessing?* (London: Arthur James, 1991)

Boyson, Rhodes (ed.), *Down with the Poor* (London: Churchill Press, 1971)

Brown, Malcolm & Ballard, Paul H., *The Church and Economic Life: A Documentary Study, 1945 to the Present* (Peterborough: Epworth Press, 2006)

Bryant, Chris, (ed.), *Reclaiming the Ground* (London: Spire, 1993)

_ _, *Possible Dreams. A Personal History of the British Christian Socialists* (London: Hodder & Stoughton, 1997)

Burn, John, *The Crisis in Religious Education*, (Harrow: Educational Research Trust, 1988)

Cohn-Sherbok, Dan, *The Salman Rushdie Controversy in Interreligious Perspective* (Lampeter: Mellen, 1990)

Covell, Charles, *The Redefinition of Conservatism, Politics and Doctrine* (Basingstoke: Macmillan, 1986)

Cowling, Maurice (ed.), *Conservative Essays* (London: Cassell, 1978)

_ _, *Mill and Liberalism* (Cambridge: Cambridge University Press, 1990)

_ _, *Religion and Public Doctrine in Modern England Vol. II Assaults* (Cambridge: Cambridge University Press, 1985)

_ _, *Religion and Public Doctrine in Modern England Vol. I* (Cambridge: Cambridge University Press, 1980)

_ _, *Religion and Public Doctrine Vol. III Accommodations* (Cambridge: Cambridge University Press, 2001)

Ecclestone, Giles, *The Church of England and Politics* (London: CIO, 1981)

Edwards, David L. (ed.), *Robert Runcie: A Portrait by His Friends* (London: Fount, 1990)

Edwards, David L. & Alison, M. (eds.), *Christianity and Conservatism: Are Christianity and Conservatism Compatible?* (London: Hodder & Stoughton, 1990)

Eliot, T. S., *The Idea of a Christian Society* (New York: Harcourt, Brace & Co, 1940)

Farnell, Rob, et al., *Hope in the City? The Local Impact of the Church Urban Fund* (Sheffield Hallam University: Centre for Regional Economic and Social Research, 1994)

Field, Frank, *The Politics of Paradise: a Christian Approach to the Kingdom* (London: Collins, 1987)

Forrester, Duncan B., *Christianity and the Future of Welfare* (London: Epworth Press, 1985)

_ _, Forrester, Duncan B, *Beliefs, Values and Policies: Conviction Politics in a Secular Age* (Oxford: Clarendon, 1989)

Forrester, Duncan B. & Danus Skene, *Just Sharing: a Christian Approach to the Distinction of Wealth, Income and Benefits* (Edinburgh: Augsburg Fortress, 1988)

Habgood, John, *Church and Nation in Secular Age* (London: Darton, Longman and Todd, 1983)

Harries, R., *Is there a Gospel for the Rich? The Christian in a Capitalist World* (London: Mowbray, 1992)

Harvey, Anthony (ed.), *Theology in the City: a Theological Response to Faith in the City* (London: SPCK, 1989)

Haseler, Stephen, *The Battle for Britain. Thatcher and the New Liberals* (London: Tauris, 1989)

Hutber, Patrick, *The Decline and Fall of the Middle Class and How it Can Fight Back* (London: Associated Business Programmes, 1976)

Gill, Robin, *Prophecy and Praxis* (London: Marshall Morgan & Scott, 1981)

Gillick, Victoria, *Dear Mrs Gillick* (Basingstoke: Marshalls, 1985)

_ _, *A Mother's Tale* (London: Hodder & Stoughton, 1989)

Griffiths, Brian, *Morality and the Market Place: Christian Alternatives to Capitalism and Socialism* (London: Hodder & Stoughton, 1982)

_ _, *The Creation of Wealth: A Christian's Case for Capitalism* (London: Hodder & Stoughton, 1984)

_ _, *Monetarism and Morality. A Response to the Bishops* (London: Centre for Policy Studies, 1985)

Gummer, John, *The Permissive Society: Fact or Fantasy?* (London: Cassell, 1971)

Gummer, John, Eric S. Heffer & Alan Beith, *Faith in Politics: Which Way Should Christian Vote?* (London: SPCK, 1987)

Jakobovits, Immanuel, *From Doom to Hope: a Jewish View on Faith in the City* (London: Office of the Chief Rabbi, 1986)

Jenkins, David, *God, Politics and the Future* (London: S.C.M Press, 1988)

_ _, *Market Whys and Human Wherefores: Thinking Again about Markets, Politics and People* (London: Cassell, 2000)

Jenkins, Roy, *Churchill* (London: Macmillan, 2001)

Jenner, Brian, *The Coal Strike: Christian Reflections on the Miners' Struggle* (Sheffield: New Urban Theology Unit, 1986)

Joseph, Keith, Reversing the Trend: A critical re-appraisal of Conservative economic and social policies: seven speeches by Keith Joseph (Chichester: Rose, 1975)

Koss, Stephen, *Nonconformity in Modern British Politics* (Connecticut: Archon Books, 1975)

Leech, Kenneth, *Struggle in Babylon. Racism in the Cities and Churches of Britain* (London: Sheldon, 1988)

Longenecker, Dwight (ed.), *The Path To Rome: Modern Journeys to the Catholic Church* (Bodmin: Gracewing, 1999)

Longford, F., *The Bishops: A Study of Leaders in the Church Today* (London: Sidgwick & Jackson, 1986)

Montefiore, Hugh, *Christianity and Politics* (Basingstoke: Macmillan, 1990)

Moore, Charles, Gavin Stamp & A. N. Wilson, *The Church in Crisis* (London: Hodder & Stoughton, 1986)

Moyser, George (ed.), *Church and Politics Today: The Role of the Church of England in Contemporary Politics* (Edinburgh: T&T Clark, 1985)

Nielson, Jorgen S. (ed., *'The 'Rushdie Affair': A Documentation* (Birmingham: Centre for the Study of Islam and Christian-Muslim Relations, 1989)

Norman, Edward R., *Church and Society in England 1770–1970* (Oxford: Clarendon, 1976)

_ _, *Christianity and the World Order* (Oxford: Oxford University Press, 1979)

Novak, Michael, *The Spirit of Democratic Capitalism* (London: Madison, 1991 edition)

Oddie, William, (ed.), *After the Deluge: Essays towards the Desecularisation of the Church* (London: SPCK, 1987)

_ _, *The Crockford's File: Gareth Bennett and the Death of the Anglican Mind* (London: Hamilton, 1989)

Ormrod, David, *Facing the Future as Christians and Socialists* (London: CSM, 1985)

_ _ (ed.), *Fellowship, Freedom and Equality Lectures in Memory of R H Tawney* (London: CSM, 1990)

Patten, Chris, *The Tory Case* (London: Longman, 1983)

Poulton, J. (ed.), *Dear Archbishop* (London: Hodder & Stoughton, 1976)

Powell, Enoch, *No Easy Answers* (London: SPCK, 1973)

_ _, *Wrestling With the Angel* (London: Sheldon Press, 1977)

Preston, R. H., *Church and Society in the Late Twentieth Century: the Economic and Political Task* (London: SCM, 1983)

Raban, Jonathan, *God, Man, and Mrs Thatcher. A Critique of Mrs Thatcher's Address to the General Assembly of the Church of Scotland* (London: Chatto & Windus, 1989)

Sachs, Jonathan, *The Persistence of Faith: Religion, Morality and Society in a Secular Age* (London: Weidenfeld & Nicolson, 1991)

Scruton, Roger, *The Meaning of Conservatism* (London: Palgrave, 1980)

_ _ (ed.), *Conservative Thoughts: Essays from The Salisbury Review* (London: Claridge, 1988)

Sheppard, David, *Bias to the Poor* (London: Hodder & Stoughton, 1983)

_ _, *The Other Britain* (Nottingham: Shaftesbury Project, 1984)

_ _, & Derek Worlock, *Better Together Christian partnership in a Hurt City* (Harmondsworth: Penguin, 1989)

Stockwood, Mervyn, *The Cross and The Sickle* (London: Sheldon Press, 1978)

Suggate, Alan M., *William Temple and Christian Social Ethics Today* (Edinburgh: T&T Clark, 1987)

Temple, William, *Christianity and Social Order* (London: SPCK, 1976 edition)

Thatcher, Margaret, *Reason and Religion: the Moral Foundations of Freedom* (London: Institute of United States Studies, 1996)

Tingle, Rachel, *Gay Lessons: How Public Funds are used to Promote Homosexuality among Children and Young People* (London: Pickwick, 1986)

_ _, *Another Gospel? An Account of the Growing Involvement of the Anglican Church in Secular Politics* (London: Christian Studies Centre, 1988)

Towler, Robert & A.P.M. Coxon, *The Fate of the Anglican Clergy* (Basingstoke: Macmillan, 1979)

Walter, Tony, *Fair Shares? An Ethical Guide to Tax and Social Security* (Edinburgh: Hansel, 1985)

Warren, Allen (ed.), *A Church For the Nation* (Leominster: Gracewing, 1992)

Watts, Michael (ed.), *Through a Glass Darkly: A Crisis Considered* (Leominster: Gracewing, 1993)

Weber, Max, (trans. Talcott Parsons) *The Protestant Ethic and the Spirit of Capitalism*, (New York: Scribner, 1958)

_ _, (trans. A. M. Henderson & Talcott Parsons), *The Theory of Social and Economic Organisation* (London: The Free Press of Glencoe, 1964)

Whiteley, Paul, 'Public Opinion and the Demand for Social Welfare in Britain', *Journal of Social policy*, Vol. 10, (1981), pp. 160–170

_ _, *Pressure for the Poor: the Poverty Lobby and Policy Making* (London: Methuen, 1987)

Wiener, Martin J., *English Culture and The Decline of the Industrial Spirit, 1850–1980* (Harmondsworth: Penguin,1981)

Williams, Dr Rowan, *Writing in the Dust: After September 11* (London: Hodder & Stoughton, 2002)

Winter, David, *Battered Bride? The Body of Faith in an Age of Doubt* (Eastbourne: Monarch, 1988)

Younkins, E. (ed.), *Three in One: Essays on Democratic Capitalism 1976–2000* (Lanham, MD: Rowman & Littlefield, 2001)

Published Secondary Material

Abse, Leo, *Margaret, Daughter of Beatrice. A Politician's Psycho-Biography of Margaret Thatcher* (London: Cape, 1989)

Adonis, Andrew, & Tim Hames (eds.), *A Conservative Revolution. The Thatcher-Reagan Decade in Perspective* (Manchester: Manchester University Press, 1994)

Alcock, Peter, *Poverty and State Support* (London: Longman, 1987)

Alderman, Geoffrey, *London Jewry and London Politics, 1889–1986* (London: Routledge, 1989)

Aldous, Richard, Reegan and Thatcher: The Difficult Relationship (New York: W. W. Norton & Company, 2012)

Anderson, Oliver, *Rotten Borough: The Real Story of Thatcher's Grantham* (London: Fourth Estate, 1989)

Appignanesi, Lisa, & Sara Maitland, *The Rushdie File* (London: Fourth Estate, 1989)

Attallah, Naim, *Singular Encounters* (London: Quartet, 1990)

Ball, Stuart, *The Conservative Party and British Politics, 1902–1951* (London: Longman, 1995)

Beckett, Francis and Hencke, David, *Marching to the Fault Line The Miners Strike and the Battle for Industrial Britain* (London: Constable, 2009)

Bentley, Michael (ed.), *Public and Private Doctrine: Essays in British History Presented to Maurice Cowling* (Cambridge: Cambridge University Press, 1993)

Berger, Peter, (ed.), *The Desecularisation of the World: Resurgent Religion and World Politics* (Washington: Eerdmans, 1999)

_ _, *The Sacred Canopy: Elements of a Sociological Theory of Religion* (New York: Doubleday & Co., 1967)

Berthoud Richard, and Kempson, Elaine, *Credit and Debt The PSI Report* (London: Policy Study Institute, 1992)

Bevir, Mark, *New Labour: A Critique* (London: Routledge, 2005)

Brown, G. Callum, *Religion and Society in Twentieth-Century Britain* (Harlow: Pearson Longman, 2006)

_ _, *The Death of Christian Britain* (London: Routledge, 2001)

Bruce, Steve, *God is Dead. Secularisation in the West* (Oxford: Blackwell, 2002)

_ _, *Religion in Modern Britain* (Oxford: Oxford University Press, 1995)

_ _, *The Rise and Fall of the New Christian Right: Conservative Protestant Politics in America, 1978–1988* (Oxford: Clarendon, 1988)

Bulpitt, J., 'The Discipline of the New Democracy: Mrs. Thatcher's Domestic Statecraft', *Political Studies*, Vol. 34, No. 1, (1986), pp. 19–39

Cameron, Helen, 'The British Government and the Inner Cities Religious Council', in Grace Davie, Linda Woodhead & Paul Heelas (eds.), *Predicting Religion: Christian, Secular, and Alternative Futures* (Aldershot: Ashgate, 2003), pp. 120–135.

Campbell, John, *Margaret Thatcher: The Grocer's Daughter Vol. I* (London: Jonathan Cape, 2001)

_ _, *Margaret Thatcher: The Iron Lady Vol. II* (London: Jonathan Cape, 2004)

Carpenter, Edward, *Archbishop Fisher: his Life and Times* (Norwich: Canterbury Press, 1991)

Carpenter, Humphrey, *Robert Runcie: the Reluctant Archbishop* (London: Hodder & Stoughton, 1996)

Casanova, José, *Public Religions in the Modern World* (Chicago: University of Chicago Press, 1994)

Chandler, Andrew, *The Church of England in the Twentieth Century The Church Commissioners and the Politics of Reform 1948–1998* (Woodbridge: Boydell, 2006)

Chadwick, Owen, *Michael Ramsey: A Life* (Oxford: Clarendon, 1990)

Clark, David, *Between Pulpit and Pew: Folk Religion in a North Yorkshire Fishing Village* (Cambridge: Cambridge University Press, 1982)

Clark, Henry, *The Church Under Thatcher* (London: SPCK, 1993)

Clarke, Peter, *Hope and Glory: Britain 1900–2000* (London: Penguin, 2004)

_ _, *A Question of Leadership; Gladstone to Thatcher* (London: Hamish Hamilton, 1991)

Cox, Jeremy, *The Churches in a Secular Society; Lambeth 1870–1930* (Oxford: OUP, 1982)

Crewe, Ivor, & Anthony King, *SDP: The Birth, Life and Death of the Social Democratic Party* (Oxford: OUP, 1995)

Crick, Michael, *The March of the Militant* (London: Faber & Faber, 1986)

Crozier, Michael, *The Making of the Independent* (London: Coronet, 1988)

Currie, R., A. D. Gilbert, & L. Horsley, *Churches and Churchgoers. Patterns of Church growth in the British Isles since 1700* (Oxford: Clarendon, 1977)

Dale, Graham, *God's Politicians: The Christian Contribution to 100 years of Labour* (London: HarperCollins, 2000)

Dale, Iain, *Memories of Maggie: A Portrait of Margaret Thatcher* (London: Politico's, 2000)

Davie, Grace, *Religion in Britain since 1945: Believing without Belonging* (Oxford: Blackwell, 1994)

Deakin, Nicholas & John Edwards, *The Enterprise Culture and the Inner City* (London: Routledge, 1993)

Denham, Andrew & Mark Garnett, *Keith Joseph* (Buckinghamshire: Acumen, 2002)

Dennis, Norman, *Uncertain Trumpet. History of Education in Church of England School Education to AD 2001* (London: Civitas, 2001)

Donnison, David, *The Politics of Poverty* (Oxford: Martin Robertson, 1982)

Durham, Martin, *Sex and Politics: The Family and Morality in the Thatcher Years* (Basingstoke: Macmillan, 1991)

Evans, Brendan, *Thatcherism and British Politics 1975–1999* (Stroud: Sutton, 1999)

Evans, Stephen, 'The Earl of Stockton's Critique of Thatcherism', *Parliamentary Affairs*, 1998, Vol. 51 (1), pp. 17–35

Fieldhouse, Roger, *Anti-Apartheid Movement: A History of the Movement in Britain* (London: Merlin, 2005)

Finlayson, Geoffrey, *Citizen, State and Social Welfare in Britain 1830–1990* (Oxford: Clarendon, 1994)

Fisher, Nigel, *Iain Macleod* (London: Deutsch, 1973)

Francis, M. & I. Zweiniger-Bargielowska (eds.), *The Conservatives and British Society 1880–1990* (Cardiff: University of Wales Press, 1996)

Furlong, Monica, *The Church of England: The State it is in,* (London: SPCK, 2nd edition, 2006)

Furnival, John & Ann Knowles, *Derek Worlock. His Personal Journey* (London: Geoffrey Chapman, 1998)

Gamble, Andrew, *The Free Economy and the Strong State. The Politics of Thatcherism* (London: Macmillan, 2nd edition, 1994)

Gardiner, George, *Margaret Thatcher: From Childhood to Leadership* (London: Kimber, 1975)

Garfield, Simon, *The End of Innocence: Britain in the Time of AIDS* (London: Faber & Faber, 1994)

Garnett, Jane, Matthew Grimley, Alana Harris, William Whyte & Sarah Williams (eds.), *Redefining Christian Britain: Post 1945 Perspectives* (London: SCM, 2007)

Garnett, Mark, *From Anger to Apathy: The British Experience since 1975* (London: Jonathan Cape, 2007)

Gilbert, Alan, *The Making of post-Christian Britain: a History of the Secularisation of Modern Society* (London: Longman, 1980)

Gilley, Sheridan, & W. J. Sheils (eds.), *A History of Religion in Britain: Practice and Belief from pre-Roman Times to the Present* (Oxford: Blackwell, 1994)

Gilmour, Ian, *Dancing with Dogma. Britain under Thatcherism* (London: Simon & Schuster, 1992)

Green, E. H. H., *Ideologies of Conservatism. Conservative Political Ideas in the Twentieth Century* (Oxford: Oxford University Press, 2002)

_ _, *Thatcher* (London: Hodder Arnold, 2006)

Green, S. J. D., *The Passing of Protestant England Secularisation and Social Change c. 1920–1960* (Cambridge: Cambridge University Press, 2011)

_ _, 'Survival and Autonomy: on the Strange Fortunes and Peculiar Legacy of Ecclesiastical Establishment in the Modern British State c.1920 to the Present Day' in Green S. J. D. & R. C. Whiting, *The Boundaries of the State in Modern Britain* (Cambridge: Cambridge University Press, 1996), pp. 299–324

Green, Stephen., *Serving God? Serving Mammon?* (London: Marshall Pickering, 1996)

Grimley, Matthew, *Citizenship, Community and the Church of England. Liberal Anglican Theories of the State between the Wars* (Oxford: Clarendon, 2004)

Grimley, Matthew, 'Law, Morality and Secularisation: The Church of England and the Wolfenden Report, 1954–1967', *Journal of Ecclesiastical History*, Vol. 60, No. 4, (October 2009), pp. 725–41

Harris, Kenneth, *Thatcher* (London: Weidenfeld & Nicolson, 1988)

Harris, Robin, *Not for Turning: The Life of Margaret Thatcher* (London: Corgi, 2013)

Harrison, Brian, 'The Rise, Fall and Rise of Political Consensus in Britain since 1940', *History*, Vol. 84, No. 274, (April 1999), pp. 301–24

Hastings, Adrian, *A History of English Christianity 1920–1990* (London: SCM Press, 4th edition, 2001)

Hatton, Derek, *Inside Left. The Story So Far* (London: Bloomsbury, 1988)

Hayter, Dianne, *Fightback! Labour's Traditional Right in the 1970s and 1980s* (Manchester: Manchester University Press, 2007)

Heffer, Simon, *Like the Roman: the Life of Enoch Powell* (London: Weidenfeld & Nicolson, 1998)

Heffernan, R. & M. Marqusee, *Defeat From the Jaws of Victory Inside Kinnock's Labour Party* (London: Verso, 1992)

Herbert, David, *Religion and Civil Society: Rethinking Public Religion in the Contemporary World* (Aldershot: Ashgate, 2003)

Hilton, Boyd, *The Age of Atonement: The Influence of Evangelicalism on Social and Economic Thought 1795–1865* (Oxford: Clarendon, 1988)

Holden, Andrew, *Makers and Manners: Politics and Morality in Post-War Britain* (London: Politico's, 2004)

Isaac, Joan, 'The Politics of Morality in the UK', *Parliamentary Affairs*, Vol. 47, No. 2, (April, 1994), pp. 175–189

_ _, 'The New Right and the Moral Society', *Parliamentary Affairs*, Vol. 43, No. 2, (April, 1990), pp. 209–27

Jeffrey-Poulter, Stephen, *Peers, Queers and Commons: the struggle for Gay Law Reform from 1950 to the present* (London: Routledge, 1991)

Jones, Ian, *Women and Priesthood in the Church of England: Ten Years On* (Manchester: Church House, 2004)

Kavanagh, D. & Anthony Seldon (eds.), *The Thatcher Effect: A Decade of Change* (Oxford: Oxford University Press, 1989)

_ _, 'Thatcher's Third Term', *Parliamentary Affairs*, Vol. 41, No. 1, (1988), pp. 1–12.

Kengor, Paul, *God and Ronald Reagan: A Spiritual Life* (New York: HarperCollins, 2004)

King, Desmond S., *The New Right: Politics, Markets and Citizenship* (London: Macmillan, 1987)

King, Roger, & Neill Nugent (eds.), *Respectable Rebels: Middle Class Campaigns in the 1970s* (London: Hodder & Stoughton, 1979)

Kirby, Dianne (ed.), *Religion and the Cold War* (Basingstoke: Palgrave, 2003)

Koss, Stephen, *Nonconformity in Modern British Politics* (London: Batsford, 1975)

Lansley, Stewart, Sue Goss & Christian Wolmar, *Councils in Conflict: the Rise and Fall of the Municipal Left* (Basingstoke: Macmillan, 1989)

Larres, Klaus (ed.), *A Companion to Europe Since 1945* (London: Wiley-Blackwell, 2009)

Leary, William, *Lincolnshire Methodism* (Buckingham: Barracuda, 1988)

Lee, Simon & Peter Stanford, *Believing Bishops* (London: Faber & Faber, 1990)

Letwin, Shirley, *The Anatomy of Thatcherism* (London: Fontana, 1992)

Lewis, Jane, *The Voluntary Sector, the State and Social Work in Britain* (Aldershot: Edward Elgar, 1995)

Lovell, Terry, *Number One Millbank: The Financial Downfall of the Church of England* (London: HarperCollins, 1998)

MacCulloch, Diarmaid, *A History of Christianity: The First Three Thousand Years* (London: Allen Lane, 2009)

Machin, G. I. T., *Church and Social Issues in the Twentieth Century* (Oxford: Clarendon, 1998)

_ _, *Politics and the Churches in Great Britain 1832 to 1868* (Oxford: Clarendon, 1977)

_ _, *Politics and the Churches in Great Britain 1869 to 1921* (Oxford: Clarendon, 1987)

Mann James, *The Rebellion of Ronald Reagan: A History of the End of the Cold War* (London: Viking, 2009)

Martin, David, *On Secularisation: Towards a Revised General Theory* (Aldershot: Ashgate, 2005)

McKibbin, *Classes and Cultures: England 1918–1951* (Oxford: Oxford University Press, 2000)

McLeod, Hugh, *The Religious Crisis of the 1960s* (Oxford: Oxford University Press, 2007)

Modood, Tariq, & Geoffrey Brahm Levey (eds.), *Secularism, Religion and Multicultural Citizenship* (Cambridge: Cambridge University Press, 2009)

Modood, Tariq, & Anna Triandafyllidou & Ricard Zapata-Barrero (eds.), *Multiculturalism, Muslims and Citizenship; A European Approach* (London: Routledge, 2006)

Modood, Tariq, (ed.), *Church, State and Religious Minorities* (London: Policy Studies Institute, 1997)

_ _, *Racial Equality: Colour, Culture and Justice* (London: IPPR, 1994)

_ _, *Not Easy Being British: Colour, Culture and Citizenship* (Stoke-on-Trent: Runneymede Trust and Trentham, 1992)

_ _, 'Minorities, Faith and Citizenship' in *Discernment: A Christian Journal for Inter-Religious Encounter*, Vol. 6, No. 2, (1992)

Moore, Charles, *Margaret Thatcher, Vol.I Not For Turning* (London: Allen Lane, 2013)

Moreton, Cole, *Is God still an Englishman? How Britain lost its faith (But found new soul)* (London: Abacus, 2010)

Morrison, David & Michael Tracey, *Whitehouse* (London: Macmillan, 1979)

Murray, Tricia, *Margaret Thatcher* (London: W. H. Allen, 1978)

Nunn, Heather, *Thatcher, Politics and Fantasy: the Political Culture of Gender and Nation* (London: Lawrence & Wishart, 2002)

O'Sullivan, John, *The President, the Pope, and the Prime Minister: Three who changed the world* (Washington: Regnery Publishing, 2006)

Owen, Chadwick, *The Christian Church in the Cold War* (London: Penguin, 1993)

Parker, Stephen G. & Lawson, Tom (eds.), *God and War: The Church of England and Armed Conflict in the Twentieth Century* (London: Ashgate, 2012)

Parry, J. P., *Democracy and Religion: Gladstone and the Liberal Party 1867–1875* (Cambridge: Cambridge University Press, 1986)

Parsons, Gerald, *The Growth of Religious Diversity: Britain from 1945* (London: Routledge, 1994)

Partington, Andrew, *Church and State: The Contribution of the Church of England Bishops to the House of Lords during the Thatcher Years* (Milton Keynes: Paternoster, 2006)

Peart-Binns, John, *Graham Leonard, A Biography* (London: Longman &Todd, 1988)

Petre, Jonathan, *By Sex Divided: The Church of England and Women Priests* (London: Fount, 1994)

Pipes, Daniel, *The Rushdie Affair, the Ayatollah, and the West* (New York: Carol Publishing Group, 1990)

Pollock, John, *The Billy Graham Story* (Michigan: Zaondervan, 2003)

Prochaska, Frank, *A Disinherited Spirit: Christianity and Social Service in Modern Britain* (Oxford: Oxford University Press, 2006)

Pugh, Martin, *We Danced All Night: A Social History of Britain Between the Wars* (London: Vintage, 2009)

Quinton, Anthony, *The Politics of Imperfection: the Religious and Secular Traditions of Conservative thought in England from Hooker to Oakeshott* (London: Faber & Faber, 1978)

Qureshi, Shoaib, *The Politics of the Satanic Verses: Unmasking Western Attitudes* (Leicester: Muslim Community Studies Institute, 1989)

Ranelagh, John, *Thatcher's People: An insiders account of the politics, the power and the personalities* (London: HarperCollins, 1991)

Rawnsley, Andrew, *Servants of the people: The Inside Story of New Labour* (London: Penguin, 2001)

Reeves, Donald, (ed.), *The Church and the State* (London: Hodder & Stoughton, 1984)

Riddell, Peter, *The Thatcher Era and its Legacy* (Oxford: Blackwell 2nd edition, 1991)

Rogers, D., *Politics, Prayer and Parliament* (London: Continuum, 2000)

Rubinstein W. D., *Left, Right and the Jews* (London: Croom Helm, 1982)

Ruthven, Malise, *A Satanic Affair: Salman Rushdie and the Rage of Islam* (London: Chatto & Windus, 1990)

Samuel, Raphael, *Island Stories: Unravelling Britain, Theatres of Memory, Vol. II* (London: Verso, 1998)

Scott, Peter Manley, Baker, Christopher R. & Graham, Elaine L., *Remoralising Britain? Political, Ethical and Theological Perspectives on New Labour* (London: Continuum, 2009)

Seldon A. & S. Ball (eds.), *The Conservative Century* (Oxford: Oxford University Press, 1994)

_ _, *Major: A Political Life* (London: Weidenfeld & Nicolson, 1997)

Seyd, Patrick, *The Rise and Fall of the Labour Left* (London: Macmillan, 1987)

Skidelsky, Robert (ed.), *Thatcherism* (London: Chatto & Windus, 1988)

Smith, Graeme, 'Margaret Thatcher's Christian Faith: A Case Study in Political Theology', *Journal of Religious Ethics*, Vol. 35, No. 3, (June 2007), pp. 233–57

Stephenson, Hugh, *Claret and Chips: the rise of the SDP* (London: Joseph, 1982)

Taaffe, Peter & Tony Mulhearn, *Liverpool: A City that Dared to Fight* (London: Fortress, 1988)

Thatcher, Carol, *A Swim-on part in the Goldfish Bowl* (London: Headline Review, 2008)

_ _, *Below the Parapet: The Biography of Denis Thatcher* (London: HarperCollins, 1997 edition)

Thorpe, D. R., *Supermac: The Life of Harold Macmillan* (London: Chatto & Windus, 2010)

Vinen, Richard, *Thatcher's Britain: The Politics and Social Upheaval of the 1980s* (London: Simon & Schuster, 2009)

Waite, Terry, *Taken on Trust: Recollections from Captivity* (London: Hodder & Stoughton, 1994)

Wearmouth, Robert, The Social and Political Influence of Methodism in the Twentieth Century (London: Epworth Press, 1957)

Webster, Wendy, *Not a Man to Match her: The marketing of a Prime Minister* (London: Women's Press, 1990)

Weeks, Jeffrey, *Coming Out: Homosexual Politics in Britain from the 19th century to the Present* (London: Quartet Books, revised edition, 1990)

Weller, Paul, *A Mirror for our Times: 'The Rushdie Affair' and the Future of Multiculturalism* (London: Continuum, 2009)

Welsby, P. A., *A History of the Church of England 1945–80* (Oxford: Oxford University Press, 1984)

Whitehouse, Mary, *Cleaning Up TV: From Protest to Participation* (London: Blandford Press, 1967)

_ _, *Whatever Happened to Sex* (Hove: Weyland, 1977)

Wilcox, Clyde, *God's Warriors: the New Christian Right in America* (Baltimore: John Hopkins University Press, 1992)

Wilkinson, Alan, *Christian Socialism: Scott Holland to Tony Blair* (London: SCM Press, 1998)

Willets, David, *Modern Conservatism* (Harmondsworth: Penguin, 1992)

Williamson, Philip, *Stanley Baldwin. Conservative Leadership and National Values* (Cambridge: Cambridge University Press, 1999)

Willner, Ann Ruth, *Charismatic Political Leadership: A Theory* (Princeton: Princeton University Press, 1968)

Wilson, Bryan, *Religion in Secular Society* (London: Penguin, 1966)

Wolffe, John (ed.), *Evangelical Faith and Public Zeal: Evangelicals and Society in Britain 1780–1980* (London: SPCK, 1995)

_ _ (ed.), *The Growth of Religious Diversity, Britain from 1945: A Reader* (Newcastle: Hodder & Stoughton, 1994)

_ _ (ed.), *Religion in History: Conflict, Conversion and Coexistence* (Manchester: Open University, 2004)

Woodhead, Linda & Catto, Rebecca, *Religion and Change in Modern Britain* (London: Routledge, 2012)

Woolley, Richard, *The Influence of William Temple and R. H. Tawney on New Labour* (Lampeter: Edwin Mellen, 2007)

Wright, Anthony, *R. H. Tawney* (Manchester: Manchester University Press, 1987)

Young, Hugo, *One of us: A biography of Margaret Thatcher* (London: Pan/ Macmillan, 1989)

Unpublished Secondary Material

Burton, Edson, 'From Assimilation to Anti-Racism: the Church of England's Response to Afro-Caribbean Migration 1948–1981' (PhD thesis, University of West of England, 2004)

La'Porte, Victoria Anne, 'The Satanic Verses Controversy: Muslim and Secular Reactions' (PhD thesis, University of Exeter, 1996)

Skinner, Robert A., 'The Roots of "Solidarity"'; Race, Religion and the Social and Moral Foundations of British Anti-Apartheid Activism 1946–58' (PhD thesis, University of Sussex, 2004)

Weiss, Antonio, *The Religious Mind of Mrs Thatcher* (2011)
http://www.margaretthatcher.org/document/112748

Weller, Paul, 'The Salman Rushdie Controversy, Religious Plurality and Established Religion in England' (PhD thesis, University of Leeds, 1996)

Website resources

Faith in the City, downloadable version: www.cofe.anglican.org/info/
socialpublic/urbanaffairs/faithinthecity

Conservative Party election manifestos: www.conservativemanifesto.com

Margaret Thatcher online archive: www.margaretthatcher.org

Office for National Statistics: www.statistics.gov.uk

ACKNOWLEDGEMENTS

W HEN YOU WERE born and where you lived undoubtedly defined your experience, and, most probably, still determines your opinion of the Thatcher years. I was born on the night of the Brixton riots in April 1981 in nearby Tooting where copycat disturbances prompted my father to start boarding up the front windows of the house, during which his frantic nail-banging triggered my mother's waters to break. I can safely say that I am a child of Thatcher, yet I have no personal tales of struggle or success associated with that tumultuous decade. I am neither the daughter of a miner nor a Sloane Ranger. I do not remember ever reading *Jenny Lives with Peter and Eric* but I do recall 'AIDS' being the ultimate curse in the playground. We lived in a house rather than a flat, which my father owned, but we were not benefactors of Thatcher's 'sale of the century', rather of a risky bet my grandfather had won on the eve of war. Margaret Thatcher was very much in the background rather than in the foreground in my youth; an absence which I have more than made up for in my adult life.

●   ●   ●

I HAVE ACCRUED many debts in the writing of this book: financial, intellectual and personal. The Department of History at King's College London proved a stimulating and rewarding environment in which to be based and thanks must go to the departmental staff, especially Richard Vinen and Pat Thane as well as my PhD supervisor Matthew Thomson at Warwick for all their support and encouragement.

Special thanks also go to all the undergraduates who took the 'Britain's Thatcher' course between 2010 and 2014. My students forced me to think and rethink my ideas about the 1980s and reaffirmed my belief that teaching is a privilege, which often benefits the teacher more than the student.

If a historian is wholly dependent on their archives, then this book is entirely indebted to the countless number of librarians and archivists who managed to unearth obscure and often uncatalogued material from their respective basements. My thanks go to all the staff at the British Library and those at John Ryland's Library, Grantham Library, Winchester Records Office, Lincolnshire Records Office, Lambeth Palace and Manchester Central Library. There are a few archivists to whom I am especially grateful: Paul Webster at Liverpool City Archives, Meg Whittle at Liverpool Catholic Cathedral Archives, Chris Collins for granting me permission to use the Margaret Thatcher papers and for creating the Margaret Thatcher Foundation website, which is unparalleled in its breadth, accessibility and comprehension. Finally, the irrepressible Andrew Riley, keeper of the Thatcher papers at Churchill College, Cambridge, for all his help and guidance in both my teaching and research. I am also extremely grateful to those who gave me permission to use such material, including the Archbishop's Council, Rt Rev. Nigel McCulloch, Enoch Powell's Literary Estate, Derek Worlock's Literary Executors for special permission to view and print his papers and the late Lady Grace Sheppard, who not only granted me full access to the David Sheppard archive but also proved a most stimulating and informative interviewee; it is privilege to be able to call their daughter, Jenny Sinclair, a friend. In conducting interviews with both Anglicans and Conservatives it really did seem as if I was encountering two different 'Englands' and yet both were characterised by their warm hospitality and enthusiasm for the project. I am incredibly grateful to the following for their time and contributions: Jonathan Aitken, Rt Hon. Lord Baker, Rt Rev. Michael Baughen,

Rt Hon. Lord Powell of Bayswater, Rt Rev. Ronnie Bowlby, Rt Rev. Tom Butler, Rt Hon. Lord Carey, Cynthia Crawford, Rt Hon. Frank Field, Rt Lord Gummer, Rt Hon. Lord Harries, Derek Hatton, Rt Hon. Lord Howe, Rt Hon. Lord Hurd, Sir Bernard Ingham, Rt Hon. Lord Jenkin, Rt Hon. Lord Lawson, Clifford Longley, Rt Rev. David Jenkins, Anthony Kilmister OBE, Prof. Diarmaid MacCulloch, Prof. David Martin, Charles Moore, Rev. Dr Edward Norman, Sir Richard O'Brien, Rt Hon. Lord Parkinson, Rt Hon. Lord Charles Powell, Hon. James Runcie, Rt Hon. Lord Sacks, Rt Rev. Mark Santer, Dr Michael Schluter, Lady Grace Sheppard, Rt Hon. Lord Tebbit, Harvey Thomas CBE, Rt Hon. Lord Wakeham and Rt Hon. Ann Widdecome. Finally, Richard O'Brien, Tony Benn, Humphrey Carpenter, Rev. Eric James and Very Reverend Alan Webster, who all unfortunately passed away while I was writing this book.

Special thanks must go to Aaron Simons for some early investigative work, Alfie Stirling for some fast and fantastic trips to the National Archives and Grantham, and Connor Lovell, whose help was invaluable as I limped over the final hurdle. I am also grateful to Ben Wright for nudging me out of my academic mindset and Hugh Dougherty for making my words palatable for popular print. To my publishers at Biteback: Iain Dale for daring to publish a book called *God and Mrs Thatcher* and my editors Victoria Godden and Olivia Beattie for all their help, encouragement and, above all, patience. I am also grateful to the anonymous reviewers for their feedback on the initial manuscript, whose suggestions greatly improved this book. I owe a great debt of gratitude to Professor Philip Williamson, Dr Dianne Kirby and Professor Linda Woodhead for their constructive feedback on the second draft and especially Rt Rev. Mark Santer who painstakingly went through the entire manuscript with great proficiency and speed. The faults that remain are of course entirely my own.

On a personal level, I am indebted to Rogan, Bharji, my sisters Kate and Alex, Debbie Giacomin, Ali Alizadeh, Victoria Lawrence,

Paul Wicks, Sarah Sanderson, Katherine Wilson and Charlotte Riley for never asking 'when's the book out?' and constantly reminding me that there is more to life than Mrs Thatcher. I am grateful, too, to 'Smugla' Brown, Steven Clarke, Leslie Joynes and Timmy Freed for both challenging my individualism and testing my altruism. Thanks also go to Carolyn Rennie and Elvis Afchu for bolstering my physical and mental faculties at times of profound stress. Wynton Marsalis has proved a constant source of inspiration throughout, not least in forcing me to consider why the story of Thatcher and the Church of England would be of interest to a trumpet player from New Orleans. Likewise my 'Renaissance Men', especially David Pearl and Martin Lovegrove, whose enthusiasm and example have been a great stimulus and Andrew St George, who embodies the concept of 'Renaissance Man' more than most. Thanks must also go to John and Kerry Fanning at La Muse Writers' Retreat and to all those at Chalosse for providing idyllic settings in which I was able to write without distraction. Finally, to the Pearly Queen of Mitcham, great aunt Phyllis Derbyshire, who did not live to see the final result and definitely would not have read it if she had. Above all, my greatest thanks must go to my parents, Susan and Leslie Filby, for encouraging a sense of history and for their unconditional and unfailing support. I am forever in their debt. It is to them that this book is dedicated.

INDEX

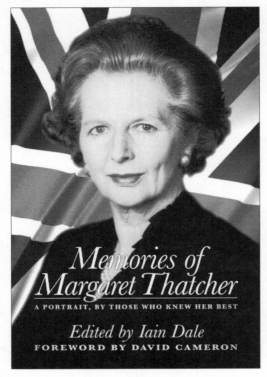